Stefanie Jung/Peter Krebs/Gunther Teubner (eds.)

# Business Networks Reloaded

Routledge
Taylor & Francis Group
LONDON AND NEW YORK

Nomos

First published 2015 by Ashgate Publishing

2 Park Square, Milton Park, Abingdon, Oxfordshire OX14 4RN
52 Vanderbilt Avenue, New York, NY 10017

*Routledge is an imprint of the Taylor & Francis Group, an informa business*

First issued in paperback 2020



**Die Deutsche Nationalbibliothek** lists this publication in the Deutsche Nationalbibliografie; detailed bibliographic data is available in the Internet at http://dnb.d-nb.de

ISBN: HB (Nomos) 978-3-8487-2038-5

**British Library Cataloguing-in-Publication Data**
A catalogue record for this book is available from the British Library.

ISBN 13: 978-1-4724-7092-8 (hbk)
ISBN 13: 978-0-367-59856-3 (pbk)

**Library of Congress Cataloging-in-Publication Data**
Business Networks Reloaded
edited by Stefanie Jung, Peter Krebs und Gunther Teubner.
424 pages
ISBN 978-1-4724-7092-8 (hardback : alk. paper) -- ISBN 978-1-4724-7093-5 (ebook) --
ISBN 978-1-4724-7094-2 (epub) CIP data has been applied for.

# Preface

Business networks are an international phenomenon. Small and medium-sized companies, i.e. SMEs, and also mid-range enterprises use business networks to compensate for the advantages of economies of scale and scope, which large companies enjoy. Therefore, business networks are of increasing importance throughout Europe. Due to their economic significance scholars have attempted to juridically account for this co-operational form for decades. But their complexity and diversity make it difficult to fully grasp business networks from a legal point of view. This might also explain why so far only Italy has established specific rules for business networks. Since it seems hard to explain business networks only with classical legal instruments such as contracts and corporations there is still much room for researchers to develop new concepts for this particular form of co-operation. Hence, basic research is still needed that is at the same time interdisciplinary as business networks are, first and foremost, an economic phenomenon. In order to have a significant impact the solutions cannot only be theoretical but need to be translated into practical advice to profit business networks.

Those challenges have prompted the Siegen Research Group, which has written a large part of the contributions in this volume, to yet again approach the essential aspects of the phenomenon of business networks. One main focus thereby was to examine how economic needs and findings can be juridically accounted for. The eponymous article "Business Networks Reloaded" *(Krebs/Aedtner/Schultes)* is central to this approach. In the legal field, it is the first contribution to deal with the question of what characterises business networks and which formations rightly bear this name. Based on economic considerations, an understanding of the term is reached that is much narrower than the ideas so far. According to this understanding, hierarchical franchising systems, supply chains and the relationship of contractors and sub-contractors to the general contractor with regard to large-scale projects are in particular not regarded as business networks (in the narrow sense). The remaining (co-operative) business networks form a more homogeneous group that is easier to capture from a legal point of view. This, however, poses the question of how to deal with the large amount of network-like relations resulting from the distinction (*Aedtner*).

In this volume, *Glückler/Hammer* present essentially new findings on the economic functioning of (co-operative) business networks. Amongst others, they show that different activities exist in networks and that the individual companies in (co-operative) networks merely participate in some specific network projects to a varying degree of intensity. Accordingly, *Krebs/Jung/Aedtner/Schultes* examine business networks from within instead of holistically and develop a corresponding network architecture, which might change our view on (co-operative) business networks. This network architecture and further economic findings are the starting point for *Krebs/Jung* to examine network governance, i.e. the appropriate degree of juridification, the different levels of regulation and the various regulatory instruments used within business networks. In this context, the new categories of "soft governance instruments" (SGI) and "hard governance instruments" (HGI) are particularly noteworthy.

Linked to the structure of business networks is the essential research question of how such entrepreneurial co-operations can be designed and which fiduciary obligations should exist to reach the network purpose. Accordingly, both *Weitzenboeck* and *Gómez Asensio* deal with the enhancement of trust through fiduciary obligations. *Crea* analyses the worldwide unique legal regulation on the organisation of business networks in Italy and the underlying concepts.

Based on their organisational structure and their activities, business networks seen from the outside often appear as an entity, which, however, does basically not exist in this way. The contributions by *Aedtner/Teubner* and *Becker* are dedicated to the indeed real threat of encountering organised irresponsibility resulting from this structure. Whereas the former discuss questions pertaining to the basis of liability, *Becker* deals with complex questions regarding causality.

With medium-sized companies and all the more with large companies, business networks pose the question of the compatibility with anti-trust law, i.e. on a European level with the prohibition of cartels according to Art 101 TFEU and the prohibition of abusive practices according to Art 102 TFEU. This important topic is dealt with in three contributions each focusing on a different aspect. It is especially worth noting the different approaches and the diverging findings of the contributions by *Schultes* and *Prosenjak*, which both deal with the prohibition of cartels. Whereas *Schultes* focuses on those network effects restricting competition that go beyond actual agreements, *Prosenjak* discusses the positive effects networks have on competition. Subsequently, *Eufinger/Dück/Schultes* address the abuse of market power, i.e. the aggregation of the network participants in particular.

The starting point for the German and international (Norwegian, Italian, Spanish) research results presented here was the Research School of Business and Economics (RSBE) at Siegen University with its general topic "Decentralised Organisations". Without the support arising from the RS-BE the Siegen Research Group would have never been established. Therefore, the University of Siegen deserves our special gratitude. Our colleagues at the Chair of Civil Law and Business Law at the University of Siegen and in particular *Dilek Bektas, Michael Matejek* and *Johannes Offergeld* contributed significantly to all the formatting work that the publication involved. Thank you very much!

From a scientific perspective, a talk by *Johannes Glückler* came as the Eureka moment to the Siegen jurists. Moreover, thanks to our colleagues *Emily M. Weitzenboeck*, *Camilla Crea* and *Carlos Gómez Asensio* this volume can also present the latest international findings. *Stefanie Jung* would not want to miss the opportunity to extend her thanks to *Richard Epstein* (NYU) and *Mario Rizzo* (NYU), who made her stay at the Classical Liberal Institute at New York University possible. Not only did this stay open new horizons, it was furthermore influential on the contribution on network governance.

*Dr. Stefanie Jung, M.A. (CoE)*
*Prof. Dr. Peter Krebs*
*Prof. Dr. Dr. h.c. mult. Gunther Teubner*

Contents

# Introductory remarks on the phenomenon of business networks and on this volume

*Prof. Dr. Peter Krebs, Dr. Stefanie Jung, M.A. (CoE)*

## A. The economic phenomenon of business networks

A greatly simplified depiction of companies may look like this: Enterprises are largely organised as corporations. Internally they are, as a rule (as default setting so to say), structured hierarchically. There are hierarchical levels that reach right up to the managing director. The larger an enterprise, the more complex and the more hierarchic is, by tendency, its structure. In the most general sense, the internal structure enables the governance of the individual activities by means of directives. From an economic point of view, it is sensible for companies to organise only a part of their activities internally whereas other transactions are conducted on the market. Regarding the latter, the company, in principle, acts freely (i.e. individually) despite its many contractual relations.

However, this possible depiction is simplifying and needs to be expanded especially in this increasingly complex economic world. To begin with, the illustrated basic structure has to be enriched by groups of companies, in which a company forms a part of a (mostly hierarchically organised) multi-corporate enterprise. The consideration, however, is not to end here since in practice a considerable approximation of individual (free) economic activity and hierarchically organised activity can be ascertained. Many companies and also some groups of companies are organised decentrally so as to achieve more effective economic activity through, the greater proximity of the locally acting persons to the subject matter and, above all, greater flexibility. This decentralisation is, considered from the other end, faced with the idea of the interlocking of activities or the cooperation of companies. The respective enterprises therewith aim to achieve economies of scale and scope but also more effective economic activities through cooperation/interlocking. This form of organised cooperation, which stands between market and hierarchy,[1] bears the name of business networks. Thereby, the concept of business networks has so far been broadly defined. Hierarchical, centralistic business affiliations such as franchising or the supply chain with powers of intervention on the part of the final manufacturer (prime example automotive industry) are, according to the so far prevailing conviction, also to be understood as business networks just as the non-hierarchical cooperation of companies on an equal footing.[2]

However, the corresponding affiliation of business activities does not automatically entail economic success. Due to the cooperation the individual enterprises partly lose their freedom of action and their flexibility. Furthermore, the interlocking of the enterprises or their cooperation is very laborious and difficult to organise. And in the case of an economically wrong decision all companies could be affected by a kind of domino effect. Accordingly, some business networks fail in practice,[3] but there are nevertheless also many successful business networks.

In any case, business networks, which are considered in the following contributions, are an important economic phenomenon of increasing practical importance throughout Europe.[4]

---

1 *Thorelli, H. B.*, Strategic Management Journal 7 (1986), 37 et seq*; Lianos, I.*, Journal of Competition Law and Economics 3 (2007), 625 (652 et seq.); *Ménard, C.*, Journal of Institutional and Theoretical Economics 160 (2004), 345 (345); *Williamson, O.*, Administrative Science Quarterly 36 (1991), 269 (271)*; Schüller, A./Krüsselberg, H. G.*, Grundbegriffe zur Ordnungstheorie und Politischen Ökonomik, Marburg 1991, p. 107.

2 Cf. *Ahlert, D./Ahlert, M.*, (eds.), Handbuch Franchising und Kooperation - Das Management kooperativer Unternehmensnetzwerke, Frankfurt a.M., 2010; *Heldt, C.*, Baukooperationen und Franchising als multilaterale Sonderverbindung, Baden-Baden, 2010; *Schimansky, A.*, Der Franchisevertrag nach deutschem und niederländischem Recht unter besonderer Berücksichtigung seines Netzcharakters und der Ansprüche bei Vertragsbeendigung, Tübingen, 2002; *Majumder, P./Srinivasan, A.*, Management Science, 54 (2008) 6, 1189 (1189 et seq.); *Vurro, C./Russo, A./Perrini, F.*, Journal of Business Ethics 90 (2009), 607 (607 et seq.).

3 *Glückler, J./Dehning, W.*, Von aktivieren der Netzwerkforschung zur Netzwerkberatung, in: Glückler et. al. (eds.), Unternehmensnetzwerke – Architekturen, Strukturen und Strategien, Berlin, Heidelberg, 2012, p. 266 et seq.

4 *Glückler, J. et al*, Organisatorische Vielfalt und Innovativität von KMU-Netzwerken: Ein bundesweites Screening, in: Glückler et. al. (eds.), Unternehmensnetzwerke – Architekturen, Strukturen und Strategien, Berlin, Heidelberg, 2012, p. 21 et seq (summary on p. 33) with regard to SME in Germany. *Becker, B./Müller, S.*, Deutsches Steuerrecht 2007, 733 (733 et seq.) with regard to SME; *Gielser, J.P.*, in:

## B. Question upon question

Business networks pose numerous economic and legal questions. A central economic question is when and under what circumstances business networks are useful.

A basic question, which may be of interest both to economists and lawyers is: How should business networks be organised and how should this organisation be backed legally? The aim thereby is to ensure that business networks can achieve the desired economies of scale and cooperational advantages through a good structure and effective work. At the same time, the disadvantages of business networks, such as the limitation of economic independence and the concomitant reduced flexibility but also the costs for the network organisation, should be kept to a minimum. Naturally, this basic question is divided into manifold individual topics. One example thereof is the prevention of free or cheap riding whereby corresponding risks primarily exist for decentralised cooperative networks.

From a legal point of view, further central questions arise. Are business networks a new legal category between contract and corporation or can they be explained with the existing legal instruments? Apparently, certain networks use corporations or contracts or gentlemen agreements. Are the applicable legal rules already largely determined by such a choice? Moreover, business networks vary greatly thus posing the question concerning the delimitation of the concept of networks. Is it convincing to have such a broad understanding of networks as it is practised at the moment? In what way should the law or also the private autonomous configuration of this organisational form take the diversity of business networks into account? In this respect, does it, for instance, make a difference whether a group of enterprises is centrally organised, as is the case with e.g. franchising, or whether companies cooperate on an equal footing?

An active business network generates profits or also losses. Accordingly, it has to be decided how the result is to be distributed among its members. Considered in more general terms, the general question arises how the relation between the network members is organised. Do fiduciary duties or duties of loyalty exist and if so to what extent? What do business

---

Beck'sches Rechtsanwalts-Handbuch, 2010, München, § 43 par. 1 et seq. with regard to franchising; *Geiser, G.*, MMR 2001, 715 concerning virtual enterprises.

networks, particularly cooperative networks, look like in practice? Which recommendations can be given to business networks regarding their legal self-organisation? Should the internal relations, such as e.g. the acceptance of a member to and the withdrawal from the network, be juridified at all?

Lastly, the organisation of enterprises with the help of business networks does not only affect its members but may also entail consequences for third parties. Can third parties that are damaged by a network activity have, for instance, claims against all network members? Who is liable under tort law if it is not clear from the outside who has done what and caused which damage?

These questions raised above illustrate the range of the legal discussion on business networks. In more abstract terms, a distinction has to be made between the internal and external relation of the network. The relation of the network or the entirety of the members to third parties is an example of a research area within the framework of the external relation. Regarding the internal relation, the organisation of the network and the relationship of the members to each other are of particular interest. Irrespective of the topic, a distinction has to be made from a legal point of view between the self-organisation of the participants and the possible legal configuration options.

The effects of business networks on the competition are interesting from both an economic as well as a legal perspective. Business networks coordinate their members' activity and thereby restrict the competition between each other. Accordingly, this at the same time raises the question concerning the violation of the ban of cartels. The companies pool their strengths in the business network, which may result in market control. Hence, at what stage does the abuse of market power come into consideration? In this way, competition law illustrates that already the basic evaluations are difficult. Should business networks be privileged from an antitrust point of view, provided they are economically useful? Or is, conversely, a new competition law approach required since not only specific agreements can have a competition restricting effect but also the participating companies will generally hold back in the competition with each other?

Regarding all these aspects mentioned above the question arises whether the legislative authority or case law should formulate rules as the Italian legislative authority has done to some extent. In the European context, the question immediately follows: To what extent should the law applicable to business networks be the same throughout the EU?

Question upon question. The complexity level of the matter is further increased by the fact that answering those questions requires both legal and economic knowledge. Therefore, research on business networks inevitably has an interdisciplinary dimension, which is also reflected in the contributions in this volume. Moreover, legal research in the EU commonly has a national character. The phenomenon of business networks can be observed in various European countries. Accordingly, national legal research on this topic has to be included. Based on contributions from Italy, Spain, Germany and Norway, this volume illustrates the European legal perspective whereby the considerations, in general, do not essentially depend on specific legal systems but are thought to be universally applicable, provided that they not already apply European law or are of a comparative nature.

## C. Attempts to provide answers

Such a research volume cannot deal with all questions mentioned above. From the perspective of the reader it would, however, be nice if it were not merely a potpourri. This is exactly the concept of the research illustrated here, which is characterised by concentrating on core themes.

### I. Cooperative business networks

The central topic of this research volume is cooperative, non-hierarchical business networks consisting of enterprises interacting on an equal footing. Even though they represent the ideal type of business networks, rather centrally organised structures such as franchising or the organised supply chain have nevertheless been at the centre of the discussion so far.[5] This may probably be due to their great economic importance as well as to the hitherto existing lack of actual knowledge about these cooperative business networks. Accordingly, the contribution by *Glückler/Hammer* deals with the latter. It contains essential empirical results regarding the organisation of cooperative business networks. From a legal point of view, the conclusion can be drawn that those networks which are outwardly often

5 Cf. *Grundmann, S./Cafaggi, F./Venturi, G.* (eds.) The Organisational Contract, Surrey, London et al., 2013, who exclusively deal with such constructions.

organised as corporation inwardly indeed act in a way which makes their explanation based on company law impossible. This aspect is particularly addressed in the contributions by *Krebs/Jung/Aedtner/Schultes* and *Krebs/ Jung* in this volume. Specifically, *Glückler/Hammer* illustrate that – as opposed to a corporation – the members do not attempt to achieve their profits in form of a dividend or the value of their shares in the company (even though such benefits are also possible) but through participating in specific activities under the umbrella of the network. The graphically illustrated activity levels thereby show that not every company participates in every kind of activity, and that in the case of participation the intensity of cooperation may considerably vary. *Glückler/Hammer* thereby particularly focus on the creation of network goods as the central possibility for the participating companies to achieve a surplus value.

*Krebs/Aedtner/Schultes* try to develop a first legal definition of business networks. This contribution was originally written irrespective of the research conducted by *Glückler/Hammer* but is in its results closely connected. The result is that the concept of business networks requires a far more narrow definition than has usually been used so far:

> A company network is every legally voluntary connection based on an economic and legal network aim of a minimum of three legally independent companies which induce a network-specific demand for organisation. The network enterprises at least partially exchange their economic independence for the co-ordination of their economic activities by means of concerted practices, agreements or the foundation of a corporation in order to implement the network aim through the bundling of resources.

This definition limits business networks to the cooperative business networks of equal companies examined by *Glückler/Hammer,* and centralistic constructions shaped by conflicts of interest such as franchising and the organised supply chain are not considered as business networks (in the narrow sense). Probably not every reader may be convinced that centralistic (and antagonistic) structures such as franchising, where one party governs everything and antagonistically faces all other participants, are not to be regarded as business networks. Nevertheless, the authors hope to encounter awareness for the fact that cooperative business networks and centralistic antagonistic structures pursue different interests and, to some extent, also exhibit different problems, which is why they should, in principle, be examined separately. Thus, the practical finding that companies participate voluntarily and to a varying degree of intensity in various activities essentially only applies to cooperative business networks. Even those not further engaged in business networks may nevertheless be interested in the attempt by *Krebs/Aedtner/Schultes* to develop a general two-step definition procedure for complex legal problems, in which a legal phenomenon is deduced from an economic phenomenon before reaching a legal definition in a second step. This contribution on the definition is eponymous for the research volume at hand since it represents the first implementation of the dichotomy resulting from the separation of cooperative business networks and centralistic antagonistic structures found in franchising, and the attempt to approach cooperative networks in an essentially new way. In the article by *Krebs/Jung/Aedtner/Schultes* a modular system of the network activities in cooperative business networks is outlined. Based on the results by *Glückler/Hammer* regarding the partial participation in various activities a specific architecture is laid out that takes these empirical findings into account. Developing a corresponding system seems necessary since neither contract law nor company law is designed for this set of problems. In the scope of the contribution, an entire architecture in the sense of a multi-module model is developed. The authors try to include the entirety of all possible network activities by means of a matrix consisting of the kind of exchange process and the kind of cooperational form. Thus, the arising modules are supposed to represent more or less homogenous business models. So as to illustrate this very abstract model each module is exemplified as business model with an example. The way of thinking in homogenous business models practiced here is inspired by codes of law on contracts from civil law jurisdictions, which generally assign every business model a contract type. This should allow the legislative authority or the judiciary to make decisions that are appropriate for the respective type. A relatively important and complementary result of this article is the proof that cooperative business networks should indeed be recognised as an independent legal category. Admittedly, this has been called for by legal scholars for a long time. But the fact that this idea has not yet prevailed in any legal order may be due to the reason that it might seem convincing with regard to cooperative business networks but not with regard to the otherwise mainly considered centralistic antagonistic relations, which have hitherto been regarded as business networks – in contrast to the definition introduced here.

In their article "Governance structures in business networks" *Krebs/Jung* try to build a bridge between foundational research on cooperative business networks and practically applicable results. Based on the results regarding the practical organisation of cooperative networks reached by

*Glücker/Hammer* and the contribution on the modular system of network activities by *Krebs/Jung/Aedtner/Schultes,* the authors develop a multi-level structure and practical suggestions how (good) governance could be implemented in cooperative business networks. Empirical findings are included in this examination even though the majority of the considerations are, due to the lack of adequate empirical foundations, suggestions based on plausibility considerations. One of the areas considered is the importance of the framework of the business network for the governance (a corporation is often used for this). Overall, the article is especially about the question whether internal regulation should actually exist and whether it should be non-binding or binding. The two terms hard governance instruments (HGI) and soft governance instruments (SGI) are developed following the differentiation between hard law and soft law. The different forms of HGI and SGI as well as their possible useful areas of application are further specified. In many articles, there are various secondary aspects that may be interesting to practitioners irrespective of business networks. In the article mentioned, these are considerations on taking the common practise in a business network into account even if this does not legitimise a binding rule.

The contribution by *Aedtner* bridges the findings on cooperative networks with research related to centralistic antagonistic structures. Based on the restriction of the concept of business networks to cooperative business networks the author raises the question how to deal with the configurations that are to be separated from cooperative business networks. Using the example of a cooperation in construction she tries to develop a similarity test, which helps to decide whether the results on cooperative business networks may be transferred to the other configurations due to sufficient similarities.

## II. Competition law

A further focus of this volume is the (European) competition law and its impact on business networks. Two of the three contributions in this area also pertain to cooperative business networks, which are in the focus of this volume. *Schultes* deals with the ban on cartels according to Art. 101 TFEU. Even though networks are often too small to cause noticeable constraints of competition, there is nevertheless the problem that in addition to the agreement immediately restricting the competition a structure can emerge that may lead to the restriction of competition. Moreover, the competition restricting effects do not necessarily have to be noticed instantly, but may be subject to delay. *Schultes*, therefore, develops a combined dynamic control of conduct and structure as a solution approach to the problem of dichotomy and statics. To a certain extent, her solution follows the regulation on merger control, which is also dynamic and conversely supplements the primary structural control of the regulation on merger control with behavioural control.

*Dück/Eufinger/Schultes* examine the scope of Art. 102 TFEU in relation to cooperative business networks. The essential issue thereby focuses on the prerequisites under which the market power can be added and on the question in how far limits also arise with regard to content due to the fact that it is a business network.

*Prosenjak* is an economist who leaves the area of cooperative business networks in his paper and tries to show that due to their positive economic effects certain network-like relations should be privileged from an antitrust point of view.

## III. The international perspective on duties of loyalty and the interpretation of agreements in particular

The three international contributions by *Weitzenboeck* (Norway), *Crea* (Italy) and *Gómez Asensio* (Spain) shall not only shed light on research in Europe. They also form a thematic unit since they deal with duties of loyalty and the interpretation of chosen regulations. Thereby, they mostly leave the area of cooperative business networks. Whereas *Weitzenboeck* uses a primarily comparative perspective focussing on common law to discuss the current state of loyalty duties and particularly the similarities and reasons for differences, *Crea* deals with the interpretational possibilities based on the Italian legal regulation. On the one hand, she regards this regulation as flexible enough to satisfy the interests of the participants. But on the other hand, this result is reached due to vagueness. From a Spanish point of view, *Gómez Asensio* examines the possibilities for governing centralistic antagonistic network structures and the role of duties of loyalty in particular.

### IV. Liability towards third parties

Lastly, the articles by *Aedtner/Teubner* and *Becker* focus on different aspects of liability towards parties outside of the network, i.e. third parties. They intend to tackle the problem of organised irresponsibility. No specific reference is made here to cooperative business networks since the liability interests of external parties are in any case merely marginally touched by this question. *Aedtner/Teubner* try to show what liability towards third parties should look like with regard to a virtual company. They see a correspondingly specific need for action, which they want to justify with a special relationship between the injuring party and the injured party, an element regarded as contract-like justification of liability in German law. Other legal systems use tort law here to legitimise and at the same time to limit the desired liability. *Becker* deals with the question whether, and if so, how the difficulties regarding proof of causality can be overcome in the event of damage caused by a business network. He advocates a form of liability where the entirety of acting network participants is liable in a parallel way and where the question regarding the extent of the liability is shifted to the internal relation of those liable.

## D. The special nature of this research volume

This research volume examines business networks from an interdisciplinary perspective. Not only does this mean that legal and economic contributions were included in this book, but also that particularly the legal contributions are based on economic findings. This approach allows an extensive consideration of business networks. Moreover, the majority of the contributions constitutes an internal unity since the scholars involved have worked together intensively in their research. This is already demonstrated by the fact that many authors have participated in several contributions and in various constellations. This approach offers the advantage that findings regarding one aspect can also be made fruitful for other questions. Accordingly, many contributions deal with a certain form of business networks, the so-called cooperative (non-hierarchical) business networks. Focussing on an economic phenomenon that has so far rarely been in the centre of discussion and including the new empirical findings related to this (*Glückler/Hammer*) enables real basic research with new results also in the legal field. As we see it, these suggested solutions put up for discussion here not only enable a new approach to the legal classification of business networks but provide practical organisational suggestions for the configuration especially of the legal structure of governance in these networks.

Also the other contributions contain manifold theoretically and practically relevant ideas. At the same time, they draw an overall picture of the problems and solutions currently discussed in Europe concerning business networks in the narrow understanding used here but also in the broad sense including centralistically organised structures such as franchising and interlocked supply chain structures, which are of particular practical relevance.

# Cooperation gains from network goods

*Prof. Dr. Johannes Glückler, Ingmar Hammer*

## A. Introduction

How can a firm increase its competitiveness? We would like to answer this question from a relational perspective that understands innovation as the result of collective effort and thus suggests the concept of the organised network. We argue that the purposeful development of organised networks enhances the individual entrepreneurial achievement and creates opportunities for collective innovation. In particular, we will try to explain which form of cooperation promises to be especially successful in order to enhance the competitiveness both of the individual members as well as the overall inter-firm network.[1]

Organised inter-firm networks emerge from the intentional cooperation of independent companies so as to jointly pursue and achieve economic objectives (Glückler 2012). The concept of the organised network represents an independent perspective on inter-firm networks that has so far attracted only little attention in research. Our analyses show that organised inter-firm networks provide an opportunity to realize cooperation gains especially from the collective creation of innovations. Based on a Germany-wide company survey we will illustrate the relevance of organised networks and their significance for the creation of knowledge and the process of learning.

Unlike sector or ego networks, which have been researched comprehensively, organised inter-firm networks offer the particular advantage of pursuing multiple yet common purposes in an organised framework of multi-

---

1 The concepts and results achieved in this contribution were developed at Heidelberg University within the scope of the research project www.kreanets.com funded by the Federal Ministry of Education and Research (Bundesministerium für Bildung und Forschung, BMBF) and carried out between 2008 and 2011 with the purpose to develop concepts and governance forms of organised inter-firm networks. The studies and concepts illustrated here are based on the book "Unternehmensnetzwerke: Architektur, Struktur und Strategien" (Glückler et al. 2012).

lateral, collaborative interaction. In the pursuit of common goals they hope to realize cooperation gains that are not achievable in isolation. Which forms of cooperation exist? We will distinguish between various activities observable in organised inter-firm networks and we will identify typical problems of the respective interaction levels. Which form of cooperation is so decisive for an organised network that it compensates for the costs of the network organisation? It is the joint development of network goods that are the property of the network. The concept of network goods allows us to identify the value added of organised networks that emerges if companies jointly create knowledge in different project groups, which can subsequently be used by all members of the network.

This chapter is structured as follows: in part two we develop the concept of the organised inter-firm network, which we qualify by comparison with existing network perspectives already discussed in extant research. In part three we demonstrate the empirical significance of organised inter-firm networks in the German economy and the opportunities they offer regarding knowledge, learning and innovation. The basis for this is a Germany-wide survey of 180,000 companies. Based on thirteen case studies of organised inter-firm networks, part four analyses the diversity of different activities among companies, which are aggregated into three activity types with regard to the value added of the network organisation. In part five we conceptualize the activity type of collective goods and develop it further into our approach of network goods that not only describes the basic mechanism of collective knowledge creation and cooperative knowledge use, but also holds it accountable for substantial cooperation gains.

## B. The concept of the organised inter-firm network

### I. General framework and the concept of entrepreneurial cooperation

Many companies only succeed in offering marketable products and services by linking their resources with those of other companies. Together companies enter new markets, reduce costs for common infrastructure, minimise entrepreneurial uncertainties or they cooperate based on the division of labour in value chains. The rise of inter-firm cooperation is the result of an increasingly dynamic environment, a functionally deepening and spatially expanding division of knowledge-oriented work as well as flexible and cooperative strategies to access resources and create value. The traditional management of innovation with its linear understanding of knowledge creation and learning seems inappropriate in light of such developments. Accordingly, linear models of innovation development give way to a reflexive understanding of the creation of novelty. The notion of innovation is increasingly replaced by the notion of learning because many innovations are to be understood as improving rather than radically breaking with existing processes or organisational principles. Especially small and medium-sized companies face the challenges of linking their limited resources with other companies and of thus compensating for the diseconomies of (small) scale. However, recent studies show that despite their need for cooperation especially small and medium-sized companies generally cooperate less with other businesses (Destatis 2003) and – if they do so – they achieve less innovation from the cooperation than large companies (Caloghiro et al. 2006). Consequently, the management of innovation-oriented networks faces serious challenges. Research on the organisation and the governance of organised inter-firm networks (Jones et al. 1997; Provan and Kenis 2008) is still in its infancy.

From the perspective of social network theory, a network is defined as a specific set of relations between a specific set of actors with the additional feature that the characteristics of these relations as a whole can be used to interpret the behaviour of the actors (Mitchell 1969). This perspective has two consequences: firstly, it places the relations centre stage of the analysis and, secondly, it shows that the structure of the relations as a whole contains information about the opportunities of individual as well as collective actors (Mizrucki 1994, Knoke and Kuklinski 1991). Thus, the network perspective is interested in the relations between the companies and the action opportunities as well as the collective effects resulting therefrom for the entire network. How can an inter-firm network be distinguished from its environment? In network analytical organisational research, various perspectives have developed depending on the focus of research that feature their own rules of delimitation.

## II. Total and focal business networks

Total networks comprise all actors that maintain relations of a specific kind. The relation rather than the actors primarily defines the network. Accordingly, an analysis of the inter-firm alliances in biotechnology will only consider those biotechnology firms that are involved in such relations

(Owen-Smith and Powell 2004; Powell et al. 2005). Total networks depict the complete structure of relations between companies and enable the analysis of network-specific characteristics such as density, connectivity, fragmentation or centre-periphery-structures and many more (Powell et al. 1996).

Focal networks and so-called ego networks each represent that part of an overall network that depicts the neighbourhood of a focal actor. The ego network contains the focal actor, its connected partners as well as the relations between these partners (Burt 1992). The research interest focuses on the question of how individual actors should organise their direct relations to achieve economic advantages. In manifold empirical studies Burt has demonstrated the positive effect a position of structural autonomy in ego networks has on the careers and salary structures of managers (Burt 1992; Burt et al. 2000; Burt 2004) or on the differential profit rates of industry sectors in the system of economic input-output-relations (Burt 1988; Burt and Carlton 1989).

Total networks comprise an overall network of relations that is neither coordinated as a whole nor perceived as a whole by the participants in the sense of a membership. In contrast, ego networks exclusively concentrate on the strategic position and the opportunities of individual actors. Neither network perspective is interested in multilateral and coordinated interaction (Glückler 2012). The disadvantage of focal networks lies in the fact that they firstly fail to take into account the complexity of the entire relations in the network and therewith secondly cannot depict networks as collective organizations. The understanding of the totality of the network and e.g. questions of collective gains, cohesion and sustainability of a network are thereby overlooked (Provan and Milward 1995).

## III. Organised inter-firm networks

Even though companies increasingly engage in collective forms of organisation, organised networks have been virtually neglected in research. Only recently has the scientific interest of structural network research focused on questions regarding the management of cooperative groups that aim at achieving permanent cooperation gains (Provan and Kenis 2008). Various approaches advance the phenomenon of multilateral, coordinated inter-firm cooperation by using different notions such as e.g. federations (Provan 1983), multilateral networks (Human and Provan 2000) or purposeful networks (Kilduff and Tsai 2003). It can be assumed that organised networks of smaller and medium-sized companies were, at least in the USA, first formed in the late 1980s at the earliest (Human and Provan 2000) and that even today many companies are able to use only little network-specific management knowledge, besides the established management concepts, to professionally, effectively and innovatively design and manage this organisational form. The starting point of the research work presented in this contribution is the notion of the organised network, which is at the same time the object of knowledge of the following case study. Organized networks are definied as: "[...] *ein freiwilliger und absichtsvoller Zusammenschluss von Mitgliedern, der die multilaterale Kooperation zwischen einer begrenzten Zahl von rechtlich unabhängigen Organisationen auf ein gemeinsam geteiltes wirtschaftliches Ziel ausrichtet*"[2] (Glückler 2012, p. 7).

Networks are here considered multilateral if they comprise of at least three members that are basically engaged in mutual cooperation so as to create or utilise collective goods. This criterion excludes the bilateral cooperation of companies as its sole characteristic feature, which has already been comprehensively researched in transaction cost theory and which neglects the incentive problems in the production of collective goods (Podolny and Page 1998). Organised networks form a type of organisation that is constituted of a certain degree of coordination and collective awareness. While, for instance, a network of strategic alliances in biotechnology includes all cooperation relations in the sector, an organised network merely refers to those companies that are organised as members of a group in which they pursue cooperative goals.

Organised networks exhibit the basic elements of an organisation. An organisation is a system of deliberately planned and coordinated actions based on the division of labour between a limited number of members with a clear line demarcating the environment or the surroundings (Bathelt and Glückler 2012, p. 201). Networks are then perceived as organised if they have an identity and if elements of governance can be recognised at the network level. A network can only be interpreted as organisation if it exhibits a minimum amount of demarcation vis-à-vis the environment and if a minimal consensus exists about who belongs to the network and who

2 "An organised network is a voluntary and purposeful affiliation of members that aligns the multilateral cooperation among a limited number of legally independent organisations with a mutually shared economic objective".

belongs to the environment. Whenever the members of a network share an understanding of a joint membership and affiliation and the other members can identify the network, then the network exhibits a collective identity that is discernable from the environment. In the empirical practice, the network identity becomes visible e.g. through brands, a corporate form or a documented description of the network as organisation (e.g. an online representation). The criterion of identity is considered to be sufficient in order to include also less institutionalised non-contractual forms of multilateral cooperation if they occur in awareness of collective actions with an assignable circle of partners. This comparably soft definition allows non-contractual forms of inter-firm networks to be considered that are based on mutual recognition, exclusive membership and governance founded on social habits and conventions (Glückler 2012).

## C. Organised inter-firm networks in Germany

### I. A Germany-wide company survey

Developing practical design concepts for long-term multilateral cooperation of companies first requires an empirical understanding of the occurrence, quality and diversity of different forms of inter-firm networks in practice. We refer to a large-scale and Germany-wide field research that screened the variety of inter-firms networks (Glückler, Janneck et al. 2012). In the scope of this screening, three questions were paramount: What is the significance of organised inter-firm networks in the German economy? Which formal features characterise these networks? Are these networks innovative and which innovation goals do their member firms pursue? A questionnaire was used to address characteristics of the geography, network size, innovation performance and relations to other networks.

177,789 small and medium-sized companies with no more than 250 employees based in the Federal Republic of Germany were invited to participate in an electronic survey. Among the 11,440 companies that responded 3,822 companies stated that they operated in networks. However, among the 3,822 identified inter-firm networks merely 1,382 companies fulfilled the criteria of the above-mentioned definition of an organized network. The following data pertains to this pool of companies. Before putting the organised inter-firm networks into the context of knowledge, learning and their significance for the entrepreneurial value creation, some typical features of organised networks shall be illustrated. Organised inter-firm networks emerge in all economic sectors and take almost all legal forms that can be chosen in Germany (Glückler, Janneck et al. 2012). Project networks are rare; the overwhelming majority of companies design their networks on a long-term basis and aim for cooperation for an unlimited period of time. Geographically, the networks are almost equally allocated in balanced proportions among regional, Germany-wide and international forms of cooperation. With regard to creation and financing, the vast majority of networks act without public subsidies or participation. The largest challenge networks face is the adequate distribution of rewards for the individual contributions to the overall network outcomes. In this chapter we argue that an opportunity emerges for companies to generate innovations by cooperating in organised networks. The role organised networks play in the development of new products, marketing concepts and organisational improvements shall be illustrated in the following part.

## II. Knowledge and learning in organised business networks

The survey results (hereafter obtained from Glückler, Janneck et al. 2012) show that irrespective of their objectives organised inter-firm networks have been conducive to innovation and therefore may be a vehicle for new knowledge and learning. Networks are created for a wide range of reasons. They can be set up to share costs or to jointly develop new knowledge or creative ideas within the entrepreneurial group. This survey inquired after the basic orientation of the networks and thereby distinguished the use of existing, the acquisition of external and the creation of new resources by joint cooperation. More than three quarters of the firms joined a network either to use or to commonly market their resources within their alliance. Only barely one-seventh of all respondents was organised in networks to jointly create new resources, i.e. to jointly develop new products or conduct research and development.

The low number of networks that built in pursuit of explicit research and development suggests a low number of innovations that arise from the resource creating business networks. Much in contrast, however, 70 per cent of the networks stated that they had already created an innovation. Consequently and irrespective of the actual founding objective, the majority of networks were capable of developing innovative products, processes as well as new organisation or marketing concepts. Apparently, learning is especially well achieved in organised networks, because their members co-create innovations even though innovativeness need not be the leitmotif for the constitution of the network.

Whereas innovations occurred as a result both in innovation-oriented as well as in purely utilisation-oriented networks, networks create different kinds of innovation depending on their network objective. Following the typecast of the OECD we distinguish four types of innovation (OECD 2005): product and process innovations more often refer to technical innovations than organisation and marketing innovations. The analysis of the screening proves a clear statistic association between the network objectives, the geography of the networks and the kind of innovation results. Utilisation networks rather create organisation and marketing innovations, are more often trans-regionally or internationally rather than locally organised and they count more members than innovation networks. The smaller innovation networks, in contrast, rather create product and process innovations and are more often than utilisation networks regionally organised.

The survey at hand is one of the largest surveys on inter-firm networks in Germany. It provides information about the relative significance and variety of networks in the cooperation of small and medium-sized companies and illustrates the significance of organised inter-firm networks as an important form of organisation to achieve entrepreneurial objectives. Organised inter-firm networks are constructed very differently. A decisive result of the survey was that organised networks not necessarily have to affiliate on an innovation-oriented basis in order to be innovative. Many networks whose main objective did not lie in researching and developing products or processes reported on the successful introduction of innovations resulting from collaborative work. Apparently, organised networks are conducive to successful learning processes and collective innovation. In the following section we use selected case studies to elaborate more deeply into the various activity levels that may emerge within multilateral cooperation and to analyse which of those are particularly important for successful collective innovation.

## D. Activities of organised business networks

In thirteen case studies of organised networks among small and medium-sized enterprises (SMEs) we have analysed the activities of the members by means of situated organizational network analysis (Glückler and Hammer 2011). Typically, firms interact with each other at multiple different levels of activity. We classify the empirical diversity of the individual activity levels into three basic types: (i) governance (ii) the exchange of resources and (iii) the production of collective goods. The following table provides an overview of the organised SME networks examined and their main features. Which opportunities and which problems are connected with the individual activity levels?

*Table 1: Characteristics of the organised SME networks examined*

| | Age | Members | Legal form | Sector | Geography | Funding | Collective good |
|---|---|---|---|---|---|---|---|
| DENTIS | 12 | 28 | Ltd. | Medical technology | National | No | Yes |
| REGIOCONSULT | 3 | 23 | Registered association | Consulting services | Regional | No | No |
| COMRA.DE | 8 | 25 | Registered association | E-Commerce | Local | No | Yes |
| BIOCL | 6 | 63 | Registered association | Biotechnology | Global | Yes | Yes |
| ZWÄG | 7 | 49 | Registered association | Health | Local | No | No |
| FORUM Z | 16 | 62 | Informal status | Waste | National | No | No |
| GKT | 7 | 43 | Ltd | Health | Local | Yes | No |
| GLASTEC | 92 | 95 | Registered association | Glass | National | No | Yes |
| CARBFIBRE | 5 | 120 | Registered association | Material | National | No | No |
| ENERGIE² | 3 | 300 | Registered association | Energy | Regional | Yes | Yes |
| BIOCON | 15 | - | Registered association | Biotechnology | Regional | Yes | No |
| RNBIOCELL | 3 | 61 | Registered association | Biotechnology | Regional | Yes | No |
| TECOP | 10 | 55 | Registered association | Optics | Regional | Yes | Yes |

All figures refer to the survey period in the year 2011. Where appropriate, networks are anonymised by pseudonyms for reasons of confidentiality.

## I. The governance of the network

All SME networks examined have formalised the governance of the organisation as a management function. Different entities take on the governance of organised affiliations. In most cases, the administration as well as the collection of contribution fees and network strategies in the business networks examined here are taken on by a central network organisation. This organisation has its own branch office with office space as well as employees in the administration and the departments. The members cover the thereby created costs with network fees. The branch office also takes on the services provided by the network. The networks under study offer their members services such as the joint purchase of production goods, the monitoring of company processes or contract research. The amount of employees varies considerably between the members. Small branch offices merely have one employee, the largest network headquarters up to twenty. It is little surprising that the extent of the work regarding the content increases the larger the size of the network organisation is, as the example of *GlasTEC* illustrates. Graduated and post-doctoral employees working in the branch office not only conduct research in commissioned work, but also within network projects. Network projects or working groups are, in addition to the organisational administration, the central means of governance in organised inter-firm networks. Network projects and network working groups thereby serve to create collective goods. They are particularly important to realize cooperation gains by developing valuable network goods. The network members monitor the governance of the joint work in projects and working groups through monitoring committees. The lateral management of network goods and the concomitant chances and problems have been hardly researched so far and remain the object of future research (Glückler and Németh 2012).

## II. The exchange of resources

The exchange of knowledge between the members is a critical network activity. From an economic perspective, various intensities of knowledge flow can be observed starting with simple tips and tricks or recommendations, successful methods or procedures reaching to firm-specific knowledge affecting its competitiveness. We shall illustrate this with examples. Members of the *BioCon* Network meet on a daily basis in the same canteen. Asked about the knowledge exchange they report that during the meetings they pass on information, which, however, never contains critical knowledge regarding the company (e.g. company processes, biotechnical procedures or corporate key figures like contribution margins of business processes). Instead, the exchange focuses on the recommendation of important external cooperation partners such as patent lawyers or investors. The exchange of less important knowledge is contrasted with forms of exchange that contain important business information. Let us take a look at the example of DENTIS and COMRA.DE. In the case of DENTIS the members exchange key performance indicators of production processes so as to jointly improve these production processes in each individual member firm (Glückler and Hammer 2012). In the case of COMRA.DE, the members pass on programme codes to other network members in agreement with their superiors (Hammer et al. 2012). Both exchange processes have in common that, firstly, they occur free of charge and that, secondly, the recipient of the information most benefits from the information. The economic benefit of these exchanges may reach significant extents. Without the exchange the companies would have to invest considerably more resources in order to achieve the same level of corporate learning. Especially due to this tangible advantage the exchange of resources as activity level is very common in all networks. The exchange of knowledge is thus able to accomplish a considerable task, but this is also exactly where one of the largest problems of bilateral knowledge exchange lies: the community hardly benefits from this form of bilateral interaction. How, then, may the community benefit as a whole? This form of interaction is called the production of collective goods.

### III. The production of collective goods

Only few of the inter-firm networks examined have created collective goods over the course of their development. Solely the network DENTIS has by means of a member-funded cooperation created common goods, which are the property of the network and can be used in the scope of a membership. The network members create collective goods by cooperating in working groups and projects. The collective goods are accompanied by the network service. Network services are offered by employees of the network and include tasks such as assisting with project proposals, organising a purchasing pool or optimising business processes. These services are subject to charge and have to be disbursed by the members. The earnings benefit the community and are used to finance joint activities.

We argue that this type of activity, which creates network goods, is the key to the cooperation gain in organised networks and generates particular value for the network as a whole. But how is new knowledge jointly created? Which contributions do the members make and how are the innovations used? We shall develop the concept of the network good for innovations created and used collaboratively. The following section is based on a detailed case study of an organised inter-firm network so as to examine the innovation-oriented design under concrete context conditions (Glückler and Hammer 2012).

## E. The network good: Creating and using knowledge collectively

### I. From the club good to the network good

Knowledge-based collective goods are interesting from an economic perspective since they create additional value and thereby offer incentives to join a network and to retain the membership on a long-term basis. Innovative marketing concepts, new production processes or exceptional technical methods that are developed in the community and at the exclusive disposal of the members provide an opportunity for the individual companies to secure competitive advantages vis-à-vis competitors outside of the network. With the concept of the club good Buchanan (1965) introduced a concept that explains how goods in the community of a club can be provided and used since the joint use of resources is afflicted with social dilemmas either by free riding or crowding.

Let us assume a set of companies wants to share the use of a machine. They can pool the financial means and acquire the resource at divided individual charges. However, if the circle of participants is not restricted then the first dilemma emerges: Free riders are members who indeed use the resource but have never contributed to its provision. Access controls solve the problem, because only those who contribute resources to the acquisition are also allowed to use the resource. However, if more members in a *club* would like to use a machine than capacities available then the common resource is either overused in the course of crowding or the individual benefit gets lost. Buchanan (1965) solves this problem with a cost-benefit model of the optimal club size at which the members achieve the best compromise of individual costs and benefits. The monitoring of the club size and the provision of the club good is ensued by third parties. The central achievement of the club good theory lies in clarifying how a collective of users can use an existing good without suffering from the dilemmas caused by free riding and crowding. Can the club good theory be applied to knowledge goods in organised inter-firm networks? Before answering this question we shall explain the concept of knowledge goods.

We assume that knowledge, similar to material goods, may be rival in its commercial use. For instance: A group of companies has developed an extensive documented repository of knowledge over the years that describes effective and efficient business processes and work flows and therewith allows individual savings as well as creates access to a certification according to DIN-ISO standard. In addition, this set of rules is updated and further developed on an annual basis. As long as only few market participants use this document they enjoy a competitive advantage vis-á-vis their competitors. The market advantage lies in the comparative cost advantages achieved by improved business processes. This advantage is based on better knowledge, and may be subject to the dilemma of crowding. If all market participants had access to this repository of knowledge, the individual competitive advantage would disappear. Just as with material goods, free riding is also possible with knowledge goods. One may only think again of the jointly created document mentioned above to improve business processes. If companies use the results of jointly created work without having contributed their own resources to its development then they act as free riders in the classical sense and gain advantage by fraud at the expense of others. Free riding and crowding are thus social dilemmas that also occur with the commercial use of knowledge goods.

Therefore, we propose to develop the concept of the club good further to that of a network good. There are three reasons for the theoretical deficit of the club good: Firstly, crowding is not a problem within the group since knowledge can be replicated any number of times. In contrast to the club theory, the problem of crowding emerges not among the members within the inter-firm network but between club members and market participants outside of the club. Secondly, the theory of club goods merely takes into account the use but not the production of collective goods by members. Imagine a network affiliates new members. The joint development of knowledge goods is at the core of the common goal of many business networks. It requires the collective project work of the member companies. As a result, not only the members involved in the project, but all other network members can learn from this if the results are made available in the entire network. However, since all members are equal partners and are not authorised to discipline or command other members, the participation in a joint project is ultimately left open to each member. This results in the possibility for the network members to free ride. While in the concept of club goods the access control successfully excludes the free rider, this is obviously not possible with a knowledge-based network good. The third problem derives from the second: If the members contribute partially to the creation of the network good, then the structure of cooperation between the members becomes important. Companies that contribute more intensively by sharing their own knowledge, lose more of their competitive advantage than those companies that contribute little or nothing at all. The theory of generalized exchange (Bearman 1997), however, indicates that commitment and knowledge transfer will be rewarded in the future in that network members are also more willing to pass on their own knowledge to active members. In the following section, the example of Dentis illustrates the creation of knowledge-based network goods, their network value, the absence of the crowding dilemma within the network, the production of network goods in the community by personal contribution and the overcoming of the free riding problem.

## II. The production of network goods

Dentis is a successful organised network of SME dental laboratories. The 27 member-companies employed overall 800 members of staff and generated about 50 million Euro revenue during the reference year of the survey. Accordingly, Dentis is one of the largest dental laboratory networks in Germany. It represents roughly 1.5 per cent of the total turnover of the dental industry in Germany. In comparison to many other dental laboratory networks, more than three times as many companies have joined Dentis. The member-companies are all competitors. As dental laboratories they operate on the same stage of the value chain between dentists and equipment providers. There are four forms of activities (see section four) in the Dentis network: the intercompany exchange of information, the bilateral leasing of production capacities, the management of joint working groups and the joint development of network goods. Figure 1 shows the networks of each of the four activities. The points represent the member-companies; the arrows between the companies indicate the actual relation between the member-companies.

*Figure 1: Four activities in the business network* DENTIS

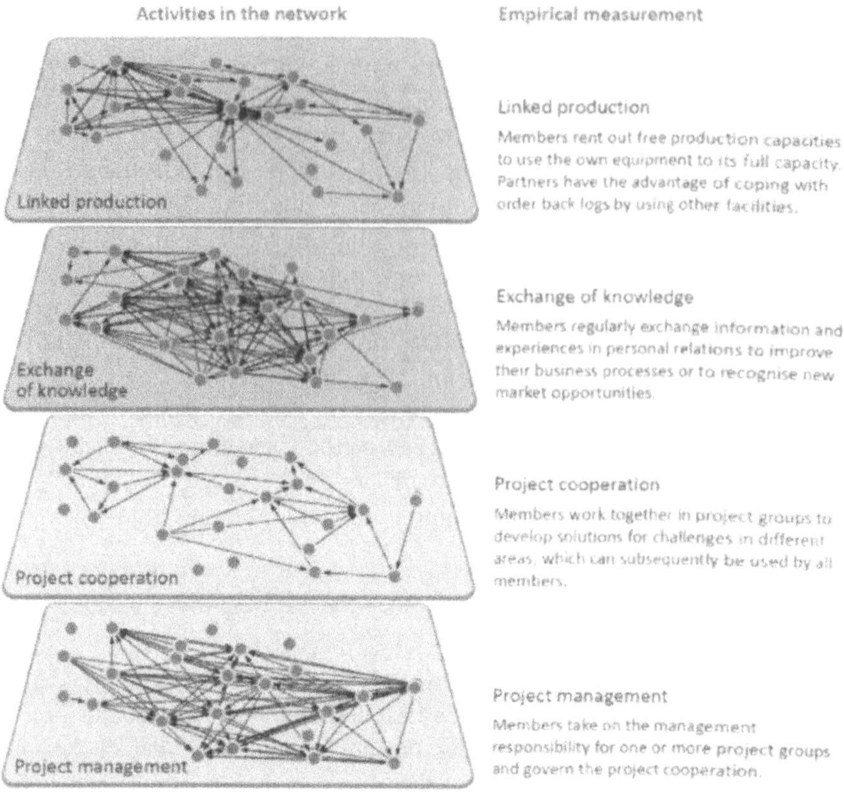


In the production of network goods, a range of different members works together. The cooperation in DENTIS is organised in project groups, in which new technologies, concepts and products are developed for the members. At the time of the survey, DENTIS had eleven project groups altogether, which cooperated in all aspects of the value chain such as procurement, manual skills, process technology and marketing. In organised networks, the development of network goods requires the multilateral input and recombination of individual skills and expertise of the members to develop new knowledge or solutions. The solutions developed in the various project groups are subsequently made available to all members. Beyond achieving purely private advantages, DENTIS thus offers its members the opportunity to be able to collectively generate and individually use additional value added at the network level. The example of the *production manual* illustrates this. With great effort and during many years, a project group has pursued the objective of collecting all important production stages and production processes in dental technology practiced by all member-companies in the network and to further develop them with external consultants. Many dental technicians and dental technician masters researched and integrated the technical details in a database, which is now available to all members in form of a production manual. The production manual is a complete template about how every dental technical product possibly imaginable is to be produced in order to combine high quality and speed. The production manual is specifically adjusted by every laboratory. The individual advantage lies in the fact that obvious rationalisation potential becomes apparent in the individual company by implementing the proposed production ways in that e.g. the same products can be produced in a shorter time. Crowding is not a possible effect for this network good since it can be reproduced as often as needed without great costs for every existing and also any new member. The competition advantage vis-à-vis non-members always remains as long as the good does not become a public good.

*What are the benefits of the network goods for the individual companies and the community?* Members of DENTIS evaluate the outcome of their project groups as profitable and lucrative. They were able to achieve savings by either improved processes, increased process quality or by innovative marketing concepts. This advantage of collective cooperation becomes apparent in the scope of a benefit assessment carried out by the members. Merely five out of the 27 members rate the project groups rather poorly. All other members evaluated their individual benefits as clearly positive. However, not only do the member-companies gain benefits from network goods, but also the network as a whole. As a limited liability company DENTIS is the proprietor of licensing rights and collective expert knowledge. The common property improves the attractiveness of a membership. Members enjoy larger incentives to stay and applicants are generally willing to accept higher fees for a new membership. Despite this very positive result the members' individual benefit assessments vary clearly. Why do the members evaluate the benefit of the network goods in different ways if it is impossible that crowding impairs the benefits? With the solution to this question we will approach the solution to the free riding problem in relation to knowledge-based network goods.

*How is the problem of free riding regarding network goods overcome?* If merely some members jointly develop a new solution, but all other members are also allowed to use it then the benefits should be distributed equally among all members. Hence, how is the individual utility indeed distributed? Those members who are highly engaged in the project cooperation at the same time report significantly higher individual benefits than lesser-involved members. In the end, the individual benefit of knowledge goods depends on the extent of the individual involvement in the production process to be able to understand and absorb new knowledge. Learning processes imply learning costs so that knew knowledge that was exclusively developed by others is sometimes possibly less well understood or less adequately used.

## F. Conclusion

The ability to initiate or affiliate with organised inter-firm networks may enhance both individual and collective competitiveness: trans-regionally, if companies are a part of nationally and internationally organised networks as well as regionally, if they are members of local networks. We develop the concept of the organised network as a specific type of multilateral organization of independent firms that is particularly conducive to the creation of network goods and thus to realize enduring cooperation gains. In organised networks, companies enjoy the possibility to create new knowledge with divided responsibilities by means of different project groups. This knowledge can be exclusively used by all network members. The observed value of knowledge is especially large if the companies use the jointly created knowledge to improve their own processes, i.e. if learning is aligned with the own company. The Germany-wide survey and the identification of roughly 4,000 networks show the empirical importance of this form of cooperation. The advantages of organised networks are underscored by the fact that most of these networks reported successful innovations in the course of their collaboration.

## Bibliography

Bathelt H, Glückler J (2012) *Wirtschaftsgeographie. Ökonomische Beziehungen in räumlicher Perspektive.* 3. ed. Stuttgart: Ulmer, UTB

Bearman P (1997) Generalized exchange. *American Journal of Sociology* 102 (5): 1383-1415

Buchanan JM (1965) An economic theory of clubs. *Economica* 32: 1-14

Burt RS (1988) The stability of American markets. *American Journal of Sociology* 94 (356-395):

Burt RS (1992) *Structural Holes: The Social Structure of Competition.* Cambridge (MA), London: Harvard University Press

Burt RS (2004) Structural holes and good ideas. *American Journal of Sociology* 110 (2): 349-399

Burt RS, Carlton DS (1989) Another look at the network boundaries of American markets. *The American Journal of Sociology* 95 (3): 723-753

Burt RS, Hogarth RM, Michaud C (2000) The social capital of French and American managers. *Organization Science* 11: 123-147

Caloghiro Y, Constantelou A, Vonortas NS (Hg) (2006) Knowledge Flows in European Industry. London: Routledge.

Destatis (2003) *Ad-hoc-Befragung über Unternehmenskooperationen. Ergebnisse für das Jahr 2003.* Wiesbaden: Statistisches Bundesamt

Glückler J (2012) Organisierte Unternehmensnetzwerke: Eine Einführung. In: Glückler J, Dehning W, Janneck M, Armbrüster T (eds.) Unternehmensnetzwerke. Architekturen, Strukturen und Strategien. Heidelberg: Springer Gabler, p. 1-18

Glückler J, Dehning W, Janneck M, Armbrüster T (2012) *Unternehmensnetzwerke. Architekturen, Strukturen und Strategien.* Heidelberg: Springer, Gabler

Glückler J, Hammer I (2012) Multilaterale Kooperation und Netzwerkgüter. In: Glückler J, Dehning W, Janneck M, Armbrüster T (eds.) Unternehmensnetzwerke. Architekturen, Strukturen und Strategien. Heidelberg: Springer Gabler, p. 139-162

Glückler J, Hammer I (2011) Situative Organisatorische Netzwerkanalyse. *Zeitschrift Führung und Organisation* 80 (6): 379-386.

Glückler J, Nemeth S (2012) Legitime Steuerungsinstanzen in lateralen Netzwerken. In: Glückler J, Dehning W, Janneck M, Armbrüster T (eds.) Unternehmensnetzwerke. Architekturen, Strukturen und Strategien. Springer Gabler, Heidelberg, p. 95-119

Glückler J, Janneck M, Dehning W, Hammer I, Staar H (2012) Organisatorische Vielfalt und Innovativität von KMU-Netzwerken: Ein bundesweites Screening. In: Glückler J, Dehning W, Janneck M, Armbrüster T (eds.) Unternehmensnetzwerke. Architekturen, Strukturen und Strategien. Heidelberg: Springer Gabler, p. 21-34

Hammer I, Beck S, Glückler J (2012) Lernen im lokalen Unternehmensnetzwerk: Imitation zwischen Konvention und Tabu. In: Glückler J, Dehning W, Janneck M, Armbrüster T (eds.) Unternehmensnetzwerke. Architekturen, Strukturen und Strategien. Heidelberg: Springer Gabler, p. 163-182

Human SE, Provan KG (2000) Legitimacy building in the evolution of small-firm multilateral networks: A comparative study of success and demise. *Administrative Science Quarterly* 45 (2): 327-365

Jones C, Hesterly WS, Borgatti SP (1997) A general theory of network governance: Exchange conditions and social mechanisms. *Academy of Management Review* 22: 911-945

Kilduff M, Tsai W (2003) *Social Networks and Organizations*. London: Sage.

Knoke D, Kuklinski JH (1991) Network analysis: Basic concepts. In: Thompson G, Frances J, Levacic R, Mitchell J (eds.) *Markets, Hierarchies and Networks*. London: Sage, p. 173-182

Mitchell JC (1969) The concept and use of social networks. In: Mitchell JC (ed.) *Social Networks in Urban Situations. Analyses of Personal Relationships in Central African Towns*. Manchester: Manchester University Press, p. 1-50

Mizruchi MS (1994) Social network analysis: Recent achievements and current controversies. *Acta Sociologica (Taylor & Francis Ltd)* 37: 329- 343

Owen-Smith J, Powell WW (2004) Knowledge networks as channels and conduits: The effects of spillovers in the Boston biotechnology community. *Organization Science* 15 (1): 5-21

Provan KG (1983) The federation as an interorganizational linkage network. *The Academy of Management Review* 8 (1): 79-89

Podolny JM, Page KL (1998) Network forms of organization. *Annual Review of Sociology* 24: 57-76

Provan KG, Kenis P (2008) Modes of network governance: Structure, management, and effectiveness. *Journal of Public Administration Research & Theory* 18: 229-252

Powell WW, White D, Koput KW, Owen-Smith J (2005) Network dynamics and field evolution: The growth of interorganizational collaboration in the life sciences. *American Journal of Sociology* 110 (4): 1132-1205

Powell WW, Koput KW, Smith-Doerr L (1996) Interorganizational collaboration and the locus of innovation: networks of learning in biotechnology. *Administrative Science Quarterly* 41 (1): 116-145

Provan KG, Milward HB (1995) A preliminary theory of interorganizational network effectiveness: A comparative study of four community mental health systems. *Administrative Science Quarterly* 40 (1): 1-33

# Company networks reloaded – putting a general functional approach to defining complex problems to the test

*Prof. Dr. Peter Krebs, Katja Aedtner, Marion Schultes*

## A. Introduction

Company networks[1] are a widespread economic phenomenon whereby companies collaborate by dividing tasks and which juridical literature has been dealing with for several decades.[2] The contributions range from dis-

---

1 Economic literature alternatively speaks of undertaking networks (Unternehmungsnetzwerk). See only *Corsten, H.H.*, Ansatzpunkte für die Koordination in heterarchischen und hierarchischen Unternehmungsnetzwerken, München 2000; *Miklis, M.*, Coopetitive Unternehmungsnetzwerke, Weimar 2010; *Sydow, J.*, Unternehmungsnetzwerke. Begriffe, Erscheinungsformen und Implikationen für die Mitbestimmung, Hans-Böckler Stiftung, HBS-Manuskript Nr. 30, Bonn 1991.

2 See *Amstutz, M.*, in: Honsell, W./Portmann, R./ Zäch, R./Zobl, D., Festschrift für Heinz Rey zum 60. Geburtstag, Zürich 2003, p. 161 (161 et seq.); id. Kritische Vierteljahreszeitschrift für Gesetzgebung und Rechtsprechung 2006, 105 (105 et seq.); *Böhner, R., R.*, Legal Issues of Multilateral Co-operations, Hart Publishing, Oxford and Portland, Oregon 2009 p. 153 et seq.; id. Kritische Vierteljahreszeitschrift für Gesetzgebung und Rechtsprechung 2006, 227 (227 et seq.); *Bräutigam, P.*, Deliktische Außenhaftung im Franchising, Baden-Baden 1994; *Collins, H.*, in: Amstutz, M., /Teubner, G., (eds.), Networks – Legal Issues of Multilateral Co-operation, Hart Publishing, Oxford, 2009, p. 187 (208 et seq.); *Druey, J. N.*, Kritische Vierteljahreszeitschrift für Gesetzgebung und Rechtsprechung 2006, 163 (163 et seq.); *Grundmann, S.*, Archiv für die civilistische Praxis 207 (2007), 718 (735 et seq.); id., in: Festschrift Westermann, Köln 2008, p. 227 (232 et seq.); *Heermann, P.W.*, Drittfinanzierte Erwerbsgeschäfte, Tübingen 1998; id. Kritische Vierteljahreszeitschrift für Gesetzgebung und Rechtsprechung 2006, 173 (173 et seq.); *Heldt, C.*, Baukooperation und Franchising als multilaterale Sonderverbindung, Baden-Baden 2010; id. Kritische Vierteljahreszeitschrift für Gesetzgebung und Rechtsprechung 2006, 208 (223 et seq.); *Kulms. R.*, Schuldrechtliche Organisationsverträge in der Unternehmenskooperation, Baden-Baden 2000; *Lange, K.W.*, Das Recht der Netzwerke, Frankfurt am Main 1998, recital 13, 380 et seq.; *Möschel, W.*, Archiv für die civilistische Praxis 186 (1986), 187 (211 et seq.); *Rohe, M.*, Netzverträge, Tübingen 1998, p. 85 et seq., esp. p. 129 et seq.; *Teubner, G.*, Zeitschrift für das gesamte Handels- und Wirtschaftsrecht 154 (1990), 295 (295 et seq.); id., in: Krohn, W./Küppers, G. (eds.), Emergenz: Die Entstehung von Ordnung, Organisa-

cussions about the autonomy of networks as juridical institute[3] to investigations of specific liability problems and duties of network participants.[4] Due to their diversity and difference compared to classic juridical institutes such as contracts or corporations jurists face significant difficulties in clarifying network problems. In this context research is considered to still be at the beginnings.[5]

These circumstances suggest approaching this topic from a completely new perspective. So far there is no juridical definition of networks.[6] Ac-

---

tion und Bedeutung, Berlin 1992, p. 210 (210 et seq.); id. Kritische Vierteljahreszeitschrift für Gesetzgebung und Rechtsprechung 1993, 367 (369, 373, 380 et seq.); id. Zeitschrift für das gesamte Handels- und Wirtschaftsrecht 165 (2001), 550 (550 et seq.); id., in: *Amstutz, M.* (ed.), Die vernetzte Wirtschaft: Netzwerke als Rechtsproblem, Zürich 2004, p. 11 (11 et seq.); id., Netzwerk als Vertragsverbund, 2004; id., in: Augsberg (ed.), Ungewissheit als Chance, Tübingen 2009, p. 109 (109 et seq.); *Wellenhofer, M.*, Kritische Vierteljahreszeitschrift für Gesetzgebung und Rechtsprechung 2006, 187 (187 et seq.); the public law discussion about networks mostly refers to networks consisting of states, networks in administration or governing authorities, see *Boysen, S.*, et al. (eds.), Netzwerke. 47. Assistententagung Öffentliches Recht, Berlin 2007.

3 First on net contracts (Netzverträge) *Möschel, W.*, Archiv für die civilistische Praxis 186 (1986), 187 (211 et seq.); further develped by *Rohe, M.*, Netzverträge, Tübingen 1998, p. 5 et seq., 65 et seq.;opposed by prevailing oppinion see only *Canaris, C. W.*, Bankvertragsrecht, Erster Teil, 4. ed., 2005, recital 393; *Einsele, D.*, Archiv für die civilistische Praxis 199 (1999), 145 (172 et seq.); *Hüffer,U.*, Zeitschrift für das gesamte Handels- und Wirtschaftsrecht 151 (1987), 93 (106 et seq.); *Koller, I.*, in: Köndgen, J. (ed.) Neue Entwicklungen im Bankhaftungsrecht, Köln 1987, p. 21 (25); *Köndgen, J.*, in: Köndgen, J. (ed.) Neue Entwicklungen im Bankhaftungsrecht, Köln 1987, p. 133 (144 et seq.); *Martinek, M.*, Moderne Vertragstypen III, München 1992, § 30 II.3.c. 4.; *Oechsler, J.*, Gerechtigkeit im modernen Austauschvertrag, Tübingen 1997, p. 353 et seq.; *Picker, E.*, Juristenzeitung 1987, 1041, 1057; *Stoffels, M.*, Gesetzlich nicht geregelte Schuldverträge, Tübingen 2001, p. 268 et seq.; *Wellenhofer, M.*, Zulieferverträge im Privat- und Wirtschaftsrecht, München 1999, p. 177.

4 Regarding the onward transfer of network discounts see: *Teubner, G.*, Netzwerk als Vertragsverbund, Baden-Baden 2004, p. 142 et seq.; *id.* Zeitschrift für das gesamte Handels- und Wirtschaftsrecht 168 (2004), 78 (92); *Böhner, R.*, Vom Franchisevertrags- zum Franchisenetzwerkrecht, Betriebs-Berater 2004, 119, 119 et seq.; *Grundmann, S.*, Archiv für die civilistische Praxis 207 (2007), 718 (747 et seq.).

5 *Grundmann, S.*, Archiv für die civilistische Praxis 207 (2007), 718 (719, 767); see also: *Martinek, M.*, in: Martinek, M./Semler, F. J./Habermeier, S./Flohr, E. (eds.), Vertriebsrecht, 3. ed., München 2010, § 1 recital 22.

6 See *Lange, K. W.*, Das Recht der Netzwerke, Frankfurt am Main 1998; *Möschel, W.* Archiv für die civilistische Praxis 186 (1986), 187 (187 et seq.); *Rohe, M.*, Netz-

cording to some contributions a juridical definition of networks may generally have no relevance for jurisprudential network research.[7] A definition is deemed insignificant based on the assumption that it is merely relevant to know in which way and with which legal consequences network participants are tied.[8] However, if one assumes that the obligations and the legal consequences are not based on agreements, but exist by virtue of objective law (extending the scope of law if need be) then it is necessary to know in order to warrant the legal consequences which cases are covered by these legal consequences and thus a definition is required.[9]

If, for instance, a network is to be evaluated under competition law it is important to know how networks are defined so as to make the distinction to other constellations within competition law clear. Similarly, this applies to the legal co-ordination of a network. In order to achieve an adequate co-ordination therewith ensuring that the network runs efficiently it has to be determined whether network-specific mechanisms can be applied to the object considered. Regarding networks as standing between the market and hierarchy[10] is useful since this serves to illustrate an approximate classification of networks. However, it does not substitute the meticulous specification of the functional preconditions for networks in form of a definition.

---

verträge, Frankfurt am Main 1998; *Teubner, G.* poses pre-conditions for the development of a legal contract network, but does not expand on the functional features of networks in: Netzwerk als Vertragsverbund, Baden-Baden 2004, p. 117; *Ruiz Peris, J. I.* in: ibid. (eds.): Nuevas Perspectivas del Derecho de Redes Empresariales,Valencia 2012, 73 (87).

7 *Zimmer, D., in: Immenga, U./Mestmäcker, E.-J.,* (eds.), Wettbewerbsrecht: GWB, Band 2, 5. ed., München 2014, § 1 recital 308; see also *Buxbaum, R. M.,* Journal of Institutional and Theoretical Economics 149 (1993), 698 (704): *„Network is not a legal concept.*“; *Teubner, G.*, Netzwerk als Vertragsverbund, Baden-Baden 2004, p. 9.

8 *Zimmer, D., in: Immenga, U./Mestmäcker, E.-J.*(eds.), Wettbewerbsrecht: GWB, Band 2, 5. ed., München 2014, § 1 recital 308.

9 See also *Druey,* in: Amstutz, M./Teubner, G. (eds.), Networks – Legal Issues of Multilateral Co-operation, Oxford 2009, p. 87 (94).

10 *Thorelli, H. B.,* Strategic Management Journal 7 (1986), 37 et seq.; *Lianos, I.,* Journal of Competition Law and Economics 3 (2007), 625 (652 et seq.); *Ménard, C.,* Journal of Institutional and Theoretical Economics 160 (2004), 345 (345); see: *Williamson, O.,* Administrative Science Quarterly 36 (1991), 269 (271); *Schüller, A./Krüsselberg, H. G.,* Grundbegriffe zur Ordnungstheorie und Politischen Ökonomik, Marburg 1991, p. 107.

But what is a functional definition and can something be determined functionally if the solution is still unknown and is a definition supposed to stand at the end instead of the beginning of a scientific analysis of a phenomenon? Juridical examinations relatively often approach matters in a way that places the definition at the end of the investigation. This is a possible, but not always necessary approach. The starting point for investigating company networks lies in the field of economy. This economic phenomenon is, generally speaking, relatively known. Especially the field of business administration has already intensively dealt with the definition of networks.[11] Due to this already existing knowledge a juridical differentiation of the phenomenon is possible by adapting it to juridical structures. For a juridical definition it is vital that it not only includes common or regular cases, but preferably all cases which belong to this phenomenon. As a consequence, a juridical definition should not only comprise the common (typical), but also the constitutive preconditions.

If the prerequisites have already been discussed for a long time and intensively as is the case with company networks albeit in a neighbouring discipline, it can be assumed that all or almost all potential preconditions have been addressed. To filter the constitutive features from the potential preconditions is a logical juridical process, which requires a certain knowledge of how the phenomenon functions, but which does not require the knowledge of solutions. In this way, a juridical definition, which is restricted to constitutive features, can and shall be derived from the attempts to define the economic phenomenon of company networks.[12]

However, this first step is – merely in the broadest sense – the derivation of a functional definition, because initially it is rather the specification of the phenomenon. More narrowly speaking, the definition would be functional if it described an independent juridical institute and not merely an actual phenomenon. But what is an independent juridical institute? The notion of juridical institute is associated with a group of connected rules that apply to an abstract issue. Accordingly, the institute is first and foremost distinguished from an individual rule. However, the matter discussed here is the point at which an abstract issue can be regarded as a juridical phenomenon, i.e. an individual juridical institute. An individual institute

11 See literature mentioned in B note 16.

12 Regarding possibilities and limits of interdisciplinary works of law and economics see *Raisch, P./Schmidt, K.*, in: Grimm, D. (ed.), Rechtswissenschaft und Nachbarwissenschaften, Bd. 1, 2. ed., München 1976, p. 143 (151 et seq.).

has the juridical right to exist only if it combines problems or chances which otherwise would not exist at all or at least not in this way. Whether company networks are individual institutes, such as a contract or a corporation, is debatable.[13] Acknowledging a company network as an institute depends on whether it shows problems and chances which would not exist otherwise. Since company networks have been discussed for a long time it can be hoped that, if specific chances and risks do exist, they already have been addressed in some form whatsoever. Accordingly, the filtering approach is also applicable here. The problems hitherto discussed therefore have to be examined as to whether they only occur in networks, i.e. whether they are network-specific. Only if this network-specific problem appears in all networks, i.e. only if the problem is constitutive, then it is also part of the network definition. Since the existence of an institute is justified by the existence of constitutive, network-specific problems it is possible, based on the problems discussed, to define whether an independent institute exits here and which limits this may have.[14] Should it turn out that no such network-specific, constitutive features exist then company networks cannot be classified as institutes, but as a phenomenon to which solely the definition developed in the first step would apply. But even if company networks turn out to be an independent institute then the first step of the definition is still not dispensable. Contrarily, it clarifies the framework, which is specified by the second (radically) functional consideration aimed at the justification as an institute.

---

13 First on network contracts *Möschel, W.*, Archiv für die civilistische Praxis 186 (1986), 187 (211 et seq.); further developed by *Rohe, M.*, Netzverträge, Tübingen 1998, p. 5 et seq., 65 et seq.; opposed by prevailing opinion see only *Canaris, C. W.*, Bankvertragsrecht, Erster Teil, 4. ed. Berlin 2005, recital 393; *Einsele, D.*, Archiv für die civilistische Praxis 199 (1999), 145 (172 et seq.); *Hüffer, U.*, Zeitschrift für das gesamte Handels- und Wirtschaftsrecht 151 (1987), 93 (106 et seq.); *Koller, I.*, in: Köndgen, J. (ed.) Neue Entwicklungen im Bankhaftungsrecht, Köln 1987, p. 21 (25); *Köndgen, J.*, in: Köndgen, J. (ed.) Neue Entwicklungen im Bankhaftungsrecht, Köln 1987, p. 133 (144 et seq.); *Martinek, M.*, Moderne Vertragstypen III, München 1992; § 30 II.3.c. 4.; *Oechsler, J.*, Gerechtigkeit im modernen Austauschvertrag, Tübingen 1997, p. 353 et seq.; *Picker, E.* Juristenzeitung 1987, 1041, 1057; *Stoffels, M.*, Gesetzlich nicht geregelte Schuldverträge, Tübingen 2001, p. 268 et seq.; *Wellenhofer, M.*, Zulieferverträge im Privat- und Wirtschaftsrecht, München 1999, p. 177.

14 Regarding a similar attempt to deduce the legitimation as legal institute from the functions of the special relations see: *Krebs, P.*, Sonderverbindung und außerdeliktische Schutzpflichten, München 2000, p. 210 et seq.

This two-step procedure applied here to deduce a definition for a juridical phenomenon and a juridical institute respectively (1. from economic to juridical phenomenon; 2. from juridical phenomenon to functional juridical institute) is, generally speaking, universally applicable. However, it requires the existence of appropriate preliminary debates about the phenomenon or the problems of the possible institute. Thereby, each of the two steps of the procedure can be usefully adapted separately. Used on its own the first step can help derive a definition for a juridical phenomenon. The second step used on its own can determine the existence of a juridical institute without having to develop a definition in advance. However, when using this second step separately it has to be known preliminarily that a juridical phenomenon is being investigated.

It is the aim of this work to firstly derive a juridical definition for company networks and therewith provide a new approach to company networks for juridical research. And secondly, a universally applicable, but so far not common, approach to derive definitions is put to the test with a specific set of problems. An additional outcome should be whether company networks can be regarded as independent institutes.[15]

## B. "Company network" – From the economic to the juridical phenomenon

There is a wide range of economic attempts to define the phenomenon of "company networks",[16] which shows enormous variation regarding the

---

15 The derivation of a network definition is thereby a part of a greater joint research project on company networks at the University of Siegen. The project's aim is, on the one hand, to provide new impulses for fundamental questions of the legal network discussion and, on the other hand, to further illuminate important individual questions.

16 See *Sydow, J.*, Unternehmungsnetzwerke, Düsseldorf 1991, p. 12; *id.*, Strategische Netzwerke, Wiesbaden 1992, p. 79; *Beck, T. C.*, Kosteneffiziente Netzwerkkooperation, Wiesbaden 1998, p. 11 et seq.; *Corsten, H.*, Ansatzpunkte für die Koordination in heterarchischen und hierarchischen Unternehmungsnetzwerken, Kaiserslautern 2000, p. 2 et seq.; *Ebertz, P.*, Risikowirkung von Unternehmenskooperationen, Aachen 2006, p. 12; *v. d. Eichen, F.* et al., Harvard Business Manager 8 (2003), 99 (101); *Jarillo, J. C.*, Strategic Management Journal 9 (1988), 31 (32); *Johanson, J./Mattsson, L.*, International Studies of Management and Organization 17 (1987), 34 (34 et seqq.); *Männel, B.*, Netzwerke in der Zulieferindustrie, Wiesbaden 1996, p. 25; *Miklis, M.*, Coopetitive Unternehmungsnetzwerke, Marburg 2010, p. 44, p. 50 et seq.; *o. V.*, zfo 1998, 242 (242); *Powell, W. W.*, Research in

language as well as the content.[17] Nonetheless, this is not the reason why the complete definitions are not reproduced here. Rather, the interesting aspects are merely the individual features discussed collectively and not the entire definitions. Accordingly, only those features discussed in business economics are used for the following analysis as a basis for a juridical definition of the phenomenon of company networks.

## I. Number of participants

Business economical literature usually requires a minimum of three,[18] seldom two[19] parties to be involved in a network. If the aim is the possibility of multilateral interactions and structures[20] then a minimum of three participants is required. Only in this case the special demand for co-ordination and specific problems regarding co-ordination arise. The requirement

---

Organizational Behaviour 12 (1990), 295 (303); *Thorelli, H. B.*, Strategic Management Journal 7 (1986), 37 (38); *Winkler, G.*, Koordination in strategischen Netzwerken, Wiesbaden 1999, p. 25; *Wipprich, M.*, Größe und Struktur von Unternehmensnetzwerken, Tübingen 2008, p. 9.

17 *Miklis, M.*, Coopetitive Unternehmungsnetzweke, Weimar bei Marburg 2010, p. 48 rightly criticises that a significant reason for the confusion regarding the term of company network lies in mixing constitutive and differentiating (here real) features.

18 *Easton, G./Håkansson, H.*, International Journal of Research in Marketing 13 (1996), 407 (408); *Beck, T. C.*, Kosteneffiziente Netzwerkkooperation, Wiesbaden 1998, p. 17; *Corsten, H.*, Ansatzpunkte für die Koordination in heterarchischen und hierarchischen Unternehmungsnetzwerken, Kaiserslautern 2000, p. 4; *Evantschisky, H.*, Erfolg von Dienstleistungsnetzwerken, Kaiserslautern 2003, p. 39; *Miklis, M.*, Coopetitive Unternehmungsnetzwerke, Weimar bei Marburg 2010, p. 50 et seq.; *Wagner, M.*, Rahmenbedingungen zur dezentralen Koordination in logistischen Netzwerken, Brandsberg 2005, p. 32; *Winkler, G.*, Konzept und Einsatzmöglichkeiten des Supply Chain Controlling, Wiesbaden 2008, p. 25; *Winkler, G.*, Koordination in strategischen Netzwerken, Wiesbaden 1999, p. 25; *Wipprich, M.* Größe und Struktur von Unternehmensnetzwerken, Tübingen 2008, p. 9.

19 *Thorelli, H. B.*, Strategic Management Journal 7 (1986), 37 (38); *Zundel, P.*, Management von Produktions-Netzwerken, Wiesbaden 1999, p. 20.

20 *Miklis, M.*, Coopetitive Unternehmungsnetzwerke, Weimar bei Marburg 2010, p. 44; *Winkler, G.*, Koordination in strategischen Netzwerken, Wiesbaden 1999, p. 25; *Lange, K. W.*, Das Recht der Netzwerke, Frankfurt am Main 1998, recital 10; see also *Männel, B.*, Netzwerke in der Zulieferindustrie, Wiesbaden 1996, p. 25; *Wertz, B.*, Management von Lieferanten-Produzenten-Beziehungen, Wiesbaden 2000, p. 9.

of at least three parties is also juridically convincing, because a juridically fully developed range of tools already exists for two-party relations in form of traditional contract law. If this two party relation exists in form of an accommodation relation the tools are less developed, but a differentiation between a normal two-party relation and a cooperative multi-party relation has to be made. Even if two parties co-operate in form of a co-operation company law holds all solutions whereas with three parties non-regulated network problems can already arise. Accordingly, a search for juridical tools to overcome these problems is not required with two-party constellations.[21] As a consequence, a juridical network definition does not entail pure two-party relations; a minimum of three participating companies is required.

## II. Companies

Company networks consist of companies. Of course, also non-profit forms of organization (NGOs, public associations) can feature network-like structures. But the effects and problems which arise with company networks are in these cases only partially existent. There is no economic network aim[22] and issues of third party liability as well as the question regarding the distribution of profits and losses are practically irrelevant. Therefore, the object of investigation here is limited to company networks.

The individual company participating in the network must be a company at the point of entering the network and remain a company for the entire duration of the network relation. If a company seizes to exist at enter-

---

21 This is also apparent in the legal discussion about liability questions in the network with the concomitant considerations regarding piercing the corporate vale see: *Bräutigam,P.*, Deliktische Außenhaftung im Franchising, Baden-Baden 1994; *Collins, H.*, in: Amstutz, M./Teubner, G. (eds.), Networks – Legal Issues of Multilateral Co-operation, 2009, p. 187 (208 et seq.); *Grundmann, S.*, Archiv für die civilistische Praxis 207 (2007), 718 (735 et seq.); *id.*, in: Festschrift H.P. Westermann, Köln 2008, p. 227 (232 et seq.); *Lange, K. W.*, Das Recht der Netzwerke, Frankfurt am Main 1998, recital 13, 380 et seq.; *Möschel, W.*, Archiv für die civilistische Praxis 186 (1986), 187 (211 et seq.); *Rohe, M.*, Netzverträge, Tübingen 1998, p. 85 et seq., esp. p. 129 et seq.; *Teubner, G.*, Zeitschrift für das gesamte Handels- und Wirtschaftsrecht 1990, 295 (295 et seq.); *id.*, Kritische Vierteljahreszeitschrift für Gesetzgebung und Rechtsprechung 1993, 367 (369, 373, 380 et seq.).

22 See below B.III.

ing a network or during the duration of the network relation, which can only happen when all company activities are completely inserted into a network organised as corporation, then this former company can no longer be regarded as an individual network participant due to the lack of company features. Instead, it is rather an inseparable part of the network.[23] The network-specific organisational questions and issues no longer exist at the point where all company activities have inseparably merged into a single corporation. The remaining issues are settled by company law.

### 1. Legal independence

The fact that all participants in a company network have to be legally independent companies is affirmed without further problems by economic literature[24] even though this prerequisite is not self-evident. There are enormous organisational similarities between the layout of an organisationally decentralised company, i.e. a decentralised network-like structure within a single legal entity, and the creation of a network between legally independent entities. At first, this may suggest that the demand for legal independence can be dispensed with.

Regarding the juridical assessment of these constellations, there are, however, considerable differences between decentralised organisations within a legal entity and networks. When the individual participants lack legal independence neither the problem regarding the legal relation between the participants nor the legal outward relation of each individual participant arises. Accordingly, if the normative measurement problems are not the same then both cases should not be comprised under the notion of networks. The fact that the notion of business networks is based on cooperating, legally independent companies is conducive to this standpoint. As a consequence, company networks are to be limited to legally independent companies.

23 If, however, a network company merges according to § 2 et seq. UmwG with a network-external company then the "new" company automatically becomes a network member.

24 So *Beck, T.C.*, Kosteneffiziente Netzwerkkooperation, Wiesbaden 1998, p. 12; *Ebertz, P.*, Risikowirkungen von Unternehmenskooperationen, Aachen 2006, p. 12; *Männel, B.*, Netzwerke in der Zulieferindustrie, Wiesbaden 1996, p. 28; *Miklis, M.*, Coopetitive Unternehmungsnetzwerke, Marburg 2010, p. 44; *Sydow, J.*, Unternehmungsnetzwerke, Düsseldorf 1991, p. 12.

## 2. Economic independence

Unlike the legal independence, economic independence as a prerequisite is indeed controversially discussed in business economics. Partly it is assumed that network companies are mostly dependent.[25] Others regard networks as economically mostly independent[26] or talk about network companies as generally economically independent.[27]

Factually, it is the economically independent companies that establish networks. This, however, cannot lead to the conclusion that the (former) economic independence of network companies is a functionally necessary prerequisite. Moreover, the question regarding economic independence also arises after establishing or entering a network.

Firstly, it has to be clarified which relation of the network companies the economic independence refers to. Thereby, a distinction has to be made between the network internal and the network external relation of the individual network companies. In determining the notion of "company network" the economic independence of network participants refers to the network internal relations to other network members. That is why group companies can function as network companies in a network with other companies not belonging to the same group even though they are dependent on their parent company (network external relation).[28] Network-internally, these affiliated companies are initially not economically dependent regarding the other (different) network companies.

Furthermore, it has to be clarified to what extent the economic independence of network companies is actually relevant. Suggestions in research literature range from economically dependent to economically autonomous.[29] From a competition point of view a company is economically independent if its decisions are not shaped by the decision of other companies due to dependences. Competition law, however, does not try to in-

25 *Sydow, J.*, Unternehmungsnetzwerke, Düsseldorf 1991, p. 12.

26 *Ebertz, P.*, Risikowirkungen von Unternehmenskooperationen, Tübingen 2006, p. 12.

27 *Backhaus, K./Mayer, M.*, Wirtschaftswissenschaftliches Studium 1993, 330 (330); *Ruiz Peris, J. I.*, in: id. (eds.): Nuevas Perspectivas del Derecho de Redes Empresariales, Valencia 2012, 73 (87).

28 *Sydow, J.*, Strategische Netzwerke, Wiesbaden 1992, p. 73 et seq.; regarding the relation between network and corporate group see C.II.3.a).

29 *Sydow, J.*, Strategische Netzwerke, Wiesbaden 1992, p. 73 et seq.; regarding the relation between network and corporate group see C.II.3.a).

tegrate this dependence within the notion of company, but rather clearly differentiates between companies and economically (competitive) dependence.[30] This suggests excluding the question of economic dependence from the notion of company. Irrespective of whether economic independence could be regarded as a feature within or without the notion of company a demand for economic independence is opposed by the fact that a legally secure, at any time recognizable categorization as a company network would no longer be possible with such prerequisites. Economic independence is, above all, also functionally not necessary. It is only functionally relevant, in order to include the chances, risks and, above all, conflicts of interests associated with company networks, that the company actually shows business establishments which result in the company's own interests. Tensions already arise here between network and individual interests constituting the network conflict. This precondition is also legally secure.

If the aim is this minor form of independent economic activity, namely after establishing or entering a network, then great importance is no longer attached to economic independence due to the fact that the individual economic activity is already comprised in the notion of company.

Summing up, it can be noted that the economic independence understood as the economic extent of the network companies' freedom is not a constitutive prerequisite for a company network. Instead, the aim has to be put on the individual economic activities of network participants, as cause for the arising network conflict, which are already guaranteed by the company feature[31] of the network members.

### 3. Economic interests of the individual network companies

Unlike the economic activities, the individual interests of network companies may be constitutive. The network companies expect to gain advantages by joining a network. The interests of the network participants are

---

30 Regarding the term network and dependent employment activities *Hengst, D.*, in: Langen, E./Bunte, H.-J. (eds.), Europäisches Kartellrecht, Band 2, 12. ed., München 2014, Art. 101 AEUV, recital 29, 33 et seq., 58 et seq.

31 See *ECJ,* Neue Juristische Wochenschrift 1991, 2891 (2891 et seq.); *ECJ,* Neue Juristische Wochenschrift 1993, 2597 (2598); *ECJ,* Neue Juristische Wochenschrift 2002, 877 (878); *ECJ,* Europäische Zeitschrift für Wirtschaftsrecht 2006, 306 (310); *ECJ,* Europäische Zeitschrift für Wirtschaftsrecht 2008, 93 (95).

thereby characterised by tensions between individual and collective interests.[32]

Furthermore, the individual interests of each network member can be very different. But the participants of a network are bound together by common collective interests, which usually manifest themselves in the aim of the network.[33]

For conflicts of interest to arise in the network between the network and the individual companies it suffices that each network company has an individual interest. Even a very intensive co-ordination normally does not lead to a complete loss of the individual economic interests. Even if the entire economic activity of a company occurs within the network and it therefore completely depends on the network from an economic point of view the network company nonetheless conducts this activity in its own interest.[34] Only if a network company no longer pursues individual interests and the collective interest exclusively controls the network company's interests then the network company has been converted into a "network corporation". As a consequence, it has forfeited its independent feature of a company as well as its economic independence. The notion of networks does not have to include this case since due to the lack of individual interests outside of the corporation company law can fully account for these issues.

Accordingly, it is constitutive for a company network that the companies participating in the network pursue their individual interests.

### 4. Provisional results regarding companies as preconditions for company networks

As a result of the analysis it can be said that their members being companies is juridically constitutive for company networks. This requires the legal independence as well as the pursuit of individual interests on part of

32 See *Teubner, G.*, in: Augsberg (ed.), Ungewissheit als Chance, Tübingen 2009, p. 109 (122); *Sydow, J.*, Strategische Netzwerke, Wiesbaden 1992, p. 90, who describes these tensions as paradox of co-operation; see. *Ruiz Peris, J. I.*, in: id. (ed.): Nuevas Perspectivas del Derecho de Redes Empresariales, p. 73 (115 et seq.).

33 Regarding the network aim see B.II.3.

34 See *Ruiz Peris, J. I.* in: id. (ed.): Nuevas Perspectivas del Derecho de Redes Empresariales, Valencia 2012, p. 73 (89 et seq.).

the network companies. The economic independence is not a constitutive feature of company networks. The conflict of interests between network interests and individual interests necessary for the notion of networks is already included in the general term of company since even the smallest individual business operations suffice for that.

## III. Network aim

Company networks are characterised by a (economic) network aim.[35] A network aim is a co-operation benefit[36] in form of a competitive advantage, which can be achieved by co-ordinating network companies.[37] This is the incentive for participating companies to be involved in a company network. The co-operation profit, which manifests itself in the realization of economic advantages, could not be realized without the network.[38] The

---

35 As *Becker, N.*, Regelungsfelder für Unternehmensnetzwerke, Wiesbaden 1999, p. 164 et seq.; *Männel, B.*, Netzwerke in der Zulieferindustrie, Wiesbaden 1996, p. 30; *Rohe, M.*, Netzverträge, Tübingen 1998, p. 76, p. 84; *Teubner, G.*, Netzwerk als Vertragsverbund, Baden-Baden 2004, p. 148; *Krebs, P.*, Sonderverbindung und außerdeliktische Schutzpflichten, München 2000, p. 315; *Bayreuther, F.*, Wirtschaftlich-existentiell abhängige Unternehmen im Konzern-, Kartell- und Arbeitsrecht, Berlin 2001, p. 289; *Lange, K. W.*, Virtuelle Unternehmen, Heidelberg 2001, p. 81 et seq.; *Schimansky, A.*, Der Franchisevertrag nach deutschem und niederländischem Recht, Tübingen 2003, p. 113, 125, 167; *Wellenhofer, M.*, Kritische Vierteljahreszeitschrift für Gesetzgebung und Rechtsprechung 2006, 187 (188); *Nicklisch, F.* Betriebs-Berater 2000, 2166 (2166 et seq.); see also *Hune, M.*, Netzwerkverträge in der Transportwirtschaft, Berlin 2010, p. 22 et seq.; *Wittig, A.*, Management von Unternehmensnetzwerken, Wiesbaden 2005, p. 29; *Heldt, C.*, Baukooperation und Franchising als multilaterale Sonderverbindung, Baden-Baden 2010, p. 70 et seq.

36 See *Messner, D.*, Die Netzwerkgesellschaft, Köln 1998, p. 170; *Powell, W.W.*, Research in Organizational Behaviour 12 (1990), 295 (303); *Sydow, J.*, Strategische Netzwerke, Wiesbaden 1992, p. 93; *Wildemann, H.* , Zeitschrift für Betriebswirtschaft 67 (1997), 417 (418); *Zhang, H.*, Ein Netzwerkansatz zur Modellierung, Analyse und Gestaltung von Konzernen, Hannover 1996, p. 188.

37 *Siebert, H.*, in: Sydow, J. (ed.), Management von Netzwerkorganisationen: Beiträge aus der „Managementforschung", Wiesbaden 2010, p. 7 (9), originally published in: Staehle, W. H./Sydow, J. (eds.), Managementforschung 1, Wiesbaden 1991, p. 291 et seq.

38 *Ahlert, D.*, Brands go East – Internationale Markenführung und Netzmarketing, Projektbericht Nr. 1 2006, p. 13; *Rohe, M.*, Netzverträge: Rechtsprobleme komplexer Vertragsverbindungen, Tübingen 1998, p. 77.

form and extent of the profit can vary for each company involved in the network.[39] The possible advantages include, amongst others, an improved access to new markets, cost advantages or quality improvement.[40] However, it is not a precondition for a network to exist that the intended advantages and therewith the network aim are actually achieved. Despite their public utility, non-profit enterprises can still feature an economic network aim since they also strive for market success, but without the intention of making profit. Therefore, this situation is related to the notion of commercial transaction where, according to the preferable view,[41] the intention of gaining income on the market, but not the intention of gaining profit is decisive.

Empirical investigations[42] partially also investigate cases of business associations. It is disputable if business associations can be considered as company networks.[43] In some cases the focus on performance based objectives or the intention of making a profit is considered as demarcation criterion for business associations as supra-company co-operations and company networks as inter-company co-operations.[44] Mainly, business

39 *Miklis, M.*, Coopetitive Unternehmungsnetzwerke, Marburg 2010, p. 163.

40 Networks also entail disadvantages in form of co-ordination costs and risks causing domino effects (see comprehensively hereon *Schultes, M.*, Unternehmensnetzwerke und das Kartellverbot des Art. 101 AEUV, forthcoming). However, this may not result in further demands regarding the notion of network.

41 *Schmidt, K.*, Handelsrecht, Köln 2014, § 9 II recital 37 et seq.; *Canaris, C. W.*, Handelsrecht, 24. ed., München 2006, § 2 recital 14; *Hopt, K.J.*, in: Baumbach, A./ Hopt, K.J., HGB, 35. ed. München 2012, § 1 recital 16; *Emmerich, V*, in: Heymann, HGB, 2. ed. Berlin, 1995-1999, § 1 HGB recital 9, 12; *Kindler, P.*, in: Ebenroth, T./Boujong, D./Joost, D., HGB, 2. ed. München 2008, § 1 recital 27; essentially *Raisch, P.*, Geschichtliche Voraussetzungen, Heidelberg 1965, p. 186 et seq.

42 See *Glückler J./Németh, S./Melot de Beauregard, P.*, DB 2011, 2701 (2707). Interviews with associations are not explicitly mentioned as company networks here. Based on the large number of members in networks, i.e. more than 1000, it can be assumed that associations are comprised here.

43 See, for instance, the differentiation between inter-company and supra-company co-operations in *Hess*, Netzwerkcontrolling Instrumente und ihre Werkzeugunterstützung (neue betriebswirtschaftliche Forschung (nbf)), Wiesbaden 2002, p. 8 et seq. and *Wohlgemuth, O.*, Management netzwerkartiger Kooperationen: Instrumente für die unternehmensübergreifende Steuerung, Wiesbaden 2002, p. 13 et seq.

44 *Hess, T.*, Netzwerkcontrolling, Wiesbaden 2002, p. 8 et seq.; *Wohlgemuth, O.*, Management netzwerkartiger Kooperationen, Wiesbaden 2002, p. 13 et seq.

associations include the co-ordination of common economic interests of the companies, but not the co-ordination of immediate business activities per se. But also when co-ordinating the common interests network-specific problems arise so that a demarcation premised on the existence of performance-based objectives does not suffice. But above all, in the scope of business associations co-operations are implemented which are typical for company networks such as the development of common terms and conditions or the exchange of information. Consequently, also business associations can be regarded as company networks if all preconditions are met.

## IV. Co-ordination and organizing the co-ordination

In order to ensure the synchronization of three or more participants and above all to achieve the network aim the activities of the network companies have to be co-ordinated.[45] The co-ordination therefore is a constitutive feature for entrepreneurial networks.

The extent of the co-ordination depends on the desired intensity of co-operation by the companies involved. The co-ordination can be organised informally, i.e. without legal ties in the sense of fulfilment obligation, but also within the scope of contractual exchange relations or in form of a corporation as co-ordinating instrument. In a network a combination of these instruments in various forms is possible. On the one hand, various network participants can take part in different forms of collaboration. On the other hand, each individual network member can be legally bound by several activities that are pursued in the network at the same time. Accordingly, one and the same network can show a wide range of legal structures.

Sometimes it is suggested to limit the notion of networks to networks with their own identity or to networks with a higher level of organisation.[46] And indeed, by drawing on such "high-level" networks certain organisational structures can be found which do not regularly exist in infor-

45 See *Becker, N.*, Regelungsfelder für Unternehmensnetzwerke, Wiesbaden 1999, p. 171; *Hune, M.*, Netzwerkverträge in der Transportwirtschaft, Berlin 2010, p. 23; *Rohe, M.*, Netzverträge, Tübingen 1998, p. 76; see *Ruiz Peris, J. I.*, in: id. (ed.): Nuevas Perspectivas del Derecho de Redes Empresariales, Valencia 2012, p. 73 (88).

46 *Glückler J./Németh, S./Melot de Beauregard, P.*, Netzwerke: Rechtsformen und Folgen für die Zusammenarbeit von Unternehmen DB 2011, 2701 (2702).

mal networks. The limitation to such high-level networks may accordingly be reasonable when looking at questions from the point of view of organisational law. For a general juridical assessment of the phenomenon of company networks these limitations cannot be justified since chances, risks and general problems not only arise in connection with high-level networks.

In competition law, the co-ordination without lawfully binding fulfilment agreements is called concerted practices.[47] Under general law of obligation an accommodation relationship emerges. If, as often is the case, essential economic values are concerned and if the law of torts can only insufficiently cope with possible damages caused,[48] then this relation can at least ex lege be regarded as a special relation in the sense of § 241 par. 2 BGB, which, however, does not entail any obligation to perform, but is associated with duties of trust and protection outside the scope of tort law.[49]

The parties can conclude real explicit or implicit contracts for the network. This case also entails, just as all special relations in the sense of § 241 par. 2 BGB, duties of trust and protection, but in addition also obligations to perform, since it can be regarded as contractual obligation within the meaning of § 241 par. 1 BGB.

Co-ordination is furthermore permissible in form of a contract of association, i.e. the foundation of a corporation. The foundation of such a corporation would entail duties of trust and protection to an increased extent as well as the application of a wide range of detailed rules under company law.

Thus, the co-ordination of the network members in form of an accommodation relationship and an exchange or association contract is a constitutive feature of a company network.

---

47 Competition law nonetheless ties consequences to such practices in Art. 101 TFEU or § 1 GWB (see *ECJ*, Neue Juristische Wochenschrift 1976, 470 (471); Europäische Zeitschrift für Wirtschaftsrecht 2009, 505 (506), according to which concerted practices result in similar effects as entailed in an agreement).

48 Regarding the prerequisits *Krebs, P.*, Sonderverbindung und außervertragliche Schutzpflichten, München 2000, p. 236 et seq. esp. 239.

49 *Krebs, P.*, Sonderverbindung und außervertragliche Schutzpflichten, München 2000, p. 236 et seq. esp. 239; other opinion for instance *Grüneberg, C.*, in: Palandt, 74. ed. München 2015, Einl v § 241 recital 8; *Heinrichs, H.*, Heldrich, A./ Koller, I./Prölls, J./ et al., Festschrift für Claus-Wilhelm Canaris zum 70. Geburtstag, München 2007, p. 421.

## V. Exchange of economic independence for co-ordination in order to achieve the network aim

Most features of the definition for company networks are static. However, there are several constitutive features in a network which mutually depend on and therefore interact with each other. A network company contributes to the network with economic activity and thereby at the same time loses factual economic independence. The loss of independence can be especially seen in the co-operation sector of the network.[50] In return for their loss of economic independence the companies, however, expect a co-operational gain, which can only be achieved through co-ordination.[51] The economic independence is therefore partially exchanged for co-ordination.[52] Accordingly, there is a functional link between economic independence, the network and the co-ordination. Only in relating to each other in a way that requires company networks to partially trade their economic independence, i.e. their capacity to freely make decisions and their freedom of action regarding the contributed economic activities, for co-operation allows the companies to achieve their network aim. For this reason, this functional connection is a constitutive feature of every company network.

## VI. Bundling of resources

Only rarely is the bundling of resources explicitly mentioned as a feature of entrepreneurial networks in economic literature.[53] However, the bundling of resources is regarded as an essential advantage of company networks.[54] At least in the case of applying a vast understanding of the term resources the bundling of resources is a mandatory prerequisite. On

---

50 See also *Eckert, S. M.*, Strategieorientiertes Kostenmanagement in Unternehmensnetzwerken, Wiesbaden 2009, p. 29 et seq.

51 See *Sydow, J.*, Strategische Netzwerke, Wiesbaden 1992, p. 90.

52 See *Sydow, J.*, Strategische Netzwerke, Wiesbaden 1992, p. 90; see *Ruiz Peris, J. I.*, in: id. (ed.), Nuevas Perspectivas del Derecho de Redes Empresariales, Valencia 2012, p. 73 (88).

53 See *Powell, W.W.*, Research in Organizational Behaviour 12 (1990), 295 (303).

54 *Teubner, G.*, Netzwerk als Vertragsverbund, Baden-Baden 2004, p. 43 et seq. See in this context also *Martinek, M.*, in: Martinek, M./Semler, F. J./Habermeier, S./ Flohr, E., Vertriebsrecht (eds.), 3. ed., München 2010, § 1 recital 22; *Sydow, J.*, Strategische Netzwerke, Tübingen 1992, p. 80 et seq., 242 et seq.; *Semlinger, K.*,

the one hand, this entails the bundling (the exchange) of know-how, information or organisational skills. Without this bundling of resources the efficient realisation of goals is unimaginable. On the other hand, the type of resources as well as the extent of their use is furthermore of importance. The underlying notion of bundling, therefore, differentiates between a loose and a close bundling of resources. The loose bundling entails the mere provision of resources[55] as well as the granting of rights of use. The full legal control over the provided resources remains with the respective company. The close bundling describes the amalgamation of the resources to an entity by contributing the resources to a corporation, which was founded for the purpose of co-ordination. A close bundling of resources is not mandatory for the affirmation of a network, but possible. For the operability a loose bundling of resources suffices.

In conclusion, the underlying wider understanding of the notion of the (required) bundling of resources has a two-fold effect.[56] Firstly, this includes the amalgamation to an entity as well as the provision, the access and the possibility to use resources. And secondly, this understanding of resources furthermore also includes know-how, information or organisational skills. It is in this way that the different manifestations of networks can be equally grasped. Due to the possibility of loose and close bundling of resources a polymorph range of legal structures can emerge in one and the same network through the participation of different members in various network activities as already shown with regard to co-ordination.

## VII. Voluntariness of the participation in a network

The economic idea of networks is associated with the voluntariness of the union. Indeed, the state could enforce network-like structures, but would then, however, be responsible for the content of internally as well as externally applicable (public) rules. One could rather consider demanding the

---

in: Staehle, W./Sydow, J. (eds.), Managementforschung 3, Berlin 1993, p. 309 (337 et seq.); *Windeler, A.*, Unternehmungsnetzwerke, Opladen 2001, 14 et seq.

55 See *Becker, N.*, Regelungsfelder für Unternehmensnetzwerke, Heidelberg 1999, p. 182.

56 Similar in terms of immaterial resources see *Ruiz Peris, J. I.*, in: id. (ed.): Nuevas Perspectivas del Derecho de Redes Empresariales, Valencia 2012, p. 73 (87 et seq.).

economic voluntariness besides the legal voluntariness as prerequisite for an entrepreneurial network,[57] since establishing and participating in a network due to economic pressure will lead to different behaviour within the network than participating in a network on purely voluntary grounds. Also the network activity is influenced by this. However, this merely modifies the network features. The basic juridical structures may not change. Above all, unsolvable problems of demarcation would emerge. When do the incentives to participate in a network become so powerful that it can no longer be regarded as economic voluntariness? Furthermore, with such preconditions, a network which is constantly growing stronger may at some point no longer be a network due to its power. Economically strong companies, which can also flourish without a network, would therefore be part of a network, whereas the economically weak companies participating in the same network would not be considered as network members due to their lack of economic voluntariness to participate. This shows that such a distinction would not be workable in any way. Therefore, the legal, but not the economic voluntariness in participating in a network should remain prerequisite for entrepreneurial networks.

## VIII. Legality

The literature apparently fails to adequately discuss the question whether merely legal networks are comprised by the notion of network. This is indicated, for instance, by the fact that the notion of trade also demands the legality[58] and it does not become evident why the legal system is supposed to look more closely at criminal networks. Additionally, each network aim could reach the quality of a corporation aim, which, as a rule, has to be legal,[59] provided the participants are willing to engage in founding a cor-

57 See *Kosiol, E.*, Die Unternehmung als wirtschaftliches Aktionszentrum, Reinbek 1972, p. 29; *Corsten, H.*, Ansatzpunkte für die Koordination in heterarchischen und hierarchischen Unternehmungsnetzwerken, Arbeitspapier Nr. 37, Kaiserslautern 2000, p. 3; *Glückler, J./Hammer, I.*, Zeitschrift Führung und Organisation 2011, 379 et seq.

58 *Kahl, G.*, in: v. Landmann, R./Rohmer, G. , Gewerbeordnung, München 1994, Einl. recital 38.

59 *Habermeier, S.*, in: Staudinger BGB, Berlin 2003, § 705 recital 18; *Westermann, H. P.*, in: Erman, G., 13. ed., 2011, § 705 recital 28; *Ulmer, P.*, in: Münchener Kommentar zum BGB, 5. ed., 2009, § 705 recital 144; *Schöne, T.*, in: Bamberger,

poration. With regard to the, practically speaking, very important breach of competition law the prerequisite of legality, however, no longer proves valuable. On the one hand, it can be very time-consuming to establish whether a network is infringing competition law. But above all, the competition law infringement itself could be affected by the existence of a network. In the end, differentiation therefore is crucial. The network must not pursue illegal aims. The classification as company network on the contrary is not affected by whether the extent of the co-operation exceeds the boundaries of the cartel ban of Art. 101 TFEU, § 1 GWB.

## IX. Duration

In economic literature authors assume without further explanation that company networks must possess a particular live span.[60] The specific duration of a network results from the fact that the achieving of co-operation aims requires a minimum of time.[61] It can be agreed to this insofar as networks are regularly aimed at a specific duration. A certain life span in the sense of long-term nature of networks, as described in the literature, is a real feature to be observed in reality. In this context the question arises whether networks require an actual duration. The existance of networks for a certain time span can be explained by the fact that the implementation of the network aim causes expenses which are supposed to be covered by the co-operation profit. Accordingly, a network is only profitable for the participants if the co-operation profit is realised. The actual realisation of the co-operation profit is, however, not a prerequisite for the existence

---

G./Roth, H. BGB, 3. ed., München 2012, § 705 recital 63; basically *Ballerstedt*, Juristische Schulung 1963, 253 (253 et seq.).

60 As, for instance, *Thorelli, H. B.*, Strategic Management Journal 7 (1986), 37 (44); *Jarillo, J. C.*, Strategic Management Journal 9 (1988), 31 (32); *Sydow, J.*, Unternehmungsnetzwerke, Düsseldorf 1991, p. 12, see also the definition of network introduced into the HGB (German commercial code) by BilMoG in connection with the freedom of inspection in § 319 b HGB in which the duration is a prerequisite. This situational definition has a protective purpose. The conflict of interest of the freedom of inspection in the network only arises if the network exists for a certain time. This would have been expressed more effectively if the legislator had used the duration as real or describing feature: "A network established on a permanent basis ...".

61 *Becker, N.*, Regelungsfelder für Unternehmensnetzwerke, Heidelberg 1999, p. 165.

of a network. The prerequisite is merely the intention to be willing to generate the co-operation profit.[62] Accordingly, the existence of a network is, at least theoretically, imaginable for a logical second. Therefore, one can already speak of a network if the co-operation profit is not obtained, because, for instance, the network has already been resolved again before reaching the aim. All in all, neither a minimal nor a maximal duration of a network can be determined since it depends on the pace of implementation of the network aim.[63] The life span of a network is, therefore, tied to the network aim and is expressed by the intention to reach the network aim. Thus, a network is, generally speaking, established on a long-term basis, but the existence of a network does not demand the actual duration as constitutive feature.

## X. Intermediate results

From a juridical perspective, the phenomenon of company networks can be defined in the following way: a company network is every legally voluntary[64] connection based on an economic[65] and legal[66] network aim[67] of a minimum of three[68] legally independent[69] companies[70] that at least partially exchange their economic independence for the co-ordination[71] of their economic activities by means of concerted practices, agreements or the foundation of a corporation in order to implement the network aim through the bundling of resources[72].

62 See above B.III.
63 *Becker, N.*, Regelungsfelder für Unternehmensnetzwerke, Heidelberg 1999, p. 165.
64 See above B.VII.
65 See above B.III.
66 See above B.VIII.
67 See above B.III.
68 See above B.I.
69 See above B.II.1.
70 See above B.II.
71 See above B.IV.
72 See above B.VI.

## C. From juridical phenomenon to juridical institute

In the scope of the two-step approach[73] developed here and after having obtained a juridical definition for the phenomenon of company networks in the first step it shall now in a second step be investigated whether or not network-specific, network-constitutive problems exist. If they do exist then company networks are not merely a phenomenon, but rather an institute. The network-specific, constitutive problems can then be used to further specify the definition of networks. Thereby it is assumed that after more than 25 years of juridical network research all essential problems that arise in relation to network-like constructions have been identified and also named. In particular, the issues regarding non-tortious liability to unaffiliated third parties,[74] direct rights of action against other unaffiliated members of the network,[75] the intensity of the duties depending on the network,[76] the distributive equality within networks,[77] as well as the complex issues of organisation in networks[78] are intensively discussed by juridical network research. In the following, these issues are to be examined as to whether they actually are network-specific as well as network consti-

73 See above A.

74 *Teubner, G.*, Zeitschrift für das gesamte Handels- und Wirtschaftsrecht 154 (1990), p. 295 (295 et seq.); *id.*, Netzwerk als Vertragsverbund, Baden-Baden 2004, p. 204 et seq.; *Wellenhofer, M.*, in: Amstutz, M./Teubner, G. (eds.): Networks – Legal Issues of Multilateral Co-operation, Oxford 2009, p. 119 (130 et seq.).

75 *Böhner, R.*, Neue Juristische Wochenschrift 1998, 109 (109 et seq.); *id.*, in: Amstutz, M./Teubner, G. (eds.), Networks – Legal Issues of Multilateral Co-Operation, Oxford 2009, p. 153 (153 et seq.); *Teubner, G.*, Zeitschrift für das gesamte Handels- und Wirtschaftsrecht 168 (2004), 78 (78 et seq.); *id.*, Netzwerk als Vertragsverbund, Tübingen 2004, p. 180 et seq.

76 *Hennemann, M.*, in: Aichberger-Beig (eds.),Vertrauen und Kontrolle im Privatrecht, Stuttgart 2011, p. 285 (285 et seq.); *Teubner, G.*, Netzwerk als Vertragsverbund, Baden-Baden 2004, p. 148 et seq.; see *Wellenhofer, M.*, in: Amstutz, M./ Teubner, G. (eds.), Networks – Legal Issues of Multilateral Co-operation, Oxford 2009, p. 119 (123 et seq.).

77 *Böhner, R.*, Neue Juristische Wochenschrift 1998, 109 (109 et seq.); *id.*, in: Amstutz, M./Teubner, G. (eds.), Networks – Legal Issues of Multilateral Co-Operation, Oxford 2009, p. 153 (153 et seq.).

78 See *Heldt, C.*, Baukooperation und Franchising als multilaterale Sonderverbindung, Baden-Baden 2010, p. 65 et seq.; see *Teubner, G.*, Zeitschrift für das gesamte Handels- und Wirtschaftsrecht 154 (1990), p. 295 (295 et seq.); siehe *id.*, in: Augsberg, I. (ed.): Ungewissheit als Chance, Tübingen 2009, p. 109 (109 et seq.).

tutive for company networks. Only if a problem is at the same time network-specific as well as constitutive for company networks then this issue has to be reflected in the preconditions for company networks. Constitutive in this case means that the problem always exists and a problem is network-specific if it only occurs in networks. However, if it only occurs in networks then this problem must have its grounds in the preconditions of the network. Therefore, network-specific and constitutive problems are an important means to review and specify the definition of networks.

## I. Constitutive, specific problems of company networks

### 1. Non-tortious liability to unaffiliated third parties

The network-specific literature predominantly assumes that the non-tortious liability of the network or of the individual network companies to unaffiliated third parties is a network-specific problem.[79] Several contributions discuss the liability of the network.[80] With regard to the "network-specific" non-tortious liability it has to be noted that liability to third parties is always required if in the scope of simple relations the system of direct liability exhibits a functional deficit.[81] From the point of view of injured third parties it does not make a huge difference if the non-affiliated infringer is either part of a network or at the end of the chain of contracts. This, at any rate, applies if the network as such does not establish confidence by virtue of insinuating it would want to be held liable as a whole. As a general rule, this may not be the case. Additionally, § 311 par. 3 (analog) BGB provides a tool which mostly accounts for the problem of liability. The question regarding non-tortious liability to third parties therefore does not depend on the existence of a company network. Accordingly, this issue is, in a strict sense, not network-specific. As a re-

---

79 *Teubner, G.*, Zeitschrift für das gesamte Handels- und Wirtschaftsrecht 154 (1990), 295 (305 et seq.); *id.*, Netzwerk als Vertragsverbund, Baden-Baden 2004, p. 204 et seq.; *Wellenhofer, M.*, in: Amstutz, M./Teubner, G. (eds.), Networks – Legal Issues of Multilateral Co-operation, Oxford 2009, p. 119 (130 et seq.).

80 See only *Teubner, G.*, Netzwerk als Vertragsverbund, Baden-Baden 2004, pp. 101–141.

81 *Krebs, P.*, Sonderverbindung und außerdeliktische Schutzpflichten, München 2000, p. 339 et seq.

sult, the problem of non-tortious liability is not suitable to functionally specify the definition of company networks.

### 2. Direct rights of action against other unaffiliated members of the network

Direct rights of action are primarily discussed in connection with franchising and in particular with regard to the franchisee's legal obligations to warn and inform other franchisees of potential damage.[82] Regardless of whether franchising systems are networks[83] this case can be considered a classical direct claims issue against third parties, which are generally not to be treated differently within or outside of the network. Accordingly, the obligations discussed here are not network-specific.

### 3. Intensity of the duties depending on the network

With regard to their intensity duties in special relations depend on the specifics of the relation.[84] This, in so far, is not network-specific. But the fact that networks seem to demand intensified loyalty and care duties is network-specific. In order to reach the common network aim it is essential that the members show particular consideration for each other whereby the exact intensity may depend on the type of actual co-operation. The correlation to the network aim at the same time shows that it is a constitutive feature. This, however, also illustrates that even though this particularity is specific as well as constitutive it is already contained in the above developed general definition for networks in form of the precondition of the network aim. A precondition of the definition is hereby asserted. The need to modify the definition is not given.

---

82 See, for instance, *Hennemann, M.*, in: Aichberger-Beig, D. a. o. (eds.), Vertrauen und Kontrolle im Privatrecht, Stuttgart 2011, p. 285 et seq.

83 See C.II.2.b.

84 *Krebs, P.*, Sonderverbindung und außerdeliktische Schutzpflichten, München 2000, p. 264 et seq., 510 et seq.

### 4. Required complex, dynamically adjusting organisation

Due to their complexity and interconnectedness networks pose specific organisational problems. If it cannot be organised then the network fails.[85] The particular need for organisation within a network results from the fact that at least three companies have to be co-ordinated[86] and have the possibility to work together on different project co-operations to a varying degree of intensity as well as with changing staff. The complexity of the problem is increased by the option to initiate new projects of co-operation whereby parallel activities emerge that respectively require other forms of organisation. Due to the availability of various co-ordinating instruments as well as the network aim additional individual and collective interests are to be brought into accordance in a network.

Each new project demands the organisation of the project content, the project participants, the choice of the co-ordinating instrument, and the alignment of the participants' co-operational needs. Even after having organised these aspects further spontaneous alignments regularly have to be made during the project. Moreover, the need for organisation further exists for the entire duration of the network with regard to the co-ordination of the parallel activities, the tensions between individual and collective interests, as well as the co-operational needs. Accordingly, not only do network companies require a new organisational structure for each project, but moreover the entire network demands an organisational structure which is flexibly adaptable to changes. Thus, this could be seen as the need for a semi-spontaneous order/organisational structure.[87] This complex and permanent need for organisation is characteristic for networks. At the same time this is also a chance as it keeps the networks flexible and dynamic. Company networks can only function if they can freely organise their need for co-ordination. This freedom, however, results in a permanent need for organisation. This specific and permanent need for organisation is network-specific. Naturally, the need for organisation also exists in other network-like constructs, but in this case the need for organisation is met with the solution for organisational problems so that the further co-

---

85 See *Teubner, G.*, in: Augsberg, I. (ed.), Ungewissheit als Chance, Stuttgart 2009, p. 109 (109 et seq.).

86 See B.I.

87 See *Heldt, C.*, Baukooperation und Franchising als multilaterale Sonderverbindung, Baden-Baden 2010, p. 67 et seq., especially p. 77 et seq.

ordination of the participants is no longer required. The network-specific need for organisation is therefore constitutive for company networks and thus has to be reflected in the definition.

### 5. Distributive equality

A further specific problem in networks mentioned by jurisdiction[88] as well as literature[89] is the distributive equality in networks.

The problem with distributive equality arises, because services in a network are often transformed into other services, which only emerge through co-operation. As a consequence, it is not always clearly defined who has provided what service to what extent and therefore it often remains unclear how emerging profits (or obligations) are to be distributed within the network. Due to the network aim individual interests of the network members as well as collective interests exist within the network. The strictly egoistic perspective on distributive equality, which is the starting point for contract law, thus does not necessarily seem adequate. The individual interests existing in a network are opposed to simply following company law when it comes to distributive equality. The impression of the network as lying between contract and corporation[90] is based on distribution equality and thus very convincing. The problem of distributive equality is aggravated by the possibility to freely choose from various forms of co-ordination such as contract, corporation and accommodation relationship to be used at the same time as well as with other activities within the network.[91] It is therefore a network-specific problem.

In this context the question arises in how far the distributive equality is a problem common to all networks. Not all networks make profits or losses so that the problem of distributive equality does not always arise. Fur-

---

88 *BGH*, Neue Juristische Wochenschrift 1999, 2671 – Sixt; *BGH* Neue Juristische Wochenschrift -RR 2003, 1635 – *Apollo-Optik; BGH* Neue Juristische Wochenschrift -RR 2006, 776 – Hertz.

89 See only *Glückler, J./Hammer, I.*, in: Glückler, J./Dehning W./Janneck, M. (eds.), Unternehmensnetzwerke – Architekturen, Strukturen und Strategien, Wiesbaden 2012, p. 139 (147 et seq.).

90 See in *Teubner, G.*, Netzwerk als Vertragsverbund, Baden-Baden 2004, p. 19 as well as p. 59.

91 *Krebs, P./Jung, S./Aedtner, K./Schultes, M.*, The modular system of network activities, in this volume, pp. 75 – 117.

thermore, especially in simply structured networks the respective co-ordination tool can already prescribe the distribution. The problem of distributive equality thus seems to frequently appear in company networks. It is therefore typical, but not constitutive. In the end, the problem of distributive equality is not suitable to further specify the definition of networks.

## II. Effects

### 1. Company networks as juridical institute

As shown above, the intensity of duties depending on the network as well as the network-specific demand for organisation are two specific and network constitutive problems. Consequently, networks are not to be regarded as a mere phenomenon, but as juridical institute since their specifics demand their own rules.

### 2. Effects on the definition

The above considerations illustrate that the definition deduced earlier has to be modified. In particular, it has to be extended by the feature of the network-specific demand for organisation. Consequently, this additional pre-condition limits the application range of networks, meaning that less constellations are considered to be networks. Therefore, the economic significance of company networks is not as great as previously assumed. Due to the limitation of the application range of company networks the definition becomes more precise and can thus possibly function as basis for an adequate solution approach.

As a result, company networks are to be defined in the following way:

A company network is every legally voluntary connection based on an economic and legal network aim of a minimum of three legally independent companies which induce a network-specific demand for organisation. The network companies at least partially exchange their economic independence for the co-ordination of their economic activities by means of concerted practices, agreements or the foundation of a corporation in order to implement the network aim through the bundling of resources.

### 3. Consequences for the application range

Based on the functional characteristics elaborated above it will be examined in the following whether corporate groups and exchange relationships as well as hierarchically organised co-operations such as franchising, supply chains or general contractors, which are classified as networks by the existing literature, are or can be regarded as company networks or whether they are to be clearly distinguished from company networks.

#### a. Corporate groups as company networks

Corporate groups exist of legally independent[92] companies.[93] The economic independence is not prerequisite for the affirmation of a company network.[94] Even though the bundling of resources[95] knows certain boundaries it is still merely a feature of corporate groups just as with company networks. Since it is the aim to achieve profit by uniting under one management the existence of a network aim[96] could also be affirmed. There are, moreover, no concerns regarding the intended duration[97] and the legality.[98]

The voluntariness of the participation in the network,[99] however, is almost completely lacking when it comes to corporate groups. The group companies do not voluntarily become (dependent) group companies, but do so due to the one-sided acquisition of leading powers by the ruling company. There are, however, also cases in which corporate groups emerge voluntarily.

92 *Emmerich, V.*, in: Emmerich, V./Habersack, M., AktG, 6. Ed., München 2010, § 1 recital 1; *Hüffer, U.*, in: *Hüffer, U.*, AktG, 10. ed., München 2012, § 18 recital 1; regarding company networks see above B.II.2.a).

93 *Emmerich, V.*, in: Emmerich, V./Habersack, M., AktG, 6. Ed., München 2010, § 1 recital 1; *Hüffer, U.*, in: Hüffer, U., AktG, 10. ed., München 2012, § 18 recital 1; regarding company networks see above B.II.2.

94 See above B.II.2.

95 See above B.VI.

96 See above B.III.

97 See above B.IX.

98 See above B.VIII.

99 See above B.VII.

Especially a voluntary company contract (without previous factual group formation) can lead to the foundation of a contract corporation.[100]

In each case of corporate groups, however, the permanent network-specific problem of organisation is missing. A corporate group does not exhibit the need for variable and flexible organisational structures which adapt to the varying individual co-operations and changes,[101] because corporate groups are centrally organised and changes in the organisational structure only occur on formal ways.

Accordingly, a corporate group cannot be, generally speaking, a company network. Corporate group companies can, however, be part of a network outside of the group.

### b. Exchange relationships as company networks?

Furthermore, it has to be clarified if pure exchange relationships suffice to be regarded as a company network. Exchange relationships, such as of services or information, are usually bilateral, independent of each other and do not have a common network aim. Through this exchange the individual companies implement their individual interests so that conflicts of interest arise. The bundling of resources is not necessary for this form or exchange relationship. The co-ordination of the parties involved in the sense of the definition criterion of co-ordination of company networks is also negligible since merely two companies are involved with the exchange in this case and both can fall back on fully developed juridical tools. Besides the already negated features of a company network, exchange relationships, furthermore, lack the network-specific demand for co-ordination or rather the specific problem of co-ordination.[102] Exchange relationships are, therefore, no networks.

In this context it is questionable whether this still applies if at least three companies co-operate in order to establish a common market, an internet platform for instance, where subsequently independent, bilateral ex-

---

100 See in general *Emmerich, V.*, in: Emmerich, V./Habersack, M., Aktien- und GmbH-Konzernrecht, 6. ed., München 2012, § 293 AktG recital 1 et seq; *Koch, J.*, in: Hüffer, U., AktG, 11. ed. 2014, § 293 recital 1 et seq; *Altmeppen, H.*, in: Münchener Kommentar zum AktG, 3. ed. München 2010, § 293 recital 1 et seq.

101 See above C.IV.

102 See above B.IV.

change relations can evolve. This form of co-operation is characterised by the fact that companies create a common, internal, outwardly closed off market and co-ordinate bilateral, and isolated exchange relationships on this market. Establishing such a market place provides the participating companies with the possibility to generate advantages which they couldn't achieve without the common marketplace, such as the reduction of transaction fees. Since an enhanced transparency dominates this common and secluded marketplace due to an improved overview the cost for finding an adequate exchange partner can thus be reduced. This represents the co-operational profit for the respective companies, which wouldn't be achieved without co-operation.[103] It is, however, questionable if the network-specific demand for organisation[104] actually is at hand in such cases. If a co-operation only exists of one trading platform which enables exchange relationships then this trading platform has to be organised. But the organisation is not required to be flexibly designed for new forms of co-operation. The network-specific problem of organisation, which also poses an advantage, does not exist in such cases. Generally speaking, the network-specific problem of organisation may only exist when a co-operation is variable in the sense of different possible forms of co-operation, which are not set in advance. This leads to the conclusion that a buying association or a R&D co-operation for specific research/development are not to be classified as company networks. The situation would be different if several companies generally affiliated in order to conduct research together in various forms and on demand. This institutional demand should suffice, because the organisation has to account for this right from the start.

### c. Hierarchically co-ordinated co-operations as company networks?

Hierarchically co-ordinated co-operations such as franchising have so far been regarded as company networks due to their complexity and density of organisational participants.[105]

---

103 See above B.III.

104 See above C.IV.

105 See, for instance, *Ahlert, D./Ahlert, M. (eds.),* Handbuch Franchising und Cooperation - Das Management Kooperativer Unternehmensnetzwerke, München 2010; *Heldt, C.,* Baukooperationen und Franchising als multilaterale Sonderverbindung, Baden-Baden 2010; *Teubner, G.,* Netzwerk als Vertragsverbund, Ba-

In its fundamental structures franchising does not meet all constitutive pre-conditions which are essential for company networks according to the definition suggested here. It is imaginable, even though in reality not observable due to the system's automatism, that a franchising system may exist between merely two parties, the franchiser and the franchisee. This already does not meet the prerequisite that a network has to exist of at least three participants. In addition, the network aim, which is to be realised and which lies in the implementation of the co-operational profit, cannot be explicitly identified with franchising. Indeed, all franchisees use the business model given by the franchiser and all franchisees intend to achieve competition advantages by using the concept. But collective interests do not emerge since the organisation is aimed at co-ordination, but not at co-operation. Franchiser and franchisee face each other in an antagonistic attitude, which is fundamentally different to the attitude within a network. The lack of a common network aim is especially apparent when the franchisees are not allowed to co-operate with each other.[106] Regarding franchising, the network-specific demand for organisation is also missing.[107] There is no demand for a flexible organisational structure, which adapts to the changes and the multitude of parallel activities. Accordingly, there is no network-specific problem of organisation.

In connection with the notion of "franchise networks" the question of distributional equality has been extensively discussed.[108] The problem of distributive equality in network-like constructions which range from contract to corporation does not merely exist in company networks, but in general with co-operative legal relationships, which are partially aimed at exchange and partially at co-operation. The existing of the problem of dis-

---

den-Baden 2004; *Schimansky, A.*, Der Franchisevertrag nach deutschem und niederländischem Recht unter besonderer Berücksichtigung seines Netzcharakters und der Ansprüche bei Vertragsbeendigung, Tübingen 2002.

106 Compare Subway, where several franchisees left in 2011 to found a purchasing co-operation named Mr. Sub.

107 The authors are aiming at the supposedly most common form of franchising – the subordination franchising. Regarding the various forms of franchising: *Martinek, M.*, Franchising Know-how-Verträge, Management- und Consultingverträge, München 1987, p. 256 – 424.

108 See, for instance, *Böhner, R.*, Neue Juristische Wochenschrift 1998, 109 (109 et seq.); *id.*, in: Amstutz, M./Teubner, G. (eds.), Networks – Legal Issues of Multilateral Co-Operation, Oxford 2009, p. 153 et seq; *Teubner, G.*, Zeitschrift für das gesamte Handels- und Wirtschaftsrecht 168 (2004), 78 (78 et seq.).

tributive equality is, therefore, no argument for classifying franchising as company network.

Similarly, this would also apply to general contractors or supply chains co-ordinated by the end buyer.

## 4. Critical reflections and further consequences

According to the above analysis company networks are not to be understood in the extent as has been assumed for a long time. After having examined constitutive features co-operations are only to be regarded as company networks if they (besides the other constitutive features) exhibit the network-specific problem of organisation. Thereby, the practical application range for company networks is immensely limited. The advantage of this is that the company networks understood in this way feature a far greater unity. This structural unity, which is reflected in the definition, makes it much easier to find adequate solutions for company networks. The cases excluded form company networks, such as franchising nevertheless share points of contact with company networks. Even though they lack the network-specific problem of organisation they nonetheless exhibit the same problem with distribution equality. Insofar as distributive equality is concerned these constellations can be included in the discussion. An important consequence of the existence of the network-specific problem of organisation is that networks are a separate legal entity.[109] For a legal entity it is characteristic to exhibit separate functions and specific problems. A further important conclusion to be drawn from this analysis is that a definition can also be reached in the functional way if the solutions are not yet known. If, as is the case here, the defining characteristics (1. economic to juridical phenomenon) or the problems (2. juridical phenomenon to defined juridical institute) have already been discussed intensively the constitutive features and problems can be extracted. The second step, however, presupposes that problems do exist.

109 Of other opinion *Buxbaum, R. M.*, Journal of Institutional and Theoretical Economics 1993, 698 – 705.

## D. Concluding statements

1. Company networks can be defined in the following way: A company network is every legally voluntary connection based on an economic and legal network aim of a minimum of three legally independent companies which induce a network-specific demand for organisation. The network companies at least partially exchange their economic independence for the co-ordination of their economic activities by means of concerted practices, agreements or the foundation of a corporation in order to implement the network aim through the bundling of resources.

2. Based on this definition, corporate groups, mere exchange relationships, and hierarchically co-ordinated co-operations in form of franchising, general contractors and supply chains co-ordinated by the end buyer are not to be classified as company networks.

3. The narrow definition of networks argued for here excludes manifold relationships which so far have been classified as networks. Rather, many forms are mere arrangements and only partially network-like. As far as this partial similarity is concerned an equal treatment can be considered. But these cases do not provide further insight for general rules and regulations within networks.

4. Based on the examples of company networks, it was shown above that a juridical definition can be deduced from an intensive economic discussion about an economic phenomenon. It was furthermore illustrated that, based on a juridical phenomenon, a functional definition can be deduced from an intensive discussion of its juridical problems by means of proving their specificity and constitutiveness. At the same time it can be justified that company networks are a juridical institute since the characteristic of an institute is the existence of separate problems and individual solutions for an abstract issue.

# The modular system of network activities[1]

*Prof. Dr. Peter Krebs, Dr. Stefanie Jung, M.A. (CoE), Katja Aedtner, Marion Schultes*

## A. Introduction

For more than 25 years attempts have been made to legally account for business networks.[2] The categorisation as a hybrid structure between mar-

---

1 This paper is a translated version of a German article („Das modulare System der Netzwerkaktivitäten") that was published in the German journal „Kölner Schrift zum Wirtschaftsrecht" (KSzW 2015, pp. 15-29).

2 See *Amstutz, M.*, in: Festschrift Rey, 2003, p. 161 (161 et seqq.); *id.*, Kritische Vierteljahresschrift für Gesetzgebung und Rechtswissenschaft 2006, 105 (105 et seqq.); *Böhner, R.*, Kritische Vierteljahresschrift für Gesetzgebung und Rechtswissenschaft 2006, 227 (227 et seqq.); *Bräutigam, P.*, Deliktische Außenhaftung im Franchising, Baden-Baden 1994; *Collins, H.*, in: Amstutz, M./Teubner, G. (eds.), Networks – Legal Issues of Multilateral Co-operation, Oxford 2009, p. 187 (208 et seqq.); *Druey, J. N.*, Kritische Vierteljahresschrift für Gesetzgebung und Rechtswissenschaft 2006, 163 (163 et seqq.); *Grundmann, S.*, Archiv für die civilistische Praxis 207 (2007), 718 (735 et seqq.); *id.*, in: Festschrift Westermann, Köln 2008, p. 227 (232 et seqq.); *Heermann, P. W.*, Drittfinanzierte Erwerbsgeschäfte, Tübingen 1998; *id,*. Kritische Vierteljahresschrift für Gesetzgebung und Rechtswissenschaft 2006, 173 (173 et seqq.); *Heldt, C.*, Baukooperation und Franchising als multilaterale Sonderverbindung, Baden-Baden 2010; *id.*, Kritische Vierteljahresschrift für Gesetzgebung und Rechtswissenschaft 2006, 208 (223 et seqq.); *Kulms, R.*, Schuldrechtliche Organisationsverträge in der Unternehmenskooperation, Baden-Baden 2000; *Lange, K. W.*, Das Recht der Netzwerke, Frankfurt am Main 1998, n. 13, pp. 380 et seqq.; *Möschel, W.*, Archiv für die civilistische Praxis 207 186 (1986), 187 (211 et seqq.); *Rohe, M.*, Netzverträge, Tübingen 1998, pp. 85 et seqq., esp. pp. 129 et seqq.; *Teubner, G.*, Zeitschrift für das gesamte Handels- und Wirtschaftsrecht 154 (1990), 295 (295 et seqq.); *id.*, in: Krohn, W./Küppers, G. (eds.), Emergenz: Die Entstehung von Ordnung, Organisation und Bedeutung, Berlin 1992, p. 210 (210 et seqq.); *id.*, Kritische Vierteljahresschrift für Gesetzgebung und Rechtswissenschaft 1993, 367 (369, 373, 380 et seqq.); *id.*, Zeitschrift für das gesamte Handels- und Wirtschaftsrecht 165 (2001), 550 (550 et seqq.); *id.*, in: Amstutz, M. (ed.), Die vernetzte Wirtschaft: Netzwerke als Rechtsproblem, Zürich 2004, p. 11 (11 et seqq.); *id.*, Netzwerke als Vertragsverbund, Baden-Baden 2004; *id.*, in: Augsberg, I. (ed.), Ungewissheit als Chance, Tübingen 2009, p. 109 (109 et seqq.); *Wellenhofer, M.*, Kritische Vierteljahresschrift für Gesetzgebung und Rechtswissenschaft 2006,

ket and hierarchy by *Oliver Williamson* is even older.[3] The apparent assumption is that their complexity and their range of variation make networks difficult to measure. Nonetheless, the search for a solution should be continued, also because the practical significance of networks keeps increasing. They especially allow small and medium-sized enterprises to gain synergetic effects, which may be of decisive importance for the competition with big enterprises.[4]

As to now, business networks are understood as consistent formation, which are difficult to explain and define[5] from a dogmatic point of view due to their diverse forms of appearance. The presentation of an empirical example by *Johannes Glückler*[6] pointed the authors' attention to the fact that business networks can comprise several parallel activities each with different participants. The empirically traceable multidimensionality may be the key to a completely new comprehension of business networks and therefore permit to legally accomplish the challenge posed by networks. If the empirical findings are generally applicable then a difference has to be made between the individual activities carried out in the business network. Taking the individual activities into account is more appropriate for answering concrete juridical questions than the attempt to come to a common result by generally categorising business networks (for example the classification of business networks between contract and corporation). Though, the general categorisation of business networks thoroughly is of interest. Based on the grounds of multidimensionality, however, the general categorisation should present itself differently as hitherto. Especially if it is certain that the different activities initially have to be distinguished,

---

187 (187 et seqq.); the network discussion in public law is mainly concerned with networks consisting of states, networks in the field of administration or authorities, see *Boysen, S. et al.* (eds.), Netzwerke. 47. Assistententagung Öffentliches Recht, Wien 2007, et passim.

3 *Williamson, O. E.*, Markets and Hierarchies. Analysis and Antitrust Implications; a study in the economics of internal organization, New York 1983.

4 For a more in depth analysis of the advantages and disadvantages see *Schultes, M.*, Company networks and the dichotomy and statics of competition law – a combined dynamic control of conduct and structure as a solution approach, pp. 198 et seqq. (in this volume).

5 For a definition see *Krebs, P./Aedtner, K./Schultes, M.*, Company networks reloaded – putting a general functional approach to defining complex problems to the test, pp. 41 et seqq. (in this volume).

6 Talk from 19.06.2012 at the University of Siegen in connection with the lecture series organised by the Research School Business and Economics.

the question arises whether this necessarily only allows for a case-by-case analysis or at the most an analysis of groups of cases. From a dogmatic point of view it would rather be desirable to develop a general system from these cases and groups of cases. A set-up of general categories also makes sense from the legislator's respectively the representing judge's perspective. For if need be, according to continental juridical understanding it is only suitable to be content with decisions on a case-by-case basis for a certain period of transition. Yet for generalised legal rules there is the need for more general constellations, to which these general legal rules shall apply. Such general legal rules are also necessary for business networks, namely to serve both as a role model for the individual drafting of contracts and as gap-filling law. Within business networks an increased necessity exists for filling gaps, although the members basically wish to regulate as less as possible which is exactly why they partially do not establish essential provisions. Moreover, non-mandatory law is necessary for a control of bones mores, i. e. according to § 138 BGB (German Civil Code) or content monitoring, i. e. according to § 307 BGB (German Civil Code). This is why it will need to be considered in a second step whether a modular system can be developed from the huge amount of conceivable activities.

The hereinafter developed solutions are designed for non-hierarchical business networks.

## B. Business networks and the phenomenon of plural activities

### I. Plural activities in business networks – empirical findings

There are various forms of cooperation within business networks. Unlike the case with business networks, the phenomenon has already been recognised regarding networks within one company. It was examined on the basis of the relation of lawyers within one multisite chancery.[7] However, a generally applicable approach has not been developed and neither have ju-

7 *Lazega, E./Pattison, P.*, Social Networks 21 (1999), 67 (67 et seqq.). As example for the capacity of the graphic representation of complex networks by way of bonding matrix see *Krempel, L.*, Visualisierung komplexer Strukturen. Grundlagen der Darstellung mehrdimensionaler Netzwerke, Frankfurt am Main 2005, pp. 134 et seqq.

ridical consequences been extrapolated from this. The question of plural activities in business networks appears to have been examined closer in the research project *kreanets*[8] for the first time. Amongst others, *Glückler et al.* have investigated a network of 28 dentistry enterprises which are organised as corporation (GmbH, German limited) in order to cooperate within a network.[9] In exploratory interviews[10] with some of the participating companies the starting point emerged for the division of four categories of activities in the investigated network (linked production, knowledge exchange, project cooperation, project management). For these four types of cooperation, which were (optically) apprehended as levels there,[11] the structure of the cooperating groups as well as the intensity of the involvement of the individual companies was thereafter measured and visualised on the basis of a survey of all network companies.[12] In the course of this, it became apparent that the network participants in all network categories are indeed engaged in diverse personnel constellations to varying extents.[13] For each of these activities resources are combined with a specific type of cooperation by various network members. In the scope of the activity of linked production,[14] for instance, companies provide available production capacities. Network members who do not have sufficient production capacities can then acquire these. In this way, two network companies combine their resources (production capacity and demand) by simply exchanging goods or services. The study showed no immediate correlation between the intensity of action and the participation in the individual activity. Therefore, the independence of these activities was concluded.

---

8 See www.kreanets.com, 30.03.2015.

9 *Glückler, J./Hammer, I.*, in: Glückler, J. et al., Unternehmensnetzwerke - Architektur, Strukturen und Strategien, Berlin, Heidelberg 2012, p. 139 (139 et seq.).

10 See *Glückler, J./Hammer, I.*, in: Glückler, J. et al., Unternehmensnetzwerke - Architektur, Strukturen und Strategien, Berlin, Heidelberg 2012, p. 139 (152, 154 et seq.).

11 See *Glückler, J./Hammer, I.*, in: Glückler, J. et al., Unternehmensnetzwerke - Architektur, Strukturen und Strategien, Berlin, Heidelberg 2012, p. 139 (155). Here, the levels are named categories of activities or kinds of activities in a more neutral manner.

12 See *Glückler, J./Hammer, I.*, in: Glückler, J. et al., Unternehmensnetzwerke - Architektur, Strukturen und Strategien, Berlin, Heidelberg 2012, p. 139 (153).

13 See *Glückler, J./Hammer, I.*, in: Glückler, J. et al., Unternehmensnetzwerke - Architektur, Strukturen und Strategien, Berlin, Heidelberg 2012, p. 139 (155).

14 See *Glückler, J./Hammer, I.*, in: Glückler, J. et al Unternehmensnetzwerke - Architektur, Strukturen und Strategien, Berlin, Heidelberg 2012, p. 139 (153).

The empirical variety of network goods and the mechanisms of their formation were further findings of the investigation.[15]

## II. Analysis and generalisation capacity of the empirical findings

In the empirical study outlined above the object of investigation was neither the generalisation capacity of the acquired knowledge nor the significance of the findings for the legal employability regarding networks.

### 1. Activity categories and influencing factors

One element to be considered is the extent to which general forms of activity are to be gained from the various activity categories distinguished in the example above (linked production, knowledge exchange, project cooperation, project management) and which further activity categories can additionally be found.

The activity form of linked production ascertained in the exemplary case stands for the immediate exchange of considerations (e.g. goods for money). This categorisation appears to be appropriate also in a legal context. Admittedly, the fact that the exchange occurs within and not without the network may have certain consequences. However, the essence of the legal regulations for the exchange of considerations, which claim validity even outside the scope of networks, may be applicable here. Modifications of this general contract law might be considered for fiduciary duties, the conclusion of the contract, but also for the termination of the contract.

The activity category of knowledge exchange in the example is not the transaction of knowledge for money in the classical sense of do ut des. Presumably, the knowledge was passed on informally in hope of a future favour. This should be a juridical independent category.

The third activity category of project cooperation distinguished in the exemplary case appears to be distinct in as far as no simple exchange exists, but something completely new is to be created by the network mem-

15 See *Glückler, J./Hammer, I.*, in: Glückler, J. et al., Unternehmensnetzwerke - Architektur, Strukturen und Strategien, Berlin, Heidelberg 2012, p. 139 in preview of the individual sections.

bers. This is indicative for the legal independence of this category even without having a clear outline of categorisation.

The "level of project management"[16] in the example does not lead to the exchange or the fabrication of new considerations. It is rather a separate part of the project cooperation which emerged in this specific case due to the fact that even though merely few companies actively participated in the project cooperation, many more enterprises wanted to have an active determining influence on the project cooperation. Such a management activity is theoretically conceivable also for a simple exchange of considerations or knowledge. Practically speaking though, such management activity might only be necessary if these activities require a great amount of organisation. Naturally, the need for management appeared particularly with regard to project cooperation, because the therefore relevant activities generally require an increased level of organisation and exhibit a higher use of resources by the network.

In any case, it seems reasonable to legally clearly distinguish the activity category of management from other activities where resources are immediately exchanged respectively brought in or new resources are created.[17]

The category which was not considered as an activity category in connection with the dentistry network examined by *kreanets* is the framework of the network. In this specific example the framework was, at least partially, a private limited liability company (GmbH).[18]

It can generally be accepted that the various activity categories have emerged in the study due to the fact that certain resources such as production capacity (regarding linked production), knowledge and network goods (regarding project work) were especially suited for networking in the view of the involved companies. Thereby, the best coordination form was implemented for each of the resources. Production capacities, for instance, were implemented within the network in the shape of a simple exchange

---

16 See *Glückler, J./Hammer, I.*, in: Glückler, J. et al., Unternehmensnetzwerke - Architektur, Strukturen und Strategien, Berlin, Heidelberg 2012, p. 73 (80 et seqq.); *Glückler, J./Hammer, I.*, in: Glückler, J. et al., Unternehmensnetzwerke - Architektur, Strukturen und Strategien, Berlin, Heidelberg 2012, p. 139 (154).

17 For the importance of governance structures see *Krebs, P./Jung, S.*, Governance Structures in Business Networks, pp. 118 et seqq. (in this volume).

18 *Glückler, J./Hammer, I.*, in: Glückler et al., Unternehmensnetzwerke - Architektur, Strukturen und Strategien, Berlin, Heidelberg 2012, p. 73 (80).

of considerations wherewith the degree of coordination in the network[19] was basically restricted to the mere provision of a marketplace. The consideration was received by the benefit recipient in the same way as it was provided by the beneficiary. With regard to project cooperation, money, know-how and personnel were coordinated in the scope of an elaborated cooperation. The considerations of the participating individual companies (e.g. provision of money, working capacity) were transformed by the interaction into a new product or a new service (e.g. benchmarking, quality management system, production handbook).[20] The recipient, in this case the network as a whole, obtained something which was completely different form the project members' contribution. Consequently, value creation through coordination has occurred.

On the one hand, the categories reflect the tangible interests of the network members, which vary according to the respective categories (e.g. maintenance of production capacity on the "level" of linked production or knowledge exchange on the eponymous "level"). On closer examination, however, the categories are also a combination of one or several resources and one form of the exchange process, i.e. of two factors influencing the activity categories.

The first possible influencing factor is the type of resources.

The second possible influencing factor is the type of exchange process (exchange of considerations, communisation, informal give and take).[21]

The third possible influencing factor is the form of cooperation, which can be described along the lines of the dichotomy transformative and non-transformative transaction. Non-transformative transaction is to be understood as an exchange without a difference between the consideration performed and the consideration received. With regard to transformative transactions (hereinafter also "transformation"), however, the participants cooperate with the result that the individual performances and the originated goods no longer concur with the initial input. For instance, the project cooperation addressed in the case study by *Glückler* includes the compilation of a quality management system.

---

19 See *Krebs, P./Aedtner, K./Schultes, M.*, Company networks reloaded – putting a general functional approach to defining complex problems to the test, B.IV. p. 41 (55 et seqq.) (in this volume).

20 *Glückler, J./Hammer, I.*, in: Glückler, J. et al., Unternehmensnetzwerke - Architektur, Strukturen und Strategien, Berlin, Heidelberg 2012, p. 139 (156).

21 For the types of exchange processes see for C.II. p. 86 et seq.

The fourth possible influencing factor is the coordinating instrument (accommodation relationship, contract, pooling, corporation).

But it could be considered whether the distinction between network good and individual good is a fifth influencing factor.[22]

The framework is no further influencing factor within the various categories, but merely has an effect on it.

The diverging categories differentiated in the example of the case study *kreanets* are neither accidental nor arbitrary. Apparently, there are typical forms of combination resulting from different influencing factors: type of recourses used, type of exchange process, type of cooperation, instruments of coordination, type of good. Due to the influencing factors which are to be considered, the distinguished categories do neither reflect all combination possibilities nor all appropriate combination possibilities which presumably are to be found in business networks.[23] Whether all considered influencing factors are necessary for the solution model is thereby not yet decided.[24]

## 2. Necessity for the distinction of the various activity categories in a network

The varying participation in the forms of activities, which the example shows,[25] reflects the diverging interests of those involved. If there are several activity categories and if participation is not compulsory for all network members, the companies will only engage in network activities which are of interest for them after having considered the assets and drawbacks. This interest is constantly subject to the recourses needed, to the profit that can be achieved and to the possible risks entailed.

Furthermore, the participation intensity might also vary. The more the member is interested in the activity, the greater will the involvement be. Therefore, if there are several activity categories, which are not connected as such, and if the companies are able to choose the categories in which they would like to participate then the enterprises will also make use of

22 See C.II.5. pp. 88 et seq.

23 It seems reasonable to suppose that the useful combination possibilities represent merely a fraction of the possible variety of combinations.

24 See further C.II. pp. 85 et seqq.

25 See B.I. pp. 77 et seq.

their flexibility. Consequently, as illustrated by the example of *kreanets*, the participants as well as the intensity of engagement will vary in each category of activity. This is a first indication of the legal relevance of this observation. Since companies engage in varying intensities it is apparent that each category of activity has to be individually considered from a legal point of view.

## III. Deductions

Before developing a system of network activities in the following, the up to now gained findings shall be summarised at this point in order to draw some first conclusions. Contrary to the previous presumption that networks are a uniform, one-dimensional construction, networks comprise of several activity categories. Not only are those categories independent from each other, they can also involve different participants, each of which can be involved in the particular activity with a different intensity and pursue different interests. The multitude of possible diverse activities may, amongst others, be due to the variety of network goods and their formation mechanisms. This plurality of different activities, which are bundled within the network, can be named plurality of activity.

From these aforementioned findings some first legal conclusions can be drawn already. At their core is the plurality of activity. The multitude of activities requires a differentiated view depending on the activity category. The type of the activity and the projects realised within the respective activity (i.e. each exchange of excess capacity) effects the legal assessment. They are the starting point for all following legal considerations.[26]

Private autonomous agreements are carried out especially at the level of the single projects and activities. However, the consideration of the single projects and activities cannot be carried out detached from the network frame. The network purpose expressed in the network frame and general rules embedded at this level have also an affect. This interaction has to be considered within the legal considerations.

The particular activities are not suitable to picture concessionary law due to their diversity. Yet there is quite a need for concessionary law since

26 For further details regarding the various levels within business networks (framework level, module level, activity level, project level) see *Krebs, P./Jung, S.*, Governance Structures in Business Networks, D. p. 118 (128 et seqq.) (in this volume).

the network members tend to frequently leave – even if unintentional – gaps because of their reluctant attitude towards a juridification. This is why it is the aim in the following to abstract the single forms of activities in order to determine the scope to which each the same concessionary rules apply, which at the same time serve for the monitoring of content and a control of bones mores.

## C. Modular system of network activities

### I. Homogenous business models as key to a modular system of network activities

As already stated, the single activities are too individual to serve as basis for concessionary law, which at the same time serves as control standard, i. e. in the meaning of § 138 BGB (German Civil Code) and § 307 BGB (German Civil Code). Hence, an approach has to be sought which allows for the derivation of a suitable, confined scope for the development of concessionary law.

While establishing the concessionary contract law (i. e. §§ 433 et seqq. BGB (German Civil Code)) including company law, legislation faced a similar task and opted for the generally separate apprehension of 'business models' with similar chance and risk structures.[27] The notion of business model as understood here implies that each participating side can systematically gain an advantage under the given circumstances and certain legal prerequisites. This idea is also applicable to the plurality of activities of networks since a defining criterion for all real activity categories (excluding the management activity) according to the definition of company networks is an economic network advantage which emerges based on the coordination of recourses.[28]

---

27 Technically speaking, the types of contracts were shaped by practice. Through the constant repetition of similar conclusions of contracts contract types evolve. The fact that the same type of contract is often concluded is based on the underlying effective business model.

28 See *Krebs, P./Aedtner, K./Schultes, M.*, Company networks reloaded – putting a general functional approach to defining complex problems to the test, B.III. p. 41 (53 et seqq.) (in this volume).

Whereas legislation faced the task of merely typifying already existing contracts therewith neglecting infrequent contracts, a comprehensive attempt at systematisation will be made in the following. This attempt aims at including the entire functioning of business networks.

As stated above, up to five possible influencing factors take effect on the complex of activities. Therefore, it is likely that by the way of their combination the possible influencing factors could also define the homogenous business models, to each of which the same concessionary law should be applicable due to their same structure of chance and risk.

## II. Categorisation and relevance of the influencing factors

It is necessary to determine whether all five influencing factors (type of cooperation, type of exchange process, instruments of coordination, recourses and the type of good)[29] are relevant for the systematisation of business models. The business models are to be homogenous with regard to their chance and risk structure. Consequently, the influencing factors are relevant if they are decisive for the classification of the chance and risk structure.

### 1. Type of cooperation

The influencing factor type of cooperation (transformative/non-transformative) may be of great importance for the systematisation of business models. In purely formal terms it may be said that any business model whatsoever falls into the two categories of either non-transformative transaction or transformative transaction respectively.[30] This dichotomy is reminiscent of the economic distinction between transaction and production economy.[31] In accordance with the business models, the cases of non-transformative transaction are characterised by the fact that the beneficia-

29 For influencing factors see B.II.1. pp. 79 et seqq.

30 See C.III. pp. 89 et seqq.

31 See *Coase, R.*, The Nature of the Firm Economica, New Series, Vol. 4, No. 16, 1937, 386 (386 et seqq.); *Williamson, O. E.*, Markets and Hierarchies. Analysis and Antitrust Implications, New York 1975; *id.*, The Economic Institutions of Capitalism. Firms, Markets, Relational Contracting, New York 1985.

ries use the good which is either made or already possessed by them and therewith achieve an easily calculable object of consideration. Especially the cooperation between various network participants is not required. Regarding the transformation, however, the resources of several network companies have to be merged in cooperation in order to achieve a value creation. In terms of business models such a transformation normally entails a considerable increase of the risk of failure.[32] And therefore a non-transformative transaction and a transformative transaction generally show a different quality of chance and risk structure. Since these systematised business models regarding their chance and risk structure should be homogenous this influencing factor is therefore relevant for the systematisation.

## 2. Exchange process

With regard to the influencing factor “exchange process” it has to be considered which forms of exchange process can exist. Thereby, “exchange of consideration”, “communisation” and "informal give and take"[33] can be distinguished. The exchange of considerations is based on the classic do ut des which is the traditional individual form of exchange. With regard to communisation two or more network participants combine their resources which can subsequently be gathered and used either individually or collectively.[34]

The informal give and take consists of two action forms, which are often combined, namely informal giving and informal taking. The defining criterion for the informal giving is the fact that initially a consideration is

32 For chances and risks see C.IV. pp. 104 et seq.

33 In the course of the research day on 17.01.2013 at Siegen University *Johannes Glückler* pointed out to the authors that the informal (tolerated) taking is a form of exchange.

34 Communisation is not congruent with corporisation, which is a form of communisation without, however, completely comprising this form of exchange. In fact, there is also a form of communisation, where the participants combine their resources mostly unjuridified und permit the reciprocal use and extraction of these resources. This form of communisation is understood here as pooling. Since the boundaries between these two forms are blurred, both forms are subsumed here under the category of communisation. See for coordinating instruments C.II.3. p. 87.

provided without claim to consideration in return. The informal giving could also be termed "generalised exchange". The consideration is not provided in the case of informal taking. Instead, the benefit recipient lawfully takes the consideration usually based on informal connivance. This taking, which can be particularly found in cases concerning knowledge, is especially common in networks in which the individual network companies are in close spatial vicinity to each other. This is an often wrongfully neglected form of exchange and straddles the boundary between implied conclusion of contract and accommodation relationship. The latter rather matches the usually unwanted juridification.

These three forms of exchange cover the scope of exchange processes completely and are considerably diverging with regard to their chance and risk structure. Accordingly, this influencing factor is additionally required for the systematisation of homogenous business models.

### 3. Coordinating instruments

The coordinating instruments comprise accommodation relationship, contract, pooling and corporation. The choice of the coordinating instrument appears to be relevant for the systematisation at first glance since the applicable legal rules are subject to the chosen coordinating instrument. This contribution, however, deals with business models, i.e. the chance and risk structure. In any case, the coordinating instruments exert a certain influence on the chance and risk structure of the individual business models, but in the exchange processes including exchange of consideration, communisation as well as informal give and take the coordinating instruments are already inherent due to the fact that the type of exchange process, to a certain extent, determines the suitable coordinating instruments. Accordingly, the range of variation in deployable coordinating instruments is, at the most, a merely small one. Ultimately, the coordinating instruments are solely the refinement of the type of exchange processes, but are not a part of the basic classification scheme of business models with homogenous chance and risk structure. Consequently, this influencing factor generally does not have to be considered in the scope of the systematisation. This does not foreclose using this factor for refinement within the scope of type of exchange process if needed.

## 4. Resources

The recourses used may influence the type of business model. As evidenced by the fact that purchase as well as business contracts practically cover each form of resources, the form of resource is, as a general rule, not decisive for the business model. Should this, however, apply to an individual case then it can be regarded as refinement, which is not decisive for the systematic basic model that is to be developed here. It should be added that the influencing factor resources itself can hardly be systematised according to a business model due to its vast scope of variation. Therefore, also this influencing factor will not be further considered in the development of the model outlined in the following.

## 5. Type of good

Individual goods or network goods[35] can be either exchanged or the result of a transformation process. If a good or a consideration is legally assigned to one or more network participants then this is termed individual good. Network goods, however, comprise goods and considerations which, in terms of property rights, can be assigned to the juridified network or the network members as a whole. The economic involvement in a network good differs from that in an individual good. Therefore, the type of good could be of influence on the chance and risk structure and subsequently on the business model. Yet the differences between individual and network good seem to be considerably less than between transformative and non-transformative transaction as a non-transformative transaction generally concerns individual goods (exchanging network goods though is permitted) and transformation primarily is related to the creation of network goods. Therewith, the differentiation between individual goods and network goods already seems to be substantially depicted in the influencing factor type of cooperation. Should this not be the case in a particular case, this could be considered in the means of refinement. The type of

35 The network good as understood here is different to the notion of network goods which is characterised by the fact that the value increases the more parties consume the same good. This is the case with internet platforms for example. See *Peters, R.*, Internet-Ökonomie, Heidelberg 2010, p. 35.

good therefore is a subordinated influencing factor, which shall not be considered in the primary systematisation to reduce complexity.

#### 6. Résumé

For the derivation of a system of network activities only the influencing factors type of cooperation and exchange process are of significant importance. The reduction of the influencing factors which are to be considered in the model from five to two leads to the positive practical effect of the decline of complexity. At the same time, however, the central chance and risk structure is covered by the two influencing factors type of cooperation and type of exchange process. In individual cases secondary influencing factors may be used for refinement.

### III. The internal structure of the network – existence of various business models

#### 1. Modularity in the network

For the systematisation modularity is proposed here. The modularity is based on the idea that each type of cooperation can be combined with each type of exchange process the outcome of this being a business model respectively a module in the meaning of a systematic description.

There are two types of cooperation which are to be differentiated within a network: transformative and non-transformative transactions. Non-transformative transaction activities are directed towards a mere exchange of existing resources. The consideration which is performed is obtained unaltered by the recipient. In this respect, a consideration contract can be regarded as a non-transformative transaction, because the consideration (the work) is received by the customer in the way the consideration provider produced it.

Transformation activities create a new good or consideration from several resources[36] by means of the participants' cooperation. Therewith, the

---

36 Resources are understood here in a wider sense. See *Krebs, P./Aedtner, K./Schultes, M.*, Company networks reloaded – putting a general functional approach to defining complex problems to the test, B.VI. p. 41 (58 et seq.) (in this volume).

recipient obtains a good that is different to those considerations which the participants have brought forth. In the area of contract law there is no specific contract type which depicts the transformation. However, *Glückler et al.*'s example can be regarded as a case of transformation since several companies issue a production manual. The fact that an adequate legal regulation is still lacking in Germany may be due to the BGB (German Civil Code) legislation from 1896 in which such a process was only imaginable in the scope of a corporation. What is required is a regulation for the modern type of cooperation within the scope of transformation in business networks as far as the participants do not express the wish for a corporation.

There are three types of exchange processes which can be assigned to each type of cooperation (transformative and non-transformative transaction) respectively, namely: exchange of considerations,[37] communisation[38] and informal give and take.[39] These types constitute the modules of the concept. In the scope of non-transformative transactions and transformation the modules exhibit a mirror-imaged structure with regard to the type of exchange process. The individual models will be treated separately in the following. Thereby, each module represents a business model.

This contribution discusses the totality of business modules in general form. The comprehensive analysis of business models also includes the depiction of those which are seldom applied in practice.

---

37 See above C.II. p. 85 as well as below C.III.2.a)aa) pp. 91 et seqq. and C.III. 2.b)aa) pp. 98 et seq.

38 See above C.II. p. 85 as well as below C.III.2.a)bb) pp. 93 et seqq. and C.II. 2.b)bb) pp. 101 et seq.

39 See above C.II. p. 85 as well as below C.III.2.a)cc) pp. 96 et seq. and C.III.2.b)cc) pp. 103 et seq.

*Figure : The modular system of network activities (modular model)*

| Type of exchange process | Form of cooperation | |
|---|---|---|
| | **Non-transformative Transaction** | **Transformative Transaction** |
| **Exchange of consideration** | Non-transformative–exchange of consideration | Transformative–exchange of consideration |
| **Communisation** | Non-transformative–communisation | Transformation–communisation |
| **Informal give and take** | Non-transformative–informal give and take | Transformation–informal give and take |

Source: Own diagram

## 2. Explanation of the individual network modules

The network modules are to be differentiated according to transaction modules (in the following simplifyingly for non-transformative transaction modules) and transformation modules. The individual modules are characterised by their mostly homogenous chance and risk structures. Hence, basically all cases which are to be comprised in the individual modules feature homogenous interests. Accordingly, the discussion can function as the foundation for the derivation of concessionary law for each module. The potential for development of individual arrangements which the network members (on the level of framework) and the specific module members (on the level of module) can agree on is, on the contrary, almost inexhaustible.[40] Just as in the case of contract law, these configurations are capable of influencing the chance and risk structures and should be measured by the legal limits to contractual freedom. They use the general dispositivity without changing the initial situation for which default rules have to be determined. Accordingly, the chance and risk structure has to be considered for each module first.

A further issue to be generally discussed is the module's suitability for specific business transactions and their illustration by way of examples. The authors can merely speculate due to the lack of empirical studies.

40 For an introduction in governance issues and challenges see *Krebs, P./Jung, S.*, Governance Structures in Business Networks, p. 118 (118 et seqq.) (in this volume).

### a. Non-transformative transaction modules

#### aa. "Non-transformative – exchange of consideration"

##### (1) Chance and risk structure of the module

The module "non-transformative – exchange of consideration" is based on the classic principle "do ut des". Individual goods are exchanged amongst the participating actors of the network by separate transactions. The prerequisites which are relevant for the chance and risk assessment are specific and transparent in this case. Participants receive a specific (initially predetermined) consideration for a specified compensation. The contract partners as well as the time of performance are likewise defined.

The difference to the exchange (do ut des) outside of the network lies in the fact that the exchange of consideration is not only to be considered in the light of pursuing the individual interests of the participants, but also in the light of the network. The module is integrated in the network and is therewith directed at achieving the implementation of the network aim arising independently of the will of the participants in the non-transformative exchange of consideration. The module is – in the same way as all others – influenced by the level of framework. In this module, the network provides at least the platform or the marketplace which creates the encounter opportunity for the exchange of considerations. Depending on the framework's configuration, its influence on the exchange of considerations can exceed the mentioned configurations and facilitate, enhance or even structure the exchange of considerations. In this module it is thus possible for the participants to establish special duties of consideration and allegiance. In extremely juridified network structures participants could be obliged to duties which bind them to the conclusion of a contract. Even though the participants achieve a direct return flow the module is nevertheless not designed with a one-off nature. Instead, the participants will hope for future exchange relations. The chance and risk structure of the module "non-transformative–exchange of consideration", however, mostly corresponds with the structure of a classical exchange of consideration which is usually coordinated by a contract.

(2) Suitability and examples

The business model is applicable to all cases in which participants within the network want to receive a specific and determinable consideration in return for their performance and in which the default risk of the return consideration should be kept as low as possible. The focus may be on opposing goods[41] which make it easily possible to exclude others from their use, such as, for instance, material goods, but also considerations which cannot be reproduced infinitely. This is not only due to the fact that these goods are especially suited for the exchange, but also due to the fact that competing approaches such as the communisation only show few advantages. Two examples will be listed in the following which illustrate the businesses that can be comprised in this module.

- **Exchange of goods.** The exchange of goods is especially applicable to such networks which provide a platform for the encounter of two different groups of companies (purchaser and seller). This should be typical especially for vertical[42] networks.
- **Linked production.** The example of linked production[43] is mentioned in *Glückler*'s study. As shown in said example, horizontal networks[44] can exchange production capacities amongst each other. A company which does not reach its full running capacity can make its production capacities available to other companies with shortages and receive a consideration in return.

bb. "Non-transformative–communisation"

(1) Chance and risk structure of the module

The module "non-transformative–communisation" exhibits a vast scope of arrangements reaching from ideally not juridified pooling to entirely jurid-

41 Generally speaking, an opposing good is a good which is no longer available to other participants due to being consumed by a participant.

42 Vertical networks in the sense of competition law.

43 *Glückler, J./Hammer, I.*, in: Glückler, J. et al., Unternehmensnetzwerke - Architektur, Strukturen und Strategien, Berlin, Heidelberg 2012, p. 139 (153).

44 Horizontal networks in the sense of competition law.

ified corporations. For illustration and refinement purposes both extremes are described in their modes of operation.

(a) Pooling

Pooling[45] within the module "non-transformative–communisation" requires several procedures in order to generate considerations. The module is based on the cooperation of at least two companies. As compensation for their performance in the pool the pool participants either receive a good or the permission to use a good from the pool. It requires at least two contributing companies for the pool to be successful. However, it can still be spoken of a pool if only one company performs a consideration without, contrary to expectations, a further company's contribution. In this case the pool has economically failed.

Each member receives a consideration in return, which is, however, not further characterised (according to amount, type, frequency or quality). Depending on the number of participants and the range of the pool each member can have the possibility to either receive a good from the pool or to use the goods in the pool in a multitude of cases.

Especially with regard to a huge amount of goods within the pool or with regard to goods which are not often utilised the chance of a generally high return flow can be envisaged for each member.

The return consideration which each individual receives is less predictable compared to the exchange of considerations. It depends on several risk factors such as the size of the pool, the amount of withdrawal possibilities for the individual participants, the arranged time for providing the consideration, the type of invested goods as well as their quality. If the communisation is arranged freely even those participants who have not (yet) contributed anything can avail themselves of the pool.[46] There is, on the other hand, the risk for early performing participants that the pool does

45 For the idea of pooling see *Ekeh, P. P.*, Social Exchange Theory The Two Traditions, Cambridge, Massachusetts 1974. Also referred to as "group-generalized exchange" by *Yamagishi, T./Cook, K. S.*, Social Psychology Quarterly, Vol. 56, No. 4, 1993, 235 (237).

46 For the problem of free-riding and cheap-riding see *Glückler, J./Hammer, I.*, in: Glückler, J. et al., Unternehmensnetzwerke - Architektur, Strukturen und Strategien, Berlin, Heidelberg 2012, p. 139 (147 et seq.).

not contain a good which they would like to use or that the pool is exhausted even before they have received their counter consideration.

Pooling can be to a large extent approximated to the exchange of consideration or the informal give and take[47]. The approximation to the exchange of consideration appears natural if, for instance, the pooling was limited by a minimal deposit or a maximal withdrawal. On the other hand, pooling can be arranged unrestrictedly so that participants do not have to provide their own contribution while still being permitted to unrestrictedly use the pool. In this case, pooling approaches the informal give and take. The possibility of approximation between the modules does not change the authority of the distinction. Such possibilities of approximation are already known from contract law and do not change the reasonableness of the contract types.

#### (b) Corporation

The corporation[48] is the most juridified form of the "non-transformative–communisation". The contribution, which is to be provided, as well as the possibility of withdrawal is usually regulated. In legally regulating the co-operation this type of coordination in form of communisation ensures the reduction of the chances of a high profit while at the same time decreasing the risks which are especially caused by the hazard of free-riding and cheap-riding.

### (2) Suitability and examples

The communisation within the realm of non-transformative transactions in form of pooling may be especially useful for the communal use of recourses such as money, technology or information. This form of exchange may be particularly used for either non- or merely partially rivalrous goods (i.e. information) or goods which cannot be used completely by only one participant, such as machines with large performance capacities.

---

47 See C.III.2.a)cc) pp. 96 et seq.

48 The term is understood in its broadest sense, so that partnerships are also included here.

Therewith, the participating company gives up nothing or only very little by joining the pool.

The communisation in form of the corporation is, on the other hand, well suited for the contribution and acquisition of resources.

- **Information pooling.** Information pooling comprises information which network companies have provided for the pool. All network participants in the poll are able to access each piece of information in the pool.[49]
- **Group purchasing organisation.** In group purchasing organisations participants bring together their demands. Therewith, better terms and conditions can be negotiated.

### cc. "Non-transformative–informal give and take"

#### (1) Chance and risk structure of the module

A further transaction module is the informal give and take ("non-transformative–informal give and take"). As outlined above,[50] the informal give and take comprises two forms of action.

When speaking of informal giving, a participant provides an individual good for a further network member without directly receiving a consideration in return.[51] When speaking of informal taking, a participant receives an individual good from a network member without directly providing a consideration in return. The other network member accepts this taking. Both forms of action can be subsumed under the notion of generalised exchange.[52]

If, when and who provides or receives which consideration is neither specified nor certain. Therewith, a high risk concerning the reflow of con-

---

49 The bundling of information may lead to new general information. This would then be conceived as network good. See C.III.2.b)aa) pp. 98 et seqq.

50 See above C.II. pp. 85 et seqq.

51 See also the principle of gift economy: *Cheal, D. J.*, The Gift Economy, New York, Oxford 1988.

52 For the idea of the generalised exchange see *Ekeh, P. P.*, Social Exchange Theory – The Two Traditions, Cambridge, Massachusetts 1974. Also referred to as "network-generalized exchange and Social Dilemmas" by *Yamagishi, T./Cook, K. S.*, Social Psychology Quarterly, Vol. 56, No. 4, 1993, 235 (237).

siderations for the participants is implied. At the same time, the informal give and take bears many chances as it often addresses those goods whose dispensation entails no or merely small immolations for the provider, but which can be of great value to the recipient. The same applies to informal taking. It is accepted especially in those cases which include merely a small loss. These considerations can be of great value to the recipient, because the considerations are, in contrast to communisation, not open to all members. Accordingly, the recipient can obtain an individually exclusive consideration. The informal give and take is (solely) in the long run designed for reciprocity.

As with the other modules, the network can influence the chance and risk structure. For instance, the object of exchange can be specified in advance. However, this does not determine who, how often, when and in what way the specified resources are to be exchanged. The generalised exchange often focuses on few network companies. This means that the benefactor provides only one or very few persons with considerations in hopes of receiving the adequate consideration especially from them in return. The informal taking, on the other hand, permits only a small amount of people who are in the long run likely to provide a compensation for the provision or the permission of taking. The intensified personal relation lowers the risk of not receiving a return consideration. As with the specification of the object of exchange, similar considerations apply to the other prerequisites. The more regulations exist, the more the informal give and take approaches one of the two other forms of exchange.

(2) Suitability and examples

The module is especially suitable for those exchanges whereby the loss of provided resources is less for the performer (or countenancer respectively) as the value of the resources for the consideration recipient (or taker respectively). In this module, particularly goods such as information, knowledge and know-how, which are not or merely partially rivalrous, can be coordinated. Those passing on a piece of information often suffer merely a small loss or none at all while it can be of great value for the recipient.

- **Exchange of transport capacities (informal giving).** Several forwarding agencies work within the same region and cover similar routes. Therefore, they can provide each other with residual transport capacity. This exchange is free of charge. The providing forwarder assumes that he can also use the available capacities of other forwarders.

- **Imitation of know-how (informal taking).** Several companies that are situated in spatial proximity by sharing the same office building permit the other companies to copy and imitate business processes.

### b. Transformation modules

In the realm of transformation within a business network, the recourses pass through a transformation process after having left the sphere of the provider. Thereby, a new good or a new service evolves. The transformation requires the cooperation of several participants and is associated with risks. There are, however, also special opportunities since the cooperation often entails synergy and learning effects. In extreme cases, the desired good can only be created by cooperation. Consequently, the transformation modules comprise two steps:

- the transformation process within the network[53] and
- the exchange of the therewith produced good

Since the part of transformation mirrors the modules of the realm of non-transformative transactions similarities to the modules of the realm of transaction can be found in the modules of transformation. Consequently, several references to the sections above can be made. This part is especially designed to particularly discuss the occurring differences and to illustrate application examples.

#### aa. "Transformation–exchange of consideration"

##### (1) Chance and risk structure of the module

The module exchange of consideration within the realm of transformation can have various forms. It can be applied for the fabrication of either an individual or a network good. Both shall be distinguished for refinement.

---

53 In transaction modules transformations may take place outside of the network. The chances and risks are - at this stage - transferred into an area outside said network.

### (a) Fabrication of individual goods

When fabricating an individual good all parties participating in the creation of the individual goods receive one of the produced goods or one part of the produced good if this can be divided. As with "exchange of non-transformative consideration–transaction" the basic principle "do ut des" is applicable here.[54] The individual participant receives an immediate return consideration for their performance. The particularity arises here in the fact that the return consideration is produced by the transformation process. This entails that the provider receives a newly emerged good by the transformation of the resources used. Through the fabrication of individual goods each participant receives a part of the transformation value (in the case of a good) or the entire transformation gain which is mirrored in the created individual good. Additionally, further information or learning effects for oneself can be gained from the fabrication of goods.

The chance and risk structure for the individual participant is similar to the exchange of considerations in the realm of non-transformative transactions.

The prerequisites, which are relevant to judge the chances and risks, are specific and transparent. The participants receive a specific (previously determined) consideration for an assigned return consideration. As with the module "non-transformative-exchange of consideration" the contract partners as well as the time of consideration are defined. The value of the return consideration, however, may be especially uncertain in as far as it yet emerges from the transformation process.

### (b) Fabrication of network goods

In the module "transformation–exchange of consideration" a network good emerges through the collective fabrication of a good which is to be assigned to the network respectively all network members in terms of property rights. Participants are permitted to use the network good and to profit from its creation.[55] This module design is also based on the principal of "do ut des". The particularity lies in the fact that all network mem-

---

54 See further C.III.2.a)aa) pp. 91 et seqq.

55 See *Glückler, J./Hammer, I.*, in: Glückler, J. et al., Unternehmensnetzwerke - Architektur, Strukturen und Strategien, Berlin, Heidelberg 2012, p. 139 (143).

bers are part of the fabrication of the network good. This is a prerequisite for the principle "do ut des" to be applicable. Otherwise a network member would receive a return consideration without providing a consideration.

The chance and risk structure is similar to the structure regarding the fabrication of an individual good. However, network goods are often more complex and therefore entail a higher level of risk in their production. On the other hand, network goods, which are not or merely partially rivalrous, can be used by several members at the same time.

(2) Suitability and examples

(a) Fabrication of individual goods

The idea of the fabrication of individual goods by exchanging considerations in the process of transformation is especially suited whenever the participating companies are not able to produce the individual good without the cooperation of the participants and whenever all participants are interested in possessing the same good. There will be even more instances in which the synergy effects combined with cooperation play a decisive part in opting for this module.

One could imagine that several companies (i.e. a steel constructor, a galvanising operator and an electronics company for shooting ranges) are in need of a new individual gate in the scope of the renovation of their respective company sites. In cooperation, they create a new company gate for each of the enterprises. The particularity of the fabrication of individual goods within the realm of transformation lies in the participants' receiving of the individual good in the form of a return consideration. Unlike supply chains or consideration pooling, which produce "a" newly created good, this case requires the fabrication of as many goods as participants. The example shows that this module feature is hardly practical for the realm of companies.

(b) Fabrication of network goods

The application of the module "transformation–exchange of consideration" is presumably especially suited for goods which are not (or scarcely) exhausted and which can therefore be used independently by all network members in (almost) the same quality (not or merely partially rivalrous goods).

If the fabrication of a good (e.g. terms and conditions) hardly allows the exclusion of the other network participants from the use of the good it is reasonable to engage the others in the preparation of the good and instead of producing an individual good to fabricate a network good. In general, so-called project cooperations can be regarded as the fabrication of network goods and are understood as the epitome of the work of business networks.

- **General terms clause.** General terms clauses could be an example of a network good which is created and used together. The legal departments of the network companies could develop general terms clauses together, which are then made available to all network companies.
- **Network good available for sale.** The procedure of the module "transformation–exchange of consideration" is furthermore suitable whenever the network would like to sell the communally produced good to a third party. The return consideration for each individual participant consists of the proceeds of the sale which are equally divided amongst the network companies or remain within the network for reinvestment.[56]

### bb. "Transformation–communisation"

#### (1) Chance and risk structure of the module

The cooperation of the participants is decisive for this form of communisation in contrast to the communisation in the realm of non-transformative transactions. Network goods as well as individual goods can be fabricated. Similar to the entire realm of transformation in general, the creation of an individual good is a rather theoretical case with regard to communisation. It is, however, imaginable if the producing group remains proprietor of the good and merely makes the rights of use available to the community. As

56 Due to the required cooperation in this module it is often difficult to determine how to evaluate the individual contributions and how the specific distribution should be made.

within the realm of non-transformative transactions, the scope of communisation reaches from pooling to corporisation.

In a network pool a group, which is smaller than the entire network, produces a network good.[57] After completion, this good is made available to all network participants for use in the network pool. For the model to be functional at least two groups have to participate in the network pool, i.e. they have to produce at least one network good each and make it available in the pool. The return flow for the individual participants of a group, who have provided the pool with a good, results firstly from the use of the co-operatively produced network good and the concomitant synergy and learning effects. And secondly, each individual participant can benefit from the provision of other network goods (produced by other groups).

Even though there are similarities to pooling in the module "non-transformative–communisation" the chance and risk structure is considerably different in this case. Unlike with pooling in the module "non-transformative–communisation", the transformation process leads to the production of a new good and, in the case of the success of the transformation process, to the occurrence of a virtually certain return flow for the group that has produced the good. Therefore, the risk primarily lies in the provision of the network good. The risk whether others also produce suitable pool goods is less relevant here since the basic return flow is secured by the successful provision of the first good. Conversely, there may hardly be any cases in which a multitude of network goods is initially produced. On the other hand, each individual pool good may, on average, be more valuable than the goods regarding communisation in the realm of non-transformative transactions. A special opportunity of participating in the fabrication of the network good lies in the learning effects for own subsequent projects.

Similar to communisation in the realm of non-transformative transaction, communisation in the realm of transformation can involve an approximation to either the exchange of considerations through, for instance, the obligational participation in the production of the network good or restrictions on the availability or to the informal give and take[58] through informally passing on the so produced goods.

57 If all network members produce a network good then this can be seen as an example of the module "transformation-exchange of considerations".

58 See C.III.2.b)cc) pp. 103 et seq.

The other extreme in the scope of this module is again the corporation even though the need for a corporation may be less urgent than in the realm of transaction due to the transformation-pooling's relatively low risk of exchange. A certain aversion may exist against the further increase of the already high complexity, which may be caused by designing the element of exchange as a corporation. This is moreover associated with costs.

(2) Suitability and examples

The module "transformation–communisation" is particularly suited for project cooperations where work distribution is reasonable. Additionally, it also appears beneficial here if the goods are not or merely partially rivalrous. The motivation for the individual to participate in this form of cooperation is especially high if the mere creation of the network in which they participate provides relatively high benefits. These benefits can either result from the return flow of the network good itself or from the learning effects gained through the production of the network good.

- **Project cooperation Dentis GmbH.**[59] Such a form of communisation can be found in *Glückler's* study in the shape of the project cooperation.[60] The results of several cooperations were made available to the network. Amongst others, quality management and a production manual were developed for the community of network members.

cc. "Transformation–informal give and take"

(1) Chance and risk structure of the module

The functioning of the informal give and take here is similar to its functioning in the module "non-transformative–informal give and take". It is likewise uncertain if, when and who provides which return consideration. In this case, however, one group produces one transformational good. The

59 For the study in general see *Glückler, J./Hammer, I.*, in: Glückler, J. et al., Unternehmensnetzwerke - Architektur, Strukturen und Strategien, Berlin, Heidelberg 2012, p. 73 (80 et seqq.).

60 *Glückler, J./Hammer, I.*, in: Glückler, J. et al., Unternehmensnetzwerke - Architektur, Strukturen und Strategien, Berlin, Heidelberg 2012, p. 139 (156).

chance and risk structure shows merely few similarities to the structure of informal give and take in the realm of non-transformative transactions. This is applicable in as far as the return flow is provided by a later return consideration of another group.

The decisive difference is that the group members who produced the transformational good have the opportunity to immediately use the produced transformational good and that the production provides learning effects for the group members. In this respect, the chance and risk structure is very similar to the communisation in the realm of transformation. The process of taking may be of only minor importance to this realm since the taking is typical for individual information.

#### (2) Suitability and examples

As a general rule, however, this module may, in contrast to the others within the realm of transformation, be suitable only for individual goods. If a group produces an individual good and subsequently makes this good available on request of another group then this happens in hopes that this other group or a third or fourth group may behave in the same way according to the approach of generalised exchange. The fact that several groups are required here entails that this form is realistically merely imaginable with larger networks. And even then it is presumably a rather rarely practiced module.

- **International lawyers' network.** One possibility would be, for instance, an international lawyers' network where subgroups are formed, which produce individual legal tools such as contract forms, lawsuit manuals or databases. Upon request, these tools are made available to other subgroups in hopes that this or other subgroups may act accordingly if required.

### IV. The relation of the modules to each other

Unlike most types of contracts which were shaped by practice the module system here is methodically designed constructively. This raises the question whether the modules stand in a legal relation to each other regarding specific features. First of all one could think of the chance–risk ratio developing in a certain direction. As the consideration of the individual modules has already shown, the chances and risks not always proceed in similar ways. Therefore, the legal analysis should refer to chances and risks separately.

According to the observations made here, the risk level rises in the realm of non-transformative transactions from the exchange of considerations to communisation and in formal give and take. This increase of risk might be connected to the growing lack of transparency regarding the return considerations. This relates to the issue if, who, when, what (and to what extent and quality) a return consideration is provided. This increase in risk can be counteracted by regulations and management tools, which enhance the transparency and strengthen trust.

Transformation exhibits a particular risk lying in either failing to produce the transformational good or requiring a disproportionately great expenditure to do so. This can be counteracted by coordination. However, in the realm of transformation the communisation and the informal give and take exhibit an opposing effect to the two according modules in the realm of non-transformative transactions. Whereas in the realm of non-transformative transactions the return consideration is uncertain for the first member when using communisation and for the first consideration using informal give and take, the transformational good is available to the performers in the shape of a return flow in the realm of transaction. Moreover, valuable experiences can be gained through cooperation which can also be regarded as return flow. On this abstract level it cannot be evaluated which of these opposing effects may generally prevail.

Basically, however, it can be said that when facing an increased level of risk for the return consideration an increased trust subserves the venture to expose oneself to this risk. This trust can be based on personal relations, but it can also be encouraged by the general legal order or the framework regulations of the network or the specific regulations of the module (or the regulation of the activities belonging to this module).

The consideration of the chances is challenging in as far as a difference has to be made between the amount of chances and the possibility to gain profit per chance and the probability of gaining profit. Thus, "non-transformative–communisation" often displays a multitude of chances. For informal give and take the profit per transaction can be extremely high particularly due to it perhaps concerning insider information. Accordingly, no clear regulations result from the realm of chances. However, it can be assumed that the module "non-transformative–exchange of consideration" exhibits the least chances as well as risks due to its transparency and the secured return flow. As a result it can be asserted that the modules differ according to their chance and risk structure, but, other than expected, do not display linear lines of development with regard to the named factors.

The modules can approximate each other and, the combination of several modules cannot be excluded. Legal typifications, such as carried out by the modular model, do not generally exclude typificational ambiguities or possible composability.

## V. The empirical findings within the modular system of network activities

The empirical findings[61] are in general also to be found in the modular model. Not all modules have to be present in one network. *Glückler's* studies seem to indicate that even advanced networks only use a few modules. If the dentistry network[62] was to be expressed by the modules then this would result in the interplay of especially the following modules: "non-transformative–exchange of consideration", "non-transformative–informal give and take", "transformation–communisation".

The exchange of the production capacities would be assigned to the module "non-transformative-exchange of consideration", while the exchange of knowledge would correspond with the module "non-transformative–informal give and take". The projects within the dentistry network were, however, organised in form of a "transformation–communisation". The dentistry network thus illustrates that the activities exercised in praxis may be assigned to the modules of the model.

Networks which are not or hardly developed will presumably, in contrast to the dentistry network, carry out their activities in applying individual modules. The modular network architecture is therefore capable of reflecting this multidimensionality which is characteristic for business networks.

The empirical findings furthermore clarify that networks are subject to a constant development and the individual modules can only be used temporarily by networks. Accordingly, the dentistry network implemented

61 *Glückler, J./Hammer, I.*, in: Glückler, J. et al., Unternehmensnetzwerke - Architektur, Strukturen und Strategien, Berlin, Heidelberg 2012, p. 139 (153 et seqq.).

62 *Glückler, J./Hammer, I.*, in: Glückler, J. et al., Unternehmensnetzwerke - Architektur, Strukturen und Strategien, Berlin, Heidelberg 2012, p. 139 (139 et seqq.).

projects, i.e. activities, for instance, which were not followed by a new project after termination. Therefore, networks can be divided into permanently integrated modules and merely temporarily integrated modules.

In *Glückler's* model each resource corresponded with one type of activity. The link between one category of activity and one resource is possible. However, the modular model shows that with adequate resources several modules can be applied simultaneously. The resource of knowledge, for instance, might be such a case.

A different question is whether the independence of the individual activity categories exhibited in *Glückler's* model can be confirmed by the modular model. In the modular model each module stands for a business model. This indeed suggests that normally each business model exists individually and that no connection whatsoever exists between the modules. However, as the hybrid type contracts in contract law show, the combination of business models is possible.[63] Also the modular model makes this possible and at least in these cases the individual modules then exhibit a connection. Moreover, it is not out of the question that certain regulations exist within the level of framework of the network, which compulsorily ensure a synchronisation of the modules within the business network.

## VI. Legal consequences resulting from the modular model

What can the field of network research gain from the knowledge that various independent network modules are to be distinguished? No consequences are entailed for the outward demarcation of networks, i.e. the definition of business networks, since the integration of one or more modules does not result in additional preconditions for the existence of networks.

However, for the understanding of business networks and for the solution of network specific questions new perspectives and possibilities arise for solving the problem. As long as business networks are considered to be one-dimensional the categorisations and therewith also the solutions will be one-dimensional, which admittedly can differ according to the network,

63 See D.I. p. 112 research questions.

but which inevitably will remain merely one-dimensional with regard to the network as a whole.[64]

## 1. Business networks as a specific legal category

The consequences of this will be shown based on the two essential questions of network research. Firstly, it has to be determined whether the network as a whole constitutes an individual legal category. And secondly, the question arises which regulations are applicable in the network.[65]

The literature so far classifies networks either as chain of contracts,[66] as corporation,[67] as a net contract,[68] as multilateral special agreement,[69] as a contract group,[70] a multilateral synallagma[71] or as a hybrid between, next to or beyond market and hierarchies,[72] or contract and corporation respec-

---

64 For example *Rohe, M.*, Netzverträge, Tübingen 1998, pp. 5 et seqq., 65 et seqq.; *Grundmann, S.*, Archiv für die civilistische Praxis 207 (2007), 718 (735 et seqq.); *Engel, C.*, Rezension: Oliver Williamson: Die ökonomischen Institutionen des Kapitalismus, Rabels Zeitschrift für ausländisches und internationales Privatrecht 57 (1993), 556 (561); *Baumgarten, A. K.*, Das Franchising als Gesellschaftsverhältnis, Göttingen 1993, pp. 114 et seqq.; critically *Druey, J. N.*, in: Amstutz, M. (ed.), Die vernetzte Wirtschaft, Zürich 2004, p. 123 (132), who considers networks as multi-piece structures consisting of combined elements. This renders legal institutions unaccountable.

65 See *Grundmann, S.*, Archiv für die civilistische Praxis 207 (2007), 718 (723).

66 *Collins, H.*, in: Amstutz, M./Teubner, G. (eds.), Networks, Oxford 2009, p. 187 (197 et seqq.); *Wellenhofer, M.*, in: Amstutz, M./Teubner, G. (eds.), Networks, Oxford 2009, p. 119.

67 *Baumgarten, A. K.*, Das Franchising als Gesellschaftsverhältnis, Göttingen 1993, pp. 114 et seqq.; *Berwanger, E.*, Der Gesellschaftsvertrag eines virtuellen Unternehmens, Homburg 2000, pp. 28 et seq.

68 *Möschel, W.*, Archiv für die civilistische Praxis 186 (1986), 187 (211 et seqq.); further developed by *Rohe, M.*, Netzverträge, Tübingen 1998, pp. 5 et seqq., 65 et seqq.

69 *Heldt, C.*, Baukooperation und Franchising als multilaterale Sonderverbindung, Baden-Baden 2010, esp. pp. 127 et seqq., 178 et seqq.

70 *Teubner, G.*, Netzwerk als Vertragsverbund, Baden-Baden 2004, p. 109, pp. 114 et seqq.

71 *Heermann, P. W.*, Drittfinanzierte Erwerbsgeschäfte, Tübingen 1998, pp. 92 et seqq., pp. 200 et seqq.

72 See *Sydow, J.*, Strategische Netzwerke, Wiesbaden 1992, p. 103 et seq.; *Powell, W. W.*, Research in Organizational Behavior 1990, 295 (295 et seqq.); *Thorelli, H. B.*, Strategic Management Journal 1986, 37 (37 et seqq.); *Corsten, H./Gössinger,*

tively.[73] Even though these solutions do not reflect the plurality of activities of networks, the conceivable combination of possible module forms and corresponding explanations can nevertheless be seen.

The modular model, in contrast, accommodates the plurality of activities in business networks by considering separate homogenous modules. The flexibility of the model developed here reflects the range of variation of business networks. Compared with other approaches existing so far, the modular model therefore shows clear benefits in functioning as an overall explanation for networks. However, this does not imply that the former explanations are rendered obsolete. It will be important to integrate the previous findings.

One of the central questions of network research is the legal assessment of networks. In effect, the evaluation lies somewhere between the conflicting priorities of divergent levels of regulation: The design of the activity and project frameworks, as well as the design of the module framework under private law,[74] is of key importance, should the legislator decide to implement non-mandatory provisions. Otherwise there probably won't be any provisions implemented on the module level. The framework comprises the network as a whole, i.e. all projects which can, in turn, be assigned to an activity or a module. Depending on its arrangement of the respective framework, this affects the network activities and projects to a greater or lesser extent.

In the sense of the terminology used here, the literature so far has intensively focused on the legal categorisation of this framework. The modular model indicates that for the consideration of the framework the general methodologies of the law of obligations, especially corporation and con-

---

*R.*, Einführung in das Supply Chain Management, München 2001, pp. 2 et seqq.; *Hune, M.*, Netzwerkverträge in der Transportwirtschaft, Berlin 2010, pp. 19 et seq.; *Scholz, C.*, in: Zentes, J./Swoboda, B./Morschett, D. (eds.), Kooperationen, Allianzen und Netzwerke, Wiesbaden 2005, p. 463 (467 et seq.); *Morschett, D.*, in: Zentes, J./Swoboda, B./Morschett, D. (eds.), Kooperationen, Allianzen und Netzwerke. Wiesbaden 2005, p. 387 (390 et seqq.); *Männel, B.*, Netzwerke in der Zulieferindustrie, Wiesbaden 1996, pp. 34 et seqq.

73 See *Teubner, G.*, in: Amstutz, M. (ed.), Die vernetzte Wirtschaft, Zürich 2004, p. 11 (11 et seqq.); *id.*, in: Amstutz, M./Teubner, G. (eds.), Networks, Oxford 2009, p. 11 (11 et seqq.).

74 See B.II.1. pp. 79 et seqq.

tract, as well as soft governance instruments (SGI)[75] should be used, but new instruments are not necessary.

Despite the modular module, the network research still has to face the question whether a business network as a whole is a new legal institution. Even though the individual modules are to be situated amongst familiar legal terms, the combination of these modules with the framework produces a new self-contained legal entity with self-contained problems. The most peculiar problem may be the need for a complex, ever adapting organisational structure.[76] To consider business networks as a new legal institution is therewith justified.

### 2. Applicable provisions in business networks

Major importance is assigned to private law arrangements in the network. The members can reach private law agreements which apply to the respective module respectively the single activity and the individual projects. In practice, private law agreements are regularly concluded for a special project.

However, private law instruments are not completely arbitrary. Basically, the contract, the corporation and the accommodation relationship, as well as soft governance instruments (SGI)[77] are available. Usually, the form of the module already determines the form of the instrument which can be used for concrete projects within the module. For the exchange of considerations the contract is generally the adequate form of coordination whereas the informal give and take is an accommodation relationship. Solely the exchange form of communisation provides a range reaching from corporation to accommodation relationship.

Less juridified business networks are basically characterised by their incomplete and not explicitly regulated modules, framework and even activities. Especially with regard to these cases, the modular approach developed here is of major significance. Due to similar interests within the

---

75 For further details see *Krebs, P./Jung, S.*, Governance Structures in Business Networks, D.II.1. p. 118 (135) (in this volume).

76 *Teubner, G.*, in: Augsberg, I. (ed.): Ungewissheit als Chance, Tübingen 2009, p. 109 (109 et seqq.).

77 For further details see *Krebs, P./Jung, S.*, Governance Structures in Business Networks, F.III. p. 118 (152 et seqq.) (in this volume).

individual modules, basic legal evaluations can be extracted which are applicable unless the framework or the private law agreements state otherwise. Therefore, the basic legal evaluations which are to be gained from the modules, function as concessionary law for the individual projects, which can be waived by framework regulations or private law agreements. The concessionary law gained in this way moreover serves as foundation for the monitoring of content, i. e. according to §§ 305 ff. BGB (German Civil Law). The modules and their basic forms of coordination are available as an approach to deduce lacking regulations and as foundation for content monitoring.

On the basis of the modular model and the basic evaluations gained from it business networks can be legally accounted for in consideration of their interaction with private law arrangements. Moreover, concessionary law can be deduced from the basic evaluations and the effects of the framework (and the provisions on the activity level). Although the modular model claims validity independent from the respective national law, it is not independent from the national law. The particular national law is a central point for the concretion for the law applicable to the modules since the modules and the business models they are based on have to consistently and normatively fit into the national law according to its system. The modular model therefore also serves legal security and renders the legal evaluation of business networks foreseeable. Instead, it appears reasonable that after adequate and preliminary academic clarification legislation should stipulate concessionary law as is often the case with practically important constructions.

## VII. Validity of the modular network architecture for economics?

The approach of the "modular network architecture" was developed from a legal perspective. It should nonetheless be addressed here whether the model could basically be of interest to economists. The modular model sets off from empirical findings whose generalisation capacity is very plausible also from an economic point of view even though further empirical studies are required. The developed network architecture based on homogenous business models is a way of constituting categories which could also be of interest for economics since business models with homogenous interests will, by tendency, have a disposition to uniform economic behaviour and phenomenona even in the absence of public legal regulations.

The modular model is basically qualified to be taken as the starting point for economic network research.

## D. Need for further research

The suggested modular model opens up a new field of research. On the one hand, the model itself reveals the need for considerable further research. On the other hand, general network issues have to be reconsidered in the light of the here suggested approach. Networks may furthermore be subject to separate or modified regulations in various other legal spheres beyond the law of obligation and corporate law. Besides, from a legal point of view, the problem arises that without empirical knowledge adequate classifications and evaluations are very difficult to make. Therefore, the modular model also requires further interdisciplinary research.

### I. The modular model and its need for further research

The legal conclusions, which can be drawn from the individual modules, were only addressed to a certain extent in this contribution. In this respect, the need for further research is widespread. For instance, distribution issues within the individual modules should be further examined. Especially with regard to transformation, the evaluation of single contributions is often difficult so that distribution issues pose special difficulties in these situations. In this respect, further research is also required regarding ownership and usage rights. Each module moreover raises the question concerning the relationship of the members amongst each other. In what way do, for instance, fiduciary duties, duties of care, obligations to inform etc. play a part?

The various possibilities of shaping the individual modules constitute a further vast field of research. This raises the question in what way the individual business models can be combined and what consequences this entails. It can be imagined that the business models are linked in a way so that the individual members not necessarily want to gain their return consideration from the module, in which they provide a consideration, but rather from a different module. This presumably practical situation will also influence the chance and risk distribution and could therefore possibly necessitate a re-evaluation.

A central aspect of the modular approach research should moreover be the consequences which the chosen coordination instruments have for the individual modules. Which legal amendments arise from the individual modules' access to the coordination forms contract or accommodation relationship or corporation?

Besides, need for further research arises regarding the consequences which the framework has for the individual modules. If, for instance, the network is organised in form of a corporation then this inevitably influences the existing modules in the network.

It also appears interesting to consider the rules concerning the beginning or ending of a module in a network, i.e. whether the general rules regarding the conclusion of a contract or the termination of a legal relation have to be modified here.

In this contribution the issue of sub-networks has been set aside. It should be examined in what way the modular model is applicable to sub-networks and in how far modifications are required. This results in further questions regarding the relationship of the sub-network to the network as a whole.

Another field of research is opened up when considering mediatisation. Mediatisation is understood here as the channelling of the members' interests regarding the use of an intermediary. Individual participants as well as the network could function as an intermediary. This raises the question – just as with regard to sub-networks – in how far the modular model accords for these problems and whether further amendments are required.

## II. General network problems in the light of the modular model

It has to be considered whether general network problems have to be re-evaluated in the light of the modular model. The need for research can be aligned by the life-cycle of the network.

Firstly, questions arise regarding the formation of networks and their modules. Subsequently, membership rights and duties have to be examined as well as organisational aspects such as decision-making processes within the network as a whole, but also in the individual modules. The modular approach furthermore poses questions concerning the entry and exit of members. In this respect it might be interesting to examine whether partial memberships are possible.

A central and much discussed aspect of network research are liability issues.[78] This especially applies to liabilities to third parties. The liability concerns firstly direct liability to third parties in special agreements[79] and secondly the tortuous liability of the network members[80] (keyword organised irresponsibility).

At the end of the network's life-cycle the question of its termination arises. How can a network be terminated and which consequences does this entail? It has to be examined, for instance, whom the network goods are to be assigned to after the termination or in how far the individual modules can be terminated if the individual member has so far not had the chance to gain profit, but has already provided the considerations. Finally, it should also be examined whether a special network law appears to be required.

## III. Network specific regulations in other fields of law

The juridical evaluation of networks can also affect other fields of law. Thus, in the sphere of competition law the question arises whether business networks, insofar as they affect the economy mostly in a positive way, are to be privileged according to Art. 101 TFEU and § 1 GWB (German Act against restraints on competition) or whether they should contrar-

---

78 See *Bräutigam, P.*, Deliktische Außenhaftung im Franchising, Baden-Baden 1994; *Collins, H.*, in: Amstutz, M./Teubner, G. (eds.), Networks – Legal Issues of Multilateral Co-operation, Oxfort 2009, p. 187 (208 et seq.); *Grundmann, S.*, Archiv für die civilistische Praxis 207 (2007), 718 (735 et seqq.); *id.*, in: Festschrift Westermann, Köln 2008, p. 227 (232 et seqq.); *Krebs, P.*, Sonderverbindung und außerdeliktische Schutzpflichten, München 2000, pp. 275 et seqq.; *Lange, K. W.*, Das Recht der Netzwerke, Frankfurt am Main 1998, n. 13, pp. 380 et seqq.; *Möschel, W.*, Archiv für die civilistische Praxis 186 (1986), 187 (211 et seqq.); *Rohe, M.*, Netzverträge, Tübingen 1998, pp. 85 et seqq., esp. pp. 129 et seqq.; *Teubner, G.*, Zeitschrift für das gesamte Handels- und Wirtschaftsrecht 1990, 295 (295 et seqq.); *id.*, Kritische Vierteljahreszeitschrift für Gesetzgebung und Rechtswissenschaft 1993, 367 (369, 373, 380 et seqq.).

79 *Krebs, P.*, Sonderverbindung und außerdeliktische Schutzpflichten, München 2000, pp. 275 et seqq.

80 See *Teubner, G.*, Zeitschrift für das gesamte Handels- und Wirtschaftsrecht 1990, 295 (295 et seqq.); *id.*, Netzwerke als Vertragsverbund, Baden-Baden 2004, pp. 204 et seqq.; *Bräutigam, P.*, Deliktische Außenhaftung im Franchising, Baden-Baden 1994.

ily rather be subjected to a stricter application due to spill-over effects, which negatively affect the willingness for competition. A similar question arises with regard to Art. 102 TFEU or § 19 f. GWB. Moreover, the question could arise how the formation of a network can be accounted for by antitrust merger control. Regarding accounting law, the allocation of items of property within the network may be difficult especially if the result were achieved that an individual network member stands in a rather fiduciary position.

### IV. Need for interdisciplinary research

Empirical studies may show under which circumstances specific modules can be considered as appropriate cooperation forms for networks. *Glückler's* studies already indicate that the type of consideration (good, service, knowledge, data, information, etc.) will be especially decisive. Thereby, network goods and individual goods are to be distinguished. Not least will the properties of the good play a part. For rivalrous goods other forms of action will be more advantageous than for merely partially or not competing goods. This approach partially addresses the issue in which situations the choice of specific modules could be reasonable. The need for further research is, however, still very high in this realm.

## E. Findings

1. The empirically detected existence of various categories of activities in business networks by *Glückler et al.* can be generalised. There are, as a general rule, several parallel conducted types of activities in business networks (plurality of activities).
2. Five possible influencing factors were found which affect the formation of an activity category, namely:
   a) the type of resources used
   b) the type of exchange process (exchange of consideration,[81] communisation,[82] informal give and take[83])

---

81 See C.III.2.a)aa) pp. 91 et seqq.; C.III.2.b)aa) pp. 98 et seqq.
82 See C.III.2.a)bb) pp. 93 et seqq.; C.III.2.b)bb) pp.101 et seqq.
83 See C.III.2.a)cc) pp. 96 et seq.; C.III.2.b)cc) pp. 10e et seq.

c) the type of cooperation (non-transformative[84] and transformative[85] transaction) and
d) the type of coordination (accommodation relationship, contract, pooling corporation[86]) and
e) type of good (individual good/network good[87]).

The framework of the network, which can be juridified to various degrees, is not an influencing factor, but affects the activity categories.[88]

3. The participation in various network activities depends on the participants' interests and regards the decision for participation as well as the intensity of participation. This implies that the various categories of activities are separate, as a general rule, and thus have to be acknowledged separately in legal terms.[89]
4. The multitude of possible activity categories within a network aggravates the systematisation. Systematisation is, however, necessary since it is the duty of objective law to provide gap-filling regulations or monitoring standards.[90] This article abstracts and systemises the possible activity categories. Similar to the legal types of contracts, systematisation is to be found in the recognition of business models with mostly congruent chance and risk structures (alignment of interests).[91]
5. Two influencing factors are essential for the systematisation. These are the type of cooperation (transformative and non-transformative transaction) and the type of exchange processes (exchange of considerations, communisation, informal give and take).[92] The specificity of communisation lies in the very large range it may exist in reaching from pooling to corporation.[93]
6. From the combination of the influencing factors type of cooperation and type of exchange process the modular system of network activities was developed here. It comprises six business models in the shape of modules. These modules are: "non-transformative-exchange of consid-

84 See C.III.1. pp. 89 et seq.; C.III.2.a) pp. 91 et seqq.
85 See C.III.1. pp. 89 et seq.; C.III.2.b) pp. 97 et seqq.
86 See B.II.1. pp. 79 et seqq.; C.II.3. p. 87.
87 See C.II.5. pp. 88 et seq.
88 See B.II.1. pp. 79 et seqq.
89 See B.II.2. pp. 82 et seq.
90 See C.I. pp. 84 et seq.
91 See C.I. pp. 84 et seq.
92 See C.II. pp. 86 et seq.
93 See C.III.2.a)bb) pp. 93 et seqq.; C.III.2.b)bb) pp. 101 et seqq.

erations",[94] "non-transformative-communisation",[95] "non-transformative-informal give and take",[96] "transformation-exchange of considerations",[97] "transformation-communisation",[98] "transformation-informal give and take".[99] Each module exhibits its individual chance and risk structure and is suited for specific constellations. These were substantiated here.[100] For further concretion the influencing factors which are not substantial for the systemisation may also be considered.

7. It was furthermore examined whether the chance and risk structures develop in a set pattern with regard to the relationship of the individual modules of the system of network activities Indeed, the risk rises in the realm of transaction starting from the module "non-transformative-exchange of consideration" to the module "non-transformative-communisation" and reaching its peak in the module "non-transformative-informal give and take". But apart from that no linearity could be assigned regarding the properties of chance, risk, transparency and trust.[101]
8. Business networks are a separate, new legal institution. Admittedly, the coordinating forms applicable to the individual modules are not generally new, but due to its plurality of activities the structure as a whole differs from all other forms to such a great extent that it has to be considered separately.
9. Based on this separate consideration of homogenous modules the model accounts for the actually existing plurality of activities of business networks. Due to the alignment of interests within the individual modules fundamental legal values can be gained which are to be applied whenever no other regulations exist under private law.

---

94 See C.III.2.a)aa) pp. 91 et seqq.
95 See C.III.2.a)bb) pp. 93 et seqq.
96 See C.III.2.a)cc) pp. 96 et seqq.
97 See C.III.2.b)aa) pp. 98 et seqq.
98 See C.III.2.b)bb) pp. 101 et seqq.
99 See C.III.2.b)cc) pp. 103 et seqq.
100 See explanations for individual modules C.III.2. pp. 91 et seqq.
101 See C.IV. pp. 106 et seq.

# Governance structures in business networks[1]

*Prof. Dr. Peter Krebs, Dr. Stefanie Jung, M.A. (CoE)*

## A. Introduction

Business networks are a popular form of co-operation in Europe especially for small and medium sized enterprises (SME),[2] but also for the sometimes neglected group of mid-range companies.[3] In contrast, large companies often do not see the need to co-operate with partners in the framework of a business network. Even if they are willing to join a business network, European and national anti-trust law (cf. Art. 101 TFEU and § 1 German anti-trust law) prohibits most forms of participation that are interesting for large firms from an economic point of view.[4] One of the few interesting opportunities for large companies are joint research co-operations, because anti-trust law is less strict concerning this aspect.

Despite being a widely used instrument, business networks so far cannot be fully grasped from a legal perspective. In a recent study on business

---

1 This paper is a translated version of a German article („Governance-Strukturen in Unternehmensnetzwerken“) that was published in the German journal „Kölner Schrift zum Wirtschaftsrecht“ (KSzW 2015, pp. 30-49).

2 SMEs are defined by the EU. The threshold to large companies is an annual turnover of not more than 50 million Euro, an overall balance sheet of not more than 43 million Euro and a workforce of not more than 250. For more information on SMEs organised in business networks see *Glückler, J. and others*, Organisatorische Vielfalt und Innovativität von KMU-Netzwerken: Ein bundesweites Screening, in: Glücker, J. and others (eds.), Unternehmensnetzwerke – Architekturen, Strukturen und Strategien, Berlin, Heidelberg, 2012, p. 21 (23 et seqq.).

3 In favour of the introduction of such a quantitative category in Germany *Krebs, P./ Jung, S.*, Große mittelständische Unternehmen - der zu Unrecht vernachlässigte Teil des Mittelstands, Der Betrieb 2013, Editorial issue 51/52. The European Commission is considering policy measures for this group of companies. See European Commission, A strong European policy to support Small and Medium-sized Enterprises (SMEs) and entrepreneurs 2015-2020 - Public consultation on the Small Business Act (SBA), 2014, question 4.3.

4 See *Schultes, M.*, Company networks and the dichotomy and statics of competition law – a combined dynamic control of conduct and structure as a solution approach, pp. 198 et seqq. (in this volume).

networks 54.3% of the responding companies stated that they encounter significant legal problems when establishing or running a business network.[5] Thus, business networks constitute an economically relevant and at the same time dogmatically interesting and challenging field of research.

This essay focuses on governance structures within business networks. Therefore, the emphasis lies on the legal relationships of the network members to one another and also to the business network as a whole. Those aspects have been relatively little researched up to now. On the one hand, this may be explained by the diversity of this form of co-operation. On the other hand, this (legal) area is dominated by freedom of contract, making it possibly less urgent to specify the governance structure from a legal perspective. However, the above mentioned practical challenges within business networks demonstrate the necessity to conduct research on possible governance structures.

One problem of business networks is, that they have not been well defined so far.[6] This is also important with regard to the governance structure, because the respective structures have to match the forms of co-operation captured by the definitions. Depending on whether business networks are to be understood in a broader sense, different governance structures will be implemented than in those cases of a more narrow definition. Thus, our research team has developed a functional legal definition of business networks.[7] This definition is much narrower than that of the prevailing opinion. In our opinion hierarchical franchise systems do not constitute a business network, as the challenges regarding dynamic self-organisation that are typically characteristic for business networks do not

5 *Glückler, J.* and others, Organisatorische Vielfalt und Innovativität von KMU-Netzwerken: Ein bundesweites Screening, in: Glücker, J. and others (eds.), Unternehmensnetzwerke – Architekturen, Strukturen und Strategien, Berlin, Heidelberg, 2012, p. 21 (29).

6 In contrast to economists lawyers mostly abstained from this discussion.

7 *Krebs, P./Aedtner, K./Schultes, M.*, Company networks reloaded – putting a general functional approach to defining complex problems to the test, D. p. 41 (73) (in this volume). Definition: „A company network is every legally voluntary connection based on an economic and legal network aim of a minimum of three legally independent companies which induce a network-specific demand for organization. The network companies at least partially exchange their economic independence for the co-ordination of their economic activities by means of concerted practices, agreements or the foundation of a corporation in order to implement the network aim through the bundling of resources."

arise.[8] In the following, these definition-centred questions will be excluded. Irrespective of the definition, hierarchical structures shall not be the subject of the research at hand, for the very reason that the structures within these organisations are very different.

However, it is safe to say about business networks that the forms and degrees of co-operation widely differ.[9] They vary due to the size and the organisational structure of the network as well as due to the network purpose and the projects conducted within the network. But even though there are so many different projects that could possibly be carried out within business networks, a recent study shows[10] that there is a tendency towards realising certain types of projects in the scope of business networks. Such a group of identical or at least very similar projects can be called an activity.[11] Among others, popular activities are buying associations (syndicates), joint research projects, the exchange of goods and services as well as the exchange of experiences and knowledge.[12]

Irrespective of the activities that are pursued within a business network, this form of organisation is generally characterised by the need for a high

---

8 *Krebs, P./Aedtner, K./Schultes, M.,*Company networks reloaded – putting a general functional approach to defining complex problems to the test, II. 3. c) p. 41 (71 et seq.) (in this volume).

9 *Glückler, J./Hammer, I.,* Multilaterale Kooperation und Netzwerkgüter, in: Glückler, J. and others (eds.), Unternehmensnetzwerke – Architekturen, Strukturen und Strategien, Berlin, Heidelberg, 2012, p. 139 (153 et seqq.); *Krebs, P./Jung, S./ Aedtner, K./Schultes, M.,* The modular system of network activities, A. p. 41 (p. 75 et seqq.) (in this volume); see for example *Beeser, S.*, Strategische Allianzen im EU-Wettbewerbsrecht, München, 1996; *Ensthaler, J./Gesmann-Nuissl, D.*, Virtuelle Unternehmen in der Praxis – eine Herausforderung für Zivil-, Gesellschafts- und Kartellrecht, Betriebs-Berater 2000, 2265 (2265 et seqq.); *Rosbenberger, H.-P.*, Verträge über Forschung und Entwicklung – F&E-Kooperationen in rechtlicher und wirtschaftlicher Sicht, Köln, 2010; *Heldt, C.*, Baukooperationen und Franchising als multilaterale Sonderverbindung, Baden-Baden, 2009; www.krea-nets.de, 30.03.2015.

10 *Glückler, J.* and others (eds.), Unternehmensnetzwerke – Architekturen, Strukturen und Strategien, Berlin, Heidelberg, 2012.

11 *Krebs, P./Jung, S./Aedtner, K./Schultes, M.,* The modular system of network activities, B. II. 1. p. 75 (79 et seqq.) (in this volume).

12 *Glückler, J./Hammer, I.,* Multilaterale Kooperation und Netzwerkgüter, in: Glückler, J. and others (eds.), Unternehmensnetzwerke – Architekturen, Strukturen und Strategien, Berlin, Heidelberg, 2012, p. 139 (153 et seqq.); see *Krebs, P./Jung, S./ Aedtner, K./Schultes, M.,* The modular system of network activities, B. II. p. 75 (79 et seqq.) (in this volume).

degree of flexibility.[13] The network members attach great importance to flowing organisational structures because activities as well as interests and members may change and they expect the network to quickly adapt to the changing needs.

Because of this need for flexibility a tendency towards a low degree of juridification can be observed.[14] The degree of juridification differs from network to network, as many influencing factors exist. One of these factors is usually related to the size of the network. Larger networks often chose a higher degree of juridification than small business networks because mutual trust is normally lower in a large network and solving conflicts on a case by case basis is often more difficult. Moreover, the degree of juridification is determined by other factors. Complex structures, great values at risk and externalities create the need for at least some form of juridification. The "life span" of the business network also plays an important role. Long-term co-operations often accumulate considerable value and, therefore, might need some legal rules.[15] At the same time, informal ties and mutual trust between network members will grow over time, which might lower the need for rules. Strong informal ties between the members (e.g. family ties) generally favour a (very) low degree of juridification. In addition, the interests of the members determine the degree of juridification. The more homogenous they are, the less binding rules they will need, as their interests will usually coincide. Also the openness of a business network towards new members might have an influence on the

---

13 *Krebs, P./Aedtner, K./Schultes, M.*, Company networks reloaded – putting a general functional approach to defining complex problems to the test, C. I. 4. p. 41 (65 et seq.) (in this volume); see *Heldt, C.*, Baukooperation und Franchising als multilaterale Sonderverbindung, Baden-Baden, 2010, pp. 67 et seqq., especially pp. 77 et seqq.; *Provan, K./Kenis, P.*, Modes of Network Governance: Structure, Management and Effectiveness, Journal of Public Administration Research and Theory 2007, 229 (244 et seqq.).

14 *Dumitrascu, V.* and others, Modern Approaches of the Business Networks, Procedia – Social and Behavioral Sciences 109 (2014), 125 (126) state that business networks have few rules.

15 In a recent study on business networks 49.2% of the responding companies stated that difficulties arise concerning the contributions to the network. Even more companies (56.2%) answered that they encounter difficulties concerning the distribution of values. *Glückler, J.* and others, Organisatorische Vielfalt und Innovativität von KMU-Netzwerken: Ein bundesweites Screening, in: Glücker, J. and others (eds.), Unternehmensnetzwerke – Architekturen, Strukturen und Strategien, Berlin, Heidelberg, 2012, p. 21 (29).

degree of juridification. A network designed for an increasing number of members requires a certain degree of juridification, e. g. concerning the admission to the network. Membership rules also point out the consequences of joining the network to prospective members.

In case members see a need for a more formal governance structure within the business network, they tend to use soft governance instruments instead of hard governance instruments.[16] Dividing governance instruments into hard governance instruments (HGI) and soft governance instruments (SGI) as introduced in this essay appears to be an important approach for the categorisation and specification of governance in business networks and will be, therefore, discussed in more detail below.

For many network members trust seems to be more important than an intense protection by legal rules.[17] But this basic attitude does not work well in all cases. If e.g. valuable assets are at risk, protective rules are required. National laws in most countries do not provide specific rules for business networks. Only general rules can be applied.[18] But these rules are so general that they cannot provide legal certainty. Furthermore, they also have difficulties in dealing with the particularities of business networks. For most governance questions the situation is even worse because of the overall lack of adequate rules. In business networks with a need for some rules members tend to establish procedural rules rather than substantive

16 The two different groups of governance instruments are discussed in more detail below.

17 This aspect is discussed in more detail in F.V.1. pp. 157 et seqq.

18 Italy has introduced a network contract as a legal instrument for business networks ("Il contratto di rete"). The instrument was established by the legislative decree on 10 February 2009, n. 5 and then converted with some amendments into law on 9 April 2009, n. 33. The law was modified thereafter by the conversion into law n. 134/2012 of the legislative decree on 22 June 2012, n. 83. On the Italian network contract see *Cafaggi, F.*, Il contratto di rete ed il diritto dei contratti, I Contratti 2009, 911 (911 et seqq.); *idem*, Il nuovo contratto di rete: learning by doing?, I Contratti 2010, 1143 (1143 et seqq.); *idem*, Il contratto di rete nella prassi prime riflessioni, I Contratti 2011, 504 (504 et seqq.); *Cafaggi, F./Iamiceli, P./Mosco, G.D.*, Il contratto di rete per la crescita delle imprese, Giuffrè, 2012; *Cafaggi, F./ Iamiceli, P./Mosco, G.D.*, Il contratto di rete e le prime pratiche: linee di tendenza, modelli e prospettive di sviluppo, I Contratti 2013, 799 (799 et seqq.). On net contracts from a German perspective *Baumgarten, A.*, Das Franchising als Gesellschaftsverhältnis - eine Studie zur spezifischen zivilrechtlichen Qualität des Rechtsverhältnisses zwischen Franchise-Geber und Franchise-Nehmer, Göttingen, 1993, pp. 114 et seqq.; *Berwanger, E.*, Der Gesellschaftsvertrag eines virtuellen Unternehmens, Münster, 2000, pp. 28 et seq.

provisions. Procedural rules are better suited to deal with future (unknown) developments and are, therefore, used to establish a governance structure within the business network. Substantive provisions are more likely to be used when it comes to a specific type of co-operation within the network.

Hence, there is at least a need for some form of self-regulation concerning the governance structure within larger and more complex networks despite the general tendency towards a low degree of juridification. These larger and more complex networks are the subject of investigation of this article. This and the emphasis on non-hierarchical structures mentioned above, constitute the scope of the analysis conducted in this essay.

It is the aim of this paper to provide a general regime for internal governance structures of business networks. We will distinguish between different levels. This will lead to a multi-level-governance structure. In the second part of this paper, we will take a closer look at the different "soft governance instruments" (SGI) and "hard governance instruments" (HGI)[19] which can be used for self-regulation within the business network. The paper will not discuss the influence of factors such as the openness of the network or (strong) informal ties between members on the governance structure. The paper will also leave aside informal structures that are based on trust, power, sympathy, reputation etc.[20]

---

19 For a closer look at these new categories see F.II. pp. 148 et seqq.; F.III. pp. 152 et seqq.

20 With respect to these aspects *Glückler, J./Németh, S.*, Legitime Steuerungsinstanzen in lateralen Netzwerken, in: *Glückler, J.* and others (eds.), Unternehmensnetzwerke – Architekturen, Strukturen und Strategien, Berlin, Heidelberg, 2012, p. 95 (100).

## B. Opening up the black box

So far, business networks have been classified in literature either as a chain of contracts,[21] a corporation,[22] a net contract,[23] multilateral special agreements,[24] a contract group ("Vertragsverbund"),[25] a multilateral synallagma[26] or as a hybrid between, next to or beyond market and hierarchies[27] or contract and corporation respectively.[28]

---

21 *Collins, H.*, The weakest Link: Legal Implications of the Network Architecture of Supply Chains, in: Amstutz, M./Teubner, G., (eds.), Networks – Legal Issues of Multilateral Co-operation, Oxford, Portland, 2009, p. 187 (197 et seqq.); *Wellenhofer, M.*, Third Party Effects of Bilateral Contracts Within the Network, in: Amstutz, M./Teubner, G., (eds.), Networks – Legal Issues of Multilateral Co-operation, Oxford, Portland, 2009, p. 119.

22 *Baumgarten, A.*, Das Franchising als Gesellschaftsverhältnis, Göttingen, 1993, pp. 114 et seqq.; *Berwanger, E.*, Der Gesellschaftsvertrag eines virtuellen Unternehmens, Münster, 2000, pp. 28 et seq.

23 *Möschel, W.*, Dogmatische Strukturen des bargeldlosen Zahlungsverkehrs, Archiv für die civilistische Praxis 186 (1986), 187 (211 et seqq.); further developed by *Rohe, M.*, Netzverträge, Tübingen, 1998, pp. 5 et seqq., 65 et seqq.

24 *Heldt, C.*, Baukooperation und Franchising als multilaterale Sonderverbindung, Baden-Baden, 2010, esp. pp. 127 et seqq., 178 et seqq.

25 *Teubner, G.*, Netzwerk als Vertragsverbund - Virtuelle Unternehmen, Franchising, Just-in-time in sozialwissenschaftlicher und juristischer Sicht, Baden-Baden, 2004, pp. 109, 114 et seqq.

26 *Heermann, P.*, Drittfinanzierte Erwerbsgeschäfte, Tübingen, 1998, pp. 92 et seqq., 200 et seqq.

27 See *Sydow, J.*, Strategische Netzwerke, - Evolution und Organisation, Wiesbaden, 2005, pp. 103 et seq.; *Powell, W.*, Neither Market nor Hierarchy – Network Forms of Organization, Research in Organizational Behaviour 1990, 295 (295 et seqq.); *Thorelli, H.*, Networks between Markets and Hierarchies, Strategic Management Journal 1986, 295 (295 et seqq.); *Thorelli, H.*, Networks between Markets and Hierarchies, Strategic Management Journal 1986, 37 (37 et seqq.); *Ménard, C.*, The Economics of Hybrid Organizations, Journal of Institutional and Theoretical Economics 2004, 345 (especially 345 et seqq.); *Corsten, H./Gössinger, R.*, Einführung in das Supply Chain Management, Oldenburg, München (and others), 2008, pp. 2 et seqq.; *Hune, M.*, Netzwerkverträge in der Transportwirtschaft - Wirtschaftliche und rechtliche Dimensionen einer modernen Vertragsverbindung zwischen Wettbewerb und Kooperation, Berlin, 2010, pp. 19 et seq.; *Scholz, C.*, Von der Netzwerkorganisation zur virtuellen Organisation – und zurück?, in: Zentes, J./ Swoboda, B./Morschett, D., (eds.), Kooperationen, Allianzen und Netzwerke– Grundlagen, Ansätze, Perspektiven, Wiesbaden, 2005, p. 463 (467 et seq.); *Männel, B.*, Netzwerke in der Zulieferindustrie, Wiesbaden, 1996, pp. 34 et seqq.

28 See *Teubner, G.*, Coincidentia oppositorum: Das Recht der Netzwerke jenseits von Vertrag und Organisation, in: Amstutz, M., (ed.), Die vernetzte Wirtschaft – Netz-

Many of these classifications are based on a rather holistic approach with regard to the organisational structure, because the network is analysed by looking at its framework in order to find a dogmatic legal explanation.[29] This article will concentrate on the internal structure of developed business networks. Hence, it is necessary to open up the "black box" called business networks and to try to draw legal conclusions from it. This approach focuses on the activities within the business network and on how the multitude of single projects (and activities) is governed.

## C. New economic findings

*Johannes Glückler* and his research team have recently conducted an interesting study on developed business networks.[30] In the paper at hand, the economic findings of this study are used as the basis for the legal regime that will be developed in the following.

*Glückler* and his team measured and visualised the structure of the cooperating groups as well as the intensity of the involvement of the individual companies on the basis of a survey of all network companies.[31] The most astounding findings of the study were, firstly, that developed (large) business networks comprise of diverse projects[32] which could be assigned to different forms of activities[33] and, secondly, that the members do not

werke als Rechtsproblem, Zürich, Basel, Genf, 2004, p. 11 (11 et seqq.); *id.*, Coincidentia Oppositorum: Hybrid Networks Beyond Contract and Organisation, in: Amstutz, M./Teubner, G., (eds.), Networks – Legal Issues of Multilateral Co-operation, Oxford, Portland, 2009, p. 3 (3 et seqq.).

29 *Krebs, P./Jung, S./Aedtner, K./Schultes, M.*, The modular system of network activities, B. III. p. 75 (83 et seq.) (in this volume).

30 See www.kreanets.de, 30.03.2015; *Glückler, J.* and others (eds.), Unternehmensnetzwerke - Architekturen, Strukturen und Strategien, Berlin, Heidelberg, 2012.

31 See *Glückler, J./Hammer, I.*, Multilaterale Kooperation und Netzwerkgüter, in: Glückler, J. and others (eds.), Unternehmensnetzwerke - Architekturen, Strukturen und Strategien, Berlin, Heidelberg, 2012, p. 139 (153).

32 *Glückler, J./Hammer, I.*, Multilaterale Kooperation und Netzwerkgüter, in: Glückler, J. and others (eds.), Unternehmensnetzwerke - Architekturen, Strukturen und Strategien, Berlin, Heidelberg, 2012, p. 139 (153 et seqq.).

33 *Krebs, P./Jung, S./Aedtner, K./Schultes, M.*, The modular system of network activities, B. II. 1. p. 75 (79 et seqq.) (in this volume).

join all sorts of activities (and, of course, not all projects).[34] Even if they do join a specific form of activity, they may participate with differing intensity in those projects. An example might help to illustrate the idea: In a given business network companies exchange knowledge (type of activity). In this context, company A met with company C in order to discuss some latest technical developments and how this new technology could be integrated in the production process (project – specific knowledge exchange). But company A did not join the conference about this topic that was organised within the network (another project within the same type of activity). In general, company A did not join any projects that were linked to the exchange of production capacity among the network members (type of activity). In contrast, company A helped to develop a quality management system (project – belonging to a type of activity called "project co-operation") and standard contracts (project - belonging to a type of activity called "project co-operation"). Company A was in need of a quality management system; hence, it sent three employees to help to develop it. Those employees significantly contributed to the success of the project. The standard contracts (project – belonging to a type of activity called "project co-operation"), in contrast, were not so important for company A. Therefore, only one employee joined the group, but was not putting much effort into this project. So even within one type of activity (project co-operation) company A worked with varying intensity on two different projects (quality management system and standard contracts).

The first important consequence which can be drawn from a legal perspective is that companies which are members of a business network do not behave like shareholders of a company. They do not expect to gain their main advantage from the network as a whole. In general, business networks are neither aimed at paying a dividend nor at exploiting the network goods as a whole, even though both aspects are perfectly admissible. Hence, members must expect another kind of return on investment. First and foremost, they want to profit from the projects they take part in. This is the level where most of the value is created for the network members. If profit (or loss) from the single project is what matters most to the members of the business network, the law applicable to these projects deserves a closer look.

34 See *Glückler, J./Hammer, I.*, Multilaterale Kooperation und Netzwerkgüter, in: Glückler, J. and others (eds.), Unternehmensnetzwerke - Architekturen, Strukturen und Strategien, Berlin, Heidelberg, 2012, p. 139 (155).

*Glückler* and his team formed categories of similar projects which correspond to the term "type of activity" used in this paper.[35] This term will be explained in more detail later on.[36] The study found that for each of these examined forms of activities resources were combined with a specific type of co-operation by various network members. In the scope of the type of activity of linked production,[37] for instance, companies offer unused production capacities. Network members who are in need of production capacities can acquire them. In this way, two network companies combine their resources (production capacity and demand) by simply exchanging goods (or services).

In exploratory interviews[38] with some of the participating companies, *Glückler* and his team (*krea.nets*) discovered three primary categories of types of activities usually lying at the core of a business network. In addition, they established a typical secondary activity.

According to the study, primary types of activities in business networks are:[39]

1. Linked production: Companies with unused production capacity sell this overcapacity to another member of the business network.
2. Knowledge exchange: Usually various forms of knowledge exchange exist in business networks. Some are very informal (phone calls) and some exhibit a more formalised structure (data bases). *Krea.nets* also found that (approved or tolerated) imitation is a crucial form of knowledge exchange in business networks.[40]

---

35 *Krebs, P./Jung, S./Aedtner, K./Schultes M.*, The modular system of network activities, B. II. 1. p. 75 (79 et seqq.) (in this volume).

36 See D.II.4. pp. 138 et seq.

37 See *Glückler, J./Hammer, I.*, Multilaterale Kooperation und Netzwerkgüter, in: Glückler, J. and others (eds.), Unternehmensnetzwerke - Architekturen, Strukturen und Strategien, Berlin, Heidelberg, 2012, p. 139 (153).

38 See *Glückler, J./Hammer, I.*, Multilaterale Kooperation und Netzwerkgüter, in: Glückler, J. and others (eds.), Unternehmensnetzwerke - Architekturen, Strukturen und Strategien, Berlin, Heidelberg, 2012, p. 139 (152, 154 et seq.).

39 *Glückler, J./Hammer, I.*, Multilaterale Kooperation und Netzwerkgüter, in: Glückler, J. and others (eds.), Unternehmensnetzwerke - Architekturen, Strukturen und Strategien, Berlin, Heidelberg, 2012, p. 139 (153 et seqq.).

40 See *Hammer, I./Beck, S./Glückler, J.*, Lernen im lokalen Unternehmensnetzwerk: Imitation zwischen Konvention und Tabu, in: Glückler, J. and others (eds.), Unternehmensnetzwerke - Architekturen, Strukturen und Strategien, Berlin, Heidelberg, 2012, p. 163 (163 et seqq.).

3. Project co-operation: In a project co-operation the network members work together in order to create something new e. g. a compilation of a quality management system or standard contracts.

The secondary activity was the management of the aforementioned primary types of activities, especially with regard to project co-operations.[41]

## D. The structure of business networks

### I. Business networks with a simple structure

In business networks, companies co-operate in order to achieve co-operative gains.[42] In general, a multitude of different co-operations can be found within networks.[43] Every single co-operation is a "project" which is why the sum of all projects can be called "project level".

In addition, there is always a "framework level". On this level the decision to establish a business network is made. In addition, rules with regard to becoming a member, as well as leaving the network, are decided here. Furthermore, rules relating to the dissolution of the business network become relevant on the framework level.

Normally, the participating companies do not want to co-operate in all forms of (possible) business activities. Therefore, a network purpose is needed to describe the aim of the business network and to give orientation to the members.[44] The purpose can be quite narrow, but it can also be very

---

41 *Krebs, P./Jung, S./Aedtner, K./Schultes, M.,* The modular system of network activities, B. I. p. 75 (77 et seqq.) (in this volume).

42 For an analysis of chances and risks of business networks see *Schultes, M.,* Company networks and the dichotomy and statics of competition law – a combined dynamic control of conduct and structure as a solution approach, C. p. 198 (202 et seqq.) (in this volume).

43 *Krebs, P./Aedtner, K./Schultes, M.,* Company networks reloaded – putting a general functional approach to defining complex problems to the test, C. I. 4. p. 41 (65 et seq.) (in this volume); *Glückler, J./Hammer, I.,* Multilaterale Kooperation und Netzwerkgüter, in: Glückler, J. and others (eds.), Unternehmensnetzwerke - Architekturen, Strukturen und Strategien, Berlin, Heidelberg, 2012, p. 139 (153 et seqq.).

44 For a closer look at the network purpose see *Krebs, P./Aedtner, K./Schultes, M.,* Company networks reloaded – putting a general functional approach to defining complex problems to the test, B. III. p. 41 (53 et seqq.) (in this volume); *Becker, N.,* Regelungsfelder für Unternehmensnetzwerke, Wiesbaden, 1999, pp. 164 et

broad. This "network purpose" does not need to be written down. It may also arise from the circumstances. The network purpose applies to the whole business network and is therefore part of the "framework level".

To sum up, simple business networks comprise of at least two levels, namely the project level and the framework level.

## II. Business networks with a complex structure

The business networks described above exhibit a very simple internal structure. But especially more developed and larger business networks are characterised by a more complex governance structure. Possible levels in those networks are:

- Framework level
- Module level
- Type of activity level (hereafter: "activity level")
- Project level
- Sub-project level/Individual level

All levels can be the source and the target of rules.

---

seqq.; *Männel, B.*, Netzwerke in der Zulieferindustrie, Wiesbaden, 1996, p. 30; *Rohe, M.*, Netzverträge, Tübingen, 1998, pp. 76, 84; *Teubner, G.*, Netzwerk als Vertragsverbund. Virtuelle Unternehmen, Franchising, Just-in-time in sozialwissenschaftlicher und juristischer Sicht, Baden-Baden, 2004, p. 148; *Krebs, P.*, Sonderverbindung und außerdeliktische Schutzpflichten, München, 2000, p. 315; *Bayreuther, F.*, Wirtschaftlich-existentiell abhängige Unternehmen im Konzern-, Kartell- und Arbeitsrecht, Berlin, 2001, p. 289; *Lange, K.*, Virtuelle Unternehmen, Recht und Wirtschaft, Heidelberg, 2001, pp. 81 et seqq.; *Schimansky, A.*, Der Franchisevertrag nach deutschem und niederländischem Recht, Tübingen, Frankfurt am Main, 2003, pp. 113, 125, 167; *Wellenhofer, M.*; Drittwirkung von Schutzpflichten im Netz, Die Kritische Vierteljahresschrift für Gesetzgebung und Rechtswissenschaft 2006, 187 (188); *Nicklisch, F.*, Vernetze Projektverträge und vernetzte Streitbeilegung, Betriebs-Berater 2000, 2166 (2166 et seqq.); see also *Hune, M.*, Netzwerkverträge in der Transportwirtschaft. Wirtschaftliche und rechtliche Dimensionen einer modernen Vertragsverbindung zwischen Wettbewerb und Kooperation, Berlin, 2010, pp. 22 et seqq.; *Wittig, A.*, Management von Unternehmensnetzwerken - Eine Analyse der Steuerung und Koordination von Logistiknetzwerken, Wiesbaden, 2005, p. 29; *Heldt, C.*, Baukooperation und Franchising als multilaterale Sonderverbindung, Baden-Baden, 2010, pp. 70 et seqq.

### 1. Framework level

The framework encompasses the business network as a whole and usually provides some general and abstract rules for the entire network. Even though business networks generally prefer more decentralised structures (self-determination),[45] some rules are useful on the framework level.

From a scientific point of view, a framework is helpful for legal scholars because it makes it easier to distinguish business networks from the market and other organisational forms like groups of companies.[46] In this respect the Italian network contract is useful.[47]

The framework level is used to determine the network purpose. Sometimes, the network purpose is implicitly assumed and not explicitly stated. In case the business network is organised with the help of a corporation on the framework level, the purpose of the corporation often reflects the purpose of the network.[48] Furthermore, many business networks opt for a very general and broad network purpose such as "technical improvement" or "improvement of the market position" of its members.[49]

In general, the framework level also serves as the "gatekeeper" to membership. Business networks often regulate the process of becoming a member, leaving the network and expelling network members. Even if no general provisions existed, the respective aspects would be discussed on the framework level. The expulsion of a member is also one of the few cases where business networks establish "hard" sanctions on the framework level. Like the network purpose this function is sometimes only implicitly assumed without lying down further provisions. But especially larger networks with a flowing membership structure will provide clear rules for be-

45 Cf. *Metzger, F. M.* and others, Koordinationsmechanismen und Innovativität von Netzwerken, in: Glückler, J. and others (eds.), Unternehmensnetzwerke – Architekturen, Strukturen und Strategien, Berlin, Heidelberg, 2012, p. 35 (38).

46 *Krebs, P./Aedtner, K./Schultes, M.*, Company networks reloaded – putting a general functional approach to defining complex problems to the test, C. II. 3. a) p. 41 (69 et seq.) (in this volume).

47 On the Italian network contract see references in footnote 18.

48 If the corporation is mostly used for management purposes, the purpose might be unrelated to the purpose of the network. For a deeper analysis of the management see below.

49 See *Schultes, M.*, Company networks and the dichotomy and statics of competition law – a combined dynamic control of conduct and structure as a solution approach, pp. 198 et seqq. (in this volume).

coming a member, expelling network members and leaving the network, as case-to-case decisions would be ineffective and too burdensome. The procedure of leaving the network is usually not as highly regulated as joining the network because it is of no value for the network to keep members who do not want to co-operate any longer. In this respect it has to be kept in mind that there are no effective tools to ensure actual co-operation.

### a. Corporations on the framework level

It is common to use corporations as part of the framework (esp. common are companies with limited liability, partnerships and associations),[50] as well as to structure the membership within the network. It is often necessary to become a shareholder in order to become a full network member.[51] The rules on membership are regularly encompassed by the articles of association. Therefore, corporations are a valuable tool to structure the network membership.

Besides structuring the membership, corporations on the framework level may also be important if "network goods"[52] exist (network goods are goods that belong to the network). In this case, corporations may be an interesting legal instrument to manage network property. Conversely, there is also the possibility of joint liabilities. A corporation with limited liability can protect the network members from personal liability. A corporation can also be used to collect money – mostly in form of membership fees – for the overall activities of the business network and to have funds ready to support (mostly) more complex and costly projects within the business network, which are expected to be beneficial to all or most of its members. If the business network finances activities within the network it is common to not only use the corporation to receive membership fees but to establish procedural rules that regulate how members decide which projects they want to finance.

Furthermore, larger business networks will structure the decision making process on the framework level. Also in this context a corporation is a

---

50 *Glückler, J./Németh, S./De Beauregard, P*, Der Betrieb 2011, 2701, 2704 et seqq., esp. 2706.

51 In some cases there is also the possibility of participation under a full membership.

52 *Krebs, P./Jung, S./Aedtner, K./Schultes, M.*, The modular system of network activities, C. II. 5. p. 75 (88 et seq.) (in this volume).

useful regulatory tool.[53] It is common to lay down rules on majorities in the statutes of the corporation. Asking for unanimity is, however, not advisable, because such a rule would threaten the business network's capacity to act. Confronted with the choice to opt for a majority (simple majority, absolute majority and qualified majority (e.g. 75% or 80%)), the choice will likely fall on qualified majority. As network members cannot be forced to actually co-operate, at least the network members' broad support for the respective undertaking is ensured in this way. Furthermore, a vast majority puts pressure on the minority to give up resistance. Even if there is no explicit pressure, the respective decision is more likely to be acknowledged by both parties, the supporting and non-supporting members, if a vast majority is in favour of the undertaking. The more decentralised a network is,[54] the fewer rules on decision making are needed on the framework level. Due to the distance between the framework level and the individual projects, the individualistic approach of network members to a project, the level of trust and the difficulties of the law of corporations to deal with such individual cases suggest that many decisions will be taken on a lower level. Especially decisions concerning the actual content of a co-operation are regulated on these levels. Besides, the level of trust between those members involved in a joint project is usually higher than that between the network members in general.

In theory, it would be possible to carry out all projects within the corporation established on the framework level. But company law was not designed to deal with shareholders (here network members) who are only interested in some of the projects within the company (encompassing the business network). There are simply no provisions for individual undertakings between shareholders within corporations as required for business networks. Also, said provisions are not necessary, as company law is not designed to regulate the individual projects of the shareholders under the umbrella of a corporation. The fact that members participate in projects in different ways and to different extents and that they want to profit primari-

53 With regard to decision making processes in general (irrespective of the level) see *Glückler, J./Németh, S.*, Legitime Steuerungsinstanzen in lateralen Netzwerken, in: Glückler, J. and others (eds.), Unternehmensnetzwerke – Architekturen, Strukturen und Strategien, Berlin, Heidelberg, 2012, p. 95 (105 et seq.).

54 *Ménard, C.*, The Economics of Hybrid Organizations, Journal of Institutional and Theoretical Economics, 2004, 345, (367) states that hybrid forms which rely on trust are usually characterised by a decentralised structure.

ly from those projects they take part in and not from the company as a whole makes it impossible to grasp business networks merely with the help of company law. Corporations are not flexible enough in this respect. Company law is not designed to deal with isolated individual projects and the flowing participation of the member companies. This is why normally most of the projects within business networks are not carried out within the corporation used on the framework level, but outside the scope of the corporation. Consequently, this means that in many cases the framework level does not merely consist of the corporation alone.

Leaving aside internal aspects, a corporation as part of the framework is a good tool to represent the network to third parties.

### b. Contracts on the framework level

Besides corporations the network members can also decide to use contracts on the framework level. Genuine multiparty contracts are not very common on this level. Such a contract would probably be most suitable if a network had only a few members who constitute a stable membership structure.[55] But even then these contracts might be too costly and complex.[56] Under these circumstances, the companies that want to form a network will generally opt for a corporation instead of a multi-party contract or use both to organise different aspects on the framework level.[57] In contrast, we assume that linked contracts might be used more often than multi-party contracts on the framework level.

---

55 On multilateral contracts see *Zwanziger, M.*, Der mehrseitige Vertrag, Tübingen, 2013; on organisational contracts see *Grundmann, S./Cafaggi, F./Vettori, G.*, The contractual Basis of Long-Term Organization – The Overall Architecture, in: Grundmann, S./Cafaggi, F./Vettori, G. (eds.), The Organizational Contract – From Exchange to Long-Term Network Cooperation in European Contract Law, Farnham, Burlington, 2013.

56 "comprehensive binding contracts tend to be far too complex and/or too costly to design and implement". *Ménard, C.*, The Economics of Hybrid Organizations, Journal of Institutional and Theoretical Economics 2004, 345, (361) on contracts in hybrid organisations in general.

57 In franchise systems, a mixture of company-owned units and franchisees can be observed. *Ménard, C.*, The Economics of Hybrid Organizations, Journal of Institutional and Theoretical Economics 2004, 345, (361). This observation might be transferable to business networks.

### c. Special relationships (Sonderverbindungen) without obligation to perform on the framework level

However, the existence of a framework does not necessarily imply a high degree of juridification. A low degree of juridification is possible as well and may sometimes be suitable for small business networks. The framework can – at least in Germany – also be structured with the help of "Sonderverbindungen"[58] (special relationships), which is a specific German legal concept. One form of a special relationship is the accommodation relation ("Gefälligkeitsschuldverhältnis"). Special relationships grant a low degree of juridification with only some basic duties, like fiduciary duties that exist to some extent (§ 242 BGB "Treu und Glauben").[59] The parties have the duty to care for each other to a certain degree. Furthermore, liability for pure economic loss (§ 280 I, § 241 II BGB) exists.[60] There is also a strict liability for vicarious agents ("Erfüllungsgehilfen") (§ 278 BGB).[61]

Outside of the German legal system, business networks will in these cases make use of a gentlemen agreement. In most legal systems, these relationships may be, unlike in Germany, merely covered by the law of torts. In particular, fiduciary duties may not play a role.

### d. "Rules of the game" on the framework level

But not only corporations, contracts and special relationships are used as instruments on the framework level. Especially "network rules" or "rules of the game" can be observed as well. Many times they are given other names like "Our philosophy", "Code of Ethics" or "The network spirit".

---

58 See *Krebs, P*, Sonderverbindung und außerdeliktische Schutzpflichten, München, 2000; the concept has been accepted as part of German Law (§ 241 II BGB) since 2002.

59 *Sutschet, H.*, in: BeckOK/ BGB, München, 2013, "§ 242", par. 14; *Grüneberg, C.* in: Palandt, München 2015, "§ 242", par. 6; *Roth, G.H./Schubert, C.*, in: MünchKomm/BGB, München, 2012, § 242, par. 86 et seqq., especially par. 89.

60 *Grüneberg, C.*, in: Palandt, München 2015, "§ 280", par. 28 a; *Schwarze*, in: Staudinger/BGB, 2014, § 280, par. E 27 et seqq.; *Ernst, W.*, in: MünchKomm/ BGB, München, 2012, "§ 280", par. 13.

61 *Grüneberg, C.* in: Palandt, München, 2015, "§ 278", par. 1; *Casper*, in: Staudinger/BGB, 2014, § 278, par. 18 et seqq.; *Grundmann, S.*, in: MünchKomm/ BGB, München, 2012, "278"; par. 3.

They are mostly not part of the corporation but part of the framework. This surprising observation mentioned above is explained by the fact that company law provisions on the framework level do not cover all network specific issues, however practical they might be.

These rules can take the form of contracts, accommodation relations, but more often they are mere "soft governance instruments" without legal binding force[62]. They elaborate on co-operative behaviour within the network and "social rules". Moreover, they sometimes describe in more detail the aim and the spirit of the business network. The rules of the game do not only describe the overall purpose but also explain activities that shall be carried out within the network like the exchange of know-how, the development of software or the development of a common marketing strategy. Besides, it is not unusual to find more specific "rules" on what kinds of companies may join the network.

Hence, it can be observed that business networks combine hard and soft governance instruments (e.g. with regard to joining the business network) on the framework level. Those soft rules shall ensure the homogeneity of the network members, which is not only important for a fruitful co-operation but also reduces the complexity of the governance structure due to the homogeneity of interests.

There is also a tendency to establish a process of dispute resolution on the framework level. Those rules are often not explicitly stated anywhere. They evolve over time through constant practice. If the business network has established a corporation on the framework level, the management is particularly suited to moderate conflicts between members because it can act as a neutral third party.

As a result, we assume that business networks will usually not only apply one governance instrument on the framework level, but a mix of the possible instruments in order to use their specific advantages for the different aspects which require regulation.

To sum up, some possible areas of regulation on the framework level are:

1. Joining and leaving the network as well as expelling network members
2. Conditions for membership

62 Soft governance instruments are discussed in more detail in F.II. pp. 148 et seqq.

3. Membership fees[63]
4. Rules on project financing
5. Decision making process
6. Organisation of activities and projects
7. Other procedural rules
8. Fiduciary duty[64] (among the network members and towards the network)
9. Co-operative behaviour (among the network members)
10. Rules for network goods[65]
11. Sanctions

2. Project level

Bilateral (two members involved) or multilateral projects (more than two members involved) are at the economic core of business networks. The individual projects are meant to create an economic benefit for the members of the network and first and foremost for the members participating in the project.

Business networks are generally designed for a multitude of projects.[66] The research group *krea.nets*[67] found that those projects are, as a matter of

63 In a recent study on business networks 49.2% of the responding companies stated that difficulties arise concerning the contributions to the network. *Glückler, J.* and others, Organisatorische Vielfalt und Innovativität von KMU-Netzwerken: Ein bundesweites Screening, in: Glücker, J. and others (eds.), Unternehmensnetzwerke – Architekturen, Strukturen und Strategien, Berlin, Heidelberg, 2012, p. 21 (29).

64 *Gómez Asensio, C.*, Los deberes derivados de la buena fe como límite al poder de dirección del cabeza de red, 2013; *Ruiz Peris, J. I.*, Derecho de la Distribución y Redes Empresariales, Valencia, 2014, V; see *Weitzenboeck, E.*, A legal framework for emerging business models – dynamic networks as collaborative contracts, Cheltenham, Northampton, 2012, pp. 238 et seqq.; on the duty to inform within contract networks see *Hennemann, M.*, Informationspflichten in Vertragsnetzwerken: Grundlagen, Reichweite und Ausgestaltung, in: Aichberger-Beig, D. and others (eds.), Vertrauen und Kontrolle im Privatrecht, Stuttgart (and others), 2010, pp. 285 – 301.

65 According to our understanding network goods belong to the business network.

66 See *Krebs, P./Jung, S./Aedtner, K./Schultes, M.*, The modular system of network activities, B. I. p. 75 (77 et seqq.) (in this volume).

67 www.kreanets.de, 30.03.2015.

principle, independent of each other.[68] Different members work on different projects with fluctuating intensity.[69]

In case problems arise within a project, specific rules that have been established for this project are particularly suited to solve the concomitant legal questions. This is why the rules on the project level should be the starting point for any legal assessment notwithstanding that rules on other levels may also have an influence on the provisions on this level.

Under German law, a project within a business network is to some extent always juridified by contract law or law of quasi-contractual relations. It is however not possible to only opt for the application of law of torts. Parties can choose between contracts,[70] corporations and a specific German instrument, the accommodation relationship ("Gefälligkeitsschuldverhältnis").[71] The latter does not imply any obligation to perform, but a duty of loyalty and a duty of care. Which tool is suitable for which situation on the project level, will be discussed in more detail below (F.III.).

### 3. Sub-project level/individual level

Especially with regard to large multilateral projects, sub-projects and individual arrangements are possible and perhaps in some cases recommendable. Sub-projects and individual arrangements are characterised by their auxiliary function for a specific project. The rules established on this level

---

68 *Glückler, J./Hammer, I.*, Multilaterale Kooperation und Netzwerkgüter, in: Glückler, J. and others (eds.), Unternehmensnetzwerke - Architekturen, Strukturen und Strategien, Berlin, Heidelberg, 2012, p. 139 (153 et seqq.); see also *Krebs, P./ Jung, S./Aedtner, K./Schultes, M.*, The modular system of network activities, B. III. p. 75 (83 et seq.) (in this volume).

69 *Krebs, P./Jung, S./Aedtner, K./Schultes, M.*, The modular system of network activities, B. p. 75 (77 et seqq.) (in this volume).

70 On multilateral contracts see *Zwanziger, M.*, Der mehrseitige Vertrag, Tübingen, 2013; on organisational contracts see *Grundmann, S./Cafaggi, F./Vettori, G.*, The contractual Basis of Long-Term Organization – The Overall Architecture, in: Grundmann, S./Cafaggi, F./Vettori, G. (eds.), The Organizational Contract – From Exchange to Long-Term Network Cooperation in European Contract Law, Farnham, Burlington, 2013.

71 For a closer look at these accommodation relationships see *Bork, R.*, in: Staudinger/BGB, Berlin, 2014, "Vorbemerkungen zu §§ 145–156", par. 79 et seqq.; *Grüneberg, C.* in: Palandt, München 2015, "Einleitung von § 241", par. 7 et seqq.; *Sutschet, H.*, in: BeckOK/BGB, München, 2013, "§ 241", par. 18 et seqq.

resemble provisions on the project level. If rules for a sub-project shall be established it has to be taken into consideration that the rules on the project level will usually influence the sub-projects and individual arrangements. In many cases it will not be necessary to establish provisions for these levels.

As this level has a pure auxiliary function for the project level, sub-projects and individual arrangements will not be further assessed in this paper. Generally, the findings for projects can be applied to this level (with some adaptation).

### 4. Activity level

In business networks, it is common to have many similar projects, e. g. exchanges of production capacity. In these cases it may be advisable to establish comprehensive rules for these homogenous projects, since the opportunities for rationalisation and know-how transfer can be seized in this way. This level is herein called activity level.

The homogeneity is not an abstract juridical one, but a natural, economic homogeneity. Also non-lawyers will perceive the similarity between the projects and, therefore, consider general rules for these homogenous projects. An example may help to illustrate the activity level:

In a given business network, members regularly exchange unused production capacities.[72] Every individual contract, i.e. every single exchange of overcapacity, is a so called "project". But if the business network establishes general provisions for all individual exchanges of overcapacity, then these rules belong to the "activity level". For instance, a duty to inform other members of available overcapacity and model contracts that help to standardise the exchange within the business network are imaginable.

---

72 *Glückler, J./Hammer, I.*, Multilaterale Kooperation und Netzwerkgüter, in: Glückler, J. and others (eds.), Unternehmensnetzwerke - Architekturen, Strukturen und Strategien, Berlin, Heidelberg, 2012, p. 139 (153); *Krebs, P./Jung, S./Aedtner, K./ Schultes, M.*, The modular system of network activities, C. III. 2. a) aa) p. 75 (91 et seqq.) (in this volume).

On this level, framework contracts[73] may be used, provided that the members accept the higher degree of juridification resulting therefrom.

## 5. Module level[74]

From a legal point of view, there could be another level between the activity level and the framework level. This level shall herein be called "module level".[75] This might be the right level for a lawmaker that wants to set network specific rules. The framework level is too abstract for encompassing legal rules. These rules would not be able to fully solve the legal problems that arise on the project level. The possible activities (activity level) and projects (project level) are not a real alternative for the lawmaker either because they are too diverse. The lawmaker would have to find legal solutions for all kinds of business networks with their diverse projects and activities. Hence, a category between these two levels is needed and may be used by the lawmaker in order to regulate business networks. Modules are the sum of different activities according to their underlying business models.[76] Since business models are used as a basis, it follows that activities and projects belonging to the same module also possess the same basic chance and risk structure.[77] The homogenous chance and risk structure may justify common rules for projects and activities within one module from a legal point of view.[78]

---

73 *Schürnbrand, J.*, in: MünchKomm/BGB, München, 2012, "§ 510", par. 14; *Ellenberger, J*, in: Palandt, München 2015, "Einführung von § 145", par. 19; *Grüneberg, C.*, in: Palandt, München 2015, "§ 305", par. 45, 51; *Graf von Westphalen, F.*, in: Graf von Westphalen, F./Thüsing, G., (eds.), Vertragsrecht und AGB-Klauselwerke, München, 2013, "Preisanpassungsklauseln", par. 60 et seqq.; *Schuhmacher, S.*, Vertragsgestaltung – Systemtechnisch für die Praxis, Zürich, Basel, Genf, 2004, par. 1015 et seqq.; *Von der Crone, H. C.*, Rahmenverträge: Vertragsrecht – Systemtheorie – Ökonomie, Zürich, Basel, Genf, 1993.

74 See *Krebs, P./Jung, S./Aedtner, K./Schultes, M.*, The modular system of network activities, pp. 75 et seqq. (in this volume).

75 For a closer look see *Krebs, P./Jung, S./Aedtner, K./Schultes, M.*, The modular system of network activities, C. I. p. 75 (84 et seq.) (in this volume).

76 *Krebs, P./Jung, S./Aedtner, K./Schultes, M.*, The modular system of network activities, C. I. p. 75 (84 et seq.) (in this volume).

77 Ibid.

78 Ibid.

Business networks will normally not provide rules on the module level because this level is too abstract and "artificial", especially if one takes the tendency to have a low degree of juridification into account. Only if the lawmaker introduced default rules based on these modules, business networks would be inclined to adjust them to their specific needs.

As the module level is not relevant for the internal structure of business networks, this aspect will not be discussed any further in this paper.

## 6. Visualised complex governance structure of business networks

The following figure illustrates a highly developed business network including all the aforementioned levels. For simplification purposes the sub-project level as well as the individual level will not be discussed at this point.

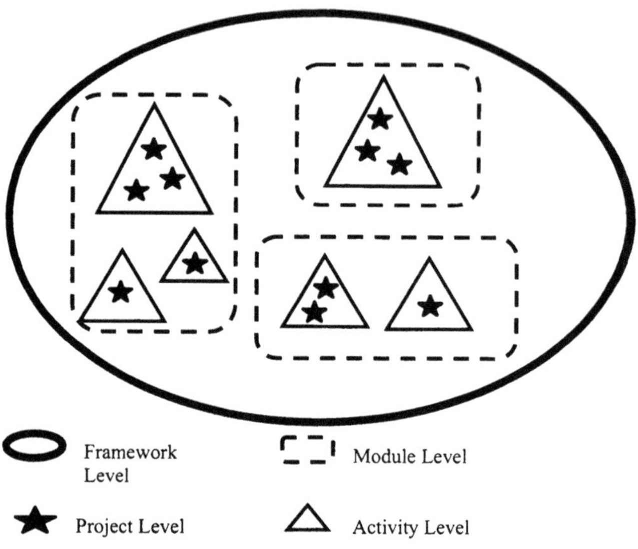


## 7. Management

So far, the management has been omitted from the analysis even though a separate management structure can be observed in major projects. "Management" is not a level itself. It rather describes the need for co-ordination and procedural rules in general. In theory, a need for management and co-ordination can exist on all levels. If one takes a closer look at the levels, it becomes clear that the framework level, the module level and the activity level are actually "management" levels. They are not at the core of the network activity. They rather try to govern the co-operation. As mentioned above, there is always a certain need for co-ordination (hence management) on the framework level. If there is an overall need for management the business network might consider establishing a central management structure on the framework level. In case the network uses a corporation on the framework level, the management board (and the employees of the corporation) might be in a good position to take over the management.

If a business network has a lot of members and these members want to have a significant influence on the management, they can establish a supervisory board or an advisory council. The representatives of the network members in these boards can advise and control the management. The power and competences of these boards can be regulated in the statutes of the corporation. But the actual power of these boards also depends on the "natural authority" of its members.

Business networks (and netlike forms of organisation[79]) which do not work with a corporation on the framework level are usually - at least partly - structured by means of contracts. In those cases the members often also introduce a management with the help of a contract.

In Germany, large innovation networks, which are supported by the Federal Ministry of Education and Research (BMBF), are obliged to have a "network manager", who is partly sponsored by the BMBF (with decreasing rates). It would be useful to describe the scope of rights and duties of managers in business networks. This is rarely done in smaller networks. In large innovation networks, some rudimentary rules are usually laid down. But in practice, the innovation network manager is often more powerful than described by these rules.[80] Especially his/her personality, experience and reputation among the members will determine the power of the network manager. In general, the aspect of informal power should

79 See *Aedtner, K.*, Network-like organizations: On their distinction and meaning exemplified by the co-operation in construction, pp. 171 et seqq. (in this volume).

80 On the influence of individuals see *Janneck, M./Staar, H.*, Mikropolitik - Informelle Einflussnahme durch individuelle Akteure in Netzwerken, in: Glückler, J. and others (eds.), Unternehmensnetzwerke – Architekturen, Strukturen und Strategien, Berlin, Heidelberg, 2012, pp. 205 et seqq.

not be underestimated in business networks. Individual actors might exercise a lot of power, which may be due to the personality of the person in charge, his/her experience and connections as well as his/her economic weight. This effect becomes especially evident in structures with a low degree of juridification even though a similar effect can also be observed in co-operations with a higher degree of juridification. Hence, (partly) juridified structures are interesting for members with little individual power as more formal processes can ensure participation to some extent. But sometimes also formal structures like supervisory boards or advisory councils grant some members more power than others.

The module level is an artificial level that most networks will not use for management purposes (as the lawmaker has so far not yet established default rules on this level). Also many forms of activities do not require a specific and costly management. Only some of them might be so complex and expensive that a special management seems necessary or at least useful (decentralised management). Participation in the management may be open to all network members irrespective of whether they are taking part in this form of activity. In this way, they gain influence on the aims and the rules that apply to the projects within this form of activity.

The same holds for projects, even though only very large projects might create the need for this kind of management structure. In cases of a (rather limited) need for management, it will often be sufficient to appoint a project spokesman who informs all the members not involved in the respective project. Especially if the project is financed by the network, other members might insist on a management in which they can take part even though they do not participate in the project itself. In those cases, a kind of advisory board for projects might constitute a suitable governance instrument.

## E. System of rules

As shown above, there are many different levels in business networks. This leads to multi-level governance problems and therefore to the question which level takes precedence over the others in which situation. The problems here are similar to the ones regarding European company law[81] and framework contracts as well as contracts for industrial plant construction or general intragroup directives. The complexity arises due to the fact that every level can be the source of provisions as well as the target of rules. Two questions follow from this fact:

- On which level do these rules apply?
- Which rules take priority in case of a conflict?

Mandatory law and (binding) case law[82] will not be considered in the following because this paper focuses on how the internal structure of the business network can be shaped by its members.

The easiest way to address the issue concerning the hierarchy of provisions would be by establishing specific network rules. The involved parties themselves would then decide on the scope as well as the priority of the individual provisions and legal sources. In industrial plant constructions, for instance, the parties always agree on a "precedence clause" containing detailed rules regarding the priority of single provisions within the whole contractual structure.[83] Even though this approach is also possible for business networks, it is rather uncommon. Therefore, it is crucial to focus on the "default system", which is applicable in those cases where no special provisions exist.

In this case, two main principles have to be reconciled. On the one hand, the principle of hierarchy[84] may have an influence on the solution. According to this principle, the higher ranking rules prevail over the lower

81 With regard to multi-level governance problems within the SE see *Manz, G./ Mayer; B./Schröder, A.*, Europäische Aktiengesellschaft – SE, Baden-Baden, 2010, Art. 9 and 10. With respect to the SPE see *Jung, S.*, Die Kapitalverfassung der Societas Privata Europaea (SPE), 2014, pp. 53 et seqq. With regard to the FE see *Jung, S.*, Grundlegende Aspekte der Europäischen Stiftung (FE), Die Privatstiftung 2013, 104 (104 et seqq.).

82 There are no binding precedents in German Law. But if a court wants to deviate from a Supreme Court Decision the decision should be properly justified. In German methodology this is called "Begründungslast" (burden of justification) see *Krebs, P.*, Archiv für die civilistische Praxis 195 (1995), 171 (171 et seqq.).

83 Cf. *Mason, L.*, Order of Precedence Clauses: An Automatic Means of Resolving Discrepancies Between Contract Documents?, Business Law Review 35 (2014), Issue 3, 106–107.

84 "Lex superior derogat legi inferiori."

ranking ones.[85] On the other hand, one has to take the principle of specialty into consideration[86] according to which the more specific rule overrules the more general rule.[87]

The conflict between hierarchy and specialty can be solved as follows: Primacy of application is granted to the more specific rule as long as the more specific rule is compatible with the higher-ranking rule. A more specific rule is also compatible with the higher-ranking rule if the latter is a default rule. The more specific rule has to be interpreted in line with the higher-ranking rule. Usually, more specific rules are set on a lower-ranking level than general rules because the parties involved on a lower-level are normally closer to the specific problems that arise. There are cases in which this "principle of specialty" does not work because none of the two rules is more specific, but both nevertheless have an area of intersection. General formal provisions on the priority regularly lead to random results. If it is not possible to determine which provisions should precede, it might be adequate to use an instrument known from constitutional law called "practical concordance" ("praktische Konkordanz").[88] The conflicting rules are delimited from each other in a way so that their respective purpose is maximally achieved.

In case the network does not clearly state on which level a rule shall apply, the rules set on one level apply to the same level and also all lower levels. If there are contradicting rules on the same level, the more specific provision overrules the more general rule. If none of the rules is more specific, the concept of practical concordance ("praktische Konkordanz") applies.

85 *Härtel, I.*, Europäische Rechtsetzung, Heidelberg, Berlin, New York, 2006, p. 311; *Katz, A.*, Staatsrecht – Grundkurs im öffentlichen Recht, Heidelberg (and others), 2010, p. 5; *Zippelius, R.*, Juristische Methodenlehre, München, 2012, p. 32; *Kramer, E.*, Juristische Methodenlehre, Bern, 2013, pp. 119 et seq.

86 "Lex specialis derogat legi generali."

87 *Larenz, K.*, Methodenlehre der Rechtswissenschaft, Berlin (and others), 1991, pp. 267 et seq.; *Härtel, I.*, Europäische Rechtsetzung, Heidelberg, Berlin, New York, 2006, p. 312; *Katz, A.*, Staatsrecht – Grundkurs im öffentlichen Recht, Heidelberg (and others), 2010, p. 5; *Zippelius, R.*, Juristische Methodenlehre, München, 2012, p. 32; *Bydlinski, F.*, Juristische Methodenlehre und Rechtsbegriff, Wien, New York, 1982, p. 465; *Kramer, E.*, Juristische Methodenlehre, Bern, 2013, pp. 111 et seqq.

88 *Zippelius, R.*, Juristische Methodenlehre, München, 2012, pp. 44 et seqq.

Within business networks, the provisions on the framework level are the highest ranking ones. These rules apply on the framework level itself and might be directed to the activity and project level as well.

The rules on the activity level are lower-ranking than provisions on the framework level, but generally overrule provisions on the project level in case of a conflict. The rules on the activity level are intended to shape the individual projects within the business network, which are related to the respective type of activity.

The project level is the lowest level of regulation of the aforementioned levels in the business network.[89]

Even though business networks do not establish formal provisions dealing with the hierarchy of provisions, the network members sometimes apply a quasi-system in practice.[90] This practical system should be respected as much as possible by the legal system.

The following graph may help to illustrate the system of rules.

Hierarchy of rules within business networks:

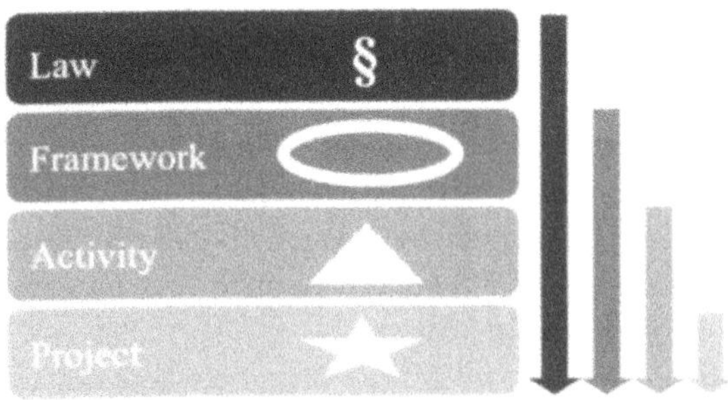


## F. Governance instruments

### I. Overview

So far, no empirical studies have been conducted on the use of different governance instruments within business networks. But since the study by

89 In order to reduce complexity, the sub-project level and the individual level (D. II. 3. pp. 137 et seq.) are both not assessed.

90 Cf. F.IV. pp. 155 et seqq.

*krea.nets* shows the needs of developed business networks,[91] this paper tries to assess the main governance instruments with regard to their advantages and disadvantages. The suitability of the different tools depends on many different factors, but not all of them can be analysed for every single governance instrument in this article. It is the aim of the article to discuss the most important factors for the two basic types of rules, namely hard governance instruments and soft governance instruments.

"Hard governance instruments" (HGI) and "soft governance instruments" (SGI) are not common juridical terms. They were developed in this paper following the terms "hard law" and "soft law". "Hard law" is the "classical" law used by the lawmaker, which has to be obeyed. "Soft law" has no or only little legal binding force and is sometimes not even developed by the lawmaker, but by another group or commission. In this case these soft law rules normally receive some form of approval by the lawmaker. But neither the term hard law nor the term soft law is used within the framework of contract law.[92] Hence, in our opinion, these terms cannot be used as categories for provisions within business networks, as the term "law" is linked to statutory law. Therefore, this paper introduces the terms hard governance instruments (HGI) and soft governance instruments (SGI) instead.

The term "soft governance instruments" refers - like soft law - to instruments which do not have legal binding force for the parties involved. They ensure rule-consistent behaviour by means of incentives or even some kind of pressure. In contrast, "hard governance instruments" - like hard law rules - possess legal binding force.

As is often the case, there is a grey area between the two categories (SGI and HGI). In the field of soft law and hard law this grey area is well known. The German Corporate Governance Codex (DCGK)[93] may serve

---

91 See www.kreanets.de, 30.03.2015; *Glückler, J.* and others (eds.), Unternehmensnetzwerke - Architekturen, Strukturen und Strategien, Berlin, Heidelberg, 2012.

92 On the freedom of contract see *Wolf, M./Neuner, J.*, Allgemeiner Teil des Bürgerlichen Rechts, München 2012, § 10, par. 33 et seqq.; *Ellenberger, J.*, in: Palandt, München, 2015, "Einführung von § 145", par. 7 et seqq.; *Busche, J.*, in: MünchKomm/BGB, München, 2012, "vor § 145", par. 2 et seqq.; *Eckert, H.-W.*, in: BeckOK/BGB, 2014, § 145, par. 8.

93 Available at http://www.dcgk.de/de/kodex.html, 30.03.2014. On corporate governance codices see *Köndgen, J.*, Privatisierung des Rechts – Private Governance zwischen Deregulierung und Rekonstitutionalisierung, Archiv für die civilistische Praxis 206 (2006), 477 (495 et seqq.).

as an example for this grey area: The obligation to provide a governance statement is based on hard law (§ 161 AktG – German stock corporation law), but the "comply or explain" approach used by the DCGK is a soft governance approach. Companies do not have to be in line with the Codex, but if they do not want to obey the guidelines of the Codex, they are obliged to state and explain this. In case of an infringement to provide a proper governance statement, German law holds legal consequences which fall in the category of hard law.[94] If a similar "comply or explain" instrument were used within business networks, it would be an example for this grey area. An even better example is a drafting task because drafting tasks are a more appropriate tool for business networks.[95] They oblige the network members to regulate a specific aspect, e.g. in the scope of project contracts. The task itself is obligatory and therefore belongs to the category of hard governance instruments (HGI), while at the same time, the drafting task guarantees full freedom of content, which rather indicates that it is a soft governance instrument (SGI). If a network has a written "philosophy" or "ethical code" these documents do not have legal binding force, but a judge would use the philosophy to interpret existing duties. This does not allow the „codes of conduct" to be categorised as HGI, but it places them closer to said grey area.

Business networks do not have to opt for either HGI or SGI as a basis for the governance structure. Both types of regulation rather complement each other within business networks.

## II. Soft governance instruments

Soft governance instruments only set incentives to comply with the (soft) rules laid down or exert gentle pressure towards the favoured behaviour. They are, however, not legally enforceable. They rather rely on and also promote intrinsic motivation and guidance instead of jeopardising it, which may be the case with HGI. Provided that an SGI possesses the po-

94 See *Mülbert, P./Schneider, U.*, Rechtsfragen rund um den Deutschen Corporate Governance Kodex, 2012, http://www.jura.uni-mainz.de/muelbert/Dateien/Muelbert_Rechtsfragen_rund_um_den_DCGK.pdf, 13.02.2014, p. 16 et seqq.

95 On drafting tasks in law see *Institut für Gesellschaftsrecht der Universität zu Köln*, Europäischer Corporate Governance-Rahmen, Neue Zeitschrift für Gesellschaftsrecht 2011, 975 (977).

tential to exert pressure, this element is only weakly developed as otherwise they should be categorised as HGI. In other words, SGI exercise behavioural control without using force. This characteristic makes them an interesting instrument for business networks. In these organisational structures, trust and co-operation are needed to work smoothly and effectively. But trust and a good "working atmosphere" which are essential for successful co-operations could be destroyed by the implementation and even more by the enforcement of HGI. This speaks, in general, for the implementation of SGI.

Besides influencing behaviour, soft governance instruments may help the network members to reduce transaction costs e.g. by offering standardisation. Standard contract models for similar projects may help to reduce information and transaction costs.

In general, SGI can work in two different ways in business networks. On the one hand, they can influence the existence of rules ("if"). Soft governance instruments can set incentives for the network members to establish rules without interfering too much by determining the actual content/ substance of the respective rules. On the other hand, soft governance instruments may also be used to shape the content of provisions ("how") or actual behaviour within business networks.

**Standard soft governance instruments** that are considered in this paper are:

- Model contract
- Tool box (of model clauses for contracts)
- Drafting task
- Best practice
- Comply or explain
- Recommendation
- Code of conduct
- Naming and shaming
- Requests for a specific behaviour (from other members or the management/supervisory board)
- (Soft) Procedural rules

A **model contract** contains all necessary rules needed for a specific type of contract. Normally, these model contracts are developed for a specific purpose, here within the business networks. A model contract helps to reduce costs through standardisation. The aim of a model contract is to save time for developing new individual contracts each time and to increase the probability of a well-designed and fair contract. There is no obligation for the network members to use a model contract for a specific project (transaction), but if the model contract is well designed and fair, it can be expected to be used without or with little alterations. Therefore, model contracts have the potential to play an important role in the way projects are carried out. It is also conceivable to develop patterns of action (i.e. with regard to dealing with certain issues).

A **tool box** (of model clauses for contracts) has the same aims as a model contract. But the tool box usually does not focus on a specific type of contract and can therefore be used in a broader context. The members may choose different clauses from said tool box for their specific contracts. But in contrast to model contracts, they are still forced to develop at least some parts of their contract on their own or hat least have to decide which clauses are integrated and which ones are left out.

**Drafting tasks** are established to remind the members of the network that in certain cases rules are needed or at least useful in order to minimise the risk of loopholes and to ensure fair dealings. Drafting tasks might be combined with a tool box or a model contract. A drafting task is classified as an HGI if it contains default rules for those cases where the network members have not dealt with the respective issues at hand, since default rules have to be categorised as HGI.

**Best practice** is not a concept limited to law. It is e.g. common as a step to technical standardisation. As a soft governance instrument it can be used as some sort of model contract or as a model for a legally relevant procedure. A further benefit of the best practice approach compared to tool boxes and model contracts is that the network saves development expenses. The problem with a best practice approach is, however, that a certain practice which worked in one occasion does not necessarily have to work in another situation. Since a practice is normally not tested systematically, one cannot be sure whether a successful practice also works as a best practice for other members. Nevertheless, this instrument might be interesting within business networks as many of them stress the importance of knowledge transfer.[96] Especially in the field of contracts and procedures this might be an interesting tool.

**Comply or explain** is a method widely used in soft law approaches for corporate government codices. Normally, a standard setting board provides rules. The companies have to either comply with them or explain their deviation. This concept works because the information is available to the public, the shareholders and other stakeholders. Besides this mild form of public pressure, there is always the threat of the lawmaker to set mandatory rules, if companies do not react to this soft law approach.[97] With regard to business networks, the "comply or explain" method does not seem very suitable. Not only is the concept too complicated and too burdensome, but also public control is missing though it is needed for pressuring companies to comply. Only the other network members could exercise this control. Furthermore, the costs for drafting such a codex within a network will normally be too high, which is why the "comply or explain" method is not likely to be frequently used within business networks. With regard to frequently used provisions[98], however, this "comply or explain"-approach might produce the desired results. As business networks aim to establish long-term co-operations, frequently used provisions will evolve. The network members could agree upon the general applicability of these provisions, unless a member states in advance that he will not comply with a certain provision.[99]

**Recommendations** are a very broad category. A model contract, a tool box and a best practice are all examples for recommendations in this broad meaning. In a more specific way, a recommendation is an advice how to deal with a certain situation (here in a legal way). A recommendation can be given well in advance and in a very general way, but there may also be

---

96 With regard to knowledge transfer within business networks *Teubner. G.*, Network as connected contracts, Oxford, 2011, pp. 19 et seq.

97 A good example for this is the so called "women quota" for supervisory boards in Germany. The German Corporate Governance Codex (DCGK) asked for an appropriate representation of women on supervisory boards. Moreover, the government encouraged companies to set themselves targets. But as the result was not sufficient for the German government, it adopted a law requiring a women quota of 30 % for supervisory boards.

98 See F.IV. pp. 155 et seqq.

99 One could refer to this solution as „default practices“.

recommendations with regard to very unique situations. It has to be kept in mind that an expert is required to be involved who is able to give valid recommendations.

A **code of conduct** is a set of rules, either adopted or developed by the members, which is aimed at influencing the behaviour inside the system. A business network may develop a code of conduct on its own.[100] But it is also possible that a group of similar business networks develops a joint code of conduct. The use of a code of conduct is more likely if a business network works in the light of the public. "Rules of the game" (also called "Our Philosophy" or "Ethical Code") are similar to codes of conduct.[101] Even if the network does not seek public visibility, rules of the game may help to establish a certain "culture" inside the business network and increase trust.

**Naming and shaming** is a strategy within business networks that is used to fight free riding or cheap riding problems. The management regularly prepares a document with every single member's contributions to the network. This document is then circulated among the members. Besides reducing the risk of free riding and cheap riding, such a document may help to foster a realistic understanding of the value of each member's own contributions, since members usually tend to overestimate their own contributions to the network while underestimating the contributions of other members. The list of contributions fights the distorted perception and as a result promotes further co-operation.

**Requests** are used to influence the behaviour of network members. The management board or powerful individual members may personally and individually address other members and request a specific behaviour. This approach works best if a powerful player of the network exercises this task.

**(Soft) procedural rules**[102] can in most cases be assigned to the grey area. For example: Negotiation clauses take the form of a HGI, but the real ef-

---

100 It could, for example, adopt the Network-Governance-Codex developed by Deutscher Franchise Verband, available at www.mittelstandsverbund.de, 06.02.2015.

101 Rules of the game can be structured either as HGI or SGI.

102 On procedural rules within business networks see *Metzger, F. M.* and others, Koordinationsmechanismen und Innovativität von Netzwerken, in: Glückler, J. and

fects are more similar to the ones of SGI. Procedural rules standardise processes within the network and stabilise business networks.[103] There are, however, also procedural rules, which are merely of an advising nature and can therefore be clearly classified as SGI.

### III. Hard governance instruments

German law offers parties within the freedom of contract three basic types of hard governance instruments from which the parties can choose:

- Corporations
- Contracts
- Accommodation relations ("Gefälligkeitsschuldverhältnisse")

In addition, there is the hard law in form of the civil code with both, default rules and mandatory rules.

#### 1. Corporation

All legal company forms might be used to govern business networks or single projects within business networks. As the study by *Glückler* shows, limited liability companies and associations are often used to structure developed business networks.[104] Corporations help to organise systems with multilateral partners that require a high degree of juridification. These characteristics make corporations a good tool for the framework level where all the members of the network interact. As mentioned before, the corporation is in most cases merely a part of the business networks's

---

others (eds.), Unternehmensnetzwerke – Architekturen, Strukturen und Strategien, Berlin, Heidelberg, 2012, p. 35 (41 et seq.).

103 *Metzger, F. M.* and others, Koordinationsmechanismen und Innovativität von Netzwerken, in: Glückler, J. and others (eds.), Unternehmensnetzwerke – Architekturen, Strukturen und Strategien, Berlin, Heidelberg, 2012, p. 35 (41).

104 *Glückler, J./Németh, S./De Beauregard, P.*, Netzwerke: Rechtsformen und Folgen für die Zusammenarbeit von Unternehmen, Der Betrieb 2011, 2701 (2704 et seqq., esp. 2706); *Glückler, J.* and others, Organisatorische Vielfalt und Innovativität von KMU-Netzwerken: Ein bundesweites Screening, in: Glücker, J. and others (eds.), Unternehmensnetzwerke – Architekturen, Strukturen und Strategien, Berlin, Heidelberg, 2012, p. 21 (29).

framework level. This is explained by the fact that only some aspects require a high degree of juridification, whereas the network members stress the importance of flexibility for other aspects.

Corporations are often used as the "gate" to membership, to structure the decision making process on the framework level and other procedural rules and to represent the network to third parties. Furthermore, it is a useful instrument to regulate the situation of network goods, i.e. of goods that belong to the business network.[105] Particularly, the articles of association and the ancillary agreements are regulatory instruments within the corporations.

Besides, corporations may be used for complex and long-term projects. On the project level, corporations are used in the same way as they would be used for projects outside the business network. Hence, they are especially suited for the co-ordination of a multitude of participants (two or more) and significant resources within long-term projects. In contrast, a simple exchange of goods or knowledge usually does not require the use of a corporation to structure the exchange process.

Overall, it can be concluded that corporations might be a useful instrument on the framework level and, under specific circumstances, on the project level.

## 2. Contracts

First and foremost, contracts are a common instrument to regulate projects, especially bilateral projects. On the project level, contracts may be used in the same way as outside the business network. Regarding the projects *krea.nets* found within business networks, the exchange of unused capacity (linked production) would usually be governed by contracts.[106] Multilateral contracts could be used for multiparty projects or to create rules of the game for all projects belonging to the same type of activity.[107]

---

105 In more detail see D.II.1. pp. 131 et seqq.

106 *Glückler, J./Hammer, I.*, Multilaterale Kooperation und Netzwerkgüter, in: Glückler, J. and others (eds.), Unternehmensnetzwerke - Architekturen, Strukturen und Strategien, Berlin, Heidelberg, 2012, p. 139 (153).

107 See *Grundmann, S./Cafaggi, F./Vettori, G.*, The contractual Basis of Long-Term Organization – The Overall Architecture, in: Grundmann, S./Cafaggi, F./Vettori, G. (eds.), The Organizational Contract – From Exchange to Long-Term Network

The discussion in the US about relational contracts might provide some insights how contracts can be structured in an environment that fosters a high level of trust between the network members.[108]

3. Accommodation relation

The accommodation relation ("Gefälligkeitsschuldverhältnis") is a specific German instrument that is in a way similar to an informal agreement or a gentlemen's agreement. The parties involved have no obligation to perform, but once they have performed they cannot reclaim their performance even if the counterpart did not perform. Within such a relation, there are no primary legal obligations (§ 241 para. 1 BGB) for either side, but a minor duty of care for the assets of the other part ("Schutzpflicht"; § 241 para. 2 BGB) and a basic duty of loyalty ("Treu und Glauben") exists. In other legal systems, the same result could be achieved if the companies in the scope of a gentlemen agreement merely agreed upon the validity of fiduciary duties and the situation-specific adjustment of tort-based obligations by means of a consideration clause.

Such an accommodation relation, for instance, could be the right instrument for knowledge exchanges, where the party providing the information normally hopes to receive needed information from the other party later on. The relationship between the parties involved is expected to remain informal.

---

Cooperation in European Contract Law, Farnham, Burlington, 2013, p. 3 (5); *Zwanziger, M.*, Der mehrseitige Vertrag, Tübingen, 2013.

108 Among others, on relational contracts in general *MacNeil, I.*, The Many Futures of Contract, Southern California Law Review 47 (1974), 691 et seqq.; *MacNeil I.*, Relational Contract: What We Do And Do Not Know, Wisconsin Law Review 483 (1985), 483 et seqq.; *Speidel, R. E.*, The Characteristics and Challenges of Relational Contracts, 94 Northwestern University Law Review 1999-2000, 823 et seqq.; *Goetz, C.J./Scott, R. E.*, Principles of Relational Contracts, Virginia Law Review, Vol. 67, No. 6, 1981, 1089 et seqq.; *Eisenberg, M. A.*, Why There Is No Law of Relational Contracts, Northwestern University Law Review, Vol. 94, No. 3, 1999, 805 et seqq.; *Baker, G./Gibbons, R./Murphy, K.J.*, Relational Contracts and the Theory of the Firm, The Quarterly Journal of Economics 2002, 39 et seqq.; *Smith Ring, P./Van De Ven, A.*, Structuring Cooperative Relationships between Organizations, Strategic Management Journal 1992, Vol. 13, No. 7, 483 et seqq. From a German perspective: *Krebs, P.*, Sonderverbindung und außerdeliktische Schutzpflichten, München, 2000, p. 611.

## IV. Customary rules and general practices

Customary rules or general practices are very relevant phenomena within business networks. They evolve over a long time due to a similar behaviour of the members in similar situations. But how do these rules fit into the presented governance structure of business networks?

There are different possibilities, how customary rules and general practices can take effect. On the one hand, there are customary rules characterised by repeated practice over a certain period of time. They usually evolve in long-term contract relations and often contradict agreed provisions or they apply to loopholes. In this context, a corresponding practice between two parties could be characterised as an (implied) agreement between said parties under certain circumstances. In this way an HGI is developed through repeated practice. But this result will be the exception because it would go against the general tendency towards a low degree of juridification in business networks, thus being, in general, contrary to the interests of both parties. Repeated practices are also not interpreted as a legally binding agreement with regard to agency by estoppel as well as to company practices.[109] However, in business networks, where a multitude of parties is involved, this contract model is in any case not applicable.

Regarding the degree of juridification it would be less problematic to view a certain practice as a rule of interpretation or substantiation of an existing provision, since this would not imply extensive juridification. But even for general contracts only little is known about the actual effect of this practice.[110] Within business networks the issue of multiparty legal relations renders the problem even more complex.

Thus, the above mentioned would suggest applying the concept of (limited) legitimate expectations, i.e. in the form that it would be considered as contradictory, if a member participated in a project for which certain practices exist, but said member would not accept these practices later on. The practice would not become a permanent provision within the network in that case, but it would still have legal implications for the individual

---

109 Cf. only *Singer, R.*, Das Verbot widersprüchlichen Verhaltens, München, 1993, pp. 235 et seqq.

110 On the unanimous decision to overrule the articles of association see *Habersack, M.*, Zeitschrift für Unternehmens- und Gesellschaftsrecht 1994, 354 (363 et seqq.); also compare *Singer, R.*, Das Verbot widersprüchlichen Verhaltens, München, 1993, pp. 235 et seqq.

project. The need for trust is higher within business networks than in general contractual relations, which speaks for the concept of (limited) legitimate expectations.

Apart from the plausible, but not court-of-law-validated effects of practices within business networks, these usages have considerable non-legal implications. When a network member breaks informal rules, he goes against the other members, which leads to the loss of trust in him. Since co-operation and trust within business networks are of utmost importance, the other members could "sanction" this behaviour with less co-operation.[111] Thus, resulting from this informal pressure, a practice will be acknowledged in general, as long as it does not result in serious disadvantages for a member of the network.

On the other hand, general practices and customary rules are supposed to evolve on the basis of soft governance instruments (SGI) like rules of the game within business networks. These instruments are meant to shape behaviour without using legal binding force. In this context, the so far developed practices and rules will also not have legal binding force most of the time. But social pressure or informal sanctions might be implied (see above).

In rare cases and under strict conditions (period and repetition of practice, acknowledgment as lawful) it could be reasonable to draw conclusions similar to cases of customary law. The effect would be complete juridification – also outside of an implied agreement between the parties in form of private customary rules ("Privatvertragsgewohnheitsrecht"). Practiced majority requirements within the decision making process could be an example of this juridified practice.

It is common that business networks stipulate majorities in the statutes of the corporation (in case a corporation is used on the framework level). But irrespective of the majorities stated in the articles of association some business networks almost only take decisions with vast majorities (over 80%). The formal requirements for an amendment of the articles of association, which are not met in the example mentioned, constitute a special problem in this case. If one assumes that the formal requirements cannot be overcome with the help of private customary rules ("Privatvertragsgewohnheitsrecht"), only one option remains, namely to bind those members

111 For more details on sanctions in business networks see G. pp. 164 et seq.

that are not complying with the practice with the help of § 242 BGB (German civil code) in the form of contradicting behaviour.

## V. Suitability of governance instruments

But not all governance tools are suitable for all purposes. In the following, this paper will discuss in which situations which instruments or which combination of instruments are suited best.

In practice, members of a business network do not only have to choose between the different instruments, but also on which level they will set the rules and to which level these provisions should apply. Hence, the choice of the governance instrument and the implementation into the multi-level governance system are the two main challenges.

### 1. Functioning of business networks as a starting point

Governance instruments aim to support the functioning of business networks. Therefore, it is useful to examine aspects that are important for the functioning of networks.

In general, the functioning of business networks is based on a high level of mutual trust between the network members.[112] Hence, mutual trust is one aspect that might have an influence on the choice of governance instruments. On the one hand, internal rules may help to establish or increase the level of trust within business networks. On the other hand, provisions – especially hard law rules, but to a certain degree also soft law rules – may also have the opposite effect. Especially overprotective provisions could be perceived as a sign of distrust.

Furthermore, members are keen on keeping the structures of the network flexible in order to be able to quickly and easily adjust it to their

---

112 *Glückler, J.*, Organisierte Unternehmensnetzwerke: Eine Einführung, in: *Glückler, J.* and others (eds.), Unternehmensnetzwerke - Architekturen, Strukturen und Strategien, Berlin, Heidelberg, 2012, p. 1 (3); *Metzger, F.* (and others), Koordinationsmechanismen und Innovativität von Netzwerken, in: *Glückler, J.* and others (eds.), Unternehmensnetzwerke - Architekturen, Strukturen und Strategien, Berlin, Heidelberg, 2012, p. 35 (40).

needs.[113] The need for flexibility suggests that in many cases HGI might not be suitable for business networks.[114] SGI usually leave more flexibility to the members, which makes them interesting tools for business networks.

But both, establishing and implementing provisions constitutes an economic burden. Especially the costs of establishing provisions could prevent network members from regulating certain aspects. This might even hold true in case the possible gains exceed the costs in the long run, because the costs occur immediately, whereas the possible gains are not only realised in the future but are usually also uncertain. Because of the *present bias* people tend to delay costs, even if this is not reasonable from an economic point of view.[115] These assumptions lead us to the conclusion that more complex tools like corporations, multiparty contracts and sophisticated soft governance instruments such as extensive model contracts are probably carefully used within business networks due to their complexity.

Secondly, the application of the rule should not cause high costs. HGI as well as SGI might create high compliance costs. Especially drafting tasks, corporations or demanding contracts might be burdensome. But in general, SGI have lower compliance costs than HGI, which is another argument for the use of SGI in business networks.

Mutual trust, flexibility and not too burdensome provisions are very important aspects for business networks. This will lead the parties tending to look for a low degree of juridifiaction. Therefore, members might prefer soft governance instruments or hard governance instruments with a low degree of juridifiaction (as in accommodation relations).

One of the main advantages of business networks is their possibility to rationalise, thus realising projects which would not be feasible for the in-

---

113 *Krebs, P./Aedtner, K./Schultes, M.*, Company networks reloaded – putting a general functional approach to defining complex problems to the test, C. I. 4. p. 41 (65 et seq.) (in this volume); see *Heldt, C.*, Baukooperation und Franchising als multilaterale Sonderverbindung, Baden-Baden, 2010, pp. 67 et seqq., especially pp. 77 et seqq.

114 Notwithstanding the fact that there are tools which make HGI more flexible. Especially clauses like change order clauses and negotiation clauses can grant the parties a certain degree of flexibility.

115 With regard to the so called „present bias“ compare among others *O'Donoghue, T./Rabin, M.*, in: Camerer, C. F./Loewenstein, G./Rabin, M., Advances in Behavioral Economics, Princeton, 2004, p. 226.

dividual company.[116] Despite the tendency towards a low degree of juridification, the benefits of rationalisation and standardisation may be a sound argument for a rule. Instruments that help standardisation are, for example, model contracts, framework contracts, best practices as well as standardised procedures and processes within the business network.

Furthermore, provisions are aimed at fostering legal certainty. But within business networks, the need for legal certainty is less urgent, especially in those cases, where an extra-legal balance between the members exists, which ensures fair dealings even without the need of legal measures. This applies to business networks in general. But even within business networks, effective and protective rules as well as procedural rules are needed for certain matters. Especially the management of valuable assets and the membership structure may create a need for rules which provide legal certainty. However, the provisions must be designed in a way that prevents enforcement through litigation, as this would destroy trust inside the business network. Here, the preventive effect of legal certainty might reduce the risk of litigation and therefore helps to maintain a better atmosphere for co-operation within the business network.

To sum up, the functioning of business networks influences the choice of governance instruments. The high level of trust within business networks required for co-operation, the need for flexibility, the avoidance of too burdensome rules, the aim of standardisation and the need for legal certainty in some specific areas characterise business networks and affect their governance structure. These characteristics are the network-specific framework in which the choice of the governance instrument takes place.

## 2. Implementation of rules into the multi-level-governance system

Not all governance instruments are suitable on all levels. The rule setters have to decide on which level they want to establish the rule and to which level these provisions should apply. This question is highly complex due

---

116 *Martinek, M.*, Franchising - Grundlagen der zivil- und wettbewerbsrechtlichen Behandlung der vertikalen Gruppenkooperation beim Absatz von Waren und Dienstleistungen, Heidelberg, 1987, p. 101; *Wildemann, H.*, Koordination von Unternehmensnetzwerken, Zeitschrift für Betriebswirtschaft 1997, 417 (418); *Eekhoff, T.*, Unternehmenskooperationen in der europäischen Wettbewerbspolitik, Köln, pp. 151 et seqq.

to three main governance levels inside business networks (framework, activity and project level).

The members have a broad choice of hard governance instruments and soft governance instruments. Which tool or which combination of instruments fits best depends on many different factors. These factors in turn also depend on the levels. If the instrument should govern an individual project, the choice of instrument is influenced, among other things, by the exchange process, by the form of co-operation and by the resources used.[117] If the governance instrument deals with organisational questions, the levels also play a role because the framework level is more abstract than the activity level. In addition to the levels, the complexity of the organisation is decisive for the choice of the governance instrument.

On top of this, the characteristics of business networks outlined above (i.e. need for flexibility, trust, co-operation) should be considered when selecting the appropriate means of regulation. The economic benefit for the network members is supposed to be created at the project level. Most rules within business networks are therefore directed towards the project level. This means that the provisions shall shape the individual projects. The rules applicable on the project level can be set on all levels. In general, the provisions established on the framework and the activity level which apply to the project level are abstract because these levels are abstract ones and only complement the specific rules set on the project level.

In a first step, we will take a look at rules that are set on the project level and shall apply to the individual projects (e.g. rules that govern an individual exchange of overcapacity). Here, the project level is the source and the target of the regulation. Soft governance instruments are generally not used in this context as they are better suited for abstract levels (the framework and the activity level). Therefore, parties of a project will normally choose between a contract, an accommodation relation[118] and a corporation (partnerships) in order to structure the individual projects.

The choice of the instrument also depends on the characteristics of the project. Important features are the form of co-operation (non-transforma-

117 *Krebs, P./Jung, S./Aedtner, K./Schultes, M.*, The modular system of network activities, C. II. p. 75 (85 et seqq.) (in this volume).

118 See the literature mentioned in footnote 59.

tive[119] or transformative[120] transaction), the type of exchange process (exchange of consideration,[121] communisation,[122] informal give and take[123]) and the type of good involved in the transaction. There are no big differences to the choice of hard governance instruments outside a business network. This paper cannot provide an extensive analysis of all the different possibilities; merely some general conclusions shall be drawn here to give an example. We will only focus on the different types of exchange processes because we assume that this is one of the main factors for choosing the best governance instrument.

A simple exchange of goods (exchange of consideration) between two parties (a buyer and a seller) is generally structured by a contract. If a project is based on the economic concept of "informal give and take",[124] the parties normally do not need and do not want any formal rules. But under German law, this type of exchange process is most of the times an ac-

---

119 Non-transformative transaction is to be understood as an exchange without a difference between the consideration performed and the consideration received. *Krebs, P./Jung, S./Aedtner, K./Schultes, M.*, The modular system of network activities, C. III. 2. a) p. 75 (91 et seqq.) (in this volume).

120 Transformative transaction is to be understood as a co-operation of members with the result that the individual performances and the originated goods no longer concur with the initial input, *Krebs, P./Jung, S./Aedtner, K./Schultes, M.*, The modular system of network activities, C. III. 2. b) p. 75 (97 et seqq.) (in this volume).

121 The exchange of considerations is based on the classic do ut des, which is the traditional individual form of exchange. *Krebs, P./Jung, S./Aedtner, K./Schultes, M.*, The modular system of network activities, C.III.2.a)aa) p. 75 (91 et seqq.) (in this volume).

122 With regard to communisation, two or more network participants combine their resources which can subsequently be gathered and used either individually or collectively. *Krebs, P./Jung, S./Aedtner, K./Schultes, M.*, The modular system of network activities, C. III.2. a) bb) p. 75 (93 et seqq.) (in this volume).

123 The informal give and take consists of two action forms which are often combined, namely informal giving and informal taking. The defining criterion for informal giving is the fact that initially a consideration is provided without claim to consideration in return. Informal giving could also be termed "generalised exchange". The consideration is not provided in the case of informal taking. Instead, the benefit recipient lawfully takes the consideration usually based on informal connivance. *Krebs, P./Jung, S./Aedtner, K./Schultes; M.*, The modular system of network activities, C. III.2. a) cc) p. 75 (96 et seq.) (in this volume).

124 See *Grant, A.*, Give and Take. A Revolutionary Approach to Success, London, 2013.

commodation relation.[125] The parties usually do not voluntarily choose this instrument. The German Civil Code rather provides that some relations are subject to these rules. Within such a relation, neither side has the obligation to perform (nor to indemnify for non-performance), but there is a minor duty of care for the assets of the other part ("Schutzpflicht") and a basic duty of loyalty ("Treu und Glauben"). The third category of exchange process is "communisation",[126] which could either work as corporation or as a contract based pooling.

SGI as well as HGI can be used on the other levels to shape the projects. In case specific projects shall be shaped, rules might be set on the activity level in order to be "closer" to the projects which shall be influenced. But in many cases, the parties to the individual projects might not want their freedom of contract to be limited too much by abstract rules set on the activity level. Hence, SGI might provide an appropriate solution on the activity level. They can maintain the members' freedom of contract while helping standardisation and shaping behaviour at least to some extent. In a second step, the network members have to decide which SGI (or HGI) they want to use. The choice of the instrument depends on the projects belonging to the activity. If the projects within this activity are usually regulated by contracts, model contracts[127] and tool boxes[128] may be particularly useful on the activity level as they might achieve standardisation. Standardisation can help members to reduce transaction costs without interfering too much with the individual projects.

The framework level is the level where rules applying to the whole network (not only the project level) are usually set. Many rules on the framework level deal with organisational questions (entering and leaving the network, expulsion of a member, decision making process etc.) and are not directly related to the different projects. In some cases, abstract "rules of the game" located on the framework level may set a framework for individual projects. These rules might be hard (i.e. corporation) or soft provisions (i.e. rules of the game).

We expect a mixture of SGI and HGI to deal with organisational questions. Most organisational rules are set on the framework level as they

125 See especially D.II,1. p. 134 and F.III.3. p. 154 et seq.

126 *Krebs, P./Jung, S./Aedtner, K./Schultes, M.*, The modular system of network activities, C. II. 2. p. 75 (86 et seq.) (in this volume).

127 See F.II. p. 149.

128 See F.II. p. 149.

shall organise the whole business network. Therefore, rules dealing with membership (how to become a member of the business network, rules for leaving the network and for expelling a network member etc.) generally apply and will be set on the framework level. Whether the network members opt for HGI or SGI will depend on the economic activity and size of the network. The higher the number of network members and the higher the values of the assets within the network, the more likely HGI are to regulate the membership. The same argumentation applies to the making process. When many parties are involved, a popular hard governance instrument is the corporation (partnership). Many developed networks set up a corporation (partnership) or association to deal with these aspects. In this case, the articles of association and corporate ancillary agreements will be used to structure the business network.

But HGI are often complemented by SGI on the framework level. Soft governance instruments could be used for setting the "rules of the game" regarding the interaction between network members.[129] Codes of conduct (or philosophies) focus on the interaction of members and[130] outline responsibilities and proper practices within the business network. These guidelines will most likely be set on the framework level and apply to all actions within the network (at the framework level, at the activity level and at the project level).

## G. Sanctions

In general, one has to differentiate between HGI and SGI and between "informal" and "formal" sanctions. Usually, HGI provide for some "formal" sanctions if the corresponding rules are not applied. In contracts, contractual penalties are common and within corporations and associations the parties usually regulate when a member can be excluded from the organisation. In contrast, there are, most of the time, no "formal" sanctions attached to SGI. Only in some grey areas SGI might have some kind of legal binding force and because of that also some kind of formal sanctions apply.

---

129 See F.II. p. 152.
130 See F.II. p. 151.

But it can be assumed that business networks will rely more on “informal” sanctions. Applying informal rather than formal sanctions is justified by the special relationship of the network members. In business networks, the relation among the members based on trust and co-operation is essential. Both could be jeopardised by formal sanctions.

A behaviour that violates rules within the network (regardless of whether these provisions can be classified as SGI or HGI) will most likely be “informally” punished by the other network members. These “sanctions” will be tailored to the individual case. There are different levels of escalation. In a first step, the partner of the party that has infringed the rule might decide to discuss the problem bilaterally. Secondly, the parties may decide to involve the management as a neutral third party, which could adopt the function of an arbitrator or a mediator. If these first steps do not help to solve the problem the partner might threaten to stop the co-operation. In case the other party does not make an attempt to change its behaviour, this member might actually end the co-operation with the misbehaving party. But the situation can escalate even further, so that all the members taking part in this specific activity might “punish” this party e.g. by not informing them about new possibilities to co-operate. In a last step, all members of a business network (or the management) might agree to “sanction” the party that has misbehaved. These sanctions may take all kind of forms (excluding a member from a project or activity, stop of information and co-operation etc.).

To sum up, we assume that there will be some kind of formal sanctions on the project level if the project is governed by HGI. On the framework level, it seems likely that the members might establish some formal rules that regulate when a member can be excluded from the network. Even if no such formal provision will be adopted on the framework level, members might choose to try to make the unwanted party leave the business network. Besides, we do not expect many formal sanctions neither on the framework level nor on the activity level. As formal sanctions destroy trust and the chances for a successful co-operation, we assume that the business network will usually work with “informal” sanctions. If these do not help to change the behaviour of the problematic party the exclusion from the network will probably be the ultima ratio.

## H. Semi-fictional example of a governance structure

A semi-fictional example[131] may illustrate how SGI and HGI may be used on the different levels within business networks.[132]

### I. Framework

Dental technicians located in one region of Germany formed a business network called "DenTech" with the purpose of technical improvement for the network members.[133] The members decided to form a GmbH (German limited liability company) and used it on the framework level. The purpose of the company in the articles of association reflected the purpose of the business network. The membership structure was governed by rules also on the framework level. The dental technicians agreed to use the GmbH as a "gate" to the business network. In order to become a member of "DenTech" it was necessary to become a shareholder of the company. In order to keep the business network running, the members transferred an annual membership fee to the GmbH. This money was used to finance, among other things, a project to develop a quality management system. The members of the business network did not expect the GmbH to pay any dividends. They hoped to profit from the projects within the business network.

### II. Projects

Technical improvement was a key for the members in order to be competitive. Nevertheless, the members did not only pursue research and develop-

---

131 Some of the rules really exist in a business network of dentists (like the body leasing contracts and the corporation on the framework level). Other provisions (like the database) are just mentioned here to illustrate the governance structure of business networks.

132 The example is based on findings by *krea.nets*. In order to illustrate the multi-level-governance structure, aspects of different existing business networks are combined in this example.

133 See *Glückler, J./Németh, S.*, Legitime Steuerungsinstanzen in lateralen Netzwerken, in: Glückler, J. and others (eds.), Unternehmensnetzwerke - Architekturen, Strukturen und Strategien, Berlin, Heidelberg, 2012, p. 95 (106).

ment within the business network, but they also invested in R&D in their own companies. Especially with regard to large research projects within one company, the demand for technical expertise sometimes peeked for a limited period of time. In these cases, the members arranged a "body leasing" inside the business network. One member "leased" a dental technician, who he did not need at that time, to another company for a limited period of time. These projects were governed by individual contracts which constitute – according to the understanding of governance structures developed in this paper – a project.

## III. Activity

But soon fierce competition for these "body leasing" contracts arose and led to some unrest among the network members. In order to mitigate the competition within the network, the dental technicians agreed on a minimum price for all body leasing contracts.[134] The entirety of the body-leasing contracts constitutes an activity. The minimum price was set on the activity level so it could affect the single body-leasing contracts (projects).[135]

In order to give every member the chance to offer their free capacities, "DenTech" established a database with the supply and demand of free capacities and recommended its members to use it (soft approach). The database fostered an atmosphere of trust and co-operation by ensuring an unrestricted flow of information.[136]

---

134 Whether these rules are compatible with anti-trust law is not part of this paper. See *Schultes, M.*, Company networks and the dichotomy and statics of competition law – a combined dynamic control of conduct and structure as a solution approach, pp. 198 et seqq. (in this volume).

135 The question, whether these provisions are consistent with anti-trust law is not within the scope of this investigation; for general information on this aspect see *Schultes, M.*, Company networks and the dichotomy and statics of competition law – a combined dynamic control of conduct and structure as a solution approach, pp. 198 et seqq. (in this volume).

136 See similarly *Hammer, I./Beck, S./Glückler, J.*, Lernen im lokalen Unternehmensnetzwerk: Imitation zwischen Konvention und Tabu, in: Glückler, J. and others (eds.), Unternehmensnetzwerke - Architekturen, Strukturen und Strategien, Berlin, Heidelberg, 2012, p. 163 (180).

Model contracts[137] for body leasing contracts were developed after a while to enhance standardisation and the reduction of transaction costs. At the same time, they were used as a "soft" approach to ensure "fair" contracts on the project level.

## IV. Conclusions

The example of "DenTech" shows that it is natural for business networks to use the framework, the activity and the project level for regulating co-operation within the business network. Many business networks establish rules on the framework and the project level right from the start. Provisions on the activity level, on the other hand, are likely to develop over time. Only if the members feel a growing need for standardisation and guidance they are likely to provide more abstract rules on the activity level.

### I.Findings

- Business networks are a popular form of co-operation for companies, which justifies more in depth analysis from an economic as well as a legal perspective.[138]
- The economic finding that there are many diverse projects and activities in developed (large) business networks has an influence on the legal perception of business networks.[139]
- Developed business networks are characterised by a multi-level governance structure. In this paper we have identified five different regulatory levels[140]
    - Framework level
    - Module level[141]
    - Activity level

---

137 No model-contracts were found in the study by Glückler.

138 Cf. A. pp. 118 et seqq.

139 Cf. C. p. 125.

140 Cf. D. II. p. 129.

141 For a closer look at this level see *Krebs, P./Jung, S./Aedtner, K./Schultes, M.*, The modular system of network activities, C. p. 75 (84 et seqq.) (in this volume).

- Project level
- Sub-project/Individual level
- The typical regulations on the framework level are[142]
  - Joining and leaving the business network, as well as expelling members
  - Conditions of the membership
  - Membership fees
  - Regulations on project financing
  - Decision making processes
  - Organisation of the activities and projects
  - Further procedural rules
  - Fiduciary duties (towards other members and the network as a whole)
  - Co-operative behaviour (between network members)
  - Regulations on network-goods
  - Sanctions
- The module level has no practical relevance for the internal and individual regulation of the internal network structure. This would only change, if the (national) legislative body implemented non-mandatory law on this level.[143]
- All levels can be the source of rules as well as the target of provisions.[144]
- As business networks are characterised by a multilevel governance structure, conflict of rules arise. The system of rules is generally characterised by two principles, namely the principle of hierarchy and the principle of speciality.[145]
- As the regulatory system of business networks can be very complex, a "good governance structure" is required within the business network.
- Business networks are likely to opt for a mixture of soft governance instruments (SGI) and hard governance instruments (HGI).[146]
- These two terms have been developed in this paper with regard to the well-known terms "soft law" and "hard law". But the latter only refers

142 Cf. D.II.1. pp. 130 et seqq.
143 Cf. D.II.5. pp. 139 et seq.
144 Cf. E. pp. 143 et seqq.
145 Cf. E. p. 144.
146 Cf. F.I. pp. 146 et seq.

to rules of law and cannot be applied in a contractual situation, which is why the terms SGI and HGI have been introduced.[147]

- In our paper, we have assessed different instruments with regard to their suitability within business networks.
- The suitability of the different tools depends on many factors. The functioning of business networks sets the conditions for the choice of the particular instrument. Especially the high level of trust within business networks required for co-operation, the need for flexibility, the avoidance of too burdensome rules, the aim for standardisation and the need for legal certainty in some specific areas affect the governance structure of business networks.[148]
- Other factors that influence the choice of governance instruments are:[149]
    - Form of exchange
    - Good that is exchanged
    - Number of members involved
    - Level on which the rule is set
    - Target level of the provision
    - Characteristics of the used tool
- In general, SGI can be used to influence behaviour and reduce costs by standardisation.[150] Interesting soft governance tools for business networks might be[151]
    - Model contracts
    - Tool boxes (of model clauses for contracts)
    - Drafting tasks
    - Best practices
    - Recommendations
    - Codes of conduct/Rules of the game
    - Naming and shaming
    - Requests
- HGI used in business networks are[152]

147 Cf. F.I. p. 146.
148 Cf. F.V.1. pp. 157 et seqq.
149 Cf. F.V.2. pp. 160 et seqq.
150 Cf. F.II. pp. 148 et seqq.
151 Cf. F.II. pp. 148 et seq.
152 Cf. F.V.2. pp. 160 et seqq.

  - Contracts
  - Corporations/partnerships/associations
  - Accommodation relations
- Habits and customs are important tools to govern a business network.

The authors hope that these preliminary results might be the starting point for further research.

# Network-like organisations: On their distinction and meaning exemplified by the co-operation in construction[1]

*Katja Aedtner*

## A. Introduction

The considerable problems occurring in many large-scale projects,[2] which in the public opinion are connected e.g. to the Elbphilharmonie in Hamburg, Stuttgart 21 or the construction of the airport in Berlin Brandenburg, have in the past years increased the interest in the organisation of the co-operation in construction.[3] According to the prevailing opinion, the co-operation in construction as a complex organisation qualifies as a network.[4]

---

1 This paper is a translated version of a German article („Netzwerkähnliche Organisationen: Zu hrer Abgrenzung und Bedeutung am Beispiel der Baukooperation") that was published in the German journal „Kölner Schrift zum Wirtschaftsrecht" (KSzW 2015, p. 62-71).

2 On the latest large-scale projects cf. only the articles at: http://www.faz.net/aktuell/politik/inland/flughafen-berlin-brandenburg/; http://www.nytimes.com/2012/09/05/business/global/airport-delays-undermine-image-of-german-efficiency.html?pagewanted=all; http://www.zeit.de/kultur/2013-04/elbphilharmonie-kosten-scholz; http://www.sueddeutsche.de/politik/protest-gegen-stuttgart-die-trillerpfeifen-verstummen-nicht-ganz-1.1874734 (last visited on 11.01.2015).

3 Cf. the Federal Ministry of Traffic and Digital Infrastructure's endeavours made in the Reformation Commission Construction of Large-Scale Projects since April 2013: http://www.bmvbs.de/SharedDocs/DE/Artikel/ UI/reformkommission-bau-von-grossprojekten.html (last visited on 11.01.2015).
Due to the increase in competition, the on-going price decline and the concomitant cost pressure the circumstances in the construction sector have drastically changed since the 90s of the 20th century. In order to meet these new basic conditions solution approaches on the classic construction agreement have already been examined. Cf. on this only: *Rosenbauer, H. K.*, Partnering und Alliancing, Berlin 2009; *Weinberger, F.*, Alliancing Contracts im deutschen Rechtssystem, Frankfurt a.M., Berlin, Bern u.a. 2010; *Eschenbruch, K./Racky, P.*, Partnering in der Bau- und Immobilienwirtschaft, Stuttgart 2008; *Heldt, C.*, who is anaysing the construction co-operation with a network background: Baukooperation und Franchising als multilaterale Sonderverbindung, Baden-Baden, 2010.

4 So *Nicklisch, F.*, in: Nicklisch, F./Weick, G., VOBB, Einl. §§ 4-13, recital 124; *Heldt, C.*, Baukooperation und Franchising als multilaterale Sonderverbindung, Ba-

However, Krebs/Aedtner/Schultes have already shown in their contribution on the definition of networks[5] that the general contractorship, which is an often-used form of contractorship (Unternehmereinsatzform)[6] in the co-operation in construction, is not included in the network definition presented.[7] Therefore, it seems obvious that this may apply to all co-operations in construction. The fact that the network definition sets stricter limits on networks than has hitherto been the case does, however, not mean that the preliminary examinations and findings of the prevailing opinion are of no significance. In this way, the prevailing opinion's classification[8] that several subcontracts in a construction project form a constructional network may hardly be accidental. A resemblance between the co-operation in construction and the network must exist at least to a certain extent. Therefore, it is worthwhile to take a closer look at the resemblance to networks and to examine whether the resemblance is, especially regarding the area of organisation, indeed so great that findings in network research could be applied to the problems occurring in the co-operation in construction.

The question why the co-operation in construction is not a network serves as a starting point. This results in the question about the network

---

den-Baden 2010, p. 70; *Sydow, J./Duschek, S.*, Interorganisationale Beziehungen, Stuttgart 2011, p. 99.

5 Network definition: "A company network is every legally voluntary connection based on an economic and legal network aim of a minimum of three legally independent companies which induce a network-specific demand for organisation. The network companies at least partially exchange their economic independence for the co-ordination of their economic activities by means of concerted practices, agreements or the foundation of a corporation in order to implement the network aim through the bundling of resources." *Krebs, P./Aedtner, K./Schultes, M.*, Company networks reloaded – putting a general functional approach to defining complex problems to the test, in this volume, p. 41 (73).

6 The form of contractorship describes the form of award to one or several contractors who the principal choses. On the various forms of contractorship see: *Kapellmann, K. D.*, Juristisches Projektmanagement, Köln 2007, p. 266; *Richter, T.*, in: Messerschmidt, B./Voith, W., Privates Baurecht, München 2012, I. Teil D. recital 196 et seqq.

7 *Krebs, P./Aedtner, K./Schultes, M.*, Company networks reloaded – putting a general functional approach to defining complex problems to the test, in this volume, p. 41 (72).

8 *Hager, G.*, in: Weyers, H.-L. (ed.), Die Verflechtung von Verträgen – Planung und Risikoverteilung bei Großprojekten, Baden-Baden 1991, col 65, 67; *Nicklisch, F.*, in: Nicklisch, F./Weick, G., VOBB, Einl. §§ 4-13, recital 81.

resemblance of the co-operation in construction. In a comparison of the network and the co-operation in construction it shall be demonstrated which areas of the network and the co-operation in construction correspond and which are at least similar.

In addition to examining the network features in the co-operation in construction, there is a further aspect with which the resemblance of both organisational forms can be measured. There are areas within the network that cannot be directly covered by contract or company law and therefore require a network-specific regulation.[9] If the co-operation in construction exhibits the same need for regulation as is required in the network and if it shows sufficient similarities to this effect then the results of network research can also provide solution approaches for problems in the co-operation in construction due to this similarity. Some aspects shall specify this. In summary, the resemblance of the co-operation in construction to the network and the effects of the similarities shall be examined.

The following considerations on the problems occurring in the co-operation in construction, which are merely deduced from similarities here, might apply all the more to those who want to follow the prevailing opinion and who assume a far wider notion of networks that also includes the co-operation in construction.[10]

## B. Network vs. co-operation in construction – indications of a network resemblance

### I. The co-operation in construction in light of the network definition

#### 1. Approach

As mentioned in the introduction, Krebs/Aedtner/Schultes have identified the constitutive features of a network in their analysis of the network defi-

---

9 Cf. on this *Krebs, P./Jung, S.*, Governance Structures in Business Networks, in this volume, p. 118 et seqq.

10 According to *Nicklisch, F.* in: Nicklisch, F./Weick, G., VOBB, Einl. §§ 4-13, recital 124; *Heldt, C.*, Baukooperation und Franchising als multilaterale Sonderverbindung, Baden-Baden 2010, p. 70; *Sydow, J./Duschek, S.*, Interorganisationale Beziehungen, Stuttgart 2011, p. 99.

nition.[11] According to this definition, the network includes far less forms of organisation than the prevailing opinion has so far assumed.[12] This may possibly also apply to the co-operation in construction in general.[13] Especially since the prevailing opinion does not take the same view a detailed analysis is required.

The usual scientific approach would be to initially determine why the co-operation in construction is not a network. Subsequently, the possible network resemblance of the co-operation in construction would have to be examined. As a result, this would, however, imply that the network definition is considered in comparison to the co-operation in construction twice in a row from various viewpoints. This successive approach is not taken here. Rather, in order to structure the examination, the following takes into consideration why the co-operation in construction is not a network based on the individual network features. In parallel, each feature is directly examined with regard to the co-operation in construction so as to determine if and in what way it is close to the network.

## 2. Analysis of the network features in the co-operation in construction based on the network definition

A network consists of **a minimum of three participants**.[14] Only with at least three participants do the network-specific organisational problems arise which cannot be covered by the classic legal instruments such as contract and corporation. In reality, however, there are usually far more partners involved in a network who form the classic network structure. The co-operation in construction is just like a network characterised by correspondingly complex organisational structures. Depending on the size

---

11 See the constitutive features of a network and the network definition above in fn. 5.

12 *Krebs, P./Aedtner, K./Schultes, M.*, Company networks reloaded – putting a general functional approach to defining complex problems to the test, in this volume, p. 41 (46 et seqq.).

13 Cf. *Krebs, P./Aedtner, K./Schultes, M.*, Company networks reloaded – putting a general functional approach to defining complex problems to the test, in this volume, p. 41 (72).

14 *Krebs, P./Aedtner, K./Schultes, M.*, Company networks reloaded – putting a general functional approach to defining complex problems to the test, in this volume, p. 41 (47).

of the project to be realised, more than 100 parties may be involved in a co-operation in construction.[15] However, the coordination problem[16] in the co-operation in construction, which is similar to the network-specific organisational problem, already emerges if a principal faces at least two contractors he has to coordinate. With merely two participants in the co-operation in construction, i.e. with one principal and one contractor, this problem does not emerge since all problems can be conclusively regulated by the set of tools provided by contract law. Accordingly, the minimum amount of three participants is in the network as well as in the co-operation in construction a decisive feature of both organisational forms.

In addition to the minimum amount of members in the network, the participants are **legally independent companies**[17] since specific organisational questions and conflicts can only arise where the entrepreneurial activities of the participants do not inseparably merge into one and the same corporation.[18] Otherwise, company law would be able to conclusively regulate these questions.[19]

Comparatively, the companies involved in the co-operation in construction also maintain their legal independence during their participation in the construction project provided they do not willingly opt for a corporation.[20]

---

15 Cf. only *Ohler, F. P.*, in: Messerschmidt, B./Voith, W., Privates Baurecht, München 2012, I. Teil D., recital 4.

16 On the classification of the network-specific organisational problem and the coordination problem in the co-operation in construction see below.

17 *Krebs, P./Aedtner, K./Schultes, M.*, Company networks reloaded – putting a general functional approach to defining complex problems to the test, in this volume, p. 41 (48 et seq.).

18 Cf. on why corporate affiliations are not a network: *Krebs, P./Aedtner, K./Schultes, M.*, Company networks reloaded – putting a general functional approach to defining complex problems to the test (in this volume), p. 41 (69 et seq.).

19 *Krebs, P/Aedtner, K./Schultes, M.*, Company networks reloaded – putting a general functional approach to defining complex problems to the test, in this volume, p. 41 et seqq. The contribution of the network members' economic activity to the business structure, which comprises and governs the entire network, has to be differentiated from the constellation that there is the possibility to found a corporation for the purpose of coordinating the network. Unlike the former constellation, the latter coordination corporation does not affect the legal independence of the network members.

20 On the implementation of construction projects by founding a corporation in form of a syndicate (ARGE) cf.: *Peters, F./Jacoby, F.*, in: Staudinger/BGB, Berlin 2013, § 631 recital 24 as well as in form of a consortium: *Schöne, T.*, in: Bamberger/Roth/BGB, München 2012, § 705 recital 185.

Usually, the participants in the co-operation in construction partially contribute their economic activities to the construction project and are connected by bilateral, independent contracts between the principal and the contractor. Therefore, the participants do not generally have to sacrifice their legal independence by participating in the co-operation in construction. This also applies to a syndicate (Arbeitsgemeinschaft/ARGE) since not the entire company is included in the syndicate.

In this respect, the network and the co-operation in construction are both complex organisational forms involving a range of legally independent companies.

A further feature of the network is the fact that the range of legally independent **companies willingly participates in the network.**[21] Neither the state nor another institution forces the network members to participate.[22] The decision to participate lies entirely within the power of the respective network member. In comparison to the network, the participation in the co-operation in construction is also legally voluntary. This is not invalidated by the fact that a principal prefers certain contractors who he definitely wants to entrust with the performance of certain services and also nominates them for the commission. The participation in the co-operation in construction is governed by the rules of the market.[23] The principal decides to which potential contractor he submits an offer and with whom he wants to undertake the construction project. Every contractor then decides individually and voluntarily whether he wants to accept the offer. This means that not everyone who wants to participate in a co-operation in construction can indeed participate, but if participation is effected then it is always legally voluntary.[24]

---

21 *Krebs, P./Aedtner, K./Schultes, M.*, Company networks reloaded – putting a general functional approach to defining complex problems to the test, in this volume, p. 41 (59).

22 *Krebs, P./Aedtner, K./Schultes, M.*, Company networks reloaded – putting a general functional approach to defining complex problems to the test, in this volume, p. 41 (59).

23 As a basic text on the market mechanism cf.: *Adam Smith*, An inquiry into the nature and causes of the wealth of nations, 1776.

24 On the classification of the legal and economic voluntariness cf. *Krebs, P./Aedtner, K./Schultes, M.*, Company networks reloaded – putting a general functional approach to defining complex problems to the test, in this volume, p. 41 (46 et seqq.).

Besides the already mentioned network features, also the **network aim** is a decisive characteristic of the network.[25] The network aim is characterised by a co-operational gain[26] e.g. in form of competition advantages for the individual network participants. The network aim and the concomitant economic advantage may be different for every network participant. However, they all have in common that an economic advantage can be gained through the network.[27] Facilitated accesses to the markets, cost advantages or quality improvement are some of the possible advantages to name but a few.[28] The network participants can implement these co-operational gains in different ways. The actual realisation is, however, not necessary for the characteristic network aim. The mere intention to achieve the network aim in form of an economic advantage suffices.[29] In order to implement the network aim the network members have the possibility to participate in different project co-operations within the network. These project co-operations may feature different compositions of network members. Moreover, a network member can participate in every co-operation in which he wants to participate to a varying intensity.[30] This variability of network activities lends the network its typical dynamic basic structure.

In contrast to the network, the aim of wanting to participate in the co-operation in construction does not manifest itself in a co-operational gain that can be seen in manifold competition advantages for the participants.

---

25 *Krebs, P./Aedtner, K./Schultes, M.*, Company networks reloaded – putting a general functional approach to defining complex problems to the test, in this volume, p. 41 (53 et seq.).

26 Cf. *Messner, D.*, Die Netzwerkgesellschaft, Köln 1998, p. 170; *Powell, W. W.*, Research in Organizational Behaviour 12 (1990), 295 (303); *Sydow, J.*, Strategische Netzwerke, Wiesbaden 1992, p. 93; *Wildemann, H.*, Zeitschrift für Betriebswirtschaft, 67 (1997), 417 (418); *Zhang, H.*, Ein Netzwerkansatz zur Modellierung, Analyse und Gestaltung von Konzernen, Hannover 1996, p. 188.

27 *Miklis, M.*, Coopetitive Unternehmungsnetzwerke, Marburg 2010, p. 163.

28 Not only are advantages, but also disadvantages connected to networks especially in form of coordination costs and domino risks resulting from network effects; see on this shortly *Schultes, M.*, Unternehmensnetzwerke und das Kartellverbot des Art. 101 AEUV, forthcoming.

29 *Krebs, P./Aedtner, K./Schultes, M.*, Company networks reloaded – putting a general functional approach to defining complex problems to the test, in this volume, p. 41 (53 et seq.).

30 *Krebs, P./Aedtner, K./Schultes, M.*, Company networks reloaded – putting a general functional approach to defining complex problems to the test, in this volume, p. 41 (54).

The principal's advantage of having individual participants in the co-operation in construction lies in the overall construction of a building that he could not build by himself. For the contractors of the principal, the advantage lies in receiving payment for their services while at the same time expecting the realisation of already calculated earnings. An actual co-operational gain, which arises for the network participants due to their participation in the network, does not, however, arise for the participants of the co-operation in construction. The difference lies in the fact that the participants in a network cooperate so as to achieve the hoped for co-operational gain. Regarding the co-operation in construction, the entire project is predetermined right from the beginning of the co-operation. The participants in the co-operation in construction are necessarily "all in the same boat"[31] and in a certain way obliged to co-operate.

Accordingly, the co-operation in construction does not exhibit a similar phenomenon that is comparable to the network aim in the sense of a network-specific co-operational gain. In the literature which attributes a network nature to the co-operation in construction, it is often stated that the network aim of the co-operation in construction is expressed in the aim to flawlessly and cost neutrally construct a building in due time.[32] Aligning all participants according to the overall project of constructing the building influences all participants and warrants the assumption of a network aim.[33] As illustrated above, this project aim is not identical to the network aim according to our network definition. Nevertheless, the understanding that the co-operation in construction exhibits an organisational aim, which exists in constructing the entire building, plays an important part for the herein pursued approach of a resemblance between the co-operation in construction and the network. Therefore, the connection of the project aim of the co-operation in construction to the network is examined closer in the following.

As already determined above, the co-operation in construction does not have a network aim, but a project aim. Thereby, a project is understood as an undertaking that is limited in time and in material, i.e., for instance, re-

---

31 *Nicklisch, F.*, in: Nicklisch, F./Weick, G., VOBB, Einl. §§ 4-13, recital 88.

32 Cf. *Heldt, C.*, Baukooperation und Franchising als multilaterale Sonderverbindung, Baden-Baden 2010, p. 66.

33 *Heldt, C.*, Baukooperation und Franchising als multilaterale Sonderverbindung, Baden-Baden 2010, p. 66 et seq.

stricted in financial and human resources.[34] As a matter of principal, a network is neither restricted in its duration[35] nor in its material. Accordingly, this does not result in sufficient similarities. Within the network, there is the possibility to participate in individual projects. Therefore, the network is the sum of its projects. The co-operation in construction could be an individual project within the network. Hence, it would merely be a part of the network.

It may be added that also an individual project can depict the network in its sum, i.e. the network only consists of one single project. However, this consideration is not convincing regarding the fact that the network as such is precisely characterised by its multitude of projects. The network-specific dynamic thus only emerges in the possibility to participate in several projects.[36] The co-operation in construction is comparable to a single project within the network and thus, taken as a whole, remains close to business networks.

Networks are aligned with a **legal network aim**.[37] This is also the case in the co-operation in construction whose project aim usually is also legal. Hence, the co-operation in construction and the network are not aimed at the same aim, but the aim of both organisations respectively must be legal.[38]

Further vital network features are the economic independence of the network participants and the coordination[39] in the network. Both stand in

34 On the notion of project see DIN 69901.

35 On the duration of the network as non-constitutive feature see: *Krebs, P./Aedtner, K./Schultes, M.*, Company networks reloaded – putting a general functional approach to defining complex problems to the test, in this volume, p. 41 (60 et seq.).

36 On this dynamic cf. the following sections below on the network-specific organisation problem.

37 *Krebs, P./Aedtner, K./Schultes, M.*, Company networks reloaded – putting a general functional approach to defining complex problems to the test, in this volume, p. 41 (60).

38 Considering networks in connection with the ban on cartels according to Art. 101 TFEU, § 1 GWB is to be differentiated from this legality. The classification is irrespective of whether the extent of the interaction exceeds the limits of the ban on cartels, see further: *Krebs, P./Aedtner, K./Schultes, M.*, Company networks reloaded – putting a general functional approach to defining complex problems to the test, in this volume, p. 41 (60).

39 The coordination is not only included in the network features but also forms an area in the network that has to be specifically regulated; see on this below II.1 and C.

close interaction to each other. The **coordination**, which is essential for the success, **requires** the **partial abandonment of the economic independence.**[40] For the exchange, the network members contribute their economic activities to the network and in return expect coordination so as to gain the network advantages.[41] There are different legal coordination instruments available for co-ordination in the network. These coordination instruments in the network are the agreement, the corporation and the accommodation relationship that all network members can use variably as required in their individual project within the network. The exchange of economic independence for coordination is a prerequisite in the network so that the network aim can be generally achieved.[42] As already shown above, the co-operation in construction does not have a network aim stricto sensu. Nonetheless, economic independence is also partially exchanged for coordination in the co-operation in construction. However, the coordinating instrument is already ex ante determined in the co-operation in construction and cannot be chosen freely. The coordination in the co-operation in construction is ensured by bilateral agreements. Thus, the coordination in the co-operation in construction is a subset of the coordination possibilities within the network. Accordingly, the exchange for coordination is not the same in the network and in the co-operation in construction but at least there is a certain similarity.

The contribution on the network definition has already shown that the network exhibits **network-specific organisational problems** as special characteristic due to its complexity and interconnectedness.[43] These network-specific organisational problems result from the multitude of participants (at least three) who within the network can participate in different projects with varying intensity and with changing personnel. A further

---

40 *Krebs, P./Aedtner, K./Schultes, M.,* Company networks reloaded – putting a general functional approach to defining complex problems to the test, in this volume, p. 41 (50 et seq.).

41 Cf. *Sydow, J.* , Strategische Netzwerke, Wiesbaden 1992, p. 90; *Ruiz Peris, J. I.,* in: idem. (ed.), Nuevas Perspectivas del Derecho de Redes Empresariales, Valencia 2012, p. 73 (88).

42 *Krebs, P./Aedtner, K./Schultes, M.,* Company networks reloaded – putting a general functional approach to defining complex problems to the test, in this volume, p. 41 (57).

43 *Krebs, P./Aedtner, K./Schultes, M.,* Company networks reloaded – putting a general functional approach to defining complex problems to the test, in this volume, p. 41 (65).

characteristic of the network is the fact that the network participants always have the possibility to initiate new other projects. In this way, not only the individual projects have to be organised, but also the parallel activities between the projects.[44] This interplay of several needs for organisation constitutes the network-specific need for organisation and the concomitant problems in the network. The described need for organisation in the network is permanent and brings about a dynamic pertaining to the entire network to which, as a result, the network must react in a flexible way. If the network-specific need for organisation is now compared to the need for organisation in the co-operation in construction then it is striking that a need for organisation does indeed exist in the co-operation in construction due to its multitude of participants and the complexity of the services. However, the special parallel activities existing in the network are lacking in the co-operation in construction. As already determined above regarding the network aim, the co-operation in construction can depict a project within the network, but the special complexity of the network, which arises due to the multitude of projects, does not exist in the co-operation in construction. The same applies also here. However, even though the network-specific need for organisation does not exist in the same way as in the network, there is a project-specific need for organisation in the co-operation in construction that is comparable to the need of a network project.

Moreover, the **bundling of resources** plays an important part in the network.[45] The bundling of resources implies the merger to one unity as well as the provision of, the access to and the possibility to use the resources[46] which also include know-how, information or organisational abilities.[47] For the operability of the network it suffices if the resources are loosely bundled and the power of disposal remains with the providing

---

44 *Krebs, P./Aedtner, K./Schultes, M.*, Company networks reloaded – putting a general functional approach to defining complex problems to the test, in this volume, p. 41 (65).

45 *Krebs, P./Aedtner, K./Schultes, M.*, Company networks reloaded – putting a general functional approach to defining complex problems to the test, in this volume, p. 41 (58).

46 *Krebs, P./Aedtner, K./Schultes, M.*, Company networks reloaded – putting a general functional approach to defining complex problems to the test, in this volume, p. 41 (58).

47 *Krebs, P./Aedtner, K./Schultes, M.*, Company networks reloaded – putting a general functional approach to defining complex problems to the test, in this volume, p. 41 (58).

company. The resources in the co-operation in construction are, in a broader understanding, bundled as in the network.[48] In general, the power of disposal over the own resources initially remains with the individual providing companies.[49] However, it is indisputable that in the construction project the power of disposal over the resources (services) ends with the transfer of the ownership of the constructor's services to the principal. A narrow bundling of resources in form of the contribution of resources to a corporation is neither in a network nor in a co-operation in construction mandatorily necessary. This is, however, not excluded if the participants decide on founding a corporation.

## 3. Concluding evaluation

As a result, both the network as well as the co-operation in construction is an incidental affiliation of at least three legally independent companies that is aimed at a legal aim by means of the bundling of resources. In addition to these corresponding network features that can be found in the co-operation in construction, there are also network features in the co-operation in construction which are not the same but sufficiently similar. These include the project aim in the co-operation in construction that exhibits similarities to the network aim, the coordination problem of the co-operation in construction in comparison to the network-specific organisational problem and the exchange of economic independence for coordination.

Thus, the network features in the co-operation in construction can be divided into two categories. The first category comprises the network features that entirely accord with the features of the co-operation in construction. The second category comprises network features that are not fully reflected in the co-operation in construction, but which exhibit a resemblance to the features in the co-operation in construction. In a simplified way, the differences lie in the fact that business networks in the sense of the definition are an especially complex form of co-operation whereas the prevailing opinion has also included simple forms co-operation in the no-

---

48 *Krebs, P./Aedtner, K./Schultes, M.*, Company networks reloaded – putting a general functional approach to defining complex problems to the test, in this volume, p. 41 (58).

49 In contrast to the organisation in a corporation such as a syndicate or consortium cf. fn. 20.

tion of network. Network features that do not have any connection to the co-operation in construction could not be determined here. As a result, there is a large extent of similarity regarding the network features between the co-operation in construction and the network.

## II. Regulatory areas in the network and in the co-operation in construction

### 1. Comparison of the regulatory areas

In addition to the examination of the similarities of the network features in the co-operation in construction, a further aspect has to be considered in order to describe the proximity of both organisations, namely the regulatory areas in the network and the co-operation in construction. As already mentioned above, there are areas in the network that cannot be directly covered by contract and company law since neither institution meets the needs of the network. In this respect, these areas have to be specifically regulated.[50] If the same areas are to be specifically regulated in the co-operation in construction as well as in the network and if sufficient similarity exists then the findings of network research can also provide solution approaches for problems in the regulatory areas of the co-operation in construction due to this similarity. Accordingly, the following will consider and examine the specific regulatory areas in the network and the extent to which the same need for regulation also exists in the co-operation in construction.

Central questions for the network are:

1. Admission to and withdrawal from the network (**status of affiliation**)
2. Decision-making process/decision finding (**level of influence**)
3. Non-tortious direct liability towards unrelated third parties (**external liability**)[51]

---

50 Cf. on this *Krebs, P./Jung, S.*, Governance Structures in Business Networks, in this volume, p. 118 et seqq.

51 *Teubner, G.*, Zeitschrift für das gesamte Handels- und Wirtschaftsrecht 154 (1990), 295 (305 et seqq.); *idem.*, Netzwerk als Vertragsverbund, Baden-Baden 2004, p. 204 et seqq.; *Wellenhofer, M.*, in: Amstutz, M./Teubner, G. (eds.), Networks – Legal Issues of Multilateral Co-operation, Oxford,2009, p. 119 (130 et seqq.).

4. Distribution of specific benefits and losses among the network members (**distributive justice**)[52]
5. Organisation/governance of the network members (**coordination**)

Firstly, the network members' **status of affiliation** shall be considered which includes the admission to and the withdrawal from the network. In this respect, the network is not governed by the regulations pertaining to (exchange) contractual provisions such as e.g. withdrawal and resignation, since the market mechanism does not hold here and the (exchange) contract is excluded as leading coordinating instrument. Admittedly, this would be an area that could be regulated by company law but company law is not as flexible as desired by the network and it is too juridified. Therefore, it is reasonable for the network to specifically regulate that the admission as well as the withdrawal of network members remains vague. The participation in the network is governed by a network mechanism in form of every single member's will to cooperate. This will to cooperate or the capability and the will of all to cooperate will decisively influence the access to the network.[53] So far, no detailed regulations exist for the network and require further research. In contrast to the network, the regulatory area regarding the network members' state of affiliation does not, however, play a part in the co-operation in construction. The participation in the co-operation in construction is induced by the market mechanism and the concomitant competition on the market. Irrespective of the form of award[54] of construction projects, only those companies will participate and be chosen which can compete successfully. The participants' withdrawal from the co-operation in construction is extensively regulated on a bilateral level in form of contractual or legal rights of withdrawal and

52 BGH, Neue Juristische Wochenschrift 1999, 2671 – Sixt; BGH, Neue Juristische Wochenschrift -RR 2003, 1635 – Apollo-Optik; BGH, Neue Juristische Wochenschrift -RR 2006, 776 – Hertz; Cf. *Böhner, R.*, Neue Juristische Wochenschrift 1998, 109 (109 et seqq.); *idem.*, in: Amstutz, M./Teubner, G. (eds.), Networks – Legal Issues of Multilateral Co-Operation, Oxford 2009, p. 153 (153 et seqq.).

53 Cf. *Aedtner, K./Teubner, G.*, Virtual corporations: Liability problems in one- and multi-level networks, in this volume, p. 382 et seqq.

54 On the various forms of award of co-operations in construction, *Kapellmann, K. D.*, Juristisches Projektmanagement, Köln 2007, p. 266; *Richter, T.*, in: Messerschmidt, B./Voith, W., Privates Baurecht, München, 2012, I. Teil D., recital 196 et seqq.

rights of termination. Therefore, there is no further need for additional regulations.

For the second regulatory area existing in the network, the network members' decision-making process and decision finding (the **level of influence**), it has to be regulated e.g. who is when and how allowed to take decisions for the network. Furthermore, there are decentred levels of decision which are located e.g. on the individual project levels and govern the decisions for the projects. Thereby, many things will be carried out rather informally.[55] In the co-operation in construction, in contrast, the central power of decision does not have to be regulated, it lies exclusively with the principal or the main contractor (usually the general contractor). The assigned contract partners do not want a further exertion of influence that goes beyond the bilateral contract relation. Accordingly, a specific need to regulate the decision-making process in the co-operation in construction does not exist.

The non-tortious direct liability towards unaffiliated third parties (**external liability**)[56] as a further regulatory area in the network captures the following problem: in the network, conflicts may arise between the network participants that are not contractually connected to each other. In literature, it has been discussed in detail according to which regulations these unaffiliated third parties should be liable to each other.[57] The non-tortious direct liability towards third parties as a problem of external liability not only arises within the network. It is rather a general problem of simple special relationships (Sonderverbindungen) and occurs if the system of direct liability exhibits a functional deficit.[58] Thus, the clarification of these liability problems is actually to be considered irrespective of the

---

55 Cf. *Krebs, P./Jung, S.*, Governance Structures in Business Networks (in this volume), p. 118 et seqq.

56 *Krebs, P./Aedtner, K./Schultes, M.*, Company networks reloaded – putting a general functional approach to defining complex problems to the test, in this volume, p. 41 (63 et seq.).

57 Cf. only *Teubner, G.*, Netzwerk als Vertragsverbund, Baden-Baden 2004, p. 101 – 141 as well as *Aedtner, K./Teubner, G.*, Virtual corporations: liability problems in one- and multi-level networks (in this volume), p. 382 et seqq.

58 *Krebs, P.*, Sonderverbindung und außerdeliktische Schutzpflichten, München, 2000, p. 339 et seqq.

network approach.[59] Nonetheless, this area has to be specifically regulated especially for the network. With § 311 para. 3 s. 1 (analogously) BGB the network and the co-operation in construction have an instrument at their disposal that can largely meet the problem of external liability. The same also applies to the co-operation in construction. If, like in the network, a simple special relationship emerges here that exhibits a functional deficit and that does not allow the direct application of regulations under contract law, then this gap can be closed with § 311 para. 3 s. 1 (analogously) BGB. Consequently, the problem of non-tortious direct liability towards unaffiliated third parties exists both in the network as well as in the co-operation in construction and can be solved with § 311 para. 3 s. 1 (analogously) BGB.

Moreover, the distribution of specific benefits and losses (**distributive justice**) is an area that has to be specifically regulated in the network. Jurisdiction[60] and literature[61] have extensively dealt with this problem. The problem with distributive justice in the network also emerges, because services are created where the extent of the individual contribution is not clearly determined due to the co-operation. Moreover, it may be in accordance with the solidary network not to conduct the distribution strictly based on profit sharing. In this way, it often remains unclear how arising benefits (or also losses) are to be distributed within the network. The regulations that are to be applied here have to be determined individually based on the structure of the specific network. In this way, the respective coordinating instrument (contract or corporation) can already determine the distribution in simply structured networks; in complex networks, however, it may be necessary that regulations beyond the coordination instruments named are to be specifically determined.

Regarding the co-operation in construction, the distribution of specific benefits and losses is not of special importance. In the co-operation in construction every single project participant has contractually determined his

---

59 *Krebs, P./Aedtner, K./Schultes, M.*, Company networks reloaded – putting a general functional approach to defining complex problems to the test, in this volume, p. 41 (63 et seq.).

60 BGH, Neue Juristische Wochenschrift 1999, 2671 – Sixt; BGH, Neue Juristische Wochenschrift -RR 2003, 1635 – Apollo-Optik; BGH, Neue Juristische Wochenschrift -RR 2006, 776 – Hertz.

61 See only *Glückler, J./Hammer, I.*, in: Glückler, J. et. al (eds.), Unternehmensnetzwerke – Architekturen, Strukturen und Strategien, Berlin, Heidelberg 2012, p. 139 (147 et seqq.).

remuneration with the principal. Any excess benefits or losses are only ascribed to those who have agreed to this based on contractual stipulations. This strictly egoistic perspective of distributive justice is appropriate for this regulatory area in the co-operation in construction due to fixed stipulations agreed upon in a contract.[62]

In conclusion, the regulatory area of **coordination** is examined with regard to its similarities between the network and the co-operation in construction. As already demonstrated for the network feature "network-specific organisational problem", several levels have to be coordinated in the network. This includes the coordination of project levels and the coordination of the network level, which is decisively influenced by the parallelism of the individual projects. For networks, specific coordination rules have to be developed so that the needs of the network participants are adequately met both on the level of projects as well as on the level of the network. This network complexity does not emerge in the same way in the co-operation in construction since merely one single project and not several projects exist here in a parallel way. Nonetheless, the co-operation in construction as an individual project is so complex with its multitude of partial services and the interlocking of these partial services that coordination is also required here. The necessary coordination is similar to the area of network coordination since also in this case contract and company law cannot adequately cover the complexity of the co-operation in construction. Accordingly, the need for co-operation arises in the co-operation in construction, which requires specific solutions.

## 2. Provisional result

There are several areas in networks that have to be specifically regulated. These are: 1. Admission to and withdrawal from the network (status of affiliation), 2. Decision-making process/decision finding (level of influence), 3. Non-tortious direct liability towards unaffiliated third parties (external liability), 4. Distribution of specific benefits and losses among the network participants (distributive justice), 5. Organisation/governance of the network members (coordination).

---

62 Similar to the distributive justice in franchising: *Böhner, R.*, Neue Juristische Wochenschrift 1998, 109 (112).

Regarding the co-operation in construction, the regulatory areas status of affiliation, level of influence and distributive justice do not require specific regulation. Contract law holds sufficient regulations for the three regulatory areas mentioned above.

With § 311 para. 3 s. 1 (analogously) BGB the area of external liability has an instrument at its disposal that leads to adequate solutions for both the network as well as the co-operation in construction.

The area of coordination requires specific regulation in the co-operation in construction and in the network since neither contract nor company law offers adequate solutions for the organisational problems.

As a result, the organisation of the co-operation in construction is in certain areas similar to the network, but not in the sense of indicating an essential uniformity. If the co-operation in construction resembled the network in every aspect then the co-operation in construction would also be a network. The question what this network resemblance implies for the co-operation in construction especially in the regulatory area of coordination will be the matter of the following.

## C. The meaning of the network resemblance of the co-operation in construction in the regulatory area of coordination

Time and again, deadlines are significantly delayed and costs increase massively in large-scale projects. Also the German Federal Government sees an essential reason for the deficient implementation and the large problems in these projects in the insufficient co-operation of the parties involved,[63] which is accompanied by inefficient coordination.[64] In the first part of this analysis it has been ascertained that the co-operation in construction features a significant resemblance to the network with regard to its organisational characteristics as well as in the area of coordination. What this resemblance may imply in detail for the co-operation in con-

63 http://www.bmvbs.de/SharedDocs/DE/Artikel/UI/reformkommission-bau-von-grossprojekten.html (last visited on 11.01.2015).

64 Cf. the endeavours made in the Reform Commission Construction of Large-Scale Projects: http://www.bmvbs.de/SharedDocs/DE/Artikel/UI/reformkommission-bau-von-grossprojekten.html, (last visited on 11.01.2015). In this connection regarding the advantages of general contractorship, see also the pending comparison by the Commission on individual awards.

struction and for overcoming the problems mentioned in the area of coordination shall be specified in the following. For this aim, the current standard coordination in the co-operation in construction is firstly presented with its far-reaching consequences. After taking the current situation into consideration, a glance at network coordination will show how the current coordination may also be improved for the co-operations in construction.

## I. Status quo of the coordination in the co-operation in construction

### 1. Duty of coordination and right of coordination of the participants

The co-operation in construction features a need for coordination that is similar to the network.[65] The co-operation in construction is accompanied by a need for co-operation from which the duties of coordination and the rights of coordination of the parties involved can be deduced. The building contract as long-term contract requires the co-operation of the parties involved.[66] Unlike within the network, where only limited legal regulations affect the duty of co-operation, the co-operation in the building contract is mandatory.[67] For the contractual parties the co-operation in the construction project includes obligations and duties of information, contribution as well as of notification.[68]

But what do these duties of co-operation mean in detail? For the contractors not affiliated by contract this means that they have the duty to co-operate in the case their service is e.g. connected to another service in the project and coordination is required here even though they are not obliged

---

65 On the other regulatory areas in the network and in the co-operation in construction cf. above B.II.1.

66 *Nicklisch, F.*, in: Nicklisch, F./Weick, G. (eds.), VOB/B, München 2014, Einl., recital 1.

67 Cf. above B.I.2, p. 174 et seq.

68 BGH, Neue Juristische Wochenschrift 1996, 2158 (2158); further specified by: BGH, Neue Juristische Wochenschrift 2000, 807 (808);
Regarding duties of co-operation, the BGH does not make a difference between single-link contracts such as in individual awards and multi-link contract chains such as in general awards. See on this also *Heldt, C.*, Baukooperation und Franchising als multilaterale Sonderverbindung, Baden-Baden 2010, p. 152.

by contract.[69] The main principal's duty of co-operation is clear even at first sight. He fulfils his duties that arise from each individual contract he has concluded in the project since, generally, he is the only contractual partner who is connected to all participants of the construction project by contract. This central position results in a special duty of co-operation for the main principal. His duty of co-operation, which results from the connection to all his employee contracts, is the duty to coordinate his contract partners.

The principal's duty of co-operation in the co-operation in construction is even further increased in the case of a general award.[70] In this case, the main principal awards the overall contract to a contractor who commits, among others, by contract to coordinate the construction. The principal (separately) pays for this service of coordination. Regarding the general award, the coordinating contractor bound by contract may be a general contractor, a general transferee, a total contractor or a total transferee (referred to as "coordination manager" in the following).[71] The forms of award named differ from each other in that they render varying extents of the actual planning or construction service. The coordination of the majority of the project or the entire project, however, is under the responsibility of them all. Due to the contractual duty of coordination owed to the principal, increased fiduciary, protection, consideration and contribution duties exist for the coordination manager in the project.[72]

Thus, not only the contractual partners affiliated by contract – usually the contractors – are obliged to cooperate in the co-operation in construction. Also for the principal or the main contractor special duties of co-operation arise which manifest themselves in the form of duties of coordination.

---

69 *Rintelen, C.*, in: Messerschmidt, B./Voith, W., Privates Baurecht, München 2012, § 631 BGB recital 115.

70 Cf. the illustration below.

71 On the individual forms of contractorship see also *Kapellmann, K. D.*, Juristisches Projektmanagement, Köln 2007, p. 266; *Richter, T.*, in: Messerschmidt, B./Voith, W., Privates Baurecht, München 2012, I. Teil D., recital 196 et seqq.

72 Cf. *Heldt, C.,* Baukooperation und Franchising als multilaterale Sonderverbindung, München 2010. p. 154 et seq., who already regards the fiduciary duty as covered by the duty of co-operation.

*Fig.: Own simplified illustration of the individual award in comparison to the general award. For a detailed description*

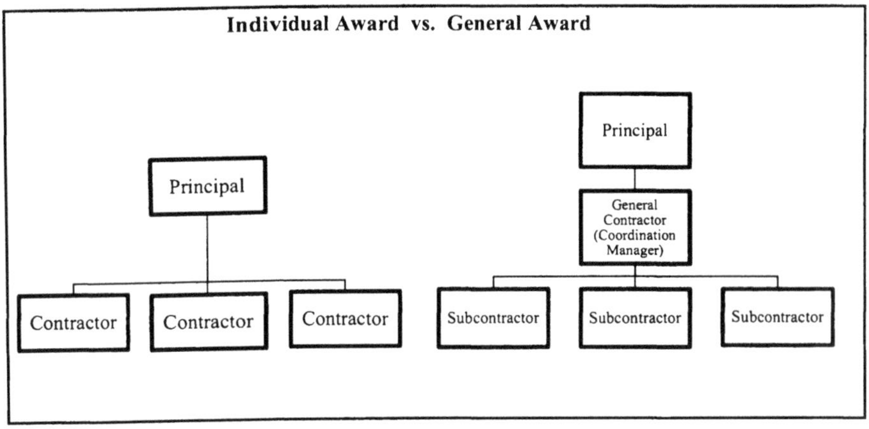


cf. *Lederer*, in: Kapellmann, Juristisches Projektmanagement, Köln 2007, recital 432 ff.

In combination with the duties of co-operation in the co-operation in construction the question regarding the rights of coordination arises. If in the case of the individual award the principal or the coordination manager has not agreed by contract that he actually has the right of coordination then to what extent is he allowed to coordinate his contractors? Even if the right of coordination does not directly result from the contract, the project aim of the co-operation in construction determines this right. As long as no disadvantage arises for the coordinated contractual partner (in case of the individual award: the individual contactor; in case of the general award: the subcontractor) through coordination then he is obliged to also perform services that are not agreed upon by contract with the coordinating contract partner if this supports the realisation of the project aim.

As a result, the principal as well as the coordination manager in the co-operation in construction have a right of coordination in addition to the duty of coordination.

## 2. The exchange agreement as coordination instrument

Network-like organisations such as the co-operation in construction are usually coordinated in bilateral independent exchange agreements.[73] In the co-operation in construction, the exchange agreements are independent service contracts between the principal or coordination manager and the contractor. The participants of the co-operation in construction have deliberately decided against the formation of a corporation e.g. in form of a syndicate or a consortium and therewith also against the risks and duties a shareholder would accept.[74]

The exchange agreement, as agreed upon in the co-operation in construction, is a coordination contract. The structure of interests in coordination contracts[75] is the classic clash of interests. One party grants another party an advantage so as to gain an advantage in return. The familiar principal: *do ut des* – I give so that you give – is reflected here. In considering the project aim of the co-operation in construction and the concomitant coordination problem it has become apparent that the parties in a construction project do not only have conflicting interests. For the implementation of the project aim they are obliged to cooperate.[76] The duty to cooperate and the combination of interests are, however, not reflected in the bilateral exchange agreement for the participants in the co-operation in construction.[77] Therefore, the necessary co-operation in form of coordination does not fully occur in the construction project. The consequences this insufficient and therewith faulty coordination can involve will be sketched out below.

---

73 Cf. *Joussen, E./Vygen, K.*, Der Subunternehmervertrag, Köln 2011, recital 30 et seqq.

74 *Nicklisch F.*, in: Nicklisch, F./Weick, G., VOBB, München, 2014, Einl. §§ 4-13, recital 124, recital 137; *Niklisch, F.*, Betriebs-Berater 2000, 2166 (2168); *Wellenhofer, M.*, Kritische Vierteljahresschrift für Gesetzgebung und Rechtswissenschaft 2006, 187 (188, 190 et seq.).

75 Cf. *Martinek, M./Habermeier, S.*, in: Martinek, M./Semler, F. J./Habermeier, S./ Flohr, E., Vertriebsrecht, München 2010, § 28 recital 39.

76 See above C.I.1.

77 *Heldt, C.*, Baukooperation und Franchising als multilaterale Sonderverbindung, Baden-Baden 2010, p. 118 et seq. Heldt identifies the co-operation in construction as a multilateral special relationship.

## 3. Consequences of a faulty coordination

### a. Economic consequences

If deadline, budget and quality risks are realised in the implementation of a construction project then this usually results in monetary disadvantages for the parties involved. The realisation of such risks often drains the calculated benefits entirely. In privately as well as publicly awarded construction projects the costs for the companies involved can even reach heights threatening their existence.

In addition to the consequences pertaining to the business, which such projects may include, especially large-scale projects managed by public authorities may have decisive consequences for the national economy.[78]

### b. Legal consequences

Flawed coordination can also have direct legal consequences for the "coordination manager". If the principal entrusts a contractor, the coordination manager, who again entrusts a subcontractor, then the contractor is responsible for the organisation of the subcontractor.[79] If the contractor does not attend to his obligation[80] to organise, then this neglect has a negative impact on the period of limitation.[81] The contractor, however, already fulfils his obligation to organise by carefully choosing the subcontractor.[82] In this respect, it is questionable to what extent the obligation to organise in-

78 Cf. http://www.zeit.de/wirtschaft/2013-01/grossprojekte-verzoegerung (last visited on 11.01.2015).

79 BGH, Neue Juristische Wochenschrift 1992, 1754 (1755); NJW 2005, 893 (894); Neue Juristische Wochenschrift 2007, 366 (367); Neue Juristische Wochenschrift 2008, 145 (145 et seq.); Neue Juristische Wochenschrift 2009, 582 (583 et seq.); Neue Juristische Wochenschrift -RR 2010, 1604 (1604); Neue Juristische Wochenschrift 2011, 2663 (2664).

80 BGH, Neue Juristische Wochenschrift 2008, 145 (145); it shall remain open here whether it really always only is a non-claimable obligation.

81 BGH, Neue Juristische Wochenschrift 2008, 145 (145) – expansion of the period of limitation to 30 years, as if he had fraudulently concealed the deficiency.

82 BGH, Neue Juristische Wochenschrift 2008, 145 (146); Neue Juristische Wochenschrift 2011, 2663 (2666).

tensifies to a secondary duty to organise[83] if the form of award, the organisational structure and the legal coordination between the principal and the contractor are designed for subcontracting.[84]

The liability for flawed organisation has been criticised in general for questioning the "werkvertragliche Ordnungsschema"[85] (contractual order scheme).[86] It especially only comes down to the success of the service.[87] Accordingly, a breach of obligation is not already attributed to the contractor if the subcontractor has not adequately organised the production of his own work. The contractor regularly uses the organisation of the subcontractor not to comply with his own duties of organisation. The attribution according to § 278 BGB shall, therefore, be eliminated. The orderly organisation of the subcontractor's service provision (production process) is regularly his affair only and is not carried out with third-party interests.[88] When taking a closer look at the organisation under the assignment of a contractor as coordination manager, this assessment has to be expanded with the increase of the obligation to a binding duty. Vis-à-vis the principal, the coordination manager has taken on the contractual task to coordinate, which therefore falls within his share of duties. If the coordination manager thus has the duty to organise and if he does not meet this obligation then this is a breach of duty for which he is liable towards his principal.

As a result, a coordination manager has to properly perform and fulfil his duty to organise the coordination taking into account his responsibility for this.

83 On the obligation in a narrower sense cf.: *Hähnchen, S.*, Obliegenheiten und Nebenpflichten, Tübingen 2010, p. 263.

84 Cf. the sections on general award C.I.1, p. 188 et seq.

85 *Bröker, J.*, in: Beck'scher VOB-Kommentar, Teil B, München 2013, § 10 Abs. 1 VOB/B recital 56.

86 See only *Kniffka, R.*, Zeitschrift für deutsches und internationales Bau- und Vergaberecht, 255, 255 et seq.

87 Cf. only BGH, Neue Juristische Wochenschrift 1992, 1754 (1754).

88 BGH, Neue Juristische Wochenschrift 2008, 145 (145 et seq.).

## II. The approach of a partial network coordination in the co-operation in construction

In the co-operation in construction, the focus of the coordination often lies on the liability regulations in the bilateral exchange agreements between principal, or rather coordination manager, and subcontractor. This is also shown, among others, by the explicit engagement of the Federal Ministry of Transport and Digital Infrastructure's Reform Commission "Bau von Großprojekten" (construction of large-scale projects) with "klaren Haftungsregeln" (clear liability regulations).[89] The approach pursued here already starts one stage earlier, namely with the successful coordination or organisation.[90] If the organisational risk can be minimised by successful coordination then the downstream liability risk regulated by the contract is also minimised. Nonetheless, liability regulations are necessary and important as part of the governance of the behaviour of those involved in the project.

How is a network approach to the coordination of the co-operation in construction structured? The coordination manager is responsible for the coordination of his subcontractors.[91] The overall coordination in those types of award that use a coordination manager, e.g. in form of a general contractor, is currently characterised exclusively by exchange agreements in form of subcontractor contracts.

The cooperative alignment thereby determines the expansion of the opposed coordination instruments (bilateral exchange agreements) with coordinating instruments that meet the combination of interests. The network governance offers a wide range of instruments that can exist on several levels, but also next to each other. These can be distinguished in Hard

---

89 BMVBS, possible reasons for exceeding estimated costs and deadlines in the implementation of large-scale projects, briefing paper for the 1st meeting of the Reform Commission Construction of Large-Scale Projects on 17.04.2013, 4.4.2013, p. 11, available at: http://www.bmvi.de/SharedDocs/DE/Anlage/VerkehrUndMobilitaet/reformkommission-bau-grossprojekte-themenpapier-erste-sitzung.pdf?__blob=publicationFile (last visited on 11.01.2015).

90 The author deals with this topic in detail in her PhD thesis in which she examines the legal coordination of general contractorship in plant constructions against the backdrop of the network.

91 Cf. above: C.I.3.b), p. 192 et seq.

Governance Instruments (HGI) and Soft Governance Instruments (SGI).[92] HGI and SGI tend to have different tasks of governance. HGI especially also attend to the extrinsic motivation of the participants by means of control whereas SGI rather emphasise the intrinsic motivation by enhancing the legally non-binding nature and therewith the self-motivation of the participants.[93] In organisations such as the co-operation in construction both governance categories of the network have to be applied in a parallel way. If the application occurred on several levels like in a network then competition would emerge between regulations in the co-operation in construction, which is not wanted here.

Against this backdrop, the approach followed here does not change the classic contractual conditions in the exchange agreements. Rather, the co-operative area in the co-operation in construction should be supported so as to ultimately contribute to a more effective and more efficient project result.

## D. Result

The co-operation in construction is not a network in the sense of the network definition presented in this volume. However, as a complex organisational form it is so similar to the network so that similar problems arise that are to be solved in a similar way. The resemblance has become apparent both in the comparison between the network features and the features of the co-operation in construction as well as in the subsequent comparison of the specifically regulated areas in the network and the co-operation in construction.

The comparison of the network features in the co-operation in construction has shown that there are features of the network that comply with the features of the co-operation in construction. Both the network and the co-operation in construction are voluntary affiliations consisting of at least three legally independent companies, which pursue a legal aim through the bundling of resources.

---

92 *Krebs, P./Jung, S.*, Governance Structures in Business Network (in this volume), p. 118 et seqq.

93 Cf. *Krebs, P./Jung, S.*, Governance Structures in Business Network (in this volume), p. 118 et seqq.

In addition to these congruent features, there are characteristics of the network that in a similar way also occur in the co-operation in construction. These features of the network are the network aim, the network-specific organisation problem as well as the exchange of economic independence for coordination by agreement, foundation of a corporation or accommodation relationship. These characteristics are reflected in a similar way in the co-operation in construction in the project aim, the complex coordination problems and the exchange of economic independence for coordination by contract.

In addition to the resemblance of the network features in the co-operation in construction, both organisations feature areas that are not covered by contract law or company law. In the network, the following areas have to be specifically regulated: 1. Admission to and withdrawal from the network (status of affiliation), 2. Decision-making process/decision finding (level of influence), 3. Non-tortious direct liability towards unaffiliated third parties (external liability), 4. Distribution of specific benefits and losses among the network participants (distributive justice), 5. Organisation/governance of the network members (coordination).

Regarding the co-operation in construction, the area of coordination has proven to be the area exhibiting a striking resemblance to the co-operation problem in the network. The area of coordination has thus been examined in detail. There are rights of coordination, but especially also duties of coordination for the participation in the co-operation in construction. The current coordination of the co-operation in construction with bilateral exchange agreements cannot display the complexity of the form of organisation. This has economically as well as legally far-reaching consequences.

Due to its resemblance to the network, this coordination problem in the co-operation in construction thus can and must be met in consideration of the results of network research. A first approach regarding the coordination in the network and the specific network regulations has already been made in the contribution on the governance of networks. Especially the juxtaposition of Soft Governance Instruments and Hard Governance Instruments can contribute to a successful coordination in the co-operation in construction.

# Company networks and the dichotomy and statics of competition law – a combined dynamic control of conduct and structure as a solution approach

*Marion Schultes*

## A. Introduction

Networks are – albeit up to now (juridically) hardly investigated – a widespread phenomenon within economic trade and therefore a praxis relevant phenomenon.[1] From the perspective of competition law, business networks[2] are of particular importance. A prerequisite for the functioning of the network is the coordination of the network participants by means of agreements and concerted practices. However, the coordination of the individual network participants therefore collides with the prohibition of cartels (Art. 101 par. 1 TFEU). This comprehensive prohibition aims at avoiding distortions of competition by restrictive agreements, decisions or concerted practices, which is why it prohibits all coordinated market conduct between independent undertakings.[3] The coordination between the members of a network though is essential for a network's success. The scope of the ban of cartels in networks therefore poses the upper threshold for coordination within a network. This is why the boundaries set by competition law determine the applicability of business networks. Since competition law also provides very strict sanctions (prohibition of the respec-

---

1 *Krebs, P./Aedtner, K./Schultes, M.*, Company networks reloaded – putting a general functional approach to defining complex problems to the test, in this volume, p. 41 (41).

2 The expression business network and company network are used with the same meaning.

3 So-called postulate of independence. See ECJ, joined cases 40/73 – 48/73, 50/73, 54/73 – 56/73, 111/73, 113/73, 114/73, Suiker Unie u. a./Commission, ECR 1975, par. 173 et seq.; ECJ, case. 172/80, Züchner/Bayerische Vereinsbank, ECR 1981, par. 13 et seq.; EC, case T-279/02, Degussa/Commission, ECR 2006 II-897, par. 132; ECJ, par. C-194/99 P, Thyssen Stahl/Commission, ECR 2003 I-10821; EC, case T-224/00, Archer Daniels Midland Company und Archer Daniels Midland Ingredients/Commission, ECR 2003 II-2597, par. 120.

tive coordination and form of cooperation, nullity of the respective agreement or decision, which are sanctioned by very high penalties) it must not be ignored. Therefore, business networks need to comply with competition law. This is why it is to be analysed in the following how the European competition rules deal with business networks and whether they are flexible enough to comprise this economic phenomenon adequately.[4]

## B. Definition company networks[5]

The underlying definition of company networks used here is the following:

A company network is every legally voluntary[6] connection based on an economic and legal[7] network aim[8] of a minimum of three[9] legally inde-

---

4 Doubtful *Ensthaler, J./Gesmann-Nuissel, D.*, Virtuelle Unternehmen in der Praxis - eine Herausforderung für das Zivil-, Gesellschafts- und Kartellrecht, Betriebs-Berater 2000, p. 2265 (2265; 2269 et seqq.).

5 For a detailed discussion see *Krebs, P./Aedtner, K./Schultes, M.*, Company networks reloaded – putting a general functional approach to defining complex problems to the test, in this volume, p. 41 (41 et seqq.).

6 In the field of economics, the idea of networks is linked to the voluntariness of merging into a network. Indeed, the state could legally enforce network-like structures, but then the state would be responsible for the internally and externally applicable (public law) rules. See *Krebs, P./Aedtner, K./Schultes, M.*, Company networks reloaded – putting a general functional approach to defining complex problems to the test, in this volume, p. 41 (59).

7 The network must not intend to pursue an illegal aim since it is not apparent why the legal system should deal with illegal networks. With regard to the practical breach of competition law it has to be noted though that the very same may be influenced by the existence of a network. As the actual interaction within the network can be of essence for the success of a network, a certain privileging of the interaction in a network therefore cannot be excluded from the start. See *Krebs, P./Aedtner, K./Schultes, M.*, Company networks reloaded – putting a general functional approach to defining complex problems to the test, in this volume, p. 41 (60).

8 The economic network aim is a co-operational gain, which manifests itself in the realisation of competitive advantages (i.e. access to new markets, cost advantages, quality improvement) and is achieved by the coordination of the participating companies. See *Krebs, P./Aedtner, K./Schultes, M.*, Company networks reloaded – putting a general functional approach to defining complex problems to the test, in this volume, p. 41 (53 et seq.).

9 The increased need for coordination or the problem of coordination only arises with three or more participants. This also applies from a juridical point of view since for

pendent companies[10] which induce a network-specific demand for organisation.[11] The network companies at least partially exchange their economic independence for the co-ordination of their economic activities[12] by means of concerted practices, agreements or the foundation of a corpora-

instances with two par.ticipants a fully developed range of tools exists in form of the traditional contract law to solve questions of coordination. With three or more par.ticipants, however, network problems, which are not regulated, may arise. See *Krebs, P./Aedtner, K./Schultes, M.,* Company networks reloaded – putting a general functional approach to defining complex problems to the test, in this volume, p. 41 (47 et seq.)

10 In order to legally assess cooperative constellations it is vital to differentiate between decentralised organisations within one legal entity (such as an affiliated group of companies) and network structures between several legal entities. If the individual participants lack their legal independence then neither the question regarding the legal relation between the participants arises nor the question regarding the legal relation of the individual companies to others. See *Krebs, P./Aedtner, K./Schultes, M.,* Company networks reloaded – putting a general functional approach to defining complex problems to the test, in this volume, p. 41(49 et seq.).

11 In particular, the network-specific need for organisation arises especially due to the need for coordination of individual projects, which require the network's cooperation. In addition, the need for organisation exists for the entire duration of the network with regard to the coordination of the parallel activities within the projects, the coordination of the tension between individual and collective interests, as well as the coordination of the cooperative needs. See *Krebs, P./Aedtner, K./Schultes, M.,* Company networks reloaded – putting a general functional approach to defining complex problems to the test, in this volume, p. 41 (65 et seq.).

12 In the case of the combination of founding a company and simultaneously joining the network, a network company contributes to the network with an economic activity while thereby losing its actual or potential economic independence at the same time. In return for the loss of economic independence the companies expect a co-operational gain which can only be achieved by the coordination. The economic independence is therefore partially exchanged for coordination. *Krebs, P./ Aedtner, K./Schultes, M.,* Company networks reloaded – putting a general functional approach to defining complex problems to the test, in this volume, p. 41 (57).

tion[13] in order to implement the network aim[14] through the bundling of resources[15].

This definition is basically kept broad, but the definition's range of application is nevertheless restricted to business networks which exhibit the network-specific problem of organisation. This entails that many network-like co-operations such as franchising or supply chains are not to be considered as company networks.[16]

---

13 In order to assure the synchronisation of three or more actors the network participants' activities have to be coordinated. Depending on the desired intensity the co-ordination may be informal, i.e. without legal ties in form of fulfilment obligations (= concerted practices, accommodation relationships under the general law of obligation), but may also be organised within the scope of contractual exchange relations (= agreements) or in form of a corporation as coordinating instrument. See *Krebs, P./Aedtner, K./Schultes, M.*, Company networks reloaded – putting a general functional approach to defining complex problems to the test, in this volume, p. 41 (55 et seq.).

14 *Krebs, P./Aedtner, K./Schultes, M.*, Company networks reloaded – putting a general functional approach to defining complex problems to the test, in this volume, p. 41 (68).

15 Without the bundling of resources the network aim cannot be pursued successfully. The underlying notion of bundling resources, which is used here, can be described as wide in a twofold way. On the one hand, this includes the bundling (the exchange) of know-how, information or organisational abilities. And on the other hand, the extent of their use is of importance besides the type of resource. The underlying notion of bundling here therefore differentiates between a loose and a tight bundling of resources. The loose bundling comprises the mere provision of resources as well as granting the right of use. The legal control over the provided resources remains with the respective company. The tight bundling describes the merger of resources to one entity by means of introducing the resources into a company which was founded for the purpose of coordination. See *Krebs, P./Aedtner, K./Schultes, M.*, Company networks reloaded – putting a general functional approach to defining complex problems to the test, in this volume, p. 41 (58 et seq.).

16 *Krebs, P./Aedtner, K./Schultes, M.*, Company networks reloaded – putting a general functional approach to defining complex problems to the test, in this volume, p. 41 (71 et seq.). With regard to franchising, the network-specific need for organisation does not exist, because the organisation and co-ordination are often comprehensively regulated in the franchise contract.

## C. Possible restraints of competition by company networks

In the following, it shall be analysed whether and if so, which restraints of competition may be caused by company networks. In this connection it shall be clarified on the one hand whether and if so, which real restraints of competition are connected with company networks. On the other hand, it shall be analysed whether and if so, which effects may be connected with company networks that indeed do not imply a real restraint of competition, but abet cartelisation and herewith constitute a potential restraint of competition.

The knowledge of real and potential restrictions of competition, which can be caused by business networks, is essential in a twofold way. Firstly, this knowledge is necessary in order to evaluate the compatibility of business networks with the ban on cartels. Company networks can vary extremely in their arrangements and therefore have different consequences for competition. A single evaluation however is opposed to an adequate assessment of business networks under competition law. Secondly, only the knowledge of all potential restrictions of competition allows taking adequate measures in order to prevent possible restrictions of competition. Therefore, all possible restrictions of competition are described here without measures to prevent them, such as a compliance system. With regard to the following illustration it has to be noted that the possible restrictions on competition mentioned hereafter are not always evoked at the same time, to the same extent, and with the same intensity by every business network. Additionally, the restrictions on competition are not to be considered as strictly isolated from each other since they can partially overlap, partially depend on each other and, depending on the arrangement, be of varying importance.

### I. Co-ordination and adjustment of economic activities

#### 1. within the business network

In business networks legally independent companies at least partially exchange their economic independence for the co-ordination of their economic activities.[17] It can generally be determined that founding and operating a business network as well as partially exchanging economic independence for the co-ordination of economic activities[18] and submitting the power over individual resources in form of bundling[19] is reasonable only if the foundation of the network entails a certain restriction of the competition between the network companies.[20] Only in this way is the idea of a network – the creation of economic advantages by co-operation[21] - actually to be implemented. Accordingly, business networks include a competition restricting component,[22] which already indicates the violation of the postulate of independence[23] and therefore a real restraint of competition.[24]

In order for the network to be successful the economic activities of the companies in the network have to be coordinated by means of agreements and/or concerted practices.[25] The successful co-ordination requires the exchange of information, which is thus also an essential component of busi-

17 See B.

18 See B.

19 See B.

20 See *Bundeskartellamt* (German federal cartel office), Sektoruntersuchung Walzasphalt, p. 73, http://www.bundeskartellamt.de/SharedDocs/Publikation/DE/Sektor untersuchungen/Sektoruntersuchung%20Walzasphalt%20-%20Abschlussbericht.pdf?__blob=publicationFile&v=3, last visited 12.07.2014.

21 See B.

22 See *Hune, M.,* Netzwerkverträge in der Transportwirtschaft Wirtschaftliche und rechtliche Dimensionen einer modernen Vertragsverbindung zwischen Wettbewerb und Kooperation, Berlin 2010, p. 261.

23 See ECJ, joined cases 40/73 – 48/73, 50/73, 54/73 – 56/73, 111/73, 113/73, 114/73, Suiker Unie u. a./Commission, ECR 1975, par. 173 et seq.; ECJ, case. 172/80, Züchner/Bayerische Vereinsbank, ECR 1981, par. 13 et seq.; EC, case T-279/02, Degussa/Commission, ECR 2006 II-897, par. 132; ECJ, par. C-194/99 P, Thyssen Stahl/Commission, ECR 2003 I-10821; EC, case T-224/00, Archer Daniels Midland Company und Archer Daniels Midland Ingredients/Commission, ECR 2003 II-2597, par. 120.

24 At the same time the immanence indicates that the co-ordination required for the operability of the network may be excluded from the ban of cartels due to the idea of immanence or rule of reason respectively or that it has the potential of being exempted due to the indispensability of the restriction of competition.

25 See B. For detailed information with regard to the special need for organisation in networks see *Krebs, P./Aedtner, K./Schultes, M.,* Company networks reloaded – putting a general functional approach to defining complex problems to the test, in this volume, p. 41 (65 et seq.).

ness networks.[26] The exchange of information can increase the trust between the network companies and, artificially, the market transparency in the business network.[27] The increased market transparency reduces the market insecurities so that consequently the network companies can align their expectations of the market and to this effect also their practices.[28] Against the background that the exchange of information is an essential component to company networks it seems realistic to say that competition is hereby restricted and that a real restraint of competition is to be seen in the exchange of information.

The alignment of practices would ultimately put the business networks in a position to influence the market structure.[29] Through the alignment of competition parameters the individual companies become homogeneous in this regard, out of which symmetric market structures can arise.[30] It can be seen here that business networks may influence the market structure. The remarkable thing is that the influence can be traced back to the co-ordination of behavior and not to a modification of the company structure. This shows that structures promoting anticompetitive behaviour amongst the members of the network can be created by the exchange of information. It seems realistic that competition between the network companies is in fact restricted due to these structures.

Additionally, the companies may, in the light of economic considerations[31], regularly withdraw or even refrain from individual or future parallel activities with regard to individual projects or within the network's

---

26 See *Beeser, S.*, Strategische Allianzen im EU-Wettbewerbsrecht, München 1996, p. 122.

27 See *Beeser, S.*, Strategische Allianzen im EU-Wettbewerbsrecht, München 1996, p. 86; see *Fuchs, A.*, Kartellrechtliche Grenzen der Forschungskooperation– Eine vergleichende Untersuchung nach US-amerikanischem, europäischem und deutschem Recht, Baden-Baden 1989, p. 79.

28 *European Commission,* Official Journal 2011, C 11/1, recital 65 et seq.

29 See also C. IV. – VI.

30 *European Commission,* Official Journal 2011, C 11/1, recital 82.

31 The aim of co-operation in the network is, amongst others, the prevention of unnecessary multiple costs by means of avoiding double activities or investments. *Basedow, J./Jung, C.*, Strategische Allianzen - Die Vernetzung der Weltwirtschaft durch projektbezogene Kooperationen im deutschen und europäischen Wettbewerbsrecht, München 1993, p. 67; *Fuchs, A.*, Kartellrechtliche Grenzen der Forschungskooperation– Eine vergleichende Untersuchung nach US-amerikanischem, europäischem und deutschem Recht, Baden-Baden 1989 p. 76; *Lee, B.*, Die Beurteilung von Forschungs- und Entwicklungsgemeinschaften im europäischen Kar-

scope of co-operation due to the co-operation of their economic activities in the network and especially within the jointly conducted projects.[32] Therewith, competition is basically exchanged for co-operation within the area of co-operation of the network so that this regularly results in the weakening of the competition intensity or at least in a factual non-competition agreement[33].[34] This is a (voluntary) restriction of the economic freedom of action and therefore a real restraint of competition.[35]

Depending on what areas of activities the co-operation in the network or the complete network entails, such as common research and development, sales or production, an alignment of competition parameters and therewith the alignment of behavior of the participants could be implemented after establishing the network or in individual areas, such as products, quantities, price or quality.[36] If, for instance, a new product is developed in the network then the market strategies as well as the cost structure may be unified,[37] whereby for example the parameters advertisement and price may be approximated. This already indicates that a network,

---

tellrecht, Frankfurt a. M. 2000, p. 40; see *European Comission,* decision from 22.12.1987, Official Journal. 1988, L 52, par. 57 d) – Olivetti/Canon.

32 *Götz, G.,* Strategische Allianzen– Die Beurteilung einer modernen Form der Unternehmenskooperation nach deutschem und europäischen Kartellrecht, Baden-Baden 1996, p. 70; *Beeser, S.,* Strategische Allianzen im EU-Wettbewerbsrecht, München 1996, p. 124; *Schäfer-Kunz, J.*, Strategische Allianzen im deutschen und europäischen Kartellrecht, Frankfurt a. M. 1995, p. 167. A prerequisite for this is that the participating companies are at least potential competitors. Reasons for the withdrawal of parallel activities may be, for instance, financial reasons or prohibitions of competition.

33 This may explicitly be agreed upon by a prohibition of competition, for instance.

34 See *Ebenroth, C./Schick, M.*, Vertikale Strategische Allianzen und Allianznetzwerke im Europäischen Recht, Europäisches Wirtschafts- und Steuerrecht 1994, p. 217 (219); see *Frie, C.,* Die wettbewerbsrechtliche Behandlung und Entwicklung von Luftverkehrsallianzen im Rahmen der Globalisierung und Liberalisierung des Luftverkehrs, Köln, München 2009, p. 202.

35 See *Götz, G.,* Strategische Allianzen– Die Beurteilung einer modernen Form der Unternehmenskooperation nach deutschem und europäischen Kartellrecht, Baden-Baden 1996, p. 70.

36 See *European Commission,* Official Journal 2011, C 11/1, par. 34, 157 et seq., 213 et seq.; *Schäfer-Kunz, J.*, Strategische Allianzen im deutschen und europäischen Kartellrecht, Frankfurt a. M. 1995, p. 167.

37 *Basedow, J./Jung, C.*, Strategische Allianzen - Die Vernetzung der Weltwirtschaft durch projektbezogene Kooperationen im deutschen und europäischen Wettbewerbsrecht, München 1993, p. 69.

which is situated at an early stage in the chain of value creation, could already bind decisive competition parameters for future markets by present behavior.[38] The present adaptation of interests could show its effects only in the future, which means that thereby the potential competition on future markets could be limited at the present time.[39] In this regard company networks can create structures allowing for potential restraints of competition.

2. In areas not connected to the network

Besides the co-ordination of their economic activities within the network the immanent exchange of information could allow the network participants to communicate beyond the network in areas and markets not connected to the network. Especially in those cases where not only information which is necessary for the co-ordination is exchanged in the network, but also information about areas not connected to the network, then the prerequisites could be established for the co-ordination of behavior also outside of the network.[40] Thereby, participants could not only gain information about the current market behavior of their partners, but also about their future behavior.[41] Business networks therefore could enable or simplify (future) co-ordinated or collusive behavior in areas and markets outside of the network[42] and hence create structure, which render possible restraints of competition.

---

38 *Basedow, J./Jung, C.*, Strategische Allianzen - Die Vernetzung der Weltwirtschaft durch projektbezogene Kooperationen im deutschen und europäischen Wettbewerbsrecht, München 1993, p. 196.

39 *Basedow, J./Jung, C.*, Strategische Allianzen - Die Vernetzung der Weltwirtschaft durch projektbezogene Kooperationen im deutschen und europäischen Wettbewerbsrecht, München 1993, p. 76.

40 *Beeser, S.*, Strategische Allianzen im EU-Wettbewerbsrecht, München 1996, pp. 86 et seq.; *Fiebig, A.*, Strategische Allianzen und ihre Herausforderungen an das Wettbewerbsrecht der Europäischen Union, Frankfurt a. M. 1996, p. 92; see *Tostmann, S.*, Containerconsortien im Seelinienverkehr – Komplexe Kooperationen als Herausforderung an die Flexibilität des EG- und US-Kartellrechts, Hamburg 1995 , p. 205.

41 *Beeser, S.*, Strategische Allianzen im EU-Wettbewerbsrecht, München 1996, p. 86.

42 *Beeser, S.*, Strategische Allianzen im EU-Wettbewerbsrecht, München 1996, p. 87; *European Commission,* Official Journal 2011, C 11/1, par. 37; 127.

Furthermore, the exchange of information in the business network determines a higher degree of market transparency.[43] As a consequence, the network members can be enabled to increasingly recognize their partners' behavior also in areas which are not connected to the network. Therefore, the network participants can be put into the position to identify the connection of reaction and therewith to co-ordinate the use of competition parameters also in areas not connected to the network.[44] This may not only cause the alignment of behavior of the network members or the assimilation of market results.[45] One consequence of the identification of the connection of reaction could furthermore be a decreased competitive pressure and a declining competition between the network companies also in the areas outside of the network, because every application of competition parameters can be counteracted by the other members.[46] This may affect several unrelated areas as well as several (related) markets. Basically, herby at first merely structures are created by the network allowing for cartelisation. Against the background that the exchange of information is an intrinsic feature of company networks and against the difficulty to distinguish information necessary for coordination and additional information, however, it rather seems to be realistic that this frequently causes real restraints of competition.[47]

## II. Group effects

Besides the possible restrictions on competition by means of the already analyzed co-ordinated effects business networks can furthermore hold the

---

43 See C. I. 1.

44 See C. I. 2; *Beeser, S.*, Strategische Allianzen im EU-Wettbewerbsrecht, München 1996, p. 86. Regarding the connection of reaction see *Jones, A./Sufrin, B.*, EU Competition Law– Text, cases, and materials, 5. ed, Oxford 2014, p. 709 et seqq.; *Röller, L.-H/Strohm, A.* in: Hirsch, G./Montag, F./Säcker, F.J (eds.), MüKo Kartellrecht vol. 1, München 2007, Introduction, par. 1537 et seqq.; *Schwalbe, U./ Zimmer, D.*, Kartellrecht und Ökonomie – Moderne ökonomische Ansätze in der europäischen und deutschen Zusammenschlusskontrolle Frankfurt am Main 2011, pp. 312 et seqq.

45 See C. I. 1.

46 *Beeser, S.*, Strategische Allianzen im EU-Wettbewerbsrecht, München 1996, pp. 86 et seq.

47 If a real coordination of behaviour occurs nevertheless remains case specific in which also other aspects, such as market structures may play a role.

danger to restrict the competition by uncoordinated effects. This includes, amongst others, the so-called group effects (spillover-effects). This describes the situation that companies which cooperate within a business network might avoid to compete with each other also on other markets and in other network unrelated areas out of consideration for their collaboration. Instead, they treat each other with care in order not to jeopardize their collaboration in the network.[48] This would result in a decreasing intensity of the competition between the network partners and could, in the extreme case, amount to the complete renunciation of the competition.[49] There is the risk that these group effects reach beyond the relevant market of the network and that they effect, depending on the structure and activity of the network, several levels of trade and levels of the value creation chain as well as future markets.[50] Especially the permanent exchange of informa-

---

48 *European Commission*, Official Journal 2011, C 11/1, par. 34; *Emmerich, V.*, Kartellrecht, München 2012, § 17, par. 18; *Basedow, J./Jung, C.*, Strategische Allianzen - Die Vernetzung der Weltwirtschaft durch projektbezogene Kooperationen im deutschen und europäischen Wettbewerbsrecht, München 1993, p. 106; *Beeser, S.*, Strategische Allianzen im EU-Wettbewerbsrecht, München 1996, p. 132; *Ebenroth, C./Schick, M.*, Vertikale Strategische Allianzen und Allianznetzwerke im Europäischen Recht, EWS 1994, p. 217 (219); *Fiebig, A.*, Strategische Allianzen und ihre Herausforderungen an das Wettbewerbsrecht der Europäischen Union, Frankfurt a. M. 1996, p. 100; *Fuchs, A.*, Kartellrechtliche Grenzen der Forschungskooperation – Eine vergleichende Untersuchung nach US-amerikanischem, europäischem und deutschem Recht, Baden-Baden 1989, p. 79; *Götz, G.*, Strategische Allianzen – Die Beurteilung einer modernen Form der Unternehmenskooperation nach deutschem und europäischen Kartellrecht, Baden-Baden 1996, p. 69; *Schäfer-Kunz, J.*, Strategische Allianzen im deutschen und europäischen Kartellrecht, Frankfurt a. M. 1995, p. 168. With regard to the group effect see only *Wollmann H./ Schedl M.* in: Hirsch, G./Montag, F./Säcker, F.J. (eds.), MüKo Kartellrecht vol. 1, München 2007, Art. 81 EG, par. 151, 213; *Pohlmann P.* in: Hirsch, G./Montag, F./Säcker, F.J. (eds.), MüKo Kartellrecht vol. 1, München 2007, Art. 81 EG, Par. 420; *Lindemann J.* in: Loewenheim, U./Meessen, K. M./ Riesenkampff A., Kartellrecht, 2. ed., München 2009, 2. Teil Gemeinschaftsunternehmen, par. 17 et seqq.

49 See *European Commission,* decision from 18.5.1994, Official Journal 1994, L 144, par. 55 et seq. – *Exxon/Shell; Ensthaler, J./Gesmann-Nuissel, D.,* Virtuelle Unternehmen in der Praxis - eine Herausforderung für das Zivil-, Gesellschafts- und Kartellrecht, Betriebs-Berater 2000, p. 2265 (2268); see *Backhaus K./Piltz K.,* Strategische Allianzen – eine neue Form kooperativen Wettbewerbs? in: ZfbF 1990, p. 1 (9 et seq.); see *Tostmann, S.,* Containerconsortien im Seelinienverkehr – Komplexe Kooperationen als Herausforderung an die Flexibilität des EG- und US-Kartellrechts, Hamburg 1995, p. 182.

tion contributes to the network members being able to communicate in every area of their activities.[51] The particularly serious consequence of these group effects is the fact that they may even emerge if the network companies are no competitors (i.e. in vertical networks) and/or if other restrictions of competition should be exempted.[52]

All in all network members could abstain from intensive competition in areas outside of the network out of consideration for their partners and their collaboration in the network so as not to jeopardize the network cooperation. Thus, the company network creates structures which favour real restraints of competition. If the network companies voluntarily decrease the intensity of competition amongst them or if they even completely resign from competing against each other, they dispense with the au-

---

50 *Beeser, S.*, Strategische Allianzen im EU-Wettbewerbsrecht, München 1996, p. 132; *Basedow, J./Jung, C.*, Strategische Allianzen - Die Vernetzung der Weltwirtschaft durch projektbezogene Kooperationen im deutschen und europäischen Wettbewerbsrecht, München 1993, p. 106; *Ebenroth, C./Schick, M.*, Vertikale Strategische Allianzen und Allianznetzwerke im Europäischen Recht, Europäisches Wirtschafts- und Steuerrecht 1994, p. 217 (225); *Fuchs, A.*, Kartellrechtliche Grenzen der Forschungskooperation – Eine vergleichende Untersuchung nach US-amerikanischem, europäischem und deutschem Recht, Baden-Baden 1989, p. 188. Therefore, the European Commission can declare the block exemption regulation on vertical agreements inapplicable on markets which are covered by networks to more than 50%, see art. 6 vertical block exemption regulation with art. 1a) reg. nr. 19/65/EEC.

51 *Beeser, S.*, Strategische Allianzen im EU-Wettbewerbsrecht, München 1996, p. 132; see C. I. 1 *Ebenroth, C./Schick, M.*, Vertikale Strategische Allianzen und Allianznetzwerke im Europäischen Recht, EWS 1994, p. 217 (220) even talk about a „schleichenden und flächendeckenden Kartellierung der Weltwirtschaft" (subtle and comprehensive cartelisation of world economy) by „diese friedliche Koexistenz auf Zeit" (this temporary peaceful co-existance). Other opinion *Schäfer-Kunz, J.*, Strategische Allianzen im deutschen und europäischen Kartellrecht, Frankfurt a. M. 1995, p. 169, who sees the competition between the involved companies also during their collaboration as an essential feature of a strategic alliance in the field of collaboration as well as in other areas. Also *Miklis, M.* assumes in Coopetitive Unternehmungsnetzwerke - Problemorientierte Erklärungs- und Gestaltungserkenntnisse zu Netzwerkbeziehungen zwischen Wettbewerbern, Marburg 2004 that the members of a business network not only cooperate, but also compete. Essential to Coopetition *Nalebuff, B./ Brandburger, A:*, Coopetition – kooperativ konkurrieren – Mit der Spieltheorie zum Unternehmenserfolg, Frankfurt am Main/New York, 1996.

52 See *Beeser, S.*, Strategische Allianzen im EU-Wettbewerbsrecht, München 1996, p. 134.

tonomous freedom of action, wherein a real restraint of competition can be seen.[53]

### III. Networking effects

Besides the group effects further uncoordinated effects in form of networking effects may arise with business networks. These may occur especially with the increasing duration of the network, when there are more business networks and the companies are (indirectly) connected by a variety of connections beyond the different networks.[54] These connections may result in the decline or even the renunciation of competition between the companies out of consideration for the matters and interests of the individual indirect partners. Basically, the networking effect is comparable to the group effect. The networking effect, however, results in an additional dimension of mutual consideration.[55] Business networks can be connected to other business networks and in their totality comprise, in a stealthy process, manifold international interrelations of entire markets as well as economic sectors and theoretically in the extreme case the worldwide cross-linking of the economy.[56]

---

53 See *Basedow, J./Jung, C.*, Strategische Allianzen - Die Vernetzung der Weltwirtschaft durch projektbezogene Kooperationen im deutschen und europäischen Wettbewerbsrecht, München 1993, p. 69; see *Ebenroth, C./Schick, M.*, Vertikale Strategische Allianzen und Allianznetzwerke im Europäischen Recht, EWS 1994, p. 217 (227).

54 *Schäfer-Kunz, J.*, Strategische Allianzen im deutschen und europäischen Kartellrecht, Frankfurt a. M. 1995, p. 170. Regarding the networking effect in joint ventures see *Lindemann, J.* in: Loewenheim, U./Meessen, K.M./Riesenkampff A., Kartellrecht, 2. ed., München 2009, 2. Teil Gemeinschaftsunternehmen, par. 20.

55 *Götz, G.*, Strategische Allianzen– Die Beurteilung einer modernen Form der Unternehmenskooperation nach deutschem und europäischen Kartellrecht, Baden-Baden 1996, p. 169.

56 See *Basedow, J./Jung, C.*, Strategische Allianzen - Die Vernetzung der Weltwirtschaft durch projektbezogene Kooperationen im deutschen und europäischen Wettbewerbsrecht, München 1993, p. 106, *Beeser, S.*, Strategische Allianzen im EU-Wettbewerbsrecht, München 1996, p. 27; *Ebenroth, C./Schick, M.*, Vertikale Strategische Allianzen und Allianznetzwerke im Europäischen Recht, EWS 1994, p. 217 (219); *Schäfer-Kunz, J.*, Strategische Allianzen im deutschen und europäischen Kartellrecht, Frankfurt a. M. 1995, pp. 164 et seq. Due to this reason the European Commission can declare the group exemption regulation on vertical agreements inapplicable on markets that are covered by networks to more than

Analogous to the group effect it may not be ruled out that network companies may reduce competition activities also in those areas which are not connected to their own network out of consideration for other connected business networks and their indirect partners.[57] This would not only affect the intensity of the competition. Networking effects may also affect the structure of the markets, because the mutual consideration due to a possible, advancing, international interconnectedness of entire economic sectors could in the long run at least theoretically lead to the oligopolisation of the markets.[58] It becomes clear here that business networks not only feature behavioral elements, but also structural elements.[59] Hence, business networks can create structures favouring cartelisation rendering potential restraints of competition possible.

## IV. Formation of market barriers

Besides the group and networking effects business networks can cause further structural changes, especially with regard to the formation of market entry barriers.[60]

---

50%, see art. 6 vertical block exemption regulation with art. 1a) reg. nr. 19/65/ EEC.

57 See *Backhaus, K./Piltz, K.*, Strategische Allianzen – eine neue Form kooperativen Wettbewerbs? in: ZfbF 1990, p. 1 (10); *Basedow, J./Jung, C.*, Strategische Allianzen - Die Vernetzung der Weltwirtschaft durch projektbezogene Kooperationen im deutschen und europäischen Wettbewerbsrecht, München 1993, p. 106; *Ebenroth, C./Schick, M.*, Vertikale Strategische Allianzen und Allianznetzwerke im Europäischen Recht, EWS 1994, p. 217 (219); see *Schäfer-Kunz, J.*, Strategische Allianzen im deutschen und europäischen Kartellrecht, Frankfurt a. M. 1995, p. 174.

58 *Basedow, J./Jung, C.*, Strategische Allianzen - Die Vernetzung der Weltwirtschaft durch projektbezogene Kooperationen im deutschen und europäischen Wettbewerbsrecht, München 1993, p. 196; *Ebenroth, C./Schick, M.*, Vertikale Strategische Allianzen, EWS (fn. 33), p. 217 (219); *Beeser, S.*, Strategische Allianzen im EU-Wettbewerbsrecht, München 1996, p. 27 et seq.

59 See *Beeser, S.*, Strategische Allianzen im EU-Wettbewerbsrecht, München 1996, p. 28; see *Ebenroth, C./Schick, M.*, Vertikale Strategische Allianzen und Allianznetzwerke im Europäischen Recht, Europäisches Wirtschafts- und Steuerrecht 1994, p. 217 (217).

60 *Beeser, S.*, Strategische Allianzen im EU-Wettbewerbsrecht, München 1996, p. 95; *Ensthaler, J./Gesmann-Nuissel, D.*, Virtuelle Unternehmen in der Praxis - eine Herausforderung für das Zivil-, Gesellschafts- und Kartellrecht, BB 2000, p. 2265

Due to the exchange of information within the network the members possess a higher market transparency compared to network external companies.[61] The more information is exchanged in the network the greater the competition advantage may be compared to non-participating companies. This development can result in the increase of market entry barriers for network externals. On the other hand it is also imaginable that business networks establish exit barriers for the network companies especially due to the costs invested into a network cooperation or due to the dependence of the individual network member on the network.[62] In both cases the economic freedom of action of the individual companies is restricted.

Furthermore, establishing standards, by leading technology or know-how for instance may create market barriers for competing technologies and network external companies.[63] On the one hand, competitors may be forced to adapt these standards if they want to prevail on the market.[64] On the other hand, they may also be excluded from the access to the respective standard.[65] Furthermore, standards may impede the technical development and innovation.[66] As soon as specific technologies are chosen to be the norm an access barrier may exist for competing technologies and companies so that they potentially may be excluded from the market.[67] This may, in the end, restrict the choice of the consumers.[68] If for the most part

---

(2269); *Schäfer-Kunz, J.*, Strategische Allianzen im deutschen und europäischen Kartellrecht, Frankfurt a. M. 1995, p. 158 et seqq.

61 *Beeser, S.*, Strategische Allianzen im EU-Wettbewerbsrecht, München 1996, p. 96. See also C. I. 1.

62 *Lange, K. W.*, Das Recht der Netzwerke - Moderne Formen der Zusammenarbeit in Produktion und Vertrieb, Heidelberg 1998, par. 1055.

63 *European Commission*, Official Journal 2011, C 11/1, par. 266; 272. Despite their competition disadvantages standards may also be pro-competitive and advantageous.

64 *Beeser, S.*, Strategische Allianzen im EU Wettbewerbsrecht, München 1996, p. 96 *Ensthaler, J./Gesmann-Nuissel, D.*, Virtuelle Unternehmen in der Praxis - eine Herausforderung für das Zivil-, Gesellschafts- und Kartellrecht, Betriebs-Berater 2000, p. 2265 (2269); *Lee, B.*, Die Beurteilung von Forschungs- und Entwicklungsgemeinschaften im europäischen Kartellrecht, Frankfurt a. M. 2000, p. 43.

65 *European Commission*, Official Journal 2011, C 11/1, par. 264.

66 *European Commission*, Official Journal 2011, C 11/1, par. 266.

67 *European Commission*, Official Journal 2011, C 11/1, par. 266.

68 *European Commission*, Official Journal 2011, C 11/1, par. 270.

only one standard is used then the customers cannot but accept this standard,[69] which as a result leads to market concentration.

At the same time, protected standards such as patents cause monopolizing effects, which may not only be considered as market barriers, but also effect the structure of the respective market as well as the structure of connected markets.[70] If new markets are made accessible by means of business networks then a strongly positioned business network may shape future markets with decisive competition parameters and may already characterize the future market decisively. Thereby the access to and the chances on the market for competitors may be reduced or even eliminated if their chances are in advance considered as too low due to the presence of the network.[71]

In comparison to the already discussed possible restrictions of competition the potential violation of competition law is in this case not to be seen in the restriction of competition parameters, but rather in the change of the market structure. Business networks could change the structure of present as well as future markets by means of present behavior. This again shows that business networks feature behavioral as well as structural elements and that they can form structures, which allow for respectively favour potential restrictions of competition.

## V. Creation or strengthening a market-dominating position[72]

Besides the possibility to establish market barriers business networks can create the prerequisites for the creation or strengthening of a market-domi-

---

69 *European Commission,* Official Journal 2011, C 11/1, par. 270.

70 *Backhaus, K./Piltz, K.,* Strategische Allianzen – eine neue Form kooperativen Wettbewerbs? in: Zeitschrift für betriebswirtschaftliche Forschung 1990, p. 1 (7); *Franz, M.,* F&E-Kooperationen aus wettbewerbspolitischer Sicht, Baden-Baden 1995, p. 121; *Schäfer-Kunz, J.,* Strategische Allianzen im deutschen und europäischen Kartellrecht, Frankfurt a. M. 1995, p. 178.

71 *Beeser, S.,* Strategische Allianzen im EU-Wettbewerbsrecht, München 1996, p. 97; p. 127; *Basedow, J./Jung, C.,* Strategische Allianzen - Die Vernetzung der Weltwirtschaft durch projektbezogene Kooperationen im deutschen und europäischen Wettbewerbsrecht, München 1993, p. 196.

72 See *Dück, H./Eufinger, A./Schultes, M.,* for business networks in the lights of European market power, in this volume, pp. 260 – 278.

nating position.[73] The establishing of market access barriers decisively contributes to this. But also the creation of competition advantages in the business network, such as size, financial assets, new technologies, capacities made available by reducing or eliminating network-internal competition pressure, access to resources and their control, efficient financial structures or the creation of monopolistic spaces, may result in the establishing or enforcing of a market-dominating position of the network companies. Additionally, group and networking effects may contribute to this. By creating or strengthening a market-dominating position the network members may alter the market situation to their advantages.[74]

When looking at the manifold factors due to which companies can gain market power by forming a network it can be seen that the potential market power does not mainly depend on the traditional market structuring criteria market share and size, but rather on company structure criteria. As a variant of external growth company networks may result in the establishing or enforcing of a market-dominating position. They can therefore produce the same results as shareholding, acquisition, or merger, but without having to resort to the variants of external growth.[75] The establishing or enforcing of a market-dominating position, which is possible within the scope of a business network, cannot be traced back to changes in the market structure, such as caused by a merger, but lies in the co-ordination of behavior. The establishing or enforcing of a market-dominating structure is often seen as a major obstacle to effective competition.[76] Altogether, company networks contribute to the creation of structures facilitating the creation or strengthening of a dominant position, wherein a potential restraint of competition can be seen.

---

73 Some business networks may deliberately aim at that, *Thorelli, H.* goes as far as to say in Networks: Between Markets and Hierarchies, SMJ 1986, p. 37 (38): „Power is the central concept in network analysis."

74 See C. IV. – VI.

75 See *Beeser, S.*, Strategische Allianzen im EU-Wettbewerbsrecht, München 1996, p. 97.

76 See art. 2 par. 3 merger control regulation.

## VI. Market concentration

Furthermore, business networks can cause market concentration. This may, on the one hand, be the result of increased market access barriers and the creation or strengthening of a market-dominating position when competitors are therewith being excluded from the market or being prevented from entering the market.[77] On the other hand, the collaboration may lead to less independent companies being active on the market in the areas of the network[78] if network members discontinue as independent providers due to reduced competition intensity or the complete renunciation of competition due to the co-operation.[79] This may have two different consequences especially for consumers. Firstly, there may be fewer providers and secondly, there may be less choice in products.[80] Insofar it becomes clear that market concentration caused by a network restricts the freedom of action of third parties in a twofold way, which can be regarded as a restriction of competition. Additionally, business networks also influence the market structure, since the decrease of the amount of individual companies on the market may be expected due to the collaboration.[81] In this case, the change in the market structure likewise cannot be traced back to merger or acquisition, but is based on the coordination of behavior. Altogether, the market concentration favoured by company networks depict a potential restraint of competition.

---

77 See C.V.

78 See *Fiebig, A.,* Strategische Allianzen und ihre Herausforderungen an das Wettbewerbsrecht der Europäischen Union, Frankfurt a. M. 1996, p. 89; see also C. I., II. and III.

79 See C. I.

80 See *European Commission,* decision from 21.12.1994, Official Journal 1994, L 378, par. 16 – *Philips/Osram;* see *European Commission,* decision from 18.10.1991, Official Journal 1991, L 306, par. 12 – *Eirpage; Beeser, S.,* Strategische Allianzen im EU Wettbewerbsrecht, München 1996, p. 128; *Fiebig, A.,* Strategische Allianzen und ihre Herausforderungen an das Wettbewerbsrecht der Europäischen Union, Frankfurt a. M. 1996, p. 103.

81 See *European Commission,* decision from 21.12.1994, Official Journal 1994, L 378, par. 16 – *Philips/Osram.*; see *Fiebig, A.,* Strategische Allianzen und ihre Herausforderungen an das Wettbewerbsrecht der Europäischen Union, Frankfurt a. M. 1996, p. 89.

## D. Structure and future related impacts of company networks on competition as a problem from an antitrust point of view

Business networks and the possible restraints of competition caused by them can affect the network members' present as well as their future behaviour. Besides, restraints of competition due to business networks may not only have implications on the present structure of the involved undertakings as well as market structures, but also on future structures of markets and undertakings. Therefore, business networks not only show behaviour specific effects, but also structure specific effects.[82] These effects are special in various respects. Firstly, to some extent they can be the consequence of a specific action conducted within the network, but they can also occur due to the network as a whole. Secondly, these effects may also arise outside the network scope, even though possible restraints of competition within the network may be exempted. Thirdly, the possible (future) changes in the structure of undertakings and markets are attributed to the coordination of conduct. Fourthly, possible future restraints of competition may be caused by a present cooperation within the network.

It becomes clear that the possible restraints of competition due to business networks comprise of a certain time element and thus of certain dynamics. Moreover, business networks combine elements of coordination of conduct and permanent structural changes,[83] which cannot only be the result of specific actions, but also of the network as a whole. The encounter of coordination of conduct and structural changes paired with future-related dynamics and the interaction between specific actions and the network as a whole render business networks a hybrid form of organisation which is difficult to grasp from an antitrust point of view.[84] What is

---

82 *Beeser, S.*, Strategische Allianzen im EU-Wettbewerbsrecht, München 1996, p. 28; *Ebenroth, C./Schick, M.*, Vertikale Strategische Allianzen und Allianznetzwerke im Europäischen Recht, Europäisches Wirtschafts- und Steuerrecht 1994, p. 217 (217, 220).

83 *Ebenroth, C./Schick, M.*, Vertikale Strategische Allianzen und Allianznetzwerke im Europäischen Recht, Europäisches Wirtschafts- und Steuerrecht 1994, p. 217 (220); *Basedow, J./Jung, C.*, Strategische Allianzen - Die Vernetzung der Weltwirtschaft durch projektbezogene Kooperationen im deutschen und europäischen Wettbewerbsrecht, München 1993, p. 25; *Beeser, S.*, Strategische Allianzen im EU-Wettbewerbsrecht, München 1996, p. 103.

84 See *Beeser, S.*, Strategische Allianzen im EU-Wettbewerbsrecht, München 1996, p. 103; *Basedow, J./Jung, C.*, Strategische Allianzen - Die Vernetzung der Welt-

more, business networks are in contradiction to the dichotomy of competition law, since competition law strictly distinguishes between the applicable controls, merger control or control of conduct, according to the form of cooperation between undertakings. Given a merger, it is subject to a structural control within the framework of merger control whereas a coordination of conduct is subject to a behavioural control according to Art. 101 TFEU.

However, the possible permanent effects business networks can have on structures cannot be traced back to a merger and in this sense they are not due to new structures in ownership.[85] They are rather attributed to coordination in form of agreements and/or concerted practices,[86] which is why they are not controlled by merger control, but according to Art. 101 TFEU. Hence, business networks do not correspond to the prevailing categorisation of competition law, which focuses on the form instead of the content of a cooperation.[87] For business networks may cause the same permanent changes in the structure of undertakings and markets as a merger regardless of their form (i. e. agreement and/or concerted practise instead of merger). Art. 101 TFEU, however, can barely capture these effects, since its focus lies on the protection of the undertakings' freedom of action and less on the protection of market structures.

Moreover, business networks are dynamic.[88] The effects of a lot of potential restraints of competition, especially those of restraints outside the scope of the network,[89] may only occur in the future despite of them being attributed to a present cooperation (which also may have been given up again in the future). Art. 101 TFEU, which the cooperation within the network is subject to, however, refers to a certain point in time. Art. 101 TFEU therefore is static. It is examined whether an interaction

---

wirtschaft durch projektbezogene Kooperationen im deutschen und europäischen Wettbewerbsrecht, München 1993, p. 25; *Ebenroth, C./Schick, M.*, Vertikale Strategische Allianzen und Allianznetzwerke im Europäischen Recht, Europäisches Wirtschafts- und Steuerrecht 1994, p. 217 (220).

85 *Beeser, S.*, Strategische Allianzen im EU-Wettbewerbsrecht, München 1996, p. 104.

86 *Beeser, S.*, Strategische Allianzen im EU-Wettbewerbsrecht, München 1996, p. 103.

87 *Beeser, S.*, Strategische Allianzen im EU-Wettbewerbsrecht, München 1996, p. 103.

88 See C.

89 See C. I. 2.

causes or has caused a restraint of competition at the point of examination.[90] So, regarding future restraints of competition it could be that no appreciable restrictions of competition by the current relevant cooperation exists at the point of examination, respectively that in the event of a future appreciable restraint of competition the cooperation causing the restraint of competition has already been suspended. Consequently, both constellations are therefore not covered by art. 101 par. 1 TFEU.

Within the framework of merger control the analysis of a merger's potential effects is undertaken orientated towards the future and therefore dynamically,[91] which would be appropriate for business networks, too. Yet merger control is not applicable to business networks. This already demonstrates that an adequate compilation of business networks under competition law fails due to networks' dynamic and hybrid form as well as to the dichotomy and statics of competition law.

Furthermore, not only the specific individual agreements within a network may need to be analysed concerning possible restraints of competition. Some possible restraints of competition may perhaps not be traced back to a specific individual agreement. In fact, restraints of competition concerning conduct as well as structures may only be attributed to the combination of all coordination and informal relationships of trust, therefore to the network as a whole. This is why the network as a whole requires analysis concerning its compliance with competition law besides the analysis of the specific individual agreements. The special thing here is the fact that restraints of competition due to the network as a whole may also only occur in the course of time, i.e. the future.

---

90 *Emmerich, V.*, in: Dauses, M. (ed.), Handbuch des EU-Wirtschaftsrechts vol. 2, München 2014, H. I. § 2 par. 71.

91 *Bardong, A.*, in: Langen, E./ Bunte, H.-J. (eds.), Kommentar zum deutschen und europäischen Kartellrecht, vol. 2 Europäisches Kartellrecht, ed. 12., Köln 2014, Art. 2 FKVO, par. 97; *Körber, T.*, in: Immenga, U./Mestmäcker, E.-J. (eds.), Wettbewerbsrecht, vol. 1 EU – Kommentar zum Europäischen Kartellrecht, 5. ed., München 2012, Art. 2 FKVO, par. 133; *Ehricke, U.*, in: Jaeger, W./Pohlmann, P./ Schroeder, D. (eds.), Frankfurter Kommentar EG Kartellrecht vol. III, Köln 2011, Art. 2 FKVO, par. 10; *European Commission*, decision from 12.4.1991, Official Journal 1991, L 122/48, par. 34, 2. indent – Alcatel/Telettra; European Commission; decision from 3.4.2001, Official Journal 2002, L 69/50, par. 21; 40; 42; 56 et seq. - Bombardier/Adtranz; European Commission, decision from 4.9.1992, M. 235 Tz. 11 – Elf Aquitaine-Thyssen/Minol.

Moreover, company networks are designed to repeatedly enable new single activities.[92] This means that future single activities and the coordination aligned to them may not be known at a present point in time. An examination of the network as a whole can be necessary also for that reason.

However, as a matter of principle, Art. 101 AEUV is intended to consider single individual agreements and concerted practises from an ex post point of view. Accordingly, the analyses within Art. 101 TFEU are isolated from each other.[93] Yet, the interaction of the individual coordination within the network and the combination of all individual activities within the network due to the network purpose may acquire the analysis of the network as a whole for the complete time of its existence. It is especially this dynamic interaction which impedes an appropriate evaluation of business networks under the scope of Art. 101 TFEU due to it being intended to statically analysing single agreements isolated from each other.

As a result it becomes clear that European competition law struggles to comprehensively encompass and adequately evaluate business networks in its present design. Business networks are dynamic and hybrid, not only encompassing elements of behavioural coordination and elements of permanent structural changes,[94] but also the need for analysing individual activities as well as the network as a whole at the same time,[95] whereas com-

92 See *Krebs, P/Jung, S./Aedtner, K./Schultes, M.*, The modular system of network activities, in this volume, pp. 75 – 117.

93 See *European Commission*, Official Journal 2011, C 11/1, par. 12, which does not contain references to an overall perspective.

94 *Ebenroth, C./Schick, M.*, Vertikale Strategische Allianzen und Allianznetzwerke im Europäischen Recht, EWS 1994, p. 217 (217); *Kartte, W.*, Wettbewerbspolitische und wettbewerbsrechtliche Probleme Strategischer Allianzen, in: Bronder, C./Pritzl, R., (eds.), Wegweiser für Strategische Allianzen – Meilen- und Stolpersteine bei Kooperationen, Wiesbaden 1992, p. 401 (408). Insofar the prescription of business networks being „between market and hierarchy" is also suitable from an anti-trust point of view. See therefor only *Powell, W.*, Neither Markets nor Hierarchy: Network Forms of Organization, ROB 1990, p. 295 – 336; *Thorelli, H.*, Networks: Between Markets and Hierarchies, Strategic Management Journal 1986, p. 37 – 51.

95 The traditional constellation that two competitors facing each other on a stable, defined market and which can be clearly distinguished from each other, cannot be taken as a basis for cooperations between businesses. This is the reason why networks challenge anti-trust law, *Ensthaler, J./Gesmann-Nuissel, D.*, Virtuelle Unternehmen in der Praxis - eine Herausforderung für das Zivil-, Gesellschafts- und Kartellrecht, BB 2000, p. 2265 (2269). *Kartte, W.*, Wettbewerbspolitische und

petition law is strictly dichotomous, static and generally designed to evaluate single agreements. This is the reason why competition law fails to deal with business networks in an appropriate way.

Yet with regard to the broad effect and the extent to which business networks may affect effective competition[96] in ways concerning the network members' (future) conduct as well as (future) market and company structures, need exists for a dynamic behavioural control of business networks on the one hand. On the other hand and at the same time, there is also the need for a dynamic structural control which analyses (future) changes of structures due to behaviour. Therefore, a dynamic structure control is required which is behaviour-specific instead of it aiming at changes within the ownership structure. Competition law in its present design does not meet these requirements.[97]

## E. A combined dynamic control of conduct and structure as a solution approach to the problem of dichotomy and statics

Due to the fact that none of the antitrust instruments (prohibition of agreements restricting competition, prohibition of abuse of a dominant position and merger control) themselves allow for an adequate assessment of com-

wettbewerbsrechtliche Probleme Strategischer Allianzen, in: C. Bronder/R. Pritzl, (eds.), Wegweiser für Strategische Allianzen – Meilen- und Stolpersteine bei Kooperationen, Wiesbaden 1992, p. 401 (406). See *Meessen, K. M.*, Gemeinschaftsunternehmen im EWG-Wettbewerbsrecht. Zwischen Markt und Hierarchie, WuW 1993, p. 901 – 909 for the problem of dichotomy and joint ventures.

96 *Beeser, S.*, Strategische Allianzen im EU-Wettbewerbsrecht, München 1996, p. 128.

97 In this way also *Ensthaler, J./Gesmann-Nuissel, D.*, Virtuelle Unternehmen in der Praxis - eine Herausforderung für das Zivil-, Gesellschafts- und Kartellrecht, Betriebs-Berater 2000, p. 2265 (2271). So also as a result for joint ventures *Meessen, K.M.*, Gemeinschaftsunternehmen im EWG-Wettbewerbsrecht. Zwischen Markt und Hierarchie, Wirtschaft und Wettbewerb 1993, p. 901 (908): „Bisher sind Gemeinschaftsunternehmen als Zwischenform begriffen und entweder einer ausschließlichen Verhaltenskontrolle oder einer ausschließlichen Strukturkontrolle unterworfen worden. Möglicherweise wird diese Betrachtungsweise der institutionellen Eigenart von Gemeinschaftsunternehmen nicht ganz gerecht." (Up to now joint ventures have been understood as an intermediate form and have been submitted to either a control of conduct or a control of structure. Maybe this point of view does not totally meet the institutional character of joint ventures.).

pany networks, it is to be considered whether a solution approach could be developed by the combination of art. 101 TFEU and one of the other two legal instruments.

As a solution to competition law's problem of dichotomy and statics a combined dynamic control of conduct and structure is proposed here.

Competition law knows an evaluation of structural changes combined with an analysis concerning coordination of conduct from merger control. When creating a full-functioned joint venture the possible effects of this creation on the conduct of the mothers' are evaluated besides the merger requirements and its effects on the market structure.[98] If a figure, whose effects on the conduct of the participants results from changes in the ownership structures and whose antitrust examination hence primarily falls under merger control, exists in the form of a cooperative full-functioned joint venture, it is not surprising that vice versa a figure exists in the form of a company network, whose effects on company and market structures lay in the coordination of the participants' conduct and whose antitrust examination therefore is primarily submitted to the control of conduct, which yet also requires a structural control.

In this respect it seems to be possible to pick up this legal notion for an analysis of business networks from an antitrust point of view. Since business networks are only subject to a control of conduct according to Art. 101 TFEU and possible changes in structures are attributed to a coordination of conduct, it appears to be appropriate to transfer the legal notion of a combined conduct and structure control form merger control to the control of conduct within the scope of art. 101 TFEU and to integrate a behaviour-specific structural control within the control of conduct. Quasi inversely to merger control where a control of conduct is undertaken in a second step within the scope of a structural control, business networks

98 See therefore *Käseberg, T.,* in: Langen, E./ Bunte, H.-J. (eds.), Kommentar zum deutschen und europäischen Kartellrecht, vol. 2 Europäisches Kartellrecht, ed. 12., Köln 2014, Art. 2 FKVO, par. 337 et seq.; *Körber, T.,* in: Immenga, U./Mestmäcker, E.-J. (eds.), Wettbewerbsrecht, vol. 1 EU – Kommentar zum Europäischen Kartellrecht, 5. ed., München 2012, VO 139/2004/EG, Art. 2, par. 608 et seqq.; *Montag, F./v. Bonin, A.*, in: *Hirsch, G./Montag, F./Säcker, F. J.* (eds.), Münchener Kommentar zum Europäischen und Deutschen Wettbewerbsrecht, Kartellrecht vol. 1, München 2007, Art. 2 FKVO, par. 11, 434; *Schröer, J.* in: Jaeger, W./Pohlmann, P./Schroeder, D. (eds.), Frankfurter Kommentar EG Kartellrecht vol. III, Köln 2011, Art. 2 FKVO, par. 252 et seqq.; *Wiedemann, G.* in: Wiedemann, G. (ed.), Handbuch des Kartellrechts, 2. ed., München 2008, § 16, par. 136.

shall also be submitted to a two-stage analysis combining the control of conduct and a structural control within the framework of art. 101 TFEU. The first stage carries out a control of conduct. Here, the single individual agreements and concerted practises within a network are evaluated with respect to their compliance to art. 101 TFEU as is the network as a whole. The second stage undertakes a behavioural-specific control of structure.

Indeed, competition law's dichotomy could be dissolved by this combined analysis. The problems the dynamics of business networks confront art. 101 TFEU with, however, remain. Yet, this problem can be faced by taking a future-orientated, i. e. a dynamic point of view for the analysis on the first stage of the combined control of conduct and structure. This can be carried out by especially taking future developments into consideration. The dynamic view of circumstances and developments is another legal notion rooted in merger control. The analysis of effects a merger may have is future-orientated and also comprises of future developments.[99] The reason therefore is the knowledge that some effects of a merger only show in the future. As already seen, some impacts business networks may have can also only take effect in the course of time.[100] For this reason it seems appropriate and justified to pick up the legal notion of taking a dynamic point of view and to incorporate it to the first stage of the combined control of conduct and structure within the scope of Art. 101 TFEU.

Alternatively, one could consider a combination of the legal instruments prohibition of agreements restraining competition and prohibition of abuse of a dominant position, i. e. a combination of art. 101 TFEU and art. 102 TFEU in order to achieve an adequate assessment of company networks from an antitrust point of view. In this respect, as explained above, in the scope of a two-stage analysis the single agreements and the

---

99 *Bardong, A.*, in: Langen, E./ Bunte, H.-J. (eds.), Kommentar zum deutschen und europäischen Kartellrecht, vol. 2 Europäisches Kartellrecht, ed. 12., Köln 2014, Art. 2 FKVO, par. 97; *Körber, T.*, in: Immenga, U./Mestmäcker, E.-J. (eds.), Wettbewerbsrecht, vol. 1 EU – Kommentar zum Europäischen Kartellrecht, 5. ed., München 2012, Art. 2 FKVO, par. 133; *Ehricke, U.*, in: Jaeger, W./Pohlmann, P./Schroeder, D. (eds.), Frankfurter Kommentar EG Kartellrecht vol. III, Köln 2011, Art. 2 FKVO, par. 10; European Commission, decision from 12.4.1991, Official Journal 1991, L 122/48, par. 34, 2. indent – Alcatel/Telettra; European Commission, decision from 3.4.2001, Official Journal 2002, L 69/50, par. 21; 40; 42; 56 et seq. - Bombardier/Adtranz; European Commission, decision from 4.9.1992, M.235 Tz. 11 – Elf Aquitaine-Thyssen/Minol.

100 See C.

network as a whole could be submitted to a dynamic control of conduct according to art. 101 TFEU on the first stage. Hereby, the conduct specific effects of networks on competition could be captured.

The conduct specific effects on market structures could then be covered by submitting the network as a whole to a dynamic analysis according to art. 102 TFEU on the second stage. For art. 102 TFEU also aims at protecting market structures, which have been weekend due to market power.[101] Yet for Art. 102 TFEU to be applicable an abusive conduct by the network is required. The possibility to create structures enhancing the creation or strengthening of a dominant position,[102] market concentration[103] and the creation of market barriers[104] with competitive instruments as such is not prohibited under Art. 102 TFEU,[105] even though effective structures of competition are thereby affected. A control of conduct on its own, even though also designed for the protection of market structures, cannot prevent the potential harmful effects on market structures caused by company networks.[106] For art. 102 TFEU does not cover all impacts, which prove to be incompatible with the claimed system of undistorted competition.[107] Particularly the uncoordinated effects such as group effects and networking effects are not encompassed by art. 102 TFEU.[108] Whereas a control of structure is aimed at already preventing the creation of market structures, which enable obstructive acts according to art. 102 TFEU (and also

---

101 *Emmerich, V.*, in: Dauses, M. (ed.), Handbuch des EU-Wirtschaftsrechts vol. 2, München 2014, H. I. § 3 Art. 102 AEUV par. 5; *Fuchs, A./Möschel, W:* in: Immenga U./Mestmäcker E. J., (eds.), Wettbewerbsrecht vol. 1, München 2012, Art. 102 AEUV par. 5; *Lübbig, T.* in: Wiedemann, G. (ed.), Handbuch des Kartellrechts, 2. ed., München 2008Art. 82 EGV par 1.

102 See C. V.

103 See C. VI.

104 See C. IV.

105 *Emmerich, V.*, in: Dauses, M. (ed.), Handbuch des EU-Wirtschaftsrechts vol. 2, München 2014, , H. I. § 3 Art. 102 AEUV par. 5; *Lübbig, T.* in: Wiedemann, G. (ed.), Handbuch des Kartellrechts, 2. ed., München 2008, Art. 82 EGV par. 1; *Weiß, W.* in: Calliess, C./Ruffert, M. (eds.), EUV/AEUV, 4. ed., München 2011, Art. 102 AEUV par. 1.

106 See *European Commission*, OJ 2004, L 24/1, EG 7; see *Lettl, T.*, Kartellrecht, München 2013, § 6, par. 2; *Mestmäcke,r E.-J./Schweitzer, H.*, Europäisches Wettbewerbsrecht, München 2004, § 23 III 2 par. 26.

107 See *European Commission*, OJ 2004, L 24/1, EG 7; *Ackermann, T.* in: Riesenhuber, K. (ed.), Europäische Methodenlehre, 2. ed. Berlin/New York, § 21 par. 9.

108 However, they are encompassed as significant restraint to effective competition by art. 2 par. 3 merger control regulation.

art. 101 AEUV),[109] art. 102 TFEU is only applicable after the creation of market power and therefor is applied to already weakened market structures. Its aim is to protect residual competition.[110] Insofar, the control of market structure is upstream to the control of market conduct. Since company networks combine conduct specific as well as structure specific elements, it becomes clear that a control of conduct, even though certain structure specific effects are also controlled by art. 102 TFEU, by itself is not sufficient to encompass all anticompetitive effects by company networks in total. For this reason priority shall be given to the first proposal for solution of a combined dynamic control of conduct and structure.

The introduction of a combined dynamic two-stage analysis that covers the need to subject business networks to both a dynamic control concerning behavioural-specific effects and structural-specific effects allows for overcoming the deficits competition law has with regard to business networks. Thereby, business networks can be assessed by an adequate analysis concerning their compliance to competition law.

## F. The combined dynamic control of conduct and structure in detail

Due to the diversity of business networks an accurate analysis remains reserved for each individual case. But generally speaking, on the first stage of the combined dynamic control of conduct and structure, a control of conduct is carried out according to art. 101 TFEU beginning with the analysis of each single activity within the network, e. g. joint development of a new product. This evaluation basically does not differ from the examination of other forms of (traditional) cooperation and shall prevent the network members from using the network to disguise a cartel.

109 See. *Körber, T.*, in: Immenga, U./Mestmäcker, E.-J. (eds.), Wettbewerbsrecht, vol. 1 EU – Kommentar zum Europäischen Kartellrecht, 5. ed., München 2012, Art. 2 FKVO par. 200; see *Montag, F./v. Bonin, A.*, in: *Hirsch, G./Montag, F./ Säcker, F. J.* (eds.), Münchener Kommentar zum Europäischen und Deutschen Wettbewerbsrecht, Kartellrecht vol. 1, München 2007, Art. 2 FKVO par. 101.

110 *Fuchs, A./Möschel, W:* in: Immenga U./Mestmäcker E. J., (eds.), Wettbewerbsrecht vol. 1, München 2012, Art. 102 AEUV par. 5; *Emmerich, V.*, in: Dauses, M. (ed.), Handbuch des EU-Wirtschaftsrechts vol. 2, München 2014, H. I. § 3 Art. 102 AEUV par. 5; Wiedemann, G. (ed.), Handbuch des Kartellrechts, 2. ed., München 2008, Art. 82 EGV par. 1.

Subsequently, the business network as a whole is subjected to a dynamic control of conduct according to art. 101 TFEU. On the one hand, this allows for encompassing restraints of competition which only take effect from the whole network, such as group effects. On the other hand, by taking a dynamic point of view future effects and developments can be detected and taken into consideration.

On the second stage, business networks are subjected to a behavioural-specific structural control. Thereby, the compilation of impacts business networks may have on the structure of undertakings and markets is rendered possible. This analysis serves as a pre-emptive control regarding market changes in order to prevent (further) impediment or single obstructive acts under art. 101 and 102 TFEU. The analysis on the second stage is dispensable if the evaluation on the first stage brought the result that the network as a whole already did not qualify for an exemption.

## G. Results

Company networks can restrict competition in many and diverse ways. Under the presumption that no measures are taken to avoid restrictions of competition within the network, company networks can restrict competition by the coordination and alignment of economic activities both within the network and in areas unconnected to the network, by group effects and networking effects, by the creation of market barriers, by the creation or strengthening of a dominant position and by market concentration.[111]

European antitrust legislation in its present design is hardly able to appropriately encompass and adequately evaluate company networks. The reasons therefore are that competition law strictly distinguishes between the applicable controls, merger control or control of conduct, according to the form of cooperation between undertakings, competition law being static and generally being based on evaluating single agreements and concerted practises separately. Company networks, however, are dynamic and hybrid. Not only do they combine elements of coordination of conduct and elements of permanent structural changes, but also the need for simultane-

111 See C.

ously analysing the compatibility of single activities and the network as a whole with antitrust law.[112]

As a solution approach to antitrust law's problem of dichotomy and static the integration of a two-stage combined dynamic control of conduct and structure in art. 101 TFEU is proposed. In this context the legal notion of an analysis combining changes of structures with an examination of coordination of conduct is picked up from merger control and transferred to Art. 101 TFEU for the analysis of company networks from an antitrust point of view. In the context of the here proposed two-stage analysis the legal notion of dynamically contemplating facts, also known from merger control, is adopted at the same time, in order to also allow for the consideration of future developments and effects of company networks on competition by a current coordination of conduct within the analysis.[113]

112 See D.

113 See F.

# Economic analysis of value-added networks: A holistic approach to the competitive effects of vertical agreements

*Jonatan Prosenjak*

## A. Introduction

In recent decades, outsourcing of business functions to third-party companies is an increasing trend. Similarly, there is a need to maintain some control of the outsourced processes, which is why firms resort to coordination instruments in the form of contractual agreements. Another recent development is the growing focus of companies to expand their business processes globally by means of contractual inclusion. In both cases, one cannot speak of an entirely organizational integration but the coordination takes place with the help of contracts. Both processes lead to a large amount of business relations that result in a network-like web of contracts. These contractual networks have great relevance along the value chain, as companies try to preserve the influence on their supply and distribution processes.[1]

In order to manage these so-called value-added networks, contractual agreements called vertical agreements, are required in upstream and downstream value-adding stages. The literature on economic analysis of vertical agreements comes to a very ambiguous assessment. It states that efficiency-enhancing and anti-competitive effects can occur simultaneously, with the result that a general statement about the welfare effect is difficult to obtain. For a sound assessment, the specific circumstances therefore have to be considered.[2]

---

1 *Williamson, O.*, The Economics of Organization: The Transaction Cost Approach, American Journal of Sociology 1981, 548 (556 et seqq.); *Sydow, J.*, Strategische Netzwerke, Wiesbaden 2005, p. 105, 136 et seq.; *Thorelli, H.*, Networks: Between Markets and Hierarchies, Strategic Management Journal 1986, 37 (44).

2 *Williamson, O.*, Antitrust Economics: Mergers, Contracting, and Strategic Behavior, Oxford, 1987, p. 178; *Kerber, W./Schwalbe, U.*, Ökonomische Grundlagen des Wettbewerbsrechts, in: Hirsch, G./ Montag, F./Säcker, F. (eds.), Münchener Kommentar zum Europäischen und Deutschen Wettbewerbsrecht, Bd. I, München, 2007, Rn. 1344, 1365.

The central objective of this article is to demonstrate the inherent advantages and disadvantages of network organization. These effects must be included in the economic analysis of vertical agreements. It is therefore a holistic assessment of vertical agreements in order to measure their welfare effects. These findings lead to a recommendation of how vertical agreements being used in value-added networks should be treated in competition law.

## B. Value-added networks in the economic theory

### I. Network - Organization between market and hierarchy

Under which circumstances is the market or the firm as coordinating instrument used for the implementation of economic activities? Coase (1937) pursued exactly this question in his seminal work "Theory of the Firm" whereby he laid the foundation stone for the research area of transaction economy.[3] Until then, it was assumed in economics that fully efficient markets exist and therewith trade free of charge, which is why, according to theory, falling back on firms would not be required for the implementation of transactions. The insight that markets cannot be used completely free of costs paved the way to the explanation for the existence of companies. If the transaction costs (costs for the use of the market) exceed the costs for the use of companies then entrepreneurial coordination is used for such activities. Within a company especially contract costs as well as future uncertainties can be considerably reduced.[4]

The realisation grew that the features of a transaction influence the choice of organizational form. The determining dimensions thereby are the frequency of the transaction, the extent of the uncertainties linked to the transaction and the specific investments which have to be made in the scope of the transaction.[5] The specificity of the investments plays a crucial

---

3 *Coase, R.*, The Nature of the Firm, Economica 1937; *Williamson, O.*, The Logic of Economic Organization, Journal of Law, Economics and Organization 1988.

4 *Coase, R.*, The Nature of the Firm, Economica 1937, 386 (388 et seqq.); *Schüller, A./Krüsselberg, H.-G.*,Grundbegriffe zur Ordnungstheorie und Politischen Ökonomik, Marburg, 2004, p. 104, 129; *Voigt, S.*, Institutionenökonomik, München, 2002, p. 30 et seq.

5 *Williamson, O.*, Antitrust Economics: Mergers, Contracting, and Strategic Behavior, Oxford, 1987, p. 165.

part in the decision for an organizational form. The more specific the investment is, which is required for the implementation of a transaction, the lower is its possibility for tertiary use. The owner of a specific resource is in a position of dependence since he runs the risk of being exploited. This is termed the hold-up problem, which can be met with the creation of an adequate control and monitoring system (governance structure).[6] For this purpose, special contract forms are predominantly used, which, according to this understanding, includes the market and the firm (hierarchy) as endpoints. In between, there lies a wide range of various contractual agreements (hybrids), which include the networks examined here.[7]

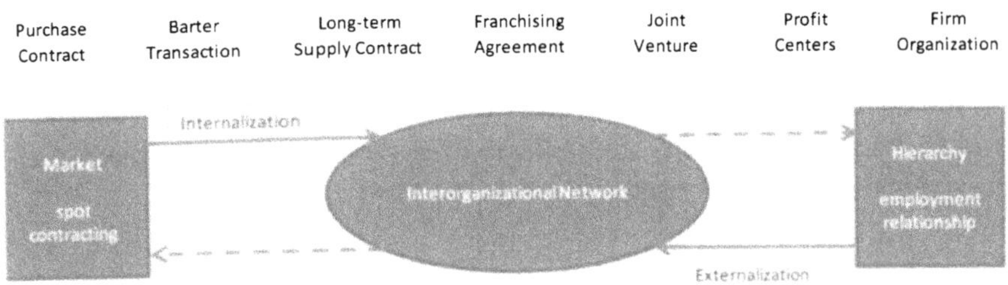


*Figure 1: The position of the network in the market-hierarchy-structure*[8]

II. Organization by contract

The transaction cost approach provides the basis for an economic theory of organization. In order to understand the many hybrid forms of organization between the endpoints market and hierarchy, it is required to draw on the insights of economic contract theory. This is because contracts are the

---

6 *Williamson, O.*, Antitrust Economics: Mergers, Contracting, and Strategic Behavior, Oxford, 1987, p. 168 et seqq.; *Voigt, S.*, Institutionenökonomik, München, 2002, p. 105 et seqq.; *Schüller, A./Krüsselberg,H.-G.*, Grundbegriffe zur Ordnungstheorie und Politischen Ökonomik, Marburg, 2004, p. 130 et seqq.

7 *Williamson, O.*, Comparative Economic Organization: The Analysis of Discrete Structural Alternatives, Administrative Science Qarterly 1991, 269 (271, 283 et seq.); *Schüller, A./Krüsselberg, H.-G.*, Grundbegriffe zur Ordnungstheorie und Politischen Ökonomik, Marburg, 2004, p. 105 et seq.; *Menard, C.*, The Economics of Hybrid Organizations, Journal of Institutional and Theoretical Economics 2004, 345 (368); *Lianos, I.*, Commercial Agency Agreements, Vertical Restraints, and the Limits of Article 81 (1) EC: Between Hierarchies and Networks, Journal of Competition Law and Economics 2007, 625 (652 et seq.).

8 Based on *Sydow, J.*, Strategische Netzwerke, Wiesbaden, 2005, p. 104.

main determinant influencing the special properties of the various governance structures.[9]

In the value-added chain, distinctions are made between suppliers, producers and distributors, who, in cooperation with each other, sell a product or a service to consumers.[10] On the one hand all actors focus on their core competencies and externalize processes that are not directly related to them. But there is still the need to maintain influence on the business relations, which take place through the aforementioned contractual agreements. One speaks of quasi-externalization. On the other hand, producers especially expand their businesses by internalizing supply and distribution channels. First and foremost, this happens in cross-border transactions without full integration. Here too, the relationship is organized by means of contractual agreements. This process is termed quasi-internalization. Consequently, the governance structure of the value-added network evolves because the variety of contractual agreements conducted between the participating parties result in a network.[11]

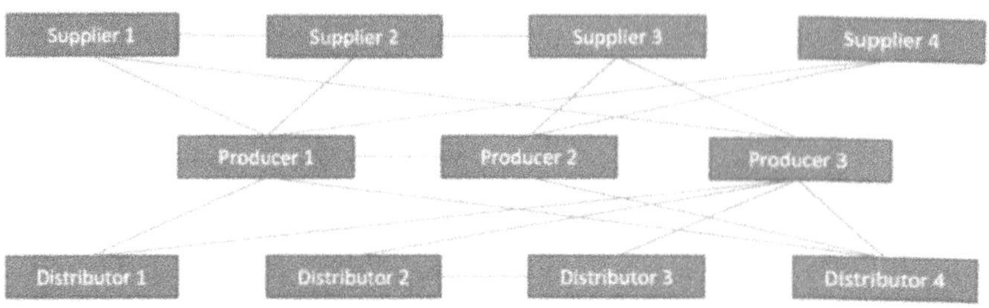


*Figure 2: The design of the value-added network*

The main purpose of contracts is to create certainty about the behaviour of the network participants. This is primarily done by assigning or limiting property rights of contracting parties and of third parties. Therefore con-

9 *Wolff, B.*, Organisation durch Verträge, München, 1994, p. 36; *Klein, B.*, Transaction Cost Determinants of „Unfair“ Contractual Arrangements, The American Economic Review 1980, 356 (361 et seq.).

10 *Kerber, W. / Schwalbe, U.*, Ökonomische Grundlagen des Wettbewerbsrechts, in: Hirsch, G. / Montag, F./ Säcker, F. (eds.), Münchener Kommentar zum Europäischen und Deutschen Wettbewerbsrecht, Bd. I, München 2007, recital 1344, 1365.

11 *Sydow, J.*, Strategische Netzwerke, Wiesbaden, 2005, p. 103 et seqq.

tracting can be principally seen as a process that defines or changes property rights.[12] The correct assignment of property rights leads to an efficient use of assets as motivation and incentive effects evolve. It may, therefore, be advantageous to transfer considerable control rights to the contract partner in order to enable him using a good more efficiently. For example, one should get the complete rights to an asset if he is the one being responsible for the functioning of the asset or the sole investor.[13]

## III. The significance of vertical agreements in value-added networks

Value-added networks make use of the efficiency-enhancing effects of contracts. They can comprise horizontal relations[14] but mostly include vertical agreements such as exclusive agreements (e.g. non-compete arrangements), selective agreements (e.g. specifications for equipment or personnel) and price/quantity agreements. All of these can impact the efficiency-raising effects. For instance, incentive problems occurring in value-added chains can be solved, which emerge as a consequence of informational asymmetries and the misallocation of property rights. In particular, vertical agreements enable the performance contributions of the contract partners to be more efficiently monitored. Overall, these special contracts ensure that adequate control and monitoring mechanisms (governance) are created according to the described considerations based on transaction cost theory.[15] Since such agreements restrict the scope of action of the contract partner, the term vertical restriction is also commonly used.[16] Effects restricting the competition can emerge if, among other

---

12 *Libecap, G.*, Contracting for Property Rights, Cambridge, 1989, p. 11; *Wolff, B.*, Organisation durch Verträge, München, 1994, p. 42.

13 *Grossman, S. / Hart, O.*, The Costs and Benefits of Ownership, Journal of Political Economy 1986, 691 (716 et seq.); *Hart, O./ Moore, J.*, Property Rights and the Nature of the Firm, Journal of Political Economy 1990, 1119 (1131 et seqq.).

14 *Martinek, M.*, Vertriebsrecht als Rechtsgebiet, in: Martinek, M. / Semler, F.-J. / Habermeier, S. / Flohr, E. (eds.), Handbuch des Vertriebsrechts, München, 2010, § 1 recital 45; *Martinek, M.*, Betriebs- und absatzwirtschaftliche Hintergründe von Vertriebsverträgen, in: Martinek, M. / Semler, F.-J. / Habermeier, S. / Flohr, E. (eds.), Handbuch des Vertriebsrechts, München, 2010, § 2 recital 14 et seq.

15 *Williamson, O.*, Antitrust Economics: Mergers, Contracting, and Strategic Behavior, Oxford, 1987, p. 172 et seqq.

16 *Kerber, W./Schwalbe, U.*, Ökonomische Grundlagen des Wettbewerbsrechts, in: Hirsch, G./ Montag, F./Säcker, F. (eds.), Münchener Kommentar zum Europä-

things, monopoly power is extended to other value-adding stages or entry-deterrent strategies are enforced by means of vertical agreements. In particular, exclusionary practices can furthermore be used to raise rival costs.[17]

Vertical agreements required for the organization of value-added networks may accordingly be restrictive of competition by effect. But they have efficiency-enhancing effects as well, which is why a consistent assessment from the point of view of competition economics is difficult.[18] Nevertheless, vertical agreements which cause price maintenance or territorial restrictions are as a basic principle critically viewed, and are regularly prohibited in competition law. For instance Article 101 of the Treaty on the Functioning of the European Union considers these agreements as hardcore restrictions.

Lafontaine and Slade (2010) show that vertical agreements are completed mostly for reasons of efficiency and not for the extension of market power.[19] They analyze several studies that examine costs and benefits of vertical restraints. Although the number of studies is small and the studies focus on certain branches of industry some essential insights can be derived. For consumers, there is a benefit gain, or at least, vertical restraints do not negatively impact them. It is shown that vertical agreements lead to lower costs, a higher consumption or a higher survival rate of businesses.[20] Menard (2004) also emphasizes that vertical agreements generally cause procompetitive effects because coordination is facilitated.[21] Vertical

---

ischen und Deutschen Wettbewerbsrecht, Bd. I, München, 2007, recital 1338, 1340.

17 *Williamson, O.*, Antitrust Economics: Mergers, Contracting, and Strategic Behavior, Oxford, 1987, p. 172 et seqq.; *Aghion, P./ Bolton, P.*, Contracts as a Barrier to Entry, The American Economic Review, 1987, 388 (398 et seq.); *Salop, S./ Scheffman, D.*, Raising Rivals' Costs, The American Economic Review 1983, 267 (267).

18 *Williamson, O.*, Antitrust Economics: Mergers, Contracting, and Strategic Behavior, Oxford, 1987, p. 178; *Kerber, W./Schwalbe, U.*, Ökonomische Grundlagen des Wettbewerbsrechts, in: Hirsch, G./ Montag, F./Säcker, F. (eds.), Münchener Kommentar zum Europäischen und Deutschen Wettbewerbsrecht, Bd. I, München, 2007, recital. 1344, 1365

19 *Lafontaine, F. / Slade, M.*, Transaction Cost Economics and Vertical Market Restrictions – Evidence, The Antitrust Bulletin 2010, 587 (598).

20 *Lafontaine, F. / Slade, M.*, Transaction Cost Economics and Vertical Market Restrictions – Evidence, The Antitrust Bulletin 2010, 607 et seq.

21 *Menard, C.*, The Economics of Hybrid Organizations, Journal of Institutional and Theoretical Economics 2004, 365 et seq.

agreements are used to overcome disincentives. The main reason to use these contracts is the governance of network relations rather than the creation of competition restrictions. A number of empirical studies prove these results.[22]

The effects of vertical agreements depend mainly on their respective market circumstances. Generally it can be stated that the essential requirement for anti-competitive effects of vertical agreements lies in an already existing, imperfectly competitive market - like for instance the presence of market power on one value-adding stage.[23] As long as there is no evidence for oligopolistic collusion and no market power exists, it can be assumed that efficiency-enhancing effects of vertical agreements will prevail.[24] In an experimental study, Smith (2011) accordingly demonstrates that exclusive agreements should be subject to exhaustive competitive examination in industries when market entry is possible only at high fixed costs. This is because foreclosure effects are more likely in such situations.[25] In addition, the nature of the good traded between the value-added stages has a significant impact on the welfare effects of vertical agreements. The rationale for vertical agreements is predominantly valid if the transaction comprises complex, heterogeneous or rarely purchased goods. Furthermore, cartel agreements are easier to enforce when a product is homogeneous. Simple industry products which can be used polyvalent in the production process are, therefore, more often affected by collusive behaviour than

22 *Henning, C. / Henningsen, G. / Henningsen, A.*, Network and Transaction Cost, American Journal of Agricultural Economics 2012, 377 (384); *Geyskens, I. / Steenkamp, J-B. / Kumar, N.*, Make, Buy, or Ally: A Transaction Cost Theory Meta-Analysis, The Academy of Management Journal 2006, 519 (520 et seqq.); *Martimort, D.*, Exclusive Dealing, Common Agency, and Multiprincipals Incentive Theory, The RAND Journal of Economics 1996, 1 (27 et seq.).

23 *Posner, R.*, Antitrust Law, Chicago University of Chicago Press 2001, 194 et seq.; *Williamson, O.*, Assessing Vertical Market Restrictions: Antitrust Ramifications of the Transaction Cost Approach, University of Pennsylvania Law Review 1979, 953 (962, 967); *Rey, P. / Stiglitz, J.*, The Role of Exclusive Territories in Producers Competition, RAND Journal of Economics 1995, 431 (440).

24 *Williamson, O.*, Assessing Vertical Market Restrictions: Antitrust Ramifications of the Transaction Cost Approach, University of Pennsylvania Law Review 1979, 953, 993.

25 *Smith, A.*, An Experimental Study of Exclusive Contracts, International Journal of Industrial Organization 29 2011, 4 (8).

heterogeneous goods. So the property of the product should be taken into account for the competitive assessment of vertical agreements.[26]

In sum, several general statements on the welfare effects of vertical agreements can be made. They are mostly used to facilitate coordination. Efficiency aspects play a crucial role. Certain preconditions must be present in the market structure so that vertical restraints can impair effective competition. But still it is mostly argued that the use of vertical agreements should lead to a case-by-case analysis.[27] In the next section the problems occurring with case-by-case analyses and the benefits of simple and generally valid rules will be illustrated.

## C. The advantage of general rules

Specific market interventions like the individual competitive assessment of business behaviour frequently result in considerable problems. It will be shown that the elaboration of generally applicable rules that form a general framework is in principle superior to the enforcement of law by individual examinations.[28] General rules should hereto fulfil the following three conditions: They must have prevalence for all market actors. Furthermore, they must be abstract, so that they may not serve any particular interests.

26 *Telser, L.*, Why should manufacturers want fair trade?, Journal of Law and Economics 1960, 86 (94 et seq.); *Ippolito, P.*, Resale Price Maintenance: Empirical Evidence from Litigation, Journal of Law and Economics 43(2) 1991, 263 (282 et seqq.).

27 *Rey, P. / Stiglitz, J.*, The Role of Exclusive Territories in Producers Competition, RAND Journal of Economics 1995, 431, 446; *Kerber, W./Schwalbe, U.*, Ökonomische Grundlagen des Wettbewerbsrechts, in: Hirsch, G./ Montag, F./Säcker, F. (eds.), Münchener Kommentar zum Europäischen und Deutschen Wettbewerbsrecht, Bd. I, München, 2007, recital 1396.

28 *Hayek, F.*, Law, Legislation and Liberty, Chicago, 2013, p. 120 et seqq., 359 et seq.; *Hoppmann, E.*, Unwissenheit, Wirtschaftsordnung und Staatsgewalt, in: V. Vanberg (eds.), Freiheit, Wettbewerb und Wirtschaftsordnung, Freiburg 1999, p. 135 (150 et seq.); *Vanberg, V.*, Rules & Choice in Economics, London, 1994, p. 178 et seqq.; *Christiansen, A / Kerber, W.*, Competition Policy With Optimally Differentiated Rules Instead Of „Per Se Rules vs. Rule of Reason", Journal of Competition Law and Economics 2005, 215 (219 et seq.).

Ultimately, general rules must be certain which ensures that the legal consequences of the regulation are objectively determinable.[29]

There are three main arguments that support the thesis that a general legal framework is superior to the use of single-case regulations. First, it is assumed that general rules stabilize expectations and guarantee predictability. This legal certainty for economic actors increases efficiency in market economies.[30] Second, a reliable legal framework prevents the enforcement of individual interests. A broad application of individual decision-making processes involves the risk that interest groups are able to influence decision-making in their favour. Rent seeking is less likely if generally applicable rules are adopted.[31] Lastly, general rules allow for the most efficient use of knowledge. A general legal framework is capable of reducing knowledge and decision problems of authorities and courts since the application of simple rules requires less provision of information in contrast to a case-by-case analysis.[32]

Therefore competition authorities must realize that not each business conduct is controllable. It should instead ensure that practices are in accordance with general rules. Economic research should not influence competition policy through the use of economic instruments during the examina-

---

29 *Hoppmann, E.*, Fusionskontrolle, Tübingen 1972, p. 68; *Schmidtchen, D.*, Property Rights, Freiheit und Wettbewerbspolitik, Tübingen, 1983, p. 11; *Hayek, F.*, Die Verfassung der Freiheit, Tübingen, 2005, p. 182 et seqq., 194 et seqq.

30 *Voigt, S. / Schmidt, A.*, Making European Merger Policy More Predictable, Heidelberg, 2005, p. 1 et seqq.; *Christiansen, A / Kerber, W.*, Competition Policy With Optimally Differentiated Rules Instead Of „Per Se Rules vs. Rule of Reason", Journal of Competition Law and Economics 2005, 215, 219.

31 *Eucken, W.*, Grundsätze der Wirtschaftspolitik, Tübingen 2004, p. 170 et seqq., *Brennan, G./ Buchanan, J.*, The Reason of Rules: Constitutional Political Economy, Cambridge, 1985, p. 72 et seq., 133 et seq.; *Christiansen, A / Kerber, W.*, Competition Policy With Optimally Differentiated Rules Instead Of „Per Se Rules vs. Rule of Reason", Journal of Competition Law and Economics 2005, 215, 219 et seq., 233 et seq.

32 *Hayek, F.*, Law, Legislation and Liberty, Chicago, 2013, p. 14 et seq., 55 et seq.; *Heiner, R.*, Rule-Governed Behavior in Evolution and Human Society, Constitutional Political Economy 1990, p. 19 (41 et seq.), *Vanberg, V.*, Rules & Choice in Economics, London, 1994, p. 186 et seq.; *Christiansen, A / Kerber, W.*, Competition Policy With Optimally Differentiated Rules Instead Of „Per Se Rules vs. Rule of Reason", Journal of Competition Law and Economics 2005, 215, 220, 233.

tion of each individual case. Instead the basic economic insights should be used to create a general institutional framework.[33]

Competition policy should therefore classify categories of business behaviours (Bx). A first category of behaviours should be clearly classified as per se harmful or beneficial for the functioning of effective competition. This category should be excluded from the examination procedure. In a second step the more complex cases should be examined. Information regarding the competitive effects of this group of agreements must be collected and the findings should then be incorporated into the design of a rule-based solution.[34]

The following figure can serve as a decision aid to create rules for different types of competition cases. If welfare (w) is depicted in a positive range - these cases have efficiency-enhancing effects - and in contrast, negative values represent competition constraining effects.[35]

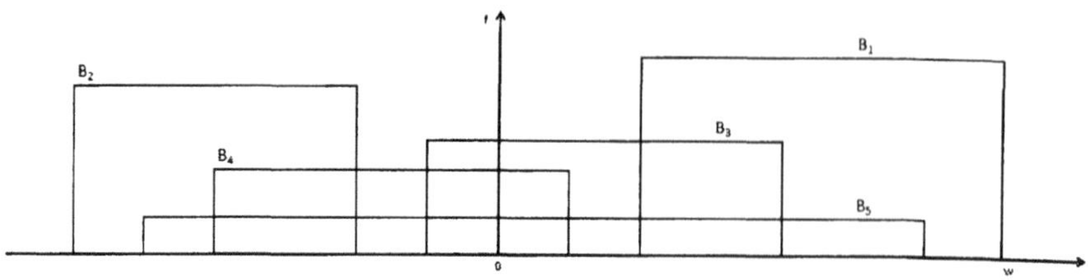


*Figure 3: Business behaviour and their welfare effects*[36]

Figure 3 shows two distinct cases that consistently lead to welfare gains on the one hand ($B_1$) and on the other hand to welfare losses ($B_2$). The de-

33 *Christiansen, A / Kerber, W.*, Competition Policy With Optimally Differentiated Rules Instead Of „Per Se Rules vs. Rule of Reason", Journal of Competition Law and Economics 2005, 215, 237.

34 *Beckner, F. / Salop, S.*, Decision Theory and Antitrust Rules, Antitrust Law Journal 1999, 41 (42, 59 et seq.); *Christiansen, A / Kerber, W.*, Competition Policy With Optimally Differentiated Rules Instead Of „Per Se Rules vs. Rule of Reason", Journal of Competition Law and Economics 2005, 215, 222.

35 *Christiansen, A / Kerber, W.*, Competition Policy With Optimally Differentiated Rules Instead Of „Per Se Rules vs. Rule of Reason", Journal of Competition Law and Economics 2005, 215, 229 et seq.

36 *Christiansen, A / Kerber, W.*, Competition Policy With Optimally Differentiated Rules Instead Of „Per Se Rules vs. Rule of Reason", Journal of Competition Law and Economics 2005, 215, 230.

rived competition rules should permit $B_1$ and prohibit $B_2$. However, most often one cannot achieve such clear results regarding the welfare effects ($B_3$, $B_4$, $B_5$). In these cases it is recommended to design differentiated rules that minimize the sum of decision errors and regulatory costs.[37] It can be stated that the design of differentiated competition rules commonly does not generate additional benefit for cases with unequal welfare allocations ($B_3$, $B_4$) because there is a small potential to reduce decision errors, whereas rising regulatory costs are not compensated. In comparison the case of $B_5$ has a high potential to reduce decision errors. For that reason it is worthwhile to create differentiated rules, even if regulatory costs rise sharply.[38]

According to the considerations made so far it can be assumed that simple and general rules are most suitable for the purposes of a perfect competition policy. An economic analysis of individual cases should, if at all, be reserved for a small number of cases where an assessment of welfare effects is very ambiguous. The trade-off between minimizing decision errors and rising regulatory costs through a higher differentiation of competition rules has to be taken into account.

Welfare effects of vertical agreements are ambiguous (see section B. III.). That is why general competition rules might not be applicable. The following passage deals with the inherent advantages and disadvantages of networks. These are to be included in the evaluation for an in depth analysis of vertical agreements used in value-added networks.

## D. Economic analysis of network organization

### I. Advantages of the network organization

Networks as an organizational form are situated between the two extremes of market and hierarchy. Thereby, as illustrated in the diagram, features of

37 *Christiansen, A / Kerber, W.*, Competition Policy With Optimally Differentiated Rules Instead Of „Per Se Rules vs. Rule of Reason", Journal of Competition Law and Economics, 2005, 215, 229 et seq.

38 *Christiansen, A / Kerber, W.*, Competition Policy With Optimally Differentiated Rules Instead Of „Per Se Rules vs. Rule of Reason", Journal of Competition Law and Economics 2005, 215. 230 et seq.

the market and the firm are combined whereas other features are deliberately omitted.

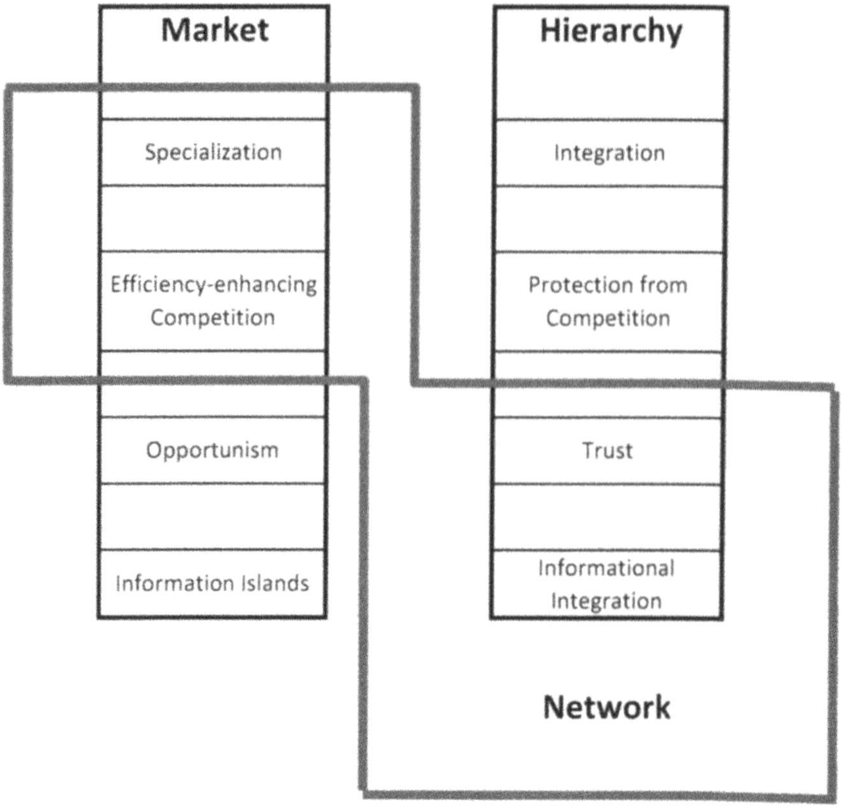


*Figure 4: Features of the enterprise network*[39]

Based on figure 2, I will hereafter describe the most important advantages of network organizations within a value-added chain. In addition, further positive features of networks are added where it is deemed suitable. Mostly, the advantages described do not occur together, but rather selectively depending on the kind of network. Advantages arise both for network participants (internal advantages) as well as for end consumers (external ad-

39 *Siebert, H.*, Ökonomische Analyse von Unternehmensnetzwerken, in: Sydow, J. (ed.), Management von Netzwerkorganisationen, Wiesbaden, 2010, p. 7 (11).

vantages) and are, for reasons of simplicity, illustrated together. It is assumed that in most cases end consumers benefit of the internal network advantages anyway so that internal and external advantages are somehow intertwined.

### 1. Economies of scale and scope

An important advantage of networks lies in the bundling of the resources of the individual network participants. By outsourcing processes economies of scale can be generated through the division of labour. In this way, each network member can specialize on their core competences.[40] Accordingly, Walker and Weber (1984 & 1987) were able to prove in examinations of entrepreneurial decisions regarding organization in the automotive industry that companies outsource production processes in the area of supplies due to comparative cost advantages.[41] Moreover capacities in the network organization are more efficiently used and unnecessary duplication of activities is avoided. In this way, it may have efficiency-enhancing effects if, for instance, the parallel operation of several sales locations is quantitatively restricted. The consumer can benefit from the reduction of fixed costs in form of reduced product prices, which can be achieved by saving costs to run the shop.[42] Research and development services are

---

40 *Siebert, H.*, Ökonomische Analyse von Unternehmensnetzwerken, in: Sydow, J. (ed.), Management von Netzwerkorganisationen, Wiesbaden, 2010, p. 21 et seq.; *Williamson, O.*, The Economics of Organization: The Transaction Cost Approach, American Journal of Sociology 1981, 548 (556 et seqq.); *Johnston, R./Lawrence, P.*, Beyond Vertical Integration – the Rise of the Value-Adding Partnership, Harvard Business Review 1988, 94 (99); *Hecker, A.*, Outsourcing als Coopetition – Eine spieltheoretische Analyse des Zusammenhangs von Kooperation und Kompetition, in: Schreyögg, G./Sydow, J (eds.), Kooperation und Konkurrenz – Managementforschung, Wiesbaden, 2007, p. 1 (9).

41 *Walker, G./Weber, D.*, A Transaction Cost Approach to Make-or-Buy Decisions, Administrative Science Quarterly 1984, 373, (385 et seq.); *Walker, G. / Weber, D.*, Supplier Competition, Uncertainty, and Make-or-Buy Decisions, The Academy of Management Journal 1987, 589 (591 et seqq.).

42 *Besanko, D./Perry, M.*, Exclusive Dealing in a Spatial Model of Retail Competition, International Journal of Industrial Organization 1994, 297 (318); *Kerber, W./ Schwalbe, U.*, Ökonomische Grundlagen des Wettbewerbsrechts, in: Hirsch, G./ Montag, F./Säcker, F. (eds.), Münchener Kommentar zum Europäischen und Deutschen Wettbewerbsrecht, Bd. I, München, 2007, recital 1357 et seq.; *Secrie-*

those corporate processes which are often not conducted by the producers themselves in value-added networks. Balakrishnan and Wernerfelt (1986) show in an empirical study that the standard of vertical integration is lower in industries with regular technological innovations, which suggests that R&D activities are rather outsourced in these cases.[43]

Furthermore, network participation allows for economies of scope since the joint use of resources and the bundling of complex and cost intensive activities lead to synergy effects and cost savings. Additionally, unsuccessful research efforts can be compensated in the network and the possibility of R&D successes is increased.[44] Risk-sharing can be a central motive to participate in a network. The costs of huge investments can be split between several network participants. Regarding planned market access, for instance, the risk of failing can be reduced for individual companies.[45]

## 2. Trust, reciprocity and social capital

Since the contracts for the coordination of networks are inevitably incomplete to a certain extent trust between the network participants becomes paramount as complementary component.[46] Long-term cooperation in net-

---

*ru, O.*, The Economic Theory of Vertical Restraints, Journal of Economic Surveys 2006, 797 (811); *Männel, B.*, Netzwerke in der Zulieferindustrie: Konzepte – Gestaltungsmerkmale – betriebswirtschaftliche Wirkungen, Wiesbaden, 1996, p. 32; *Habermeier, S./ Ehlers, J.*, Art. 81 EG Vertikale Wettbewerbsbeschränkungen, in: Hirsch, G./Montag, F./Säcker, F. (eds.), Münchener Kommentar zum Europäischen und Deutschen Wettbewerbsrecht, Bd. I, München 2007, recital 248.

43 *Balakrishnan, S./Wernerfelt, B.*, Technical Change, Competition and Vertical Integration, Strategic Management Journal 1986, 347 (351 et seq., 357); *Siebert, H.*, Ökonomische Analyse von Unternehmensnetzwerken, in: Sydow, J. (ed.), Management von Netzwerkorganisationen, Wiesbaden, 2010, p. 22.

44 *Siebert, H.*, Ökonomische Analyse von Unternehmensnetzwerken, in: Sydow, J. (ed.), Management von Netzwerkorganisationen, Wiesbaden, 2010, p. 17, 21 et seq.

45 *Menard, C.*, The Economics of Hybrid Organizations, Journal of Institutional and Theoretical Economics 2004, 345, 357 et seq.; *Männel, B.*, Netzwerke in der Zulieferindustrie: Konzepte – Gestaltungsmerkmale – betriebswirtschaftliche Wirkungen, Wiesbaden, 1996, p. 32.

46 *Männel, B.*, Netzwerke in der Zulieferindustrie: Konzepte – Gestaltungsmerkmale – betriebswirtschaftliche Wirkungen, Wiesbaden, 1996, p. 363; *Bradach, J./ Eccles, R.*, Price, Authority, and Trust: From Ideal Types to Plural Forms, Annual Review of Sociology 1989, 97 (104 et seqq.); *Powell, W.*, Weder Markt noch Hie-

work relations leads to increased trust between the partners of interaction and facilitated cooperation. One speaks of dynamic transaction costs, which are reduced due to the cooperation.[47] Long-term exchange relations develop in contrast to simple transactions.[48] In this way, repeated interactions allow legal relations without agreements fixed by contract. By means of the general bonding of the network partners an attitude of standardised social expectations develops within the network whereby self-supporting sanctioning mechanisms emerge, which makes it possible for the entire system to function without external institutions. Therefore internal Institutions, like conventions or private rules, which do not have to rely on the state for the enforcement of contracts play a more dominant role.[49]

If services are performed by the network participants without expecting immediate counter services this is referred to as general reciprocity. The participants are aware of the long-term gain of the cooperation, which is why one-sided services are provided with the knowledge about future compensation. This principle is supported by an effective sanctioning

---

rarchie: Netzwerkartige Organisationsformen, in: Kenis, P./Schneider, V., (eds.), Organisation und Netzwerk: Institutionelle Steuerung in Wirtschaft und Politik, Wien, 1996, p. 222; *Teubner, G.*, Netzwerk als Vertragsverbund – Virtuelle Unternehmen, Franchising, Just-in-time in sozialwissenschaftlicher und juristischer Sicht, Baden-Baden, 2004, p. 49.

47 *Langlois, R./Richardson, P.*, Firms, Markets and Economic Change – A Dynamic Theory of Business Institutions, New York, 1995, p. 35 et seqq.; *Kerber, W./ Schwalbe,U.*, Ökonomische Grundlagen des Wettbewerbsrechts, in: Hirsch, G./ Montag, F./Säcker, F. (eds.), Münchener Kommentar zum Europäischen und Deutschen Wettbewerbsrecht, Bd. I, München, 2007, recital 1363; *Morgan, R./ Hunt S.*, The Commitment-Trust Theory of Relationship Marketing, Journal of Marketing 1994, 20 (25).

48 *Morgan, R./Hunt S.*, The Commitment-Trust Theory of Relationship Marketing, Journal of Marketing 1994, 20, 21; *Dwyer, R./Schurr, P./Oh, S.*, Developing Buyer-Seller Relationships, Journal of Marketing 1987, 11 (12 et seqq.).

49 *Teubner, G.*, Netzwerk als Vertragsverbund – Virtuelle Unternehmen, Franchising, Just-in-time in sozialwissenschaftlicher und juristischer Sicht, Baden-Baden, 2004, p. 33, 44; *Powell, W.*, Weder Markt noch Hierarchie: Netzwerkartige Organisationsformen, in: Kenis, P./Schneider, V. (eds.), Organisation und Netzwerk: Institutionelle Steuerung in Wirtschaft und Politik, Wien, 1996, p. 255 et seq.; *Voigt, S.*, Institutionenökonomik, München, 2002, p. 39; *Uzzi, B.*, Social Structure and Competition in Interfirm Networks: The Paradox of Embeddedness, Adminstrative Science Quarterly 1997, 35 (43, 61); *Geyskens, I. / Steenkamp, J-B. / Kumar, N.*, Make, Buy, or Ally: A Transaction Cost Theory Meta-Analysis, The Academy of Management Journal 2006, 519, 522.

mechanism since network members run the risk of being excluded from the profitable network if services are not performed.[50] It is common to include clauses in the contracts within networks which make the exclusion from the network possible in case the rules are breached or certain norms are not accepted.[51] Likewise, the network member's possibility to voluntarily withdraw also has its advantages. Hirschman (1970) points out that such feedback processes provide important information about the attractiveness of the organizational form. In general though, the cooperation within the network is designed as long-term, which is why the option exit is rather rarely used compared to referring to problems (voice),[52] since stable, repeated transactions within a network reduce the potential benefit gained from opportunistic behaviour. The informal institutions, which evolve in a network, have the potential to overcome the commitment problem by means of a multilateral reputation mechanism.[53] Trust and the commitment to cooperative behaviour are therefore factors which preferably emerge in networks. Morgan and Hunt (1994) prove in an empirical study that trust and commitment to the business relation have positive effects on the cooperation between the actors participating in the network

50 *Teubner, G.*, Netzwerk als Vertragsverbund – Virtuelle Unternehmen, Franchising, Just-in-time in sozialwissenschaftlicher und juristischer Sicht, Baden-Baden, 2004, p. 121, 125; *Morgan, R./Hunt S.*, The Commitment-Trust Theory of Relationship Marketing, Journal of Marketing 1994, 20, 24 et seq.; *Telser, L.*, A Theory of Self-Enforcing Agreements, The Journal of Business 1980, 27 (43 et seq.); *Kali, R.*, Endogenous Business Networks, The Journal of Law Economics & Organization 1999, 615 (619).

51 *Lianos I.*, Commercial Agency Agreements, Vertical Restraints, and the Limits of Article 81 (1) EC: Between Hierarchies and Networks, Journal of Competition Law and Economics 2007, 625, 659; *Menard, C.*, The Economics of Hybrid Organizations, Journal of Institutional and Theoretical Economics 2004, 345, 351.

52 *Hirschman, A.*, Exit, Voice, and Loyalty – Responses to Decline in Firms, Organizations, and States, Cambridge, 1970, p. 182 et seqq.; *Uzzi, B.*, Social Structure and Competition in Interfirm Networks: The Paradox of Embeddedness, Adminstrative Science Quarterly 1997, 35, 61; *Semlinger, K.*, Effizienz und Autonomie in Zulieferungsnetzwerken – Zum strategischen Gehalt von Kooperation, in: Sydow, J. (eds.), Management von Netzwerkorganisationen, Wiesbaden 2010, p. 52 et seq.

53 *Greif, A.*, Contract Enforceability and Economic Institutions in Early Trade: The Maghribi Traders' Coalition, The American Economic Review 1993, 525 (533 et seqq.); *Kali, R.*, Endogenous Business Networks, The Journal of Law Economics & Organization 1999, 615, 616 et seq.

and thereby significantly contribute to the success of the business.[54] Bodensteiner, Hünerberg and Mann (2009) reach similar results by discovering in an empirical study of distributor-producer-relations that trust has positive effects on the willingness to cooperate.[55]

Furthermore, the formation of social capital is favoured within network structures. An additional advantage, for instance, lies in the matching of suitable pairs. In this way, employees and assets are employed in their most productive way within the network.[56] In order to strengthen these mechanisms specific measures are suitable such as, for instance, setting up communication platforms.[57] This includes horizontal and vertical cooperational relations for the planning of joint promotion measures, for the design of the strategic marketing concept or also for the cooperation with respect to competitors.[58] In distribution systems the sales organs exchange their experiences or appear in an advisory function before the head office. These functions need not be explicitly agreed upon and often emerge out of the on-going cooperation. Advisory boards may emerge, which, depending on the situation, also take on managing tasks in the system.[59] Moreover, Smith (2011) shows in an experiment that communication be-

---

54 *Morgan, R./Hunt S.,* The Commitment-Trust Theory of Relationship Marketing, Journal of Marketing 1994, 20, 22, 24, 29 et seq.

55 *Bodensteiner, K./Hünerberg, R./Mann, A.*, Partnerbindung in Hersteller-Händler-Kooperationen – Das Beispiel der Automobilwirtschaft, in: Hünerberg, R./Mann, A. (eds.), Ganzheitliche Unternehmensführung in dynamischen Märkten, Wiesbaden, 2009, p. 435 (443 et seq., 452 et seq.).

56 *Fafchamps, M./ Minten, B.*, Returns to Social Network Capital Among Traders, Oxford, 2002, p. 173 (176 et seq., 196); *Kranton, R.*, Reciprocal Exchange: A Self-Sustaining System, The American Economic Review 1996, 830 (845 et seq.); *Kali, R.*, Endogenous Business Networks, The Journal of Law Economics & Organization 1999, 615 617, 634.

57 *Bodensteiner, K./Hünerberg, R./Mann, A.*, Partnerbindung in Hersteller-Händler-Kooperationen – Das Beispiel der Automobilwirtschaft, in: Hünerberg, R./Mann, A. (eds.), Ganzheitliche Unternehmensführung in dynamischen Märkten, Wiesbaden, 2009, p. 455 et seq.

58 *Martinek, M.,* Vertriebsrecht als Rechtsgebiet, in: Martinek, M. / Semler, F.-J. / Habermeier, S. / Flohr, E. (eds.), Handbuch des Vertriebsrechts, München, 2010, § 2, recital 14 et seq.

59 *Martinek, M.,* Vertriebsrecht als Rechtsgebiet, in: Martinek, M. / Semler, F.-J. / Habermeier, S. / Flohr, E. (eds.), Handbuch des Vertriebsrechts, München, 2010, § 1, recital 45.

tween distributors rather leads to less foreclosure effects.[60] Furthermore, the solidarity between the network participants can be strengthened with mutual specific investments and change barriers whereby a trustful cooperation develops.[61] Additionally, granting economic advantages such as, for example, quantity or loyalty discounts or also assurances of exclusive contracts have positive effects on the cooperation.[62]

Especially for cross-border business the organizational form of a network is chosen so as to revert to the benefits of informal institutions. One advantage is that networks can be established and dissolved quickly.[63] But foremost, the absence of legal frameworks or missing jurisdiction can be compensated with informal institutions. Networks therefore serve as efficient instruments for contract enforcement.[64]

**Excursus: Historical examples for trust and multilateral reputation mechanisms in networks**

The Maghribi-Traders researched by Greif (1993) form a network underpinned with informal institutions. This 11th century coalition of Mediterranean merchants reverted to informal institutions so as to overcome the informational asymmetries between merchants and their travelling salesmen. They further developed a multilateral reputation mechanism, which allowed them to exclude agents who were not operating in the interest of the principals. In this way, an effective sanctioning mechanism was estab-

60 *Smith, A.*, An Experimental Study of Exclusive Contracts, International Journal of Industrial Organization 29 2011, 4, 7 et seq.

61 *Masten, S.*, Equity, Opportunism, and the Design of Contractual Relations, Journal of Institutional and Theoretical Economics 1988, 180 (189 et seqq.); *Siebert, H.*, Ökonomische Analyse von Unternehmensnetzwerken, in: Sydow, J. (ed.), Management von Netzwerkorganisationen, Wiesbaden, 2010, p. 13; *Bodensteiner, K./ Hünerberg, R./Mann, A., Partnerbindung in Hersteller-Händler-Kooperationen – Das Beispiel der Automobilwirtschaft*, in: Hünerberg, R./Mann, A. (eds.) Ganzheitliche Unternehmensführung in dynamischen Märkten, Wiesbaden, 2009, p. 446 et seq., 452 et seq.

62 *Bodensteiner, K./Hünerberg, R./Mann, A.*, Partnerbindung in Hersteller-Händler-Kooperationen – Das Beispiel der Automobilwirtschaft, in: Hünerberg, R./Mann, A. (eds.), Ganzheitliche Unternehmensführung in dynamischen Märkten, Wiesbaden, 2009, p. 444 et seqq., 452 et seq., 456.

63 *Schüller, A./Krüsselberg, H.-G.,*Grundbegriffe zur Ordnungstheorie und Politischen Ökonomik, Marburg, 2004, p.106.

64 *Kali, R.*, Endogenous Business Networks, The Journal of Law Economics & Organization 1999, 616, 618 et seq.; *Thorelli, H.*, Networks: Between Markets and Hierarchies, Strategic Management Journal 1986, 37. 45.

lished, which allowed for a long-distance trade without formal contracts and therefore with low transaction costs.[65]

In the scope of the transformations of the economic system in China, which have been taking place since 1979, it could be ascertained that network-like relations were increasingly resorted to. This organizational form also termed Guanxi is based on long-term relations and therefrom emerging mutual trust. Boisot and Child (1996) trace this development back to the fact that the missing institutional framework is compensated by informal institutions emerging in the networks.[66] In an empirical study Xin and Pearce (1996) show that such informal relations are increasingly established as protection against risks such as, for instance, expropriation by the government.[67]

In a study on the contract design of African businesses Bigsten with other authors (1998) ascertained that long-term contracts based on trust are more frequently closed between producers, suppliers, and purchasers so as to protect themselves against undeveloped institutional frameworks. Multilateral reputation mechanisms play a likewise important part in the assertion of contractual claims.[68]

### 3. Efficient use of knowledge

Networks take on a productive role in the scope of knowledge utilization since companies are exposed to the problem of having to permanently assert themselves on the market as well as adapt through innovation and flexibility. Knowledge thereby poses an essential competition parameter

---

65 *Greif, A.*, Contract Enforceability and Economic Institutions in Early Trade: The Maghribi Traders' Coalition, The American Economic Review 1993, 525. 525 ff; *Kali, R.*, Endogenous Business Networks, The Journal of Law Economics & Organization 1999, 615. 616 et seq.

66 *Boisot, M/Child, J.*, From Fiefs to Clans and Network Capitalism: Explaining China's Emerging Economic Order, Administrative Science Quarterly 1996, 600 (604 et seqq., 612 et seqq.).

67 *Xin, K./Pearce, J.*, Guanxi: Connections as Substitutes for Formal Institutional Support, Academy of Management Journal 1996, 1641 (1644 et seq., 1652 et seq.).

68 *Bigsten, A./Collier, P./Dercon, S./Fafchamps, M./Gauthier, B./Gunning, J./Oduro, A./ Oostendorp, R./Patillo, C./Soderbom, M./ Teal, F./ Zeufack, A.*, Contract Flexibility and Dispute Resolution in African Manufacturing, The Journal of Development Studies 2000, 1 (11 et seqq., 22 et seqq.).

for companies, which is why the allocation and the use of knowledge is a central task for companies.[69] Companies often establish cooperation so as to gain access to knowledge.[70] A starting point for efficient knowledge utilization is offered by Hayek (1945), who ascertains that knowledge is available in a decentralised way with every single actor. Consequently, centralised knowledge utilization is no superior solution and the use of knowledge should occur in a decentralised way.[71] Networks offer a structural arrangement which can contribute to using the decentrally existing knowledge efficiently. Additionally, the will for experimentation and the creativity of the interacting agents is sustained while at the same time maintaining a mutual order of action in the scope of the network organization. Modern information technology plays an important role in the use of distributed knowledge, which allows the connected actors to access the network knowledge.[72] Furthermore, learning and spillover effects are favoured by network structures. The best prerequisites are created within the network for the fast implementation of superior production processes or innovative organizational structures.[73] Accordingly, Gnyawali, He and Madhavan (2006) show that companies have a better competition position by participating in networks.[74]

---

69 *Picot, A./Reichwald, R./Wigand, R.*, Die grenzenlose Unternehmung – Information, Organisation und Management, Wiesbaden 2001, p. 22 et seqq.; *Hayek, F.*, The Use of Knowledge in Society, The American Economic Review 1945, 519 (524); *Williamson, O.*, Comparative Economic Organization: The Analysis of Discrete Structural Alternatives, Administrative Science Qarterly 1991, 277 et seq.

70 *Richardson, G.*, The Organization of Industry, Economic Journal 1972, 883 (893 et seqq.); *Staber, U.*, Sleeping with the Enemy, oder Vorsicht vor falschen Freunden? – Sozioökonomische Überlegungen zum Dilemma der Coopetition, in: Schreyögg, G./Sydow, J. (eds.): Kooperation und Konkurrenz – Managementforschung, Wiesbaden, 2007, p. 259.

71 *Hayek, F.*, The Use of Knowledge in Society, The American Economic Review 1945, 519, 521 et seqq.

72 *Richter, N.*, Das Unternehmen als dezentrale Wissensordnung und die Vernetzung durch digitale Informationstechnologien, Open Journal of Knowledge Management 2010, 29 (32).

73 *Siebert, H.*, Ökonomische Analyse von Unternehmensnetzwerken, in: Sydow, J. (ed.), Management von Netzwerkorganisationen, Wiesbaden, 2010, p. 7, 17; *Männel, B.*, Netzwerke in der Zulieferindustrie: Konzepte – Gestaltungsmerkmale – betriebswirtschaftliche Wirkungen, Wiesbaden, 1996, p. 32.

74 *Gnyawali, D./He, J./Madhavan, R.*, Impact of Co-Opetition on Firm Competitive Behavior: An Empirical Examination, Journal of Management 2006, 507 (521).

The efficient supply of information for the actors participating in the network is indispensable for supplier networks, especially just-in-time-systems, and the progress in information and communication technology has a positive effect on this.[75] The idea of superior knowledge utilization can be clearly illustrated on the distribution side of value-added networks. An important advantage of contractual distribution systems is the ability to flexibly adapt to various changes in the environment. It can be instantly reacted to new client requests or technological change and organizational innovations can be quickly implemented. It is especially positive that distribution systems regularly possess well-functioning communication processes, which puts them into the position to promptly react to market and competition developments.[76] In this way, also Rey and Tirole (1986) show that a distribution area exclusively assigned to distributors leads to the optimal use of decentralised information. Distributors react efficiently to demand and supply shocks.[77] In the international distribution of products producers are often unfamiliar with the market circumstances of the individual countries, which is why they rely on distribution intermediaries who are more familiar with the local circumstances. Developing new markets particularly requires profound knowledge of the legal circumstances, the particularities of consumer needs and the compatible marketing strategy.[78]

---

75 *Siebert, H.*, Ökonomische Analyse von Unternehmensnetzwerken, in: Sydow, J. (ed.), Management von Netzwerkorganisationen, Wiesbaden, 2010, p. 7 13 et seq.; *Altmann, N. /Deiß, M /Döhl, V./Sauer, D.*, Ein „Neuer Rationalisierungstyp" – neue Anforderungen an die Industriesoziologie, Soziale Welt 1986, 191 (192 et seq.).

76 *Martinek, M.*, Betriebs- und absatzwirtschaftliche Hintergründe von Vertriebsverträgen, in: Martinek, M./Semler, F.-J./Habermeier, S. / Flohr, E. (eds.), Handbuch des Vertriebsrechts, München, 2010, § 2 recital 92.

77 *Rey, P./Tirole, J.*, The Logic of Vertical Restraints, The American Economic Review 1986, 921 (928).

78 *Mestmäcker, E.-J./Schweitzer, H.*, Europäisches Wettbewerbsrecht, München, 2004, § 12 recital 1; *Blair, B./Lewis, T.*, Optimal Retail Contracts with Asymmetric Information and Moral Hazard, The RAND Journal of Economics 1994, 284 (284).

## 4. Coopetition

Networks are characterised by cooperative behaviour, since continuity is required in the relation between the network members for the jointly carried out transactions. However, a too one-sided orientation for harmony prevents the useful incentive effect of conflicts, because a conflict-laden discussion culture stimulates the questioning of the actions and obliges to look for superior innovations.[79] This is why the network participants preserve their autonomy to a certain extent. In contrast to entities within a company, they see themselves exposed to competitive pressure also in relation to the participants of their own network. Since they make their decisions independently an efficient incentive effect develops.[80] Networks unfold dynamic character traits, since boundaries between and within the network are permanently blurred. Network members are constantly keen to optimally position themselves within the network. Competing endeavours to assert themselves lead to the development of a constructive, market-based efficiency pressure.[81] Accordingly, networks combine components of cooperation and competition in an efficient way. Thus, the term coopetition has emerged.[82]

---

79 *Messner, D.*, Fallstricke und Grenzen der Netzwerksteuerung, PROKLA 1994, 563 (589 et seqq.); *Hirschman, A.*, Wieviel Gemeinsinn braucht die liberale Gesellschaft? Berlin, 1994, p. 293 (296 et seqq.), *Morgan, R./Hunt, S.*, The Commitment-Trust Theory of Relationship Marketing, Journal of Marketing 1994, 20, 26.

80 *Menard, C.*, The Economics of Hybrid Organizations, Journal of Institutional and Theoretical Economics 2004, 345, 352 et seq.; *Männel, B.*, Netzwerke in der Zulieferindustrie: Konzepte – Gestaltungsmerkmale – betriebswirtschaftliche Wirkungen, Wiesbaden, 1996, p. 134.

81 *Thorelli, H.*, Networks: Between Markets and Hierarchies, Strategic Management Journal 1986, 37. 42 et seq.; *Siebert, H.*, Ökonomische Analyse von Unternehmensnetzwerken, in: Sydow, J. (ed.), Management von Netzwerkorganisationen, Wiesbaden, 2010, p. 7. 11 et seq.

82 *Nalebuff, B./Brandenburger, A.*, Coopetition – kooperativ konkurrieren: mit der Spieltheorie zum Unternehmenserfolg, Frankfurt a.M., 1996, p. 23 et seqq.; *Hecker, A.*, Outsourcing als Coopetition – Eine spieltheoretische Analyse des Zusammenhangs von Kooperation und Kompetition, in: Schreyögg, G./Sydow, J (eds.), Kooperation und Konkurrenz – Managementforschung, Wiesbaden, 2007, p. 3 et seq., 22 et seqq.; *Menard, C.*, The Economics of Hybrid Organizations, Journal of Institutional and Theoretical Economics 2004, 345, 351 et seq.; *Siebert, H.*, Ökonomische Analyse von Unternehmensnetzwerken, in: Sydow, J. (ed.), Management von Netzwerkorganisationen, Wiesbaden, 2010, p. 12 et seq.; *Messner, D.*, Fallstricke und Grenzen der Netzwerksteuerung, PROKLA 1994, 563, 594; *Mor-*

The incentive advantages of the market are used and at the same time the coordinating instruments of the hierarchy are preserved. Furthermore, due to the long-term cooperation transaction costs are saved, since the permanent search for business partners is eliminated and thereby the costs for initiating and implementing contracts are reduced.[83] The mutual aim of the network further leads to the reduction of monitoring costs. Despite their long-term relations networks pose a flexible instrument to be able to adequately react to fast changing surrounding circumstances. The problem of instable surrounding circumstances especially occurs in industries with short product cycles and fast changing customer preferences.[84] The feature of coopetition thus especially applies to value-added networks. The actors participating in the network are aware that the group success can only be realised through cooperative interaction. The mutual interest of the system is the economic success of the business model. Despite the system consistency, the autonomous, sometimes even the competing actions of the subsystems are thereby accepted. The individual subsystems offer contributions, which are then mostly aligned by the head of the system so as to generate a benefit for the entire system in a channelled way. The network system has to watch by means of adequate coordinating instruments, especially including the vertical agreements described above, that the threshold

---

*gan, R./ Hunt, S.*, The Commitment-Trust Theory of Relationship Marketing, Journal of Marketing 1994, 20, 26.

83 *Picot, A./Dietl, H. /Franck, E.*, Organisation – Eine ökonomische Perspektive, Stuttgart, 2005, p. 368 et seq.; *Sydow, J.*, Strategische Netzwerke, Wiesbaden, 2005, p. 100 et seq., 130 et seqq., 268 et seqq.; *Männel, B.*, Netzwerke in der Zulieferindustrie: Konzepte – Gestaltungsmerkmale – betriebswirtschaftliche Wirkungen, Wiesbaden, 1996, p. 80, 83.

84 *Ouchi, W.*, Markets, Bureaucracies, and Clans, Administrative Science Quarterly 1980, 129 (132 et seqq.); *Picot, A./Reichwald, R.*, Auflösung der Unternehmung? Vom Einfluss der IuK-Technik auf Organisationsstrukturen und Kooperationsformen, Zeitschrift für Betriebswirtschaft 64 1994, 547 (563 et seqq.); *Männel, B.*, Netzwerke in der Zulieferindustrie: Konzepte – Gestaltungsmerkmale – betriebswirtschaftliche Wirkungen, Wiesbaden, 1996, p. 81 et seq.; *Kim, S./Mcfarland, R./ Kwon, S./Son, S./ Griffith, D.*, Understanding Governance Decisions in a Partially Integrated Channel: A Contingent Alignment Framework, Journal of Marketing Research 2011, 603 (604, 609 et seq.).

to harmful effects of the self-interest oriented actions of the individual actors is not exceeded.[85]

Various empirical studies were able to ascertain the useful effects of networks. Kim et al. (2011) show that networks are a flexible organizational form, which is able to react quickly to changing circumstances in the environment. Monitoring instruments are established in networks ensuring the business success of the distribution system by controlling for the sales force activities. Control becomes necessary if sales force performance is difficult to monitor and protection of brand reputation is required.[86] Henning et al. (2012) further ascertain that transaction costs, which arise due to the commitment problem, and search costs, are reduced within networks.[87] In a meta-analysis, in which 200 studies from transaction and organization theory were examined, the efficiency-increasing effects of networks could also be ascertained. Accordingly, companies increasingly revert to contractual instruments and relational cooperation so as to overcome problems which arise as a consequence of specific investments and uncertainties.[88] Geysken et al. (2006) in this analysis furthermore ascertain that the organization in the network has a positive effect on the performance indicated for instance by faster growth of sales or profits.[89]

## II. Disadvantages of the network organization

Despite the described variety of advantages that can evolve in value-added networks, the occurrence of disadvantages is possible in the network orga-

85 *Martinek, M.*, Betriebs- und absatzwirtschaftliche Hintergründe von Vertriebsverträgen, in: Martinek, M./Semler, F.-J./Habermeier, S. / Flohr, E. (eds.), Handbuch des Vertriebsrechts, München, 2010, § 2 recital 89 et seqq.

86 *Kim, S./Mcfarland, R./Kwon, S./Son, S./ Griffith, D.*, Understanding Governance Decisions in a Partially Integrated Channel: A Contingent Alignment Framework, Journal of Marketing Research 2011, 603, 606, 609.

87 *Henning, C. / Henningsen, G. / Henningsen, A.*, Network and Transaction Cost, American Journal of Agricultural Economics 2012, 377, 380, 384.

88 *Geyskens, I./Steenkamp, J-B./Kumar, N.*, Make, Buy, or Ally: A Transaction Cost Theory Meta-Analysis, The Academy of Management Journal 2006, 519, 522 et seqq., 530 et seq.

89 *Geyskens, I./Steenkamp, J-B./Kumar, N.*, Make, Buy, or Ally: A Transaction Cost Theory Meta-Analysis, The Academy of Management Journal 2006, 519, 523, 531.

nization. These disadvantages are illustrated in the next section. It will be shown that these disadvantages are mostly manageable by the network participants themselves or that they can be solved with the help of a suitable institutional framework.

### 1. Internal network problems

Scharpf (1993) shows that benefit can only be maximised by entrepreneurial coordination decisions, since the benefit of the individual actors, which can be positive and negative, is aggregated. Actors whose position is worsened by the decision are ignored due to the decision of the coordinating head for the good of the entire business. In contrast, options are basically excluded if they worsen the position of an individual network participant, despite the fact that they would maximise the overall welfare within the network. Compromises are merely reached through complex conflict solving instruments. Accordingly, the increasing complexity is mirrored in higher transaction costs.[90] Therefore, internal network problems primarily arise due to the complexity of network control.[91] This problem becomes clearly apparent if the number of members in the network is high, since the coordination is made difficult due to the individual and interacting options. Difficulties may then arise in the scope of negotiating processes. In this way, agreements have to be often reached in networks on standards (e.g. quality standards).[92] A further problem for value-added networks pertains to the alignment of subsequent processes or processes determined by priority. The network participants have to agree upon the time to fulfil certain tasks. In both cases, the coordinational problems are considered to be controllable since by means of a one-time agreement, at the time the network was constituted for instance, a solution can be found. It is more problematic if ongoing activities of the network are

---

90 *Scharpf, F.*, Coordination in Hierarchies and Networks, in: F. Scharpf (ed.), Games in Hierarchies and Networks: Analytical and Empirical Approaches to the Study of Governance Institutions, Frankfurt 1993, p. 131 et seqq.; *Messner, D.*, Fallstricke und Grenzen der Netzwerksteuerung, PROKLA 1994, 563, 577 et seqq.

91 *Messner, D.*, Fallstricke und Grenzen der Netzwerksteuerung, PROKLA 1994, 563 et seqq., 577.

92 *Thompson, J.*, Organizations in Action, New York, 1967, p, 54 et seqq., 70 et seq., 128 et seq.; *Messner, D.*, Fallstricke und Grenzen der Netzwerksteuerung, PROKLA 1994, 563, 567.

intertwined and decisions can only be made together and by mutual consent.[93]

Furthermore, unequally distributed power relations or asymmetrically allocated information pose problems, which may especially emerge between the head of the network and the decentralised affiliated and autonomously acting network members. The thereby emerging complex relations of dependencies may lead to a wrongful distribution of network advantages or to an unjustifiable allocation of the risks with a weak network member. In the worst case, such problems may lead to the network's inability to act.[94]

The benefits of the combination of cooperation and competition in networks (coopetition) have already been illustrated. At the same time, a negotiating dilemma may arise hereof. On the one hand, the way of negotiating resulting from the strive for competition advantages, which, for instance, includes the manipulation of information or threatening gestures, may counteract the necessary prerequisites for a trustful relation. On the other hand, the flexibility of networks is at risk due to the requirement of stable cooperation relations for the creation of trustful relations. Thereby, the adaptability of the system may be reduced since decisions are rather taken by consensus to avoid conflicts. Stable structures are preserved whereby necessary reorientations as reaction to external changes are made more difficult.[95]

> "»Kooperation« kann sich demnach in interaktiven Prozessen sowohl außerordentlich produktiv, als Entwicklungsmotor, aber eben auch als Blockade-

93 *Messner, D.*, Fallstricke und Grenzen der Netzwerksteuerung, PROKLA 1994, 563, 567 et seq.

94 *Bayreuther, F.*, Wirtschaftlich-existenziell abhängige Unternehmen im Konzern-, Kartell- und Arbeitsrecht: zugleich ein Beitrag zur rechtlichen Erfassung moderner Unternehmensverträge, Berlin, 2001, p. 338 et seqq.; *Teubner, G.*, Netzwerk als Vertragsverbund – Virtuelle Unternehmen, Franchising, Just-in-time in sozialwissenschaftlicher und juristischer Sicht, Baden-Baden 2004, 46 et seq., 51 et seq.; *Messner, D.*, Fallstricke und Grenzen der Netzwerksteuerung, PROKLA 1994, 563, 584 et seq.

95 *Scharpf, F.*, Coordination in Hierarchies and Networks, in: F. Scharpf (ed.), Games in Hierarchies and Networks: Analytical and Empirical Approaches to the Study of Governance Institutions, Frankfurt 1993, p. 153 et seq.; *Messner, D.*, Fallstricke und Grenzen der Netzwerksteuerung, PROKLA 1994, 563, 570 et seq., 582 et seq.

mechanismus auswirken."[96] (Translation by the author: "»Cooperation« may, accordingly, have extremely productive effects as engine for development, but also as blocking mechanism.")

A problem linked to the continuation of the cooperation relations lies in the creation of mutual dependencies, which lead to increased exit costs. Accordingly, the once made decision of founding a network may lead to path dependencies, a sequence of inefficient decisions, which inhibits the initially realised short-term efficiency advantages.[97] Such an obstacle to withdrawal for the companies within a network furthermore prevents the useful feedback effect of the exit option.[98] Moreover, domino effects may occur due to the high degree of dependency of the companies within the network. If a network member encounters financial problems, which prevent it from fulfilling its delivery commitment, then this puts the entire network at risk as it is threatened by a landslide-like expansion of insolvencies.[99] Likewise, measures of the network head detrimental to reputation may expand to the entire network. At this point, it may be referred to the so-called shock adverts by the fashion manufacturer Benetton, who jeopardized the sales turnover of the retailers participating in the network by shocking adverts.[100] The current labour law disputes of Burger King[101] or the practices of tax evasion of McDonald's or Starbucks[102] may have similar effects on the business of franchise branches belonging to the sys-

96 *Messner, D.*, Fallstricke und Grenzen der Netzwerksteuerung, PROKLA 1994, 563, 590.

97 *Messner, D.*, Fallstricke und Grenzen der Netzwerksteuerung, PROKLA 1994, 563, 572 et seq.; *Thorelli, H.*, Networks: Between Markets and Hierarchies, Strategic Management Journal 1986, 37, 42 et seq.

98 *Hirschman, A.*, Exit, Voice, and Loyalty – Responses to Decline in Firms, Organizations, and States, Cambridge, 1970, p. 182 et seqq.

99 *Battiston, S./Delli Gatti, D./Gallegati, M./Greenwald, B./Stiglitz, J.*, Credit chains and bankruptcy propagation in production networks, Journal of Economic Dynamics and Control 2007, 2061 (2072 et seq., 2082).

100 *Imbusch, P.*, Benetton – Authentizität oder Massenbetrug?, in: Imbusch, P./ Rucht, P. (eds.), Profit oder Gemeinwohl? Fallstudien zur gesellschaftlichen Verantwortung von Wirtschaftseliten, Wiesbaden 2007, p. 271 et seqq.; *Martinek, M./Habermeier, S.*, Abschluss und Durchführung von Franchiseverträgen, in: Martinek, M./Semler, F.-J./Habermeier, S. /Flohr, E. (eds.), Handbuch des Vertriebsrechts, München, 2010, § 27 recital 63.

101 *Voss, O.*, Beflecktes Image, Wirtschaftswoche 45 2013, p. 62.

102 „Französische Steuerfahnder nehmen McDonald's unter die Lupe", Wirtschaftswoche online 22.01.2014 [online: 02.08.2014].

tem. Similarly, business practices of supply companies may have negative effects on the network system if, for instance, poor working conditions come to light or standards of environmental protection are ignored.

It was already mentioned in section B. I. that organizational decisions are made according to the kind of transaction. Accordingly, it can be assumed that the participating network actors include the potential imponderables described (e.g. coordinational problems, complex relations of dependencies, asymmetrically distributed power relations and information) in their calculations and, based on this, take an organizational decision optimised for the implementation of their transaction, which, in accordance with the theory of transaction cost economics, is situated on a range between market and hierarchy. It has to be furthermore assumed that network cooperations are in most cases formed due to common interests and therefore a mutual interest in a long-term cooperation exists. Brickley et al. (2006) accordingly show that asymmetrical power relations between the contract partners not necessarily lead to the exploitation of the weaker network partners.[103] The potential coordination problems in networks described above can in this way be put into perspective. Furthermore, the protection of weaker contract partners can be assured by legal regulations in general civil law and commercial law like the assurance of an adequate participation in the business success or in competition law by means of the prohibition of the exploitation of a market dominating position.[104]

### 2. External network problems

The decision of actors to carry out their economic activities through a network organization may in certain cases lead to risks for society. For instance, it is sometimes difficult for the end consumer to recognize with whom the business is being concluded since networks exhibit a uniform market appearance, but in the end are an organizational entity with a range of independent companies. Furthermore, the boundaries of the participating companies in networks are partially fluent, which puts them in the pos-

103 *Brickley, J./Misra, S./van Horn, R.*, Contract Duration: Evidence From Franchising, Journal of Law and Economics 2006, 173 (180 et seq., 190 et seq.).

104 *Bayreuther, F.*, Wirtschaftlich-existenziell abhängige Unternehmen im Konzern-, Kartell- und Arbeitsrecht: zugleich ein Beitrag zur rechtlichen Erfassung moderner Unternehmensverträge, Berlin, 2001, p. 149 et seqq.

ition to change their appearance as required.[105] In connection with this, occurring disturbances or failures cannot be unambiguously ascribed if they occur at the interface between individual network partners.[106] There are concerns that responsibilities are difficult to assign thus leading to an increase of risk as well as a transfer of risks to third parties. Furthermore, the contractual self-implementing agreements based on trust may lead to a reduced use of formal assurances. Since an informal assurance is inferior to a formal assurance regarding the spread of risks, inefficient risk transfer may occur.[107] These external costs must be internalised by an adequate legal framework. Liability rules are suitable for this purpose because the liability of the entire organization can in that way be dissolved in the individual liability of the system members.[108] Besides the legal solution of the

105 *Teubner, G.*, Netzwerk als Vertragsverbund – Virtuelle Unternehmen, Franchising, Just-in-time in sozialwissenschaftlicher und juristischer Sicht, Baden-Baden, 2004, p. 55 et seq.; *Duschek, S./Ortmann, G. /Sydow, J.*, Grenzmanagement in Unternehmungsnetzwerken: Theoretische Zugänge und der Fall eines strategischen Dienstleistungsnetzwerks, in: Ortmann, G./Sydow, J. (eds.), Strategie und Strukturation. Strategisches Management von Unternehmen, Netzwerken und Konzernen, Wiesbaden, 2001, p. 191 (193, 206 et seq.); *Picot, A./Reichwald, R.*, Auflösung der Unternehmung? Vom Einfluss der IuK-Technik auf Organisationsstrukturen und Kooperationsformen, Zeitschrift für Betriebswirtschaft 64 1994, 547, 560 et seq.; *Ortmann, G./Sydow, J.*, Grenzmanagement in Unternehmensnetzwerken: Theoretische Zugänge, Die Betriebswirtschaft 1999, 205 (214).

106 *Teubner, G.*, Netzwerk als Vertragsverbund – Virtuelle Unternehmen, Franchising, Just-in-time in sozialwissenschaftlicher und juristischer Sicht, Baden-Baden 2004, p. 56; *Endres, E./Wehner, T.*, Störungen zwischenbetrieblicher Kooperation – Eine Fallstudie zum Grenzstellenmanagement in der Automobilindustrie, in: Sydow, J. (ed.), Management von Netzwerkorganisationen, Wiesbaden, 2010, p. 295 (312 et seq.).

107 *Arnott, E. /Stiglitz, J.*, Moral Hazard and Nonmarket Institutions: Dysfunctional Crowding Out or Peer Monitoring?, The American Economic Review 1991, 179 (188 et seq.).

108 *Picker, E.*, Vertragliche und deliktische Schadenshaftung – Überlegungen zu einer Neustrukturierung der Haftungssysteme, JZ 1987, 1041 (1057 et seq.); *Noll, J.*, Who Should Be Liable in a Virtual Enterprise Network? Social Science Research Network 2002, http://ssrn.com/abstract=319965 [online: 02.08.2014], p. 9 et seq.; *Teubner, G.*, Netzwerk als Vertragsverbund – Virtuelle Unternehmen, Franchising, Just-in-time in sozialwissenschaftlicher und juristischer Sicht, Baden-Baden, 2004, p. 47 et seqq.; *Teubner, G.*, Netzwerke als kollektive Akteure höherer Ordnung, in: Kenis, P. /Schneider, V. (eds.), Organisation und Netzwerk: Institutionelle Steuerung in Wirtschaft und Politik, Wien, 1996, p. 553 et seq., *Kali, R.*, Endogenous Business Networks, The Journal of Law Economics & Or-

network boundary problem it can also be resorted on boundary management within the network organization addressing liability risks. This includes for example the precise definition of boundaries or the clear allocation of responsibilities.[109] In the context of quality control the assignment of responsibilities to the right network participants is particularly an important task.[110]

It is furthermore feared that the benefit of the network is gained at the expense of those not participating in the group. This is regarded as the ingroup-outgroup effect. For instance, a rising number of exchange relations initiated by networks may increase the search costs for those actors remaining in the market.[111] Kali (1999) further concludes that the existence of networks may exert a negative influence on the markets since "honest" market actors are integrated in the network and a greater amount of "nonhonest" individuals remain on the market. Network participants accordingly profit at the expense of the actors remaining in the market. From the view of the overall welfare once established networks therefore may lead to inefficient path dependencies. They continue to exist despite their

---

ganization 1999, 615. 616 et seq.; *Eucken, W.*, Grundsätze der Wirtschaftspolitik, Tübingen, 2004, p. 279 et seqq.

109 *Duschek, S./Ortmann, G./Sydow, J.*, Grenzmanagement in Unternehmungsnetzwerken: Theoretische Zugänge und der Fall eines strategischen Dienstleistungsnetzwerks, in: Ortmann, G./Sydow, J. (eds.), Strategie und Strukturation. Strategisches Management von Unternehmen, Netzwerken und Konzernen, Wiesbaden, 2001, p. 195 et seqq., 201 et seqq.; *Modrow-Thiel, B./Roßmann, G./Wächter, H.*, Netzwerkanalyse – ein sozialwissenschaftliches Konzept zur Untersuchung komplexer Entscheidungsstrukturen, Zeitschrift für Personalforschung 1992, 97 (99 et seq.); *Duschek, S./Ortmann, G./Sydow, J.*, Grenzmanagement in Unternehmungsnetzwerken: Theoretische Zugänge und der Fall eines strategischen Dienstleistungsnetzwerks, in: Ortmann, G./Sydow, J. (eds.), Strategie und Strukturation. Strategisches Management von Unternehmen, Netzwerken und Konzernen, Wiesbaden, 2001, p. 207 et seq.

110 *Endres, E./Wehner, T.*, Störungen zwischenbetrieblicher Kooperation – Eine Fallstudie zum Grenzstellenmanagement in der Automobilindustrie, in: Sydow, J. (ed.), Management von Netzwerkorganisationen, Wiesbaden, 2010, p. 314 et seqq.; *Beck, P.*, Qualitätsmanagement und Transaktionskostenansatz: Instrumente zur Optimierung Vertraglicher Vertriebssysteme, Wiesbaden 1997, p. 80 et seq., 147.

111 *Scharpf, F.*, Games Real Actors Could Play: The Challenge of Complexity, Journal of Theoretical Politics 1991, p. 277 (295 et seqq.), *Kranton, R.*, Reciprocal Exchange: A Self-Sustaining System, The American Economic Review 1996, 830, 840 et seq.

macroeconomic inefficiency, because network participants have an increased interest in maintaining the network due to their isolated benefit.[112] However, in this model it is assumed that the only rational for the use of network organization is to overcome a missing legal framework. Other beneficiary aspects of networks are neglected which is why the results have to be put into perspective.[113]

Especially the cumulative use of vertical agreements may negatively influence the competition, since the extensive use of exclusive relation agreements, such as often occurs with the value-added networks examined here, may result in the fact that competitors have no access to the market or the access is tied to high costs. The end consumer is faced with welfare deficits caused by this market dominance.[114] Contradicting this, Besanko and Perry (1993) in their model show that from the perspective of consumer welfare it is preferable if all producers, and not only some or none at all, use exclusive dealing agreements. In this case they have higher incentives to make brand-enhancing investments.[115] Similarly, Kali (1999) argues that positive welfare effects are only realised if a sufficiently high amount of market actors participates in the network,[116] because in general the personalised exchange relations in a network are easier to assert, which is why efficiency-increasing effects occur. These, however, com-

112 *Kali, R.*, Endogenous Business Networks, The Journal of Law Economics & Organization 1999, 615, 617 et seqq., 633.

113 *Kali, R.*, Endogenous Business Networks, The Journal of Law Economics & Organization 1999, 615, 628 et seq., 634.

114 *Lafontaine, F./Slade, M.*, Transaction Cost Economics and Vertical Market Restrictions – Evidence, The Antitrust Bulletin 2010, 587, 601; *Comamor, W./Rey, P.*, Vertical Restraints and the Market Power of Large Distributors, Review of Industrial Organization 2000, 135 (150); *Habermeier, S./ Ehlers, J.*, Art. 81 EG Vertikale Wettbewerbsbeschränkungen, in: Hirsch, G./Montag, F./Säcker, F. (eds.), Münchener Kommentar zum Europäischen und Deutschen Wettbewerbsrecht, Bd. I, München 2007, recital 243.

115 *Besanko, D./Perry M.*, Equilibrium Incentives for Exclusive Dealing in a Differentiated Products Oligopoly, The RAND Journal of Economics 1993, 646 (646, 662); *Secrieru, O.*, The Economic Theory of Vertical Restraints, Journal of Economic Surveys 2006, 797, 813.

116 *Kali, R.*, Endogenous Business Networks, The Journal of Law Economics & Organization 1999, 615, 632.

pensate the efficiency losses of the participants remaining on the market only if the network reaches a certain size.[117]

## E. Conclusion

Competition authorities are confronted with a major challenge concerning the legal treatment of network organizations.[118] With regard to the variety of hybrid organizational forms it is stated that their advantages and disadvantages should be noted on the basis of an individual examination.[119] But as discussed the enforcement of law by individual examinations has shortcomings (section C.). For that reason the aim was to formulate a generally valid statement in relation to the welfare effects of value-added networks. Therefore two elements of value-added networks were under scrutiny - vertical agreements that are utilized between the value-added stages and the inherent properties of network governance.

Vertical agreements can have restrictive effects on competition, or they can achieve efficiency-enhancing effects (section B. III.). Several empirical findings lead to the supposition that efficiency aspects seem to prevail. In addition, the market structure already requires certain preconditions (e.g. high market entry costs, low number of market participants) in order for vertical restraints to harm competition.

On the basis of these results the inherent advantages and disadvantages of the network organization were taken into account to reach a general statement (section D.). The analysis revealed that the inherent advantages of network organizations seem to outweigh the disadvantages. Shortcomings of network governance can for the most part be overcome. It has been illustrated that the potential disadvantages of networks are manageable, or can be resolved due to legal regulations. When no resolution is possible within pre-existing legal regulations, further legal developments in the re-

---

117 *Kali, R.*, Endogenous Business Networks, The Journal of Law Economics & Organization 1999, 615, 618, 620 et seqq.

118 *Menard, C.*, Maladaption of Regulation to Hybrid Organizational Forms, International Review of Law and Economics 1998, 403 (403 et seqq.); *Menard, C.*, The Economics of Hybrid Organizations, Journal of Institutional and Theoretical Economics 2004, 345, 357.

119 *Masten, S.*, Case Studies in Contracting and Organization, Oxford University Press 1996, p. 12; *Menard, C.*, Maladaption of Regulation to Hybrid Organizational Forms, International Review of Law and Economics 1998, 403, 347 et seq.

spective fields of law would be required (e.g. liability law). In general, interorganizational networks are predominantly considered as an efficient coordination device.

By visualizing the position of value-added networks in the figure which was introduced in section C. the following conclusion can be drawn. The welfare effects of the usage of vertical agreements ($B_{vr}$) are ambiguous so that the application of differentiated competition rules might be reasonable. Still it might be preferable to apply general rules if regulatory costs are too high. However it has been previously stated that an individual analysis of the market circumstances may assist in filtering out business behaviours obviously harming effective competition.

If vertical agreements, in contrast, are utilized in value-added networks ($B_{van}$), welfare effects will move mainly in the positive range. It cannot be ruled out that business behaviours with negative welfare effects may still occur, but because of the above-mentioned shortcomings of differentiated competition rules, welfare losses will not be compensated due to higher regulatory costs.

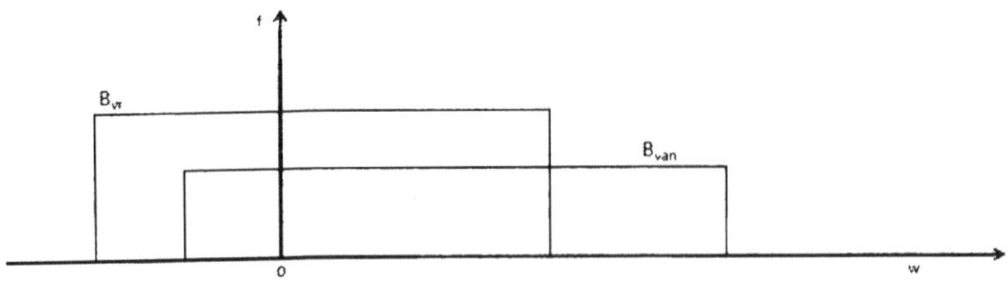


*Figure 5: The welfare effect of value-added networks*

Consequently, for the governance of value-added networks an appropriate control and monitoring system is required. It is primarily setup by a net of horizontal and in particular vertical agreements. Because of the restrictive treatment of certain vertical agreements in competition law, the optimal functioning of the efficient network governance is compromised. Thus a move away from the restrictive assessment of vertical agreement in the context of vertical network systems is recommended. Vertical agreements in value-added networks nurture procompetitive effects and should therefore be handled in a less restrictive way by competition authorities.[120]

120 *Menard, C.*, Maladaption of Regulation to Hybrid Organizational Forms, International Review of Law and Economics 1998, 403, 416 et seq.

# Company networks in the light of European market power[1]

*Hermann Dück, Dr. Alexander Eufinger, Marion Schultes*

The authors examine the complex structures of business networks from an antitrust point of using the example of networks with potential market power, which may fall under the scope of the European prohibition of abuse of a dominant position (Art. 102 TFEU). Therewith, initially the question arises whether business networks are a single undertaking with market power or a collective consisting in several single undertakings with market power. Moreover, it is necessary to clarify to what extent the criteria for market power on the level of European law can be tied in with the business network as a whole or as to single components.

## A. Introduction

Networks are a widespread and therefore practically relevant – although (juridically) little researched – phenomenon in the conduct of business.[2] Especially from the perspective of competition law importance is attached to company networks. The connection of several participants in a network organisation inevitably entails a certain restriction of competition. If a network possesses market power then this circumstance requires a closer consideration with regard to the prohibition of misuse of a market dominating position. In the following company networks are considered in the light of the European prohibition of abusive practice according to Art. 102 TFEU, whereby the special structural features of networks or the specific network characteristics are taken into account.

---

1 The following paper results from a research week (organised by *Teubner, G.* and *Krebs, P.* at the University of Siegen) dealing with the juridical compilation of company networks which led to valuable findings.

2 *Krebs, P./Aedtner, K./Schultes, M.*, Company networks reloaded – putting a general functional approach to defining complex problems to the test, in this volume, p. 41 (41).

Thereby, the phenomenon of networks is first defined and illustrated by means of selected examples. At the same time, a differentiation is established to network similar, but not identical forms of cooperation. Based on the question important for the differentiation between single and collective dominance[3] whether company networks as a whole are to be considered as an individual company or as a group of several independent companies, the existing criteria for market dominance are subsequently presented. On this basis, it is then debated how the case of networks can be tied in with the criteria for market power.

3 *Fuchs, A./Möschel, W.*, in: Immenga, U./Mestmäcker, E.-J. (eds.), EU-WettbR, 5. ed., München 2012, AEUV, Art. 102 recital 73 et seq., 115 et seq.; *Bergmann, H.*, in: Loewenheim, U./Meessen, K./Riesenkampff, A. (eds.), Kartellrecht, 2. ed., München 2009, EGV, Art. 82 recital 91 et seq., 121 et seq.; *de Bronett, G.*, in: Wiedemann, G. (ed.), Handbuch des Kartellrechts, 2. ed., München 2008, § 22 recital 10 et seq., 25 et seq.

## B. Company networks

### I. Definition and concretion of the network phenomenon

A company network is every legally voluntary[4] connection based on an economic and legal[5] network aim[6] of a minimum of three[7] legally independent companies[8] which induce a network-specific demand for organi-

---

4 In the field of economics, the idea of networks is linked to the voluntariness of merging into a network. Indeed, the state could legally enforce network-like structures, but then the state would be responsible for the internally and externally applicable (public law) rules. See *Krebs, P./Aedtner, K./Schultes, M.*, Company networks reloaded – putting a general functional approach to defining complex problems to the test, in this volume, p. 41 (59).

5 The network must not intend to pursue an illegal aim since it is not apparent why the legal system should deal with illegal networks. With regard to the practical breach of competition law it has to be noted though that the very same may be influenced by the existence of a network. As the actual interaction within the network can be of essence for the success of a network, a certain privileging of the interaction in a network therefore cannot be excluded from the start. See *Krebs, P./Aedtner, K./Schultes, M.*, Company networks reloaded – putting a general functional approach to defining complex problems to the test, in this volume, p. 41 (60).

6 The economic network aim is a co-operational gain, which manifests itself in the realisation of competitive advantages (i.e. access to new markets, cost advantages, quality improvement) and is achieved by the coordination of the participating companies. See *Krebs, P./Aedtner, K./Schultes, M.*, Company networks reloaded – putting a general functional approach to defining complex problems to the test, in this volume, p. 41 (53 et seqq.).

7 The increased need for coordination or the problem of coordination only arises with three or more participants. This also applies from a juridical point of view since for instances with two participants a fully developed range of tools exists in form of the traditional contract law to solve questions of coordination. With three or more participants, however, network problems, which are not regulated, may arise. See *Krebs, P./Aedtner, K./Schultes, M.*, Company networks reloaded – putting a general functional approach to defining complex problems to the test, in this volume, p. 41 (47 et seq.).

8 In order to legally assess cooperative constellations it is vital to differentiate between decentralised organisations within one legal entity (such as an affiliated group of companies) and network structures between several legal entities. If the individual participants lack their legal independence then neither the question regarding the legal relation between the participants arises nor the question regarding the legal relation of the individual companies to others. See *Krebs, P./Aedtner, K./Schultes, M.*, Company networks reloaded – putting a general functional approach to defining complex problems to the test, in this volume, p. 41 (49 et seq.).

sation.[9] The network companies at least partially exchange their economic independence for the co-ordination of their economic activities[10] by means of concerted practices, agreements or the foundation of a corporation[11] in order to implement the network aim[12] through the bundling of resources.[13]

---

9 In particular, the network-specific need for organisation arises especially due to the need for coordination of individual projects, which require the network's cooperation. In addition, the need for organisation exists for the entire duration of the network with regard to the coordination of the parallel activities within the projects, the coordination of the tension between individual and collective interests, as well as the coordination of the cooperative needs. See *Krebs, P./Aedtner, K./Schultes, M.*, Company networks reloaded – putting a general functional approach to defining complex problems to the test, in this volume, p. 41 (65 et seq.).

10 In the case of the combination of founding a company and simultaneously joining the network, a network company contributes to the network with an economic activity while thereby losing its actual or potential economic independence at the same time. In return for the loss of economic independence the companies expect a co-operational gain which can only be achieved by the coordination. The economic independence is therefore partially exchanged for coordination. See *Krebs, P./Aedtner, K./Schultes, M.*, Company networks reloaded – putting a general functional approach to defining complex problems to the test, in this volume, p. 41 (57).

11 In order to assure the synchronisation of three or more actors the network participants' activities have to be coordinated. Depending on the desired intensity the coordination may be informal, i.e. without legal ties in form of fulfilment obligations (= concerted practices, accommodation relationships under the general law of obligation), but may also be organised within the scope of contractual exchange relations (= agreements) or in form of a corporation as coordinating instrument. See *Krebs, P./Aedtner, K./Schultes, M.*, Company networks reloaded – putting a general functional approach to defining complex problems to the test, in this volume, p. 41 (55 et seqq.).

12 *Krebs, P./Aedtner, K./Schultes, M.*, Company networks reloaded – putting a general functional approach to defining complex problems to the test, in this volume, p. 41 (68).

13 Without the bundling of resources the network aim cannot be pursued successfully. The underlying notion of bundling resources, which is used here, can be described as wide in a twofold way. On the one hand, this includes the bundling (the exchange) of know-how, information or organisational abilities. And on the other hand, the extent of their use is of importance besides the type of resource. The underlying notion of bundling here therefore differentiates between a loose and a tight bundling of resources. The loose bundling comprises the mere provision of resources as well as granting the right of use. The legal control over the provided resources remains with the respective company. The tight bundling describes the merger of resources to one entity by means of introducing the resources into a company which was founded for the purpose of coordination. See *Krebs, P./Aedt-*

This definition is basically kept broad, but the definition's range of application is nevertheless restricted to business networks which exhibit the network-specific problem of organisation. This entails that many network-like co-operations such as franchising or supply chains are not to be considered as business networks.[14]

## II. Company networks as addressees of competition law

### 1. Elements of the definition of undertaking

In competition law, the so-called functional definition of "undertaking" is applied according to which an undertaking is a legal independent unit performing a permanent economic activity irrespective of its legal form or kind of financing.[15] This general definition hence contains the necessity of a *legal independent unit*.

Furthermore, it is European practice to attribute infringements (of competition law) by subsidiary companies to the parent company.[16] This requires several legal personalities acting as an *economic unit* and therefore as a single entity according to Art. 102 TFEU.[17] Besides cases in which

---

*ner, K./Schultes, M.*, Company networks reloaded – putting a general functional approach to defining complex problems to the test, in this volume, p. 41 (58 et seq.).

14 *Krebs, P./Aedtner, K./Schultes, M.*, Company networks reloaded – putting a general functional approach to defining complex problems to the test, in this volume, p. 41 (71 et seq.). With regard to franchising, the network-specific need for organisation does not exist, because the organisation and co-ordination are often comprehensively regulated in the franchise contract.

15 See ECJ ECR 1991, I-1979 recital 21 – Höfner und Elser; EGC ECR 1992, II-1403 recital 358 – SIV and others; *Emmerich, V.*, in: Immenga, U./Mestmäcker, E.-J. (eds.), EU-WettbR, 5. ed., München 2012, Art. 101 par. 1 recital 7; *Nordemann, J. B.* , in: Loewenheim, U./Meessen, K./Riesenkampff, A. (eds.), Kartellrecht, 2. ed., München 2009, § 1 recital 19 et seq.

16 ECJ ECR 1972, 619 recital 132 et seq. – *ICI*; ECJ ECR 2000, I-10065 recital 27 – Metsä-Serla and others; EGC ECR 2006, II-1887 recital 117 – Hoek Loos; *Dieckmann, H.*, in: Wiedemann, G. (ed.), Handbuch des Kartellrechts, 2. ed., München 2008, § 46 recital 2a; *Weitbrecht, A./Mühle, J.*, Europäisches Kartellrecht 2009, EuZW 2010, p. 327 (333).

17 ECJ ECR 1974, 1147 recital 41 – Centrafarm und de Peijper; ECJ ECR 2003, I-11005 recital 99 – Aristrain; ECJ ECR 2009, I-8237 recital 39, 59 – Akzo Nobel and others; EGC ECR 2007, II-5049 recital 60 – Akzo Nobel and others; *Emme-*

the parent company holds nearly 100 %[18] of the shares of the particular subsidiary company there are circumstances that indicate the existence of an economic unit and entitle the European Commission to take action against each of the participants.[19] According to court ruling such neither exhaustive[20] nor cumulative[21] circumstances are, for example, the parent company's responsibility for the pricing policy,[22] the sales targets, the gross margin, the selling costs, the cash flow, the goods in stock[23] or the production and distribution activities.[24]

If there are several participants, an economic unit contains "undertakings"[25] which are legally independent but which at the same time depend

---

*rich, V.*, in: Immenga, U./Mestmäcker, E.-J. (eds.), EU-WettbR, 5. ed., München 2012, Art. 101 par. 1 recital 43; *Nordemann, J.B.*, in: Loewenheim, U./Meessen, K./Riesenkampff, A. (fn. 3), § 1 recital 94; *Säcker, F.J*, Gesellschafts- und dienstvertragsrechtliche Fragen bei Inanspruchnahme der Kronzeugenregelung, Wirtschaft und Wettbewerb 2009, p. 362 (362).

18 *Emmerich, V.*, in: Immenga, U./Mestmäcker, E.-J. (eds.), EU-WettbR, 5. ed., München 2012, Art. 101 par. 1 recital 47 et seq.; in the European Commission's practice it has regularly been sufficient for the parent company to hold 98 % of the shares of the subsidiary company, see *European Commission*, Decision of 19 January 2005 relating to a proceeding pursuant to Art. 81 ECT and Art. 53 EEAA, COMP/E-1/37.773 – *MCAA*, COM (2004), 4876 final, recital 258.

19 EGC ECR 1998, II-1727 recital 45 – Metsä-Serla and others; *Emmerich, W.*, in: Immenga, U./Mestmäcker, E.-J. (eds.), EU-WettbR, 5. ed., München 2012, Art. 101 par. 1 recital 46.

20 EGC ECR 2007, II-5049 recital 65 – Akzo Nobel and others; ECJ ECR 2009, I-8237 recital 74 – Akzo Nobel and others.

21 *Dück, H./Eufinger, A.*, Dezentrale Antitrust-Compliance und europäische Entscheidungspraxis zur kartellrechtlichen Haftungszurechnung im Konzern, CCZ 2012, p. 131 (132).

22 See ECJ ECR 1972, 619 recital 137 – ICI; ECJ ECR 1972, 787 recital 45 – Geigy.

23 See ECJ ECR 1996, I-5457 recital 15 – Viho; EGC ECR 1995, II-17 recital 48 – Viho.

24 See ECJ ECR 1974, 223 recital 37 et seq. – Istituto Chemioterapico Italiano and Commercial Solvents.

25 *Lübbig, T.*, in: Wiedemann, G. (ed.), Handbuch des Kartellrechts, 2. ed., München 2008, § 7 recital 2; „undertaking" here means the objective-personnel affiliation beyond the definition of undertaking of the economic unit; see *Thomas, S.*, Unternehmensverantwortlichkeit und -umstrukturierung nach EG-Kartellrecht, 2005, p. 36; *Dück, H./M. Schultes, M.*, Bußgeldhaftung und Rechtsnachfolge – Schlupfloch für Kartellsünder?, WM 2013, p. 9 (9); for a functional consideration beyond the definition of undertaking of the competition law see *Krebs, P./Aedtner, K./Schultes, M.*, Company networks reloaded – putting a general functional ap-

economically on the superordinate unit.[26] A(n) (independent) undertaking therefore also requires *economic independence*. Otherwise the particular unit would be part of an undertaking and not an undertaking on its own.

Apart from that the definition of undertaking used in the field of competition law can be specified by the fact that an undertaking is regarded as dependent if the *management* of a subsidiary company is determined by the parent company.[27] This corresponds with Art. 5 par. 4 EC Merger Regulation (ECMR) according to which the turnovers of subsidiary companies and the parent company have to be added (together) calculating the aggregate turnover of all participating undertakings.[28] In its Jurisdictional Notice under Council Regulation (EC) no. 139/2004 on the control of concentrations between undertakings the European Commission has explicitly declared that if an undertaking concerned directly or indirectly has such links with other undertakings, these are to be regarded as part of its group for purposes of turnover calculation under the ECMR.[29]

---

proach to defining complex problems to the test, in this volume, B. II. „Economic independence".

26 *Emmerich, V.*, in: Immenga, U./Mestmäcker, E.-J. (eds.), EU-WettbR, 5. ed., München 2012, Art. 101 par. 1 recital 10; see *Nordemann, J.B.*, in: Loewenheim, U./Meessen, K./Riesenkampff, A. (eds.), Kartellrecht, 2. ed., München 2009, § 1 recital 36, 96, in the context of group-related law; for a detailed analysis of the topic of the economic unit see *Thomas, S.*, Unternehmensverantwortlichkeit und -umstrukturierung nach EG-Kartellrecht, 2005, p. 133 et seq.; *Kersting, C.*, Wettbewerbsrechtliche Haftung im Konzern, Der Konzern 2011, p. 445 (456); *Dück, H./M. Schultes, M.*, Bußgeldhaftung und Rechtsnachfolge – Schlupfloch für Kartellsünder?, WM 2013, pp. 9 et seq.

27 *European Commission*, Decision of 10 December 2003 relating to a proceeding under Art. 81 ECT and Art. 53 EEAT, COMP/E-2/37.857 – Organic Peroxides, COM (2003), 4570 final, recital 386; see in this context the remarks concerning the principle of personal liability by *Emmerich, V.*, in: Immenga, U./Mestmäcker, E.-J. (eds.), EU-WettbR, 5. ed., München 2012, Art. 101 par. 1 recital 46; see also *Nordemann,J.B*, in: Loewenheim, U./Meessen, K./Riesenkampff, A. (eds.), Kartellrecht, 2. ed., München 2009, § 1 recital 94 et seq., with regard to intra-group competition.

28 *Ablasser-Neuhuber, A.*, in: Loewenheim, U./Meessen, K./Riesenkampff, A. (eds.), Kartellrecht, 2. ed., München 2009, VO 139/2004/EG, Art. 5 recital 24, 28; *Körber, T.*, in: Immenga, U./Mestmäcker, E.-J. (eds.), EU-WettbR, 5. ed., München 2012, FKVO, Art. 5 recital 59.

29 *European Commission*, Consolidated Jurisdictional Notice under Council Regulation (EC) no. 139/2004 on the control of concentrations between undertakings, OJEU 2009, C 43/09, marginal no. 176; see also *Körber, T.*, in Immenga, U./Mestmäcker, E.-J. (eds.), EU-WettbR, 5. ed., München 2012, FKVO, Art. 5 recital 59.

Consequently, there are three elements which are constitutive for network members representing a company according to competition law's definition. The network members have to be legally as well as economically independent (positive criteria) and there must not be central management power by the network regarding the undertakings which belong to the network (negative criterion). In this case the network as a whole is no undertaking according to competition law. The network as a whole inversely is a company if one of the mentioned criteria is missing.

### 2. Subsumption with regard to the network definition

Regarding the fact that the network members are legally independent according to the definition of network, the first criterion can be accepted as given. The question whether the network members are economically independent can be problematic, because according to the definition of network they *partially* give up their economic independence. In the end, it is decisive to what extent the network members are allowed to give up sovereignty without losing their feature as economically independent undertakings.

Referring to the wording of the term of economic *independence* of a company it is plausible to demand that the network members give up their economic independence completely[30] to become a dependent (on the network) unit. As a general rule, the network members expect to gain (economically) from their participation in the network so that (economic) advantages are the reason for the participation. In this context, there is a particular tension between the individual interests (of the network members) and the collective interests (of the network).[31]

In order to be able to pursue own interests, a minimum of economic independence in relation to the other network companies has to be kept. The opportunity to make decisions independently from other network com-

---

30 *Nordemann, J.-B.* in: Loewenheim, U./Meessen, K./Riesenkampff, A. (eds.), Kartellrecht, 2. ed., München 2009, § 1 recital 96, uses the final abandonment of economic independence referring to *European Commission*, 7th report on competition policy, 1977, recital 30.

31 See *Teubner, G.*, in: Augsberg, I. (ed.), Ungewissheit als Chance – Perspektiven eines produktiven Umgangs mit Unsicherheit im Rechtssystem, Tübingen 2009, p. 109 (122); *Sydow, J.*, Strategische Netzwerke, Wiesbaden 1992, p. 90, describes the tension as paradox of cooperation.

panies needs to be given at all times.[32] When a network member no longer pursues individual interests and when the collective interest of the network becomes the decisive interest, then the network company turns into a "network company".[33] In this case the economic independence of the single company no longer exists. If a minimum of economic independence still exists, the network members however are to be considered as economically independent undertakings.[34]

If a network is centrally managed, classifying a company as economically independent depends on the question whether the network members (primary) participate in the network to pursue their individual interests or whether the collective interest of the whole network outweighs the individual interests. As a rule, a central management will at least *also* reflect the interests of the network members. Furthermore, the fact that all network members *voluntarily*[35] accept a uniform management indicates that such a management can be ruled out if individual interests of the network companies (still) exist.

### 3. Interim Result

Company networks have to fulfil high requirements to be accepted as a single entity (undertaking). Besides the legal independence the term of the single undertaking requires the members to be economically independent of the network, respectively the economic dependence of the network members on the network. The particular network members generally remain undertakings according to the definition of undertaking in competition law regardless of the exchange of economic independence for coordi-

---

32 *Krebs, P./Aedtner, K./Schultes, M.*, Company networks reloaded – putting a general functional approach to defining complex problems to the test, in this volume, p. 41 (50 et seq.).

33 *Krebs, P./Aedtner, K./Schultes, M.*, Company networks reloaded – putting a general functional approach to defining complex problems to the test, in this volume, p. 41 (52).

34 See *Krebs, P./Aedtner, K./Schultes, M.*, Company networks reloaded – putting a general functional approach to defining complex problems to the test, in this volume, p. 41 (52).

35 See from this point of view *Krebs, P./Aedtner, K./Schultes, M.*, Company networks reloaded – putting a general functional approach to defining complex problems to the test, in this volume, p. 41 (69 et seq.).

nation within the network. There are further doubts about the feature of networks being undertakings, because the criterion of a uniform management can be missing given the fact that network members may voluntarily accept a uniform management and keep pursuing individual interests.

As a general rule, a company network as a whole is not to be considered as a single entity (undertaking). In fact, the single network members represent independent undertakings. Because of their connection within the network the particular network members could form an oligopoly if they reach the necessary market share and therefore could be addressees of Art. 102 TFEU in the case of infringements. According to this, in the following the criteria for collective market dominance are analysed.

## C. Criteria of collective dominance

Under Art. 102 TFEU, the abuse of a dominant position by one or more undertakings is incompatible with the internal market insofar as it may affect trade between Member States. A dominant position of several companies is presumed when the companies are in a position to prevent effective competition on the relevant market due to their dominant position, which allows them to behave autonomously toward their competitors, their trading partners and their consumers.[36] The Commission and European case law determine market power based on a number of factors stated below.

### I. Airtours criteria

According to the jurisprudence of the European Court three conditions must be satisfied cumulatively (known as the Airtours criteria) for collective dominance.[37] First, each member of the oligopoly must be in a position to find out about the market behavior of other companies to determine whether they commonly act on the market or not.[38] For this purpose the

36 ECJ ECR 1979, 461 recital 38 – Hoffman-La Roche; ECJ ECR 1980, 3775, 3793 recital 26, 30 – L'Oréal.

37 See ECJ ECR 2002, II-2585 recital 62 – Airtours; EGC ECR 2005, II-209 recital 111 – Piau; Ch. Höhn, EGC, RIW 2003, p. 63 (63).

38 EGC ECR 2002, II-2585 recital 62 – Airtours; EGC ECR 2005, II-209 recital 111 – Piau; *Eilmansberger, T.*, in: Münchener Kommentar zum Europäischen und

respective market needs to come with a transparent structure, enabling each member of the dominant oligopoly to determine the development of all the other firms' behavior in the market with reasonable accuracy and speed.[39] Secondly, it is required that a permanent tacit coordination can take place – at least hypothetically. Therefore, adequate incentives have to persist for the involved companies not to deviate from the agreed procedure on the market

This is the case when sufficient deterrence in the long term provides an incentive not to diverge from the agreed procedures and to adhere to the collective market behavior.[40] A network requires coordination for it to function and this necessary coordination in return requires the exchange of information[41] in order to enable the network members to coordinate with each other. This information exchange causes an increase in transparency within the network. Increased transparency in turn facilitates monitoring the network companies involved regarding the compliance of agreements. Due to the enabled monitoring the partners know which network company does not adhere to agreements and therefore know when to reprimand it.[42] To avoid such measures it is reasonable to assume that network companies tend to adhere to agreements and thus hold on collective market behavior.

Finally, the foreseeable reaction of customers and actual or potential competitors must not question the anticipated success of joint action.[43]

---

Deutschen Wettbewerbsrecht (Kartellrecht): Europäisches Wettbewerbsrecht, München 2007, EG, Art. 82 recital 88.

39 EGC ECR 2002, II-2585 recital 62 – Airtours; *Eilmansberger, T.*, in: Münchener Kommentar zum Europäischen und Deutschen Wettbewerbsrecht (Kartellrecht): Europäisches Wettbewerbsrecht, München 2007, EG, Art. 82 recital 88; *Wessely, T.*, in: Frankfurter Kommentar zum Kartellrecht, Köln 2012, EG, Art. 82 recital 143.

40 EGC ECR 2002, II-2585 recital 62 – Airtours; EGC ECR 2005, II-209 recital 111 – Piau; *Wessely, T.*, in: Frankfurter Kommentar zum Kartellrecht, Köln 2012, EG, Art. 82 recital 143.

41 *Krebs, P./Aedtner, K./Schultes, M.*, Company networks reloaded – putting a general functional approach to defining complex problems to the test, in this volume, B. V. „Exchange of economic independence for co-ordination in order to achieve the network aim".

42 *European Commission*, Communication – Guidelines on the applicability of Art. 101 of the Treaty on the Functioning of the European Union to horizontal cooperation agreements, 2011/C 11/01, recital 67; see *H.-Rosenberger, P.*, Verträge über Forschung und Entwicklung, 2. ed., Köln 2010, chap. 2, recital 49.

43 EGC ECR 2002, II-2585 recital 62 – Airtours; EGC ECR 2005, II-209 recital 111 – Piau.

Against this background it is to be analysed, whether a company would have to face countermeasures by competitors when conducting an autonomous and highly competitive measures, for example exercising an aggressive pricing policy, which would render such a deviation from the common action unattractive.Considering that network companies probably tend to abstain from (intensive) competition both within and outside the network in the course of time during their network cooperation out of consideration for the cooperation in the network, the common action is unlikely to be questioned.

## II. Criteria of dominance under Art. 2 par. 1 lit. b) of the EUMR

If it is established that several companies act as a collective unit on the market according to the Airtours criteria, is to be examined in a second step whether this collective actually holds a dominant position on the relevant market and whether it abused this position.[44] The existence of a dominant position generally results from the interplay of several factors which, taken separately, are not necessarily decisive.[45] Rather, an overall view of the various criteria is required, whereby focus in particular lays on the market position and the economic and financial strength of the companies involved, the alternatives available to suppliers and users, their access to supplies or markets and the development of supply and demand. Therefore, one usually differentiates between market-related and business-related criteria for collective dominance.[46]

With regard to the criteria referring to the market structure focus is particularly directed to the companies' market share in the relevant market.[47] When the companies have a combined market share of more than 85%,

---

44 ECJ ECR 2000, I-1365 recital 39 – Compagnie maritime belge transports.

45 ECJ ECR 1979, 461 recital 41 – Hoffman-La Roche; ECJ ECR 1991, I-3359 recital 60 – AKZO; ECJ ECR 1994, I-5641 recital 47 – DLG.

46 Art. 2 par. 1 lit. b) EUMR cannot be applied analogously, because it is not allowed to change European primary law by applying secondary law analogously as the legislator of the secondary law does not possess the competence to change primary law. However, the criteria mentioned in Art. 2 par. 1 lit. b) ECMR could serve as points of reference for developing the law in conformity with the system.

47 *Bunte, E.*, in: Langen, H.-J./Bunte,E., Kartellrecht, 11. ed. 2010, EG, Art. 82 recital 44; *Wessely, T.*, in: Frankfurter Kommentar zum Kartellrecht, Köln 2012, EG, Art. 82 recital 106; *Eilmansberger, T.*, in: Münchener Kommentar zum Europä-

they can behave independently of the other companies in the market readily, so that the existence of a collective dominant position can be approved.[48] This also applies to market share of 70 to 80%, which is a clear indication of the existence of a dominant position on the relevant market.[49] A dominant position can be affirmed for a market share of 55 % when it results in being ca. 10 – 15 % higher than the combined market shares of the two major competitors. Given the relation between the market shares a dominant position of this collective can be assumed in such a case.[50] Anyway, it is often referred to the relationship between the market shares of the company in question and those of its competitors. Thus, the evidentiary effect of a relatively high market share increases when a considerable distance between the respective shares is additionally given.[51]

However, a high market share is not immutable for the existence of a dominant position by more than one company. In fact, the relevance varies from market to market and depends on the particular production, supply and demand structure.[52] This follows from the fact that an interaction between the level of the market share and the structure of the market exists. A particularly important factor in this context are barriers to entry for third parties as well as barriers to expansion for companies already active on the market (see here explicitly the Airtours criteria).[53]

---

ischen und Deutschen Wettbewerbsrecht (Kartellrecht): Europäisches Wettbewerbsrecht, München 2007, EG, Art. 82 recital 104.

48 For the single dominance see ECJ ECR 1975, 1663 recital 379/380 – Suiker Unie; ECJ ECR 1996, I-5951 recital 28 – Tetra Pak II; *Wessely, T.*, in: Frankfurter Kommentar zum Kartellrecht, Köln 2012, EG, Art. 82 recital 109; *Bunte. E.*, in: Langen, H.-J./Bunte,E., Art. 82 recital 52.

49 EGC ECR 1991, II-1439 recital 92 – Hilti; *Eilmansberger, T.*, in: Münchener Kommentar zum Europäischen und Deutschen Wettbewerbsrecht (Kartellrecht): Europäisches Wettbewerbsrecht, München 2007, EG, Art. 82 recital 104; *T. Wessely*, in: Frankfurter Kommentar zum Kartellrecht, Köln 2012, EG, Art. 82 recital 109.

50 EGC ECR 1994, II-755 recital 119 – Tetra Pak.

51 ECJ ECR 1978, 207 recital 108, 110 – United Brands; ECJ ECR 1979, 461 recital 42, 48 – Hoffman-La Roche; EGC ECR 2003, II-5917 recital 210 – British Airways; *Bunte*, *E.* in: Langen, H.-J./Bunte,E., Kartellrecht, 11. ed. 2010, EG, Art. 82 recital 55.

52 ECJ ECR 1979, 461 recital 40 – Hoffman-La Roche.

53 Vgl. *Lettl, T.*, Kartellrecht, 2007, § 3 recital 18; *Mestmäcker, E.-J./ Schweitzer H.*, Europäisches Wettbewerbsrecht, 2004, § 16 recital 33; *de Bronett, G.* in: Wiedemann, G. (ed.), Handbuch des Kartellrechts, 2. ed., München 2008, § 22 recital 22;

The factor of the corporate structure includes criteria such as technological advantages, economies of scale, industrial property or resources (e.g. production and delivery capacity, access to commodity markets, economic and financial power, locational advantages, etc.).[54] A wide product range of businesses is also an indicator for collective dominance. This is especially the case when the product range of the dominant company is more diverse than that of its main competitors, since this fact gives the respective company the possibility to selectively respond to individual customer needs and to diversify economic risks in a better way.[55] In addition, a high level of productivity and profitability of the company - for example caused by advantages in the field of investment and research –can indicate a strong market position.[56]

The economic and financial power of oligopolists also plays a major role, since it can enable companies to prevent new competitors from entering the respective market effectively.[57] For instance, by flexibly increasing production and supply capacities and the creation of artificial barriers to market entry dominant companies can retain or even expand their dominant position in relation to their competitors. A further business-related

---

*Fuch S../Möschel, W.* in: Immenga, U./Mestmäcker, E.-J. (eds.), EU-WettbR, 5. ed., München 2012, Art. 102 recital 98.

54 See *Riesenkampff, A./ Lehr, S.*, in: Loewenheim, U./Meessen, K./Riesenkampff, A. (eds.), Kartellrecht, 2. ed., München 2009, VO 139/2004/EG, Art. 2 recital 7; *Körber, T.*, in: Immenga, U./Mestmäcker, E.-J. (eds.), EU-WettbR, 5. ed., München 2012, FKVO, Art. 2 recital 219 mentioning the undertaking related criteria of economic and financial power.

55 ECJ ECR 1983, 3461 recital 55 – Michelin; ECJ ECR 1991, I-3359 recital 58 – *AKZO*; *Bunte, E.*, in: Langen, H.-J./Bunte,E., Kartellrecht, 11. ed. 2010, EG, Art. 82 recital 61; *Wessely, T.*, in: Frankfurter Kommentar zum Kartellrecht, Köln 2012, EG, Art. 82 recital 119; *Eilmansberger, T.*, in: Münchener Kommentar zum Europäischen und Deutschen Wettbewerbsrecht (Kartellrecht): Europäisches Wettbewerbsrecht, München 2007, EG, Art. 82 recital 113.

56 ECJ ECR 1978, 207 recital 82, 84 – United Brands; *Bunte, E.*, in: Langen, H.-J./ Bunte,E., Kartellrecht, 11. ed. 2010, EG, Art. 82 recital 61; *Wessely, T.*, in: Frankfurter Kommentar zum Kartellrecht, Köln 2012, EG, Art. 82 recital 119; *Eilmansberger, T.*, in: Münchener Kommentar zum Europäischen und Deutschen Wettbewerbsrecht (Kartellrecht): Europäisches Wettbewerbsrecht, München 2007, EG, Art. 82 recital 113.

57 ECJ ECR 1978, 207 recital 121, 124 – United Brands; ECJ ECR 1983, 3461 recital 59 – Michelin.

factor for a dominant position is owning a respected and well-known brand.[58]

## D. Network specific link to the criteria of market power

The assessment of possibly existing market power by means of applying the market power criteria to company networks can ultimately only happen on a case-by-case basis. An overall evaluation can already be eliminated, because networks are diverse and at best can merely be evaluated schematically and non-universally. It seems important to engage with the question what to apply the criteria for market power to, i.e. which points of contact in company networks can be identified. This is carried out exemplarily by means of the market power criterion "market share" as well as the criterion "resources" related to the company structure.

### I. Market share

Regarding the question of market shares it is questionable whether the market shares of all companies participating in the network are to be taken into account or whether merely the market shares of those companies are to be considered which especially work in smaller groups[59] within the network. Considering the fact that the intention of some networks is to improve their market position due to their affiliation in a network then this already indicates that the market shares of all network companies are to be considered in the assessment of market power.

58 ECJ ECR 1978, 207 recital 93 – United Brands; European *Commission*, Decision of 14 May 1997 relating to a proceeding pursuant to Art. 86 ECT, IV/34.621, 35.059/F-3 – Irish Sugar plc, ABl. 1997, L 258/1, Tz. 109; *Wessely, T.,*: in: Frankfurter Kommentar zum Kartellrecht, Köln 2012, EG, Art. 82 recital 119; *Eilmansberger, T.*, in: Münchener Kommentar zum Europäischen und Deutschen Wettbewerbsrecht (Kartellrecht): Europäisches Wettbewerbsrecht, München 2007, EG, Art. 82 recital 113.

59 See *Krebs, P./Jung, S./Aedtner, K./Schultes, M.*, The modular system of network activities, in this volume, p. 75 (77 et seqq.).

Moreover, achieving cooperational profit in form of economic advantages is an essential feature of company networks.[60] In order to achieve advantages it is, however, not necessary that each network company always acts itself. The network companies can also profit from other cooperational groups, their activities and the thereby gained advantages, if, for instance, a cooperational group develops a new technology, which is then made available to all network companies. In this way, it seems appropriate to include all those companies and their market shares in the assessment of market power that benefit from the potential network advantages.

If, however, the advantages remain with merely a smaller group of network companies and are not available for all companies then only the market shares of the companies involved are to be considered. In general it can be expected that all companies profit from the advantages which is why in principle all market shares of all companies are to be included in the assessment of market power.

## II. Resources

Also regarding the criteria of company structure the question arises in connection to the examination of market power to what extent the individual features may be taken into account. The individual features which are to be considered in general can be broadly defined as resources. The bundling of resources is an essential feature of the definition of company networks.[61] The network companies have to provide the network with resources or integrate resources into the network so as to render it functional in the first place.

Regarding the assessment of market power, the question especially arises in this connection whether only the bundled resources are to be included in the evaluation or all resources which the individual networks possess. By bundling their resources in the network the individual network

60 *Krebs, P./Aedtner, K./Schultes, M.*, Company networks reloaded – putting a general functional approach to defining complex problems to the test, in this volume, p. 41 (53 et seqq.).

61 *Krebs, P./Aedtner, K./Schultes, M.*, Company networks reloaded – putting a general functional approach to defining complex problems to the test, in this volume, p. 41 (58 et seq.).

members relinquish their unlimited control over the respective resources.[62] However, they can still freely dispose of the resources which are not bundled in the network. The company network and the participating companies therefore have no actual possibility to access the resources which are not bundled. Accordingly, the possibility to access the resources depends on the respective network members. In this way, it seems appropriate to initially merely consider the resources bundled in the network for the assessment of market power of company networks.

Furthermore, potential resources are to be included in the question regarding market power if actual access possibilities exist in the network. If, for instance, agreements exist according to which individual network members have to provide the network with specific resources, e.g. in the case of financial constraints, then these should also be taken into account.

Basically, the resources bundled in the network and not the entire resources of the network companies are to be taken as a basis for the assessment of market power. If, moreover, the network has the actual possibility to access resources which are not bundled then the latter are also to be taken into account. This requires the actual possibility to access the resources which are not bundled, meaning the individual network companies have to relinquish their control over the resources.

## E. Result

Whilst company networks are an acknowledged phenomenon in practice the (juridical) research into networks is still at the beginning.[63] Reliable rules are especially needed when it comes to the juridical evaluation of company networks.[64] In the context of competition law this applies to the argumentation of market power as the preliminary stage of the prohibition of the misuse of a market dominating position according to Art. 102 TFEU.[65]

---

62 At least that applies to a „close“ bundeling where the resources are contributed to the network, see thereto *Krebs, P./Aedtner, K./Schultes, M.*, Company networks reloaded – putting a general functional approach to defining complex problems to the test, in this volume, p. 41 (58 et seq.).

63 See A.

64 See A.

65 See A.

The prohibition of market misuse is addressed to the company network in its entirety.[66] In general, this does not regard an individual company in the sense of an economic entity, but an affiliation of several legally and economically independent companies.[67] Moreover, the criterion of uniform management may be missing regularly in order to confirm the company feature of a network as a whole.[68] A consequence of the classification as a network affiliation is the fact that the assessment of market power is conducted according to the rules of collective market dominance.[69]

The collective market dominance is on the one hand determined on the basis of the *Airtours* criteria of the GC,[70] which are based on the three criteria market transparency, the lack of an incentive to divert from joint actions, and no impairment by the probable behaviour of competitors as well as consumers.[71] Furthermore, an assessment according to Art. 2 par. 1 lit. b) EUMR[72] follows which contains a feature catalogue of the market and company structure.[73] The market share and the resources of those involved are thereby of particular importance.[74]

As a general rule, the network as a whole is to be addressed when linking to the mentioned criteria.[75] This also applies irrespective of which network companies become active in specific cases as long as all members benefit from the advantages.[76] Regarding the criterion of the resources, the question additionally arises to what extent they should be included.[77] In this case, it depends on the resources already bundled in the network unless further access possibilities exist for the network.[78]

66 See B. II.
67 See B. II. 1., 2.
68 See B. II. 1., 2.
69 See B. II. 3.
70 See C. I.
71 See C. I.
72 See C. II.
73 See C. II.
74 See C. II., D.
75 See D.
76 See D. I.
77 See D. II.
78 See D. II.

# The scope of loyalty duties in dynamic networks

*Dr. Emily M. Weitzenboeck*

## A. Introduction[1]

The last three decades have witnessed the growth of new forms of entrepreneurial cooperation such as dynamic networks like virtual enterprises. Large firms disintegrate and reorganise into smaller units, focusing on core competences and outsourcing the other areas of business. In dynamic networks, small and medium businesses, including freelancers, link up together or with larger firms and form networks that respond quickly to business opportunities. These networks are often hybrid, having elements of contract-based organizations and corporate forms.

Three models of dynamic networks may be identified: (i) spontaneous and temporary virtual enterprises, i.e. co-operation forms of legally independent businesses and freelancers that are set up to specifically to address a business opportunity and disbanded once that has been addressed and the project completed;[2] (ii) virtual enterprises that are created for a limited time out of a pre-established pool of firms that provides an underlaying basis of trust to enable virtual enterprises to be quickly set up, and (iii) long-term dynamic networks with a lead partner.[3]

This paper will analyse the legal relationship that is created between participants in a dynamic network and will assess the standard of behaviour that is expected of them towards each other. In civil law countries, there is usually a general principle that contracts should be performed in

1 This paper is largely based on parts of *Weitzenboeck, E.M.*, A New Legal Framework for Emerging Business Models: Dynamic Networks as Collaborative Contracts, Edward Elgar Publishing, Cheltenham, Northampton , 2012.

2 This is based on the definition of the virtual enterprise by *Mertens, P./Faisst, W.*, Virtuelle Unternehmen - Idee, Informationsverarbeitung, Illusion, 1997, 18 Saarbrücker Arbeitstag für Industrie, Dienstleistung und Verwaltung.

3 For more on these three models of dynamic networks, see *Weitzenboeck, E.M.*, A New Legal Framework for Emerging Business Models: Dynamic Networks as Collaborative Contracts, 2012, pp. 5-9.

good faith. What, in practice, does this mean for the dynamic networks examined in this article?

This article will first analyse the civil law notion of good faith in contract performance, that is, the operation phase of the dynamic network when the parties are collaborating to perform the task or service to the client. It will enquire what behaviour is required from the contracting parties and what behaviour is proscribed. The enquiry will then look at the notion of good faith in common law countries and the different approaches taken in various common law jurisdictions ranging from England (where scholars are traditionally reluctant to admit such a notion in contract performance), the United States (where there is a statutory duty to perform contracts in good faith) and Australia (where there has not been a clear adoption as yet in Australian common law, though some states appear to have accepted the principle of good faith in contract performance).

This paper will then look at whether certain dynamic networks give rise to additional good faith duties than the classical, core, good faith duties required during contract performance, that is, whether they give rise to duties which are akin to fiduciary duties under partnership and company law. To what extent do or could members of a virtual enterprise owe fiduciary or fiduciary-like duties to the other members, and what are the implications of this?

## B. Good faith in the performance of collaborative contracts

Much of the literature on the notion of good faith in contract performance is based on the presumption that the contract in question is a bilateral contract where the parties very often have opposing interests, for example, between service provider and customer or between buyer and seller. An analysis of the duty of good faith in contract performance in this literature, therefore, must be viewed in this light, that is, that the legal scholar in question is discussing good faith duties in bilateral exchange contracts.

Virtual enterprises are usually made up of more than two parties. The typical contract used is a multilateral contract. However, a virtual enterprise may be made up of a nexus of contracts such as a contract between a virtual enterprise party and the client, and a series of subcontracting contracts between the other virtual enterprise parties, together with an underlying association, company or partnership-like structure for the enterprise pool.[4] A nexus of contracts is what is most typical for long-term dynamic networks with a lead partner.

In order to examine and understand fully the content and extent of the duty of good faith in contract performance, the literature on bilateral (exchange-type) contracts is first examined. As we shall see, legal scholars have generally discussed the notion of good faith in contract performance as consisting of two main duties (i) the duty to co-operate and (ii) the duty to provide information. The extent and manner in which such duties are applied to the operation phase of a dynamic network will then be examined. Extensive reference will be made to French doctrine where the duty of good faith in contract performance, in particular disclosure duties, has been greatly developed by the courts. Reference will also be made to legal scholars in other civil law jurisdictions (Germany and Italy) and in Norway. Such reference is made not just to show how certain countries have interpreted each of these good faith duties (*de lege lata*) but also to see how such good faith duties could be interpreted in other countries with a similar legal tradition and culture but which have not yet done so or felt the need to do so (*de lege ferenda*). For ease of reference, these two good faith duties will be referred to as the **core** good faith duties in contract performance.

Two other loyalty-related duties that come to the fore in collaborative contracts and that are often discussed in literature on joint ventures – in particular but not exclusively, in common law literature – are the extent to which there is a duty (iii) to keep confidential certain information provided by the other parties and to refrain from misusing it, and (iv) to refrain from competing with the other joint venture parties.[5] These are referred to as **additional** good faith duties in this article, again for ease of reference. These two matters are usually regulated in the joint venture or consortium or other collaborative agreement through, respectively, a confidentiality clause and a non-competition clause, or through statutory provisions, e.g.

4 See, for example, the Virtuelle Fabrik and the VirtuellBau networks in *Weitzenboeck, E.M.*, A New Legal Framework for Emerging Business Models: Dynamic Networks as Collaborative Contracts, 2012, pp. 42-49.

5 See, for example, *Nordtveit, E.*, Oppdragssamarbeid – Joint Ventures: Samarbeidsformer innenfor entreprenørverksemd, konsulenttenester og leverandørindustri, Oslo, 1992, chapter 10 entitled *''Lojalitetsplikter' i samarbeidstilhøvet'*; *Hewitt, I.*, Hewitt on Joint Ventures, London (and others), 2011, para 11-06 on 'Misuse of confidential information', para 11-07 and 11-08 on 'Non-compete'.

through trade secret law. These two loyalty-related duties are derived from the fiduciary duties discussed in partnership law and company law and are owed by partners to each other and to the partnership, and by officers of the company (directors, managers) to the company (and, in some countries, to the shareholders).[6] However, what happens if there is no statutory protection or contractual clause to regulate these matters, i.e. the use of confidential information and the duty not to compete? The rest of this paper will examine to what extent, in the case of collaborative networks like the dynamic networks, one could argue that these additional good faith duties apply to the contractual parties *in the absence of specific statutory recognition or contractual provision*. It will be shown that these additional good faith duties are fiduciary obligations, and that a collaborative contract *may* – depending on the type of network – give rise to fiduciary obligations even though the collaborative contract itself is not a fiduciary contract in the sense that a partnership or a (common law) trust is. To better discuss the notion of fiduciary obligations, we will also examine fiduciary relationships and look closely at the fiduciary duties in partnerships and companies.

Before proceeding with this discussion, it is important to clarify that even where a contractual relationship is not a fiduciary relationship, certain parts of the relationship could still give rise to fiduciary obligations. As Bean states:

> We can consider a relationship as fiduciary not only on a general level, dealing with the attendant features of the relationship, but in respect of a particular matter or matters. Where the relationship is only fiduciary in respect of a particular matter, it is apt not to refer to it as a fiduciary relationship but as a fiduciary duty since the whole relationship is not fiduciary.[7]

That is why Finn emphasised that

> it is meaningless to talk of fiduciary relationships as such. Once one looks to the rules and principles which actually have been evolved, it quickly becomes apparent that it is pointless to describe a person – or for that matter a power –

---

6 *Nordtveit, E.*, Oppdragssamarbeid – Joint Ventures: Samarbeidsformer innenfor entreprenørverksemd, konsulenttenester og leverandørindustri, Oslo, 1992, p. 280 holds that the duty not to compete, to keep information that can harm the other partners confidential and similar duties are often called *lojalitetsplikter* because they are the typical result of the general duty of loyalty in partnership/company law.

7 *Bean, G.M.D*, Fiduciary Obligations and Joint Ventures, Gloucestershire, 1995, p. 36.

> as being fiduciary unless at the same time it is said for the purposes of which particular rules and principles that description is being used.[8]

He added that '[t]hese rules are everything. The description "fiduciary" nothing.'[9] He explained further that '[i]t is not because a person is a "fiduciary" or a "confidant" that a rule applies to him. It is because a particular rule applies to him that he is a fiduciary or confidant *for its purpose.*' [Finn's emphasis][10] Further on in his book – which he called *Fiduciary Obligations* and not, it must be observed, fiduciary relationships – he reiterates this principle.[11]

In the forthcoming discussion, one should distinguish between three types of contracts:

1. *discrete or exchange contracts* where each party pursues its own commercial interest which can be seen as antagonistic to that of the other party: in civil law countries and in the US, the parties must nevertheless observe the core good faith duties discussed above and which will be examined in more detail below.
2. *collaborative contracts* where parties collaborate together to provide one product or service or to jointly discover, develop or create a product or service: even here the parties are not precluded from having and pursuing their own commercial interests when performing the contract as long as this does not go against the core and additional good faith duties discussed above;
3. *fiduciary contracts or fiduciary relationships* such as agency, insurance, partnership or company. With regards to the latter two types of relationships, as a rule, fiduciary duties are owed by partners in a partnership towards the other partners and the partnership, and also by the directors and managers of a company towards the company, as discussed below (section E). The reason is because the fiduciary is serving and protecting the interest of the partnership (and the other partners) or, in the case of a director, of the company, is in a relationship of trust and dependency.

---

8 See *Finn, P.D.*, Fiduciary Obligations, Sydney, 1977, para 2.

9 *Ibid.*

10 *Ibid,* para 3.

11 Finn states that 'a person is *not* a "fiduciary" – or a "confidant" – until a duty applies to him. When one does, he then becomes a "fiduciary" – or a "confidant" – but for the purposes of that duty only.' *Ibid*, para 159.

In other words, what I have called 'additional good faith duties' – in civil law jargon – are fiduciary duties in common law jargon. A sharp distinction should be kept between these three different types of commercial relationships highlighted above. Moreover, it should be borne in mind that although, in general, collaborative contracts such as those underlying dynamic networks do not give rise to fiduciary relationships, certain fiduciary duties – or additional good faith duties – may arise with respect to some particular matter or matters, to the extent discussed below.

### I. Good faith distinguished from the notion of abuse of rights

Some authors have linked the notion of good faith in the performance of contract with the theory of abuse of rights, in the sense that the good faith of a contracting party consists in not abusing one's rights.

Good faith, through the theory of abuse of right, is thus seen as a negative right imposing certain limits on the exercise of one's rights. In German law this is known as the *Schrankenfunktion*[12] of good faith. An application of the theory of abuse of rights in German law mentioned by Markesinis *et al* is the prohibition of *venire contra factum proprium*, that is, a person exercising a right must not contradict his own previous conduct which induced reliance by the other party.[13]

This notion is abstract and difficult to define and many of the cases referred to by scholars are more akin to other legal notions like waiver and the common law notion of estoppel.[14] There is no unitary interpretation of *abus de droit* by the French courts.[15] Picod, in his doctoral thesis on good faith in contract performance in French law, sees a very limited applica-

---

12 *Markesinis, B.S./Unberath, H./Johnston*, A., The German Law of Contract: A Comparative Treatise, Oxford (and others), 2006, p. 123 refer to this as the 'internal' limits of rights. In this sense, good faith limits the enforcement of existing rights.

13 *Ibid.*

14 *Ibid. Markesinis, B.S./Unberath, H./Johnston, A.*, cite, for example, BGHZ 18, 340 (26.10.1955) where a lawyer was not entitled to charge more than he suggested on an earlier occasion; BGHZ 50, 191 (20.5.1968) concerning a person who invoked an arbitration clause before the ordinary court after having previously opposed arbitration on grounds of jurisdiction.

15 See *Picod, Y.*, Le Devoir de Loyauté dans l'Exécution du Contrat, Paris, 1989, p. 37.

tion of the theory of *abus de droit* – as distinct from good faith – in contract performance, namely in the area of rescission of a contract.[16]

The prohibitory function of the notion of abuse of rights applies not just to the manner of performance by the debtor but also to the enforcement of a right by the creditor of an obligation. As Markesinis et al observe, 'The right as such is not contested but merely the manner in which its enforcement is attempted.'[17]

Ripert applies a narrow interpretation of abuse of right as requiring the intention to harm.[18] However, if one were to interpret abuse of right as 'intentional fault', this takes us back to the general notion of contractual fault. As Picod explains, this would mean that good faith consists in not committing fault in the exercise of contractual prerogatives,[19] and does not take us much further than the general notion of performing a contract diligently.

## II. Duty to co-operate

Picod states that the duty to co-operate in the performance of a contract does not imply any particular sacrifice on the contracting parties.[20] This duty refers to a minimal degree of loyalty of each contracting party to take into consideration the interests of the other contracting party, in order to make things easier for him.[21] In France, the courts have recognised a duty

16 *Ibid*, p. 35. The general rule in the *Code Civil* is that contracts have the effect of law between the contracting parties, and a party is not allowed to unilaterally get out of a contract. This rule has two exceptions: (i) where a party has reserved the right to rescind a contract by the insertion of a rescission clause in the contract; (ii) where the law expressly allows a party to rescind a contract in certain circumstances such as by choosing to forfeit earnest money instead of entering into a contract of sale (article 1590). According to *Picod, Y.*, the only claim against the exercise of a right of rescission is for the other party to prove that this right was exercised disloyally, and was thus an abuse of a right.

17 *Markesinis, B.S./Unberath, H./Johnston, A.*, The German Law of Contract: A Comparative Treatise, Oxford (and others), 2006, p. 125.

18 See further *Picod, Y.*, Le Devoir de Loyauté dans l'Exécution du Contrat, Paris, 1989, p. 35; *Ripert, G.*, La règle morale dans les obligations civiles, Paris, 1949, para 92.

19 *Picod, Y.*, Le Devoir de Loyauté dans l'Exécution du Contrat, Paris, 1989, p. 36.

20 *Ibid*, p. 101.

21 *Ibid*, p. 102.

of co-operation on both the obligation-debtor[22] and the obligation-creditor: (i) the obligation-creditor has a duty to facilitate the execution of the obligation by the obligation-debtor and (ii) the obligation-debtor has a duty to co-operate with his creditor in order to allow the creditor to obtain the maximum benefit desired from his execution.[23]

The creditor of an obligation must abstain from manoeuvres which will make the performance of the contract impossible or more onerous for the debtor. He is also deemed to be in breach of his duty of loyalty if he imposes pecuniary hardships on the debtor which are disproportionate to the usefulness of the object which the contract is aimed to achieve. Therefore, he should refrain from causing the debtor useless expenses. For example, French jurisprudence has held that a carrier should send merchandise on the itinerary which is most advantageous for the shipper.[24]

The duty on the obligation-debtor to co-operate was illustrated in a case decided by the Court of Appeal of Paris which held that a firm that had to furnish a software application to its contracting party was bound, on one hand, to aid its client to define and clarify its needs and requirements, and on the other hand, to carry out a preliminary and serious study of the defined requirements to create a software which satisfies those needs as closely as possible.[25]

In other words, each party has a duty to facilitate the performance of the contract by the other party. Thus, in a publishing contract, the author must correct the proofs and return them.[26]

German law has also recognised a duty of co-operation between the parties.

> The parties are under an obligation to assist each other in respect of the performance of the contract where good faith requires it. Such an obligation is

---

22 The debtor of an obligation or 'obligation-debtor' is the party who has the duty to carry out performance of an obligation. The creditor of an obligation or 'obligation-creditor' is the party to whom or to whose benefit performance is carried out.

23 See further *Picod, Y.,* Le Devoir de Loyauté dans l'Exécution du Contrat, Paris, 1989, p. 107-110.

24 *Weill, A./Terré, F.*, Droit Civil: Les Obligations, Paris, 1986, p. 360.

25 Paris, 18.6.1984, cited by *Picod, Y.*, Le Devoir de Loyauté dans l'Exécution du Contrat, Paris, 1989, p. 110.

26 Trib. Civ Seine 15.4.1863, Pataille 1865 p. 47 cited by *Picod, Y.,* Le Devoir de Loyauté dans l'Exécution du Contrat, Paris, 1989, p. 107.

likely to arise where it is necessary to secure the effectiveness of that performance.[27]

As to the precise scope of this obligation under German law, this depends on the particular circumstances of the case. Thus, for example, one party may be under an obligation to provide documentation where this is necessary in dealing with tax authorities (e.g. BGH NJW 1992, 1695),[28] or where it is needed to procure a loan (e.g. BGH NJW 1973, 1793).[29] Where the performance of the contract hinges on some act by the other party, the latter is required to co-operate, for instance where the required authorities' approval of the transaction depends on it (e.g. BGH NJW 1989, 1607).[30]

Cian and Trabucchi, commenting on Italian law, describe good faith as *un generale dovere di solidarietà* – a general duty to show solidarity – which obliges each of the parties to act in such as way as to preserve the interests of the other party insofar as this does not import an appreciable sacrifice of one's reasons for contracting.[31]

An important point that should be highlighted is that the more technically complex the subject-matter of the contract is, the more there is need for collaboration between the parties. Picod illustrates this with the example of a provider of a software system who should not just deliver the software programmes, but should also have carried out preliminary studies to help the user determine his needs, and who should also provide assistance in the use of the software, its maintenance and in the training of personnel.[32] It should be pointed out that the provision of bespoke or tailor-made software is a specialised field of information technology law and many of the issues mentioned by Picod are very often the subject of detailed clauses in the software contract (e.g. clauses on delivery, commissioning and acceptance of software) or of separate, ancillary computer contracts (e.g. maintenance agreements, training contracts).

---

27 *Markesinis, B.S./Unberath, H./Johnston, A.*, The German Law of Contract: A Comparative Treatise, Oxford (and others), 2006, p. 128.

28 Judgment dated 13.2.1992.

29 Judgment dated 1.6.1973.

30 Judgment dated 3.2.1989. See further on these cases *Markesinis, B.S./Unberath, H./Johnston, A.*, The German Law of Contract: A Comparative Treatise, Oxford (and others), 2006, pp.128-129.

31 See *Cian, G./Trabucchi, A.*, Commentario Breve al Codice Civile, Padua, 2009, para 1375 commenting on the Italian Civil Code article 1375 (a contract must be executed in good faith).

32 *Picod, Y.*, Le Devoir de Loyauté dans l'Exécution du Contrat, Paris, 1989, p. 110.

Similarly, the more technically complex a virtual enterprise contract is, in particular one between parties in an enterprise pool, the more heightened is the need for collaboration between the virtual enterprise parties.

Applied to virtual enterprises, this duty will import that each party must participate in the performance of the task which forms the object of the contract, because each party's effort is determining for the successful performance of the task and hence of the contract. As Nordtveit opines, writing on joint ventures in Norwegian law, the duty to take part in the management body, such as a steering committee, of the virtual enterprise is of paramount importance since this will enable the collaboration to reach its aims.[33]

## III. Duty to provide information/duty to disclose

The duty to co-operate is linked with the duty of disclosure in virtue of which one party may be deemed to have a duty to bring to the knowledge of the other party certain facts which he has an interest to know in order to perform the contract. Picod sees the obligation to disclose or to provide information as a corollary of the duty to co-operate.[34] The French courts have extensively developed the duty to provide information (*obligation de renseignement*), and therefore detailed reference is made to the content and extent of this obligation in French law to explore the content of this duty.

In France, the obligation to inform at first arose in the context of contracts of sale,[35] was further developed in jurisprudence, and today it 'has attained a degree of independence and unity that has emancipated it from

33 *Nordtveit, E.*, Oppdragssamarbeid – Joint Ventures: Samarbeidsformer innenfor entreprenørverksemd, konsulenttenesterog leverandørindustri, Oslo, 1992, p. 279.

34 *Picod, Y.*, Le Devoir de Loyauté dans l'Exécution du Contrat, Paris, 1989, pp. 101-102, 111-127.

35 In particular, in the statutory warranty against latent defects of the object sold – see *Picod, Y.*, Le Devoir de Loyauté dans l'Exécution du Contrat, Paris, 1989, p. 113. Similarly, a lessor should inform the lessee about known defects in the property leased. See *Weill, A./Terré, F.*, Droit Civil: Les Obligations, Paris, 1986, p. 361.

its parent, good faith'.[36] The party's mutual duty to carry out a contract in good faith requires 'a sort of association, of collaboration,' between them to enable them to achieve their particular aspiration.[37] Thus, the obligation-debtor should perform in a way which facilitates the enjoyment of the performance by the obligation-creditor, and the obligation-creditor should facilitate for his debtor the execution of his obligations. Consequently, each time that some information could be useful to a contracting party, jurisprudence will charge the other party with an obligation to disclose.[38]

In France, the courts have recognised stricter duties of disclosure in contracts where one party has certain specialist knowledge or technical competence and the product forming the object of the execution is dangerous or where the performance of the contract will give rise to a certain risk (of danger). Thus, where these two criteria are combined: (i) specialist knowledge or technical competence coupled with (ii) danger or risk of danger, there is a stricter duty of disclosure. The Court of Cassation has clearly affirmed that every manufacturer or seller of a dangerous product has a contractual duty to inform the buyer of the danger.[39] With regards to the duty to provide information on risk of danger, the example often cited by jurists is the duty of medical doctors to provide their patients with precise and complete information prior to medical intervention.[40]

Another situation where the French courts have recognised duties of disclosure is where a person, again having specialist knowledge or technical competence, has a duty to provide advice or counsel. If one examines the cases and examples cited by jurists, it emerges that these are situations where one of the parties – the person having specialist knowledge or tech-

---

36 *Whittaker, S./Zimmermann*, R., Good Faith in European Contract Law: Surveying the Legal Landscape, in: Zimmermann, R./Whittaker, S. (eds), Good Faith in European Contract Law, Cambridge, 2000, p. 36.

37 *Alisse* (1975) 90, cited by *Picod, Y.*, Le Devoir de Loyauté dans l'Exécution du Contrat, Paris, 1989, p. 114.

38 See further, *Picod, Y.*, Le Devoir de Loyauté dans l'Exécution du Contrat, Paris, 1989, p. 114.

39 Judgment of 31.01.1973, cited by *Picod, Y.*, Le Devoir de Loyauté dans l'Exécution du Contrat, Paris, 1989, p. 117. Weill and Terré similarly cite French jurisprudence which has held that the manufacturer or the seller of a piece of equipment should indicate its mode of use and the dangers that its use may bring. See Weill, A./Terré, F., Droit Civil: Les Obligations, Paris, 1986, p. 361.

40 See *Picod, Y.*, Le Devoir de Loyauté dans l'Exécution du Contrat, Paris, 1989, p. 119.

nical competence – *is in a position of trust*. These include medical doctors, notaries, estate agents, bankers, insurers and also car mechanics and professional (i.e. expert) sellers. Thus, for example, it was held in France that a car mechanic should warn the client against carrying out expenses which are disproportionate to the market value of the car. Similarly, expert sellers must inform their client of any inherent inconveniences of the material or fabric chosen by the client for the manufacture of the product (e.g. furniture).[41]

It should be noted that it is the non-expert party who is protected by the French courts. Such party benefits from a sort of presumption of legitimate ignorance (*presumption d'ignorance légitime*), in particular because the other contracting party is an expert in whom he could have confidence. However, this is not a right acquired from passivity in the sense that the non-expert party is not exempted from the duty to find out information. To treat the non-expert party as an incapable adult (*un incapable majeur*) is to encourage his bad faith. As Picod states, he should show 'a minimum degree of curiosity'.[42] Moreover, he also has the duty to engage in dialogue with the expert party. Thus, the duty to inform of the latter is counter-balanced by the duty to co-operate on the part of the other party.[43]

Up to now, we have seen that the two broad categories in which the French courts have recognised a duty to provide information are linked with the quality of one of the parties, i.e. that one of the parties is a specialist who has expert knowledge or technical competence. There is a third category, discussed by Picod,[44] which is independent of the quality of the parties. In contracts whose performance is not instantaneous but spread out in time (e.g. contract of works or lease) each party should inform the other party of any event which is susceptible of modifying the execution of the contract by the other party or of any fact which could facilitate the execution of the other party. Picod holds that any change in the execution should be pointed out, whether it is a change of risks, of a difficulty in performance or of an overrun of a contractual expectation.[45]

---

41 *Picod, Y.*, Le Devoir de Loyauté dans l'Exécution du Contrat, Paris, 1989, p. 122.

42 *Picod, Y.*, Le Devoir de Loyauté dans l'Exécution du Contrat, Paris, 1989, p. 126.

43 *Picod, Y.*, Le Devoir de Loyauté dans l'Exécution du Contrat, Paris, 1989, p. 126.

44 *Picod, Y.*, Le Devoir de Loyauté dans l'Exécution du Contrat, Paris, 1989, pp. 123-125.

45 *Picod, Y.*, Le Devoir de Loyauté dans l'Exécution du Contrat, Paris, 1989, p. 123.

How could these three categories be applied among virtual enterprise parties? First and foremost, each party should provide sufficient information on its part of the performance (i.e. on the part of the whole task which that party performed) to enable the other virtual enterprise parties to carry out their part of the task so that together they achieve the aim or object of the virtual enterprise contract, such as to provide a product or service to the customer. This includes providing information on any danger or special risks of danger in handling or using some item being produced or some dangerous equipment put at the disposal of the virtual enterprise, in cases where the other virtual enterprise parties have no technical expertise in using such item or equipment, or cannot be expected to have such expertise. Most importantly are the third category duties identified by Picod. Thus, a party should inform the other virtual enterprise parties of any event which could impinge on the successful or timely execution of the contract. Any change or potential change in the execution of the contract should be pointed out. In addition to this, any information which could facilitate the execution of any or all of the other parties should also be provided.

The parties may also specifically agree in the contract that certain information should be provided by one or some of the parties. Such a provision is binding by virtue of it being a contractual provision, having thus 'the force of law' between the contracting parties[46] and there is no need to further analyse whether such information should be disclosed as a corollary of the duty to co-operate.[47]

## IV. Non-misuse of confidential information

The duty not to misuse confidential information includes both a duty to keep the information confidential and also a duty to use that information for the project purposes only. The duty of confidentiality, like the duty to disclose discussed in the preceding section, also concerns information. However, whereas the duty to inform is an *active* duty involving the duty

46 See *Weitzenboeck, E.M.*, A New Legal Framework for Emerging Business Models: Dynamic Networks as Collaborative Contracts, Cheltenham, Northampton, 2012, pp. 156-159.

47 See further *Picod, Y.*, Le Devoir de Loyauté dans l'Exécution du Contrat, Paris, 1989, p. 112.

to provide information to the other contracting parties, the duty of confidentiality involves both a *passive* duty (to keep information that was disclosed in confidence secret) and an *active* duty (the duty not to misuse that confidential information by, for example, producing a similar product or service).

An important concern of a virtual enterprise party, as indeed any other project party, is that any confidential information disclosed to the other parties is kept confidential and used for the project purposes only. This concern applies with regard to information disclosed during the negotiation stage as well as during the performance of the project. The fear is that a party will use for its own purposes information or technology that has been disclosed which either is another party's property or was developed in the project and intended to be used only for the project. Some countries have a statutory duty to keep certain information confidential where trade secrets are protected either as part of unfair competition law or through a specific law.[48] Such statutory provisions are very often supplemented by contractual provisions protecting intellectual property and confidential information. In fact, many of the enterprise pool rulebooks or statutes have detailed provisions on the use of proprietary information including intellectual property both during a particular project and afterwards.[49]

The length of time that a co-operative venture has been running is also an important factor, when determining the nature of the relationship of the parties. In (Rt 1997 p 199) the Norwegian Supreme Court held that where a joint venture had run for a long period of time, as was the case before them, the collaboration between the former parties could give rise to a special loyalty (*en særlig lojalitet*). The court cited with approval Stuevold Lassen (1988), and held that businesses that are in a contractual relationship with each other, or had been, or are negotiating to enter into such a relationship, must show a greater consideration than outsiders. 'He who has been trusted, has a special duty to show consideration.'[50]

48 See, in particular, *Weitzenboeck, E.M.*, A New Legal Framework for Emerging Business Models: Dynamic Networks as Collaborative Contracts, Cheltenham, Northampton, 2012, pp. 105-108.

49 Such provisions could be simple or detailed, depending on the scope of the collaborative project, and whether any intellectual property or other confidential information is expected to be developed in such project.

50 My translation; see *Stuevold Lassen, B.*, Om Tyveri av Bygninger og Anlegg – Idébeskyttelse og Vern mot Etterligning, 1988.

Bean, writing on fiduciary obligations and joint ventures in common law, holds that a fiduciary duty requiring the fiduciary not to disclose confidential information may exist.[51] He distinguishes between fiduciary law and the law of confidential information. The former is solely a creation of equity, the latter has its roots in both common law and equity. Bean explains that a fiduciary duty and a duty of confidentiality arising out of the same facts may co-exist. However, they need not do so and the types of duty have differences. Thus, a breach of duty of confidentiality may require damage to be proved whereas a breach of a duty of confidentiality, if treated as fiduciary, does not require damages.[52]

## V. Non-competition

Having joined a virtual enterprise, one of the main concerns of a participant is that another participant will not compete with it with regards to the same business opportunity. This concern exists both during the time that such a firm is a participant in a virtual enterprise and, even more, if such a firm is no longer a participant, having either been expelled or allowed to withdraw from the virtual enterprise. It is therefore common to find a non-competition clause in a virtual enterprise agreement prohibiting a party who had been expelled or allowed to withdraw from trying to take over or otherwise complete work which fell within the virtual enterprise agreement.

It is likely that there is a higher risk of such recalcitrant behaviour from a party in a spontaneous, one-off virtual enterprise, than a party in a virtual enterprise formed out of an enterprise pool. In the latter case, the party is also risking expulsion from the enterprise pool for such behaviour, seriously prejudicing chances of future collaboration not just with the virtual enterprise parties but with all the other members in the enterprise pool.

The difficulty that arises is with regards to the extent and limit of the obligation not to carry out competing activity. One should bear in mind that for many parties, a specific virtual enterprise agreement would just be

51 *Bean, G.M.D.*, Fiduciary Obligations and Joint Ventures, Gloucestershire, 1995, p. 42.

52 *Bean, G.M.D.*, Fiduciary Obligations and Joint Ventures, Gloucestershire,1995, p. 42.

a part of its whole business activity, and that such party would also be involved in a number of other business ventures and deals.

This matter has been extensively discussed by Nordtveit with regards to the position in Norway in the case of joint venture agreements.[53] He is against a general, sweeping prohibition of carrying out any activity in the same business field. In a joint venture agreement, the parties are obliged to collaborate on a very specific task for a certain (limited) period of time, but will otherwise also carry out their own business operations irrespective of each other, both during the performance of the joint venture and afterwards. Therefore, he explains, it is difficult to start from the premise that parties cannot carry out an activity that is similar to that being carried out in the joint venture.[54]

One should distinguish between prohibiting a party from taking over work that is being specifically carried out by a virtual enterprise from a general prohibition of a party to compete in the same line of business. The former prohibition is justifiable and in some countries, such as Norway, it is deemed to fall within the general duty of loyalty (*lojalitetsplikten*) that joint venture parties owe to each other. The latter prohibition, however, is likely to be in restraint of trade.[55] This is, probably, even more true in the case of virtual enterprises where the parties are usually small and medium-sized enterprises, and have one, or a few, special competence(s) or expertise. Prohibiting a party from using or exercising that expertise is tantamount to ordering it to close down the rest of its business activities. In England, if one of the virtual enterprise parties were to take over work that is being specifically carried out by the virtual enterprise, it or they are likely to be considered in breach of contract. However, in English law, where there is no generally-recognised duty to carry out contracts in good faith, the extent of any general duties not to compete 'are, in very many cases, not sufficiently clear to provide any remedy.'[56] It is thus common to find recommendations in common law publications on joint ventures that

53 *Nordtveit, E.*, Oppdragssamarbeid – Joint Ventures: Samarbeidsformer innenfor entreprenørverksemd, konsulenttenester og leverandørindustri, Oslo, 1992, p. 280 *et seq.*

54 *Nordtveit, E.*, Oppdragssamarbeid – Joint Ventures: Samarbeidsformer innenfor entreprenørverksemd, konsulenttenester og leverandørindustri, Oslo, 1992, p. 282.

55 *Hasaas, O.*, Lojalitetsplikt i Norsk og Internasjonale Kontraktsforhold, in: Industribygging og Rettsutvikling: Juridisk Festskrift i Anledning Hydros 100-årsjubileum, Bergen, 2005, pp. 337-338, concurs.

56 *Hewitt, I.*, Hewitt on Joint Ventures, London (and others), 2011 para 11-07.

are mainly addressed to practitioners, to be clear in the contract between the parties as to what can and cannot be undertaken by each party in its separate business. Hewitt, who has written one of the main publications on joint ventures for practitioners in common law, has listed a number of issues that need to be addressed such as: whether the non-compete obligation is intended to apply also to any subsidiaries, what the scope of the prohibited activity is, and whether there are to be any exceptions to the non-compete prohibition.[57]

Another question that arises is with regards to new projects or business opportunities in the same line of business and requiring similar skills that may arise while a virtual enterprise is in operation. A distinction should be made between a virtual enterprise, where the collaboration is carried out on the basis of a virtual enterprise contract and also, possibly, on a nexus of contracts or other legal mechanisms as explained earlier, and a corporate joint venture. In the latter case, the parties would have specifically set up a partnership or company to carry out their collaboration and thus, any business activity in the same subject-matter (i.e. according to the objects of the partnership or company) or the same geographical area could be harmful to the partnership or company as it could deprive it of some of its market.[58] In the case of a contractual collaboration such as a virtual enterprise, the parties would naturally expect to be free to offer their services, perhaps even together with some of the other parties in the virtual enterprise, in response to a new business opportunity. Of course, the virtual enterprise agreement could impose some limitations on this.

What about the case where there is a new business opportunity to establish a new project that is intricately linked with an existing project being carried out by a virtual enterprise? Is there a duty, on the party who is approached by the client with the project proposal, to invite the current project parties to also form part of a new virtual enterprise to bid for the new project?

This matter arose in the United States in *Meinhard v Salmon* with regards to a joint venture.[59] Salmon had leased a piece of property for 20 years, backed by funds from a joint venture with Meinhard where the lat-

57 *Hewitt, I.*, Hewitt on Joint Ventures, London (and others), 2011, para 11-08.

58 See further on this *Nordtveit, E.*, Oppdragssamarbeid – Joint Ventures: Samarbeidsformer innenfor entreprenørverksemd, konsulenttenester og leverandørindustri, Oslo, 1992, pp. 282-283.

59 New York Court of Appeals, 1928, 249 NY 458, 164 NE 545.

ter was to pay Salmon half of the money required for the project. When the lease was near its end, the new owner of the reversion wanted to lease other property in the neighbourhood, for a long term to someone who would destroy the buildings and put up another in their place. He approached Salmon and a property controlled by Salmon leased the property. When Meinhard found out about the new project, he wanted the lease to be held in trust as an asset of his venture with Salmon, making offer in the trial to share the personal obligations incidental to the guaranty. Salmon refused. The New York Court of Appeals held that 'joint adventurers, like copartners, owe to one another, while the enterprise continues, the duty of the finest loyalty.' The court held as very significant the fact that Salmon kept Meinhard in the dark and 'appropriated to himself in secrecy and silence'. Had he informed Meinhard that the plan had been submitted and that he could also compete for the award, the court would have decided differently:

> If he had done this, we do not need to say whether he would have been under a duty, if successful in the competition, to hold the lease so acquired for the benefit of a venture then about to end, and thus prolong by indirection its responsibilities and duties. *The trouble about his conduct is that he excluded his coadventurer from any chance to compete, from any chance to enjoy the opportunity for benefit that had come to him alone by virtue of his agency. This chance, if nothing more, he was under a duty to concede.* [my emphasis]

Nordtveit, writing on joint ventures in Norway, holds that what might give a basis for holding that there is a duty to have the other project parties (in our case, the other virtual enterprise parties) in the new project, is that there is a close inner connection between the current project and the new project, and that the existence of the current contract with the client is the reason why that party was approached with the new project.[60] Nordtveit, in a footnote, then continues that this seems to have been the defining reasoning in *Meinhard v Salmon.*

However, I would suggest that what the Court of Appeal in *Meinhard v Salmon* objected to was that Salmon kept Meinhard in the dark and 'appropriated to himself in secrecy and silence' the new business opportunity. In fact, the Court clearly stated that had Salmon informed Meinhard and

60 See *Nordtveit, E.*, Oppdragssamarbeid – Joint Ventures: Samarbeidsformer innenfor entreprenørverksemd, konsulenttenester og leverandørindustri, Oslo, 1992, pp. 284-285.

given him the chance to make a competing bid, the dispute would not have arisen.[61]

I hold that what the US Court of Appeal recognised was *a duty to inform* the other co-adventurer(s) of the new, closely knit, project, and not a duty on the party approached with the spin-off project to have them as project partners also in the new project. Giving them a chance or opportunity to compete, by informing them of the business opportunity, is what the court required. Whether that is done through a joint project with the party who informed them of the spin-off opportunity, or whether the other parties or some of them decide to compete alone or in other co-operative ventures (or other virtual enterprises), is not the matter at issue.

I would also further qualify the duty to inform current parties of a spin-off business opportunity as per *Meinhard v Salmon*. In this American case there were two other important factors to which the court gave weight in its decision: (1) the fact that the customer who approached the party in the previous joint venture with a new project *did not know of the existence of the other co-adventurers* and (2) the court defined the relationship between joint venturers as a fiduciary one with a higher standard of care: 'not honesty alone, but the punctilio of an honor the most sensitive, is then the standard of behaviour.' The fiduciary notion is discussed in greater detail in section D below.

I would argue that good faith requires that a virtual enterprise participant who is approached with a request for a follow-up or spin-off project, which could be carried out by the same virtual enterprise members, would have a duty to inform the other parties. This would be especially the case in an enterprise pool where very often what happens is that a client first approaches a member of the enterprise pool with a project or business opportunity and that member takes the project to the enterprise pool when it cannot carry out that project on its own.[62] However, it is essential that the project is a follow-up or spin-off project, in the sense that it arose from and because of the previous collaboration with that client, as 'a pre-emptive opportunity' as the Court held in *Meinhard v Salmon*.

61 *Meinhard v Salmon,* New York Court of Appeals, 1928, 249 NY 458, 164 NE 545, p. 464.

62 See, for example, the Virtuelle Fabrik, *Weitzenboeck, E.M.*, A New Legal Framework for Emerging Business Models: Dynamic Networks as Collaborative Contracts, Cheltenham, Northampton, 2012, pp. 42-46.

In any case, a new virtual enterprise would have to be formed for the new collaboration since a virtual enterprise is deemed to be connected to a mission and ends with that mission.[63] Of course, the parties could quickly adapt or extend the use of the previous virtual enterprise contract to the follow-up project. However, where the client contacts a party of a virtual enterprise and makes it clear that he only wants that specific party to carry out the new project and does not desire any of the other virtual enterprise parties, the party contacted by the client has no obligation to involve the other parties in the new project.[64] This is even more the case where such a party is capable of addressing that business opportunity on its own.[65]

What was said above with regards to there not being a general duty to not compete in the same line of business, applies equally, I would submit, to the long-term dynamic network with a lead partner. In fact, such concerns are usually specifically addressed through non-competition or exclusivity clauses in the lead partner's alliance contracts with the other business partners.[66] In the case of such long-term dynamic networks, I find it difficult to extrapolate any duty on the lead partner to inform the other network members of any new, closely linked project. This is because of the very nature of these type of dynamic networks, in particular that the lead partner usually keeps control of the brand and of any related intellectual property and also decides and controls what orders to accept, what should be farmed out, and to which other network members.

---

63 See the definition of a virtual enterprise by Mertens/Faisst in *Weitzenboeck, E.M.*, A New Legal Framework for Emerging Business Models: Dynamic Networks as Collaborative Contracts, Cheltenham, Northampton, 2012, pp. 26-27.

64 *Nordtveit, E.*, Oppdragssamarbeid – Joint Ventures: Samarbeidsformer innenfor entreprenørverksemd, konsulenttenester og leverandørindustri, Oslo, 1992, p. 285, appears to concur.

65 In fact, in the Virtuelle Fabrik and VirtuellBau networks, an enterprise pool member approached with a business opportunity would take it to the enterprise pool only if that member is unable to carry out that task alone. See *Weitzenboeck, E.M.*, A New Legal Framework for Emerging Business Models: Dynamic Networks as Collaborative Contracts, Cheltenham, Northampton, 2012, pp. 42-46.

66 See, for example, the alliance agreement between Cisco and KPMG Consulting, Inc available online in EDGAR, which contains an exclusivity clause whereby KPMG undertakes not to 'directly or indirectly enter into any agreement, understanding or arrangement with a Cisco competitor to offer services or products competing with those offered by Cisco' during five years after the end of Cisco's investment in KPMG.

## VI. Contractual provision vs. general law principles

The four good faith duties discussed above, that is, the duty to co-operate, the duty to provide information, the duty of confidentiality and the duty not to compete, are often also expressly regulated in the virtual enterprise contract through specific clauses. Where these matters are expressly regulated in the contract, the question may arise whether one could still supplement these provisions by the general good faith duties in the background law (i.e. according to general rules in the governing law). One should here examine the exact wording of these clauses in the contract to determine whether the contract was meant to be exhaustive. However, as indeed Nordtveit states, one could initially assume that the parties did not intend to have lower standards of loyalty than those found in the general law.[67]

## C. Good faith in common law jurisdictions

The traditional law of contract, as it became established in England in the second half of the nineteenth century, did not impose or recognise a general duty of good faith. As Mason explains, the classical theory of contract, which assumed contracting parties to be in an adversarial position, was hostile to the emergence of a general doctrine of good faith in common law.[68] However, he continues, there is a recent move away from the adversarial emphasis on the freedom of the parties to pursue in an uninhibited fashion their own interests. Instead the general law 'is moving towards a conception of contract which places more emphasis, if not on co-operation, at least on conduct which takes account of the interests of the other party to the contract. This movement is associated with a new focus on the reasonable expectations of the parties ...'[69] Steyn L.J., writing extra-judicially, observed that:

---

67 See *Nordtveit, E.*, Oppdragssamarbeid – Joint Ventures: Samarbeidsformer innenfor entreprenørverksemd, konsulenttenester og leverandørindustri, Oslo, 1992, p. 280.

68 *Mason, A.F.*, Contract, Good Faith and Equitable Standards in Fair Dealing, Law Quarterly Review (116) 2000, pp. 66, 70.

69 *Mason, A.F.*, Contract, Good Faith and Equitable Standards in Fair Dealing, Law Quarterly Review (116) 2000, p. 72.

> Undoubtedly, good faith has a subjective requirement: the threshold requirement is that the party must act honestly. That is an unsurprising requirement and poses no difficulty for the English legal system. But good faith additionally sets an objective standard, viz. the observance of reasonable commercial standards of fair dealing in the conclusion and performance of the transaction concerned. ... Used in this sense, judges in the greater part of the industrialised world usually have no great difficulty in identifying a case of bad faith. It is not clear why it should perplex judges brought up in the English tradition.[70]

He concludes that 'there is not a world of difference between the objective requirement of good faith and the reasonable expectations of parties'.

Harrison, in her extensive analysis of good faith in sales under English law, mentions a number of principles recognised by English judges which are based on notions of fairness or fair dealing, such as: (1) the obligation of the vendor to be reasonable in giving or withholding approval in situations where the vendor's approval is required for some act to be done by, on or in relation to the subject matter of the contract; (2) the principle that 'a man is not permitted to rely on his own wrong'; (3) a positive duty of contractual parties to take steps to achieve the purpose of the contract.[71]

Commenting on developments in other common law countries, Mason states that 'in various jurisdictions, the courts have had recourse to equitable principle[s] to fill the void. This movement in the law of contract is not as visible in the United Kingdom as it is in Canada, Australia and New Zealand.'[72] He attributes the United Kingdom's isolation from this movement 'with the importance that United Kingdom judges and lawyers attach to London's position as a centre of international commerce and finance.'[73]

There has been no clear adoption of the principle of good faith in Australian common law and, in particular, no express consideration of the issue by the High Court of Australia. However, the obligation of good faith in contract performance appears to have been accepted in New South

70 *Steyn, J.*, Contract law: Fulfilling the Reasonable Expectations of Honest Men, Law Quarterly Review (113) 1997, pp. 433, 438.

71 *Harrison, R.*, Good Faith in Sales, London (and others), 1997, p. 508 et seq.

72 *Mason, A.F.*, Contract, Good Faith and Equitable Standards in Fair Dealing, Law Quarterly Review (116) 2000, p. 83.

73 *Mason, A.F.*, Contract, Good Faith and Equitable Standards in Fair Dealing, Law Quarterly Review (116) 2000, p. 83.

Wales,[74] but in another state – Victoria – the Supreme Court there unanimously declared that it was 'reluctant to conclude that commercial contracts are a class of contracts carrying an implied term of good faith as a legal incident, so that an obligation of good faith applies indiscriminately to all the rights and power conferred by a commercial contract.'[75] Though the court found it difficult to construe a duty of good faith in a contract between parties which it described as 'commercial leviathans', it declared *obiter* that an obligation of good faith may be implied where the relationship between the parties is unbalanced or one party is at a substantial disadvantage or is particularly vulnerable. The court ultimately held that in contracts between commercial partners,

> [i]f one party to a contract is more shrewd, more cunning and out-manoeuvres the other contracting party who did not suffer a disadvantage and who was not vulnerable, it is difficult to see why the latter should have greater protection than that provided by the law of contract.[76]

With regards to the United States, the American Uniform Commercial Code imposes an obligation of good faith in the performance or enforcement of a contract (article 1-304),[77] an obligation mirrored in section 205 of the Restatement of Contracts Second. When article 1 was revised, the definition of good faith was changed from the narrow 'honesty in fact' to the broader 'honesty in fact and the observance of reasonable commercial standards of fair dealing.'[78] The broader definition of good faith couples 'honesty in fact' (subjective honesty) with the 'observance of reasonable commercial standards of fair dealing' (objective commercial reasonableness).[79]

---

74 See, for example, *Renard Constructions (ME) Pty Ltd v Minister for Public Works* (1992) 26 NSWLR 234; *Wilmott, L. et al*, Contract Law, Oxford, 2009, p. 262-265.

75 Buchanan, J.A. at para 25 in *Esso Australia Resources Pty Ltd v Southern Pacific Petroleum* decided by the Supreme Court of Victoria (Court of Appeal), 15 September 2005, [2005] VSCA 228.

76 Warren, C.J. at para 4, Esso Australia Resources Pty Ltd v Southern Pacific Petroleum, Supreme Court of Victoria (Court of Appeal), 15 September 2005, [2005] VSCA 228.

77 Formerly section 1-203 of the UCC.

78 See section 1-201(b)(20) of the UCC.

79 See the drafter's comments to the new definition of good faith in the UCC. See also *Farnsworth, A.E.*, Farnsworth on Contracts – Vol II, New York, 2004, para 7.17.

Farnsworth holds that there is both a proscriptive and a prescriptive side to good faith.[80] He explains that the good faith duty both proscribes undesirable conduct, such as subterfuge and evasion, and requires affirmative action as well:

A party may thus be under a duty not only to refrain from hindering or preventing the occurrence of conditions of the party's own duty or the performances of the other party's duty, but also to take some affirmative steps to cooperate in achieving these goals. A promisee, as one court put it, 'must not only not hinder the promisor's performance, he must do whatever is necessary to enable him to perform.'[81]

In the United States, terms imposing a duty of good faith may be implied in a contract, in the sense that the terms may be supplied by the courts. As Farnsworth explains, the implied duty of good faith is based on a fundamental notion of fairness.[82]

The requirement for affirmative action is similar to the duty to co-operate discussed above. Farnsworth also explains that US courts have often supplied a term requiring a party to exercise good faith when that party has been given a discretionary power to determine certain terms of the contract such as quantity, price or time. Farnsworth holds that in exercising 'a good faith business judgment', the judgment may be 'to some extent in one's self-interest and that far less is expected than is expected of fiduciaries.'[83]

A pertinent question concerns the scope of the good faith notion. The notion of good faith should not be over-stretched as to lose its elasticity. Scholars have veered from pure scepticism about its usefulness (is it merely the absence of bad faith?) to attempting to classify as 'good faith' issues which fall under other areas of law (e.g. under the heading of the standard duty of care).

---

80 On the proscriptive and prescriptive sides of good faith, see further the debate between Summers and Burton, *Weitzenboeck, E.M.*, A New Legal Framework for Emerging Business Models: Dynamic Networks as Collaborative Contracts, Cheltenham, Northampton, 2012, pp. 221-222.

81 See *Farnsworth, A.E.*, Farnsworth on Contracts – Vol II, New York, 2004, para 7.17. Farnsworth was citing *Kehm Corp. v United States*, 93 F Supp 620, 623 (Ct Cl 1950). See also See *Dalton v Educational Testing Service*, 663 NE2d 294 (NY 1995).

82 *Farnsworth, A.E.*, Farnsworth on Contracts – Vol II, New York, 2004, para 7.17.

83 *Farnsworth, A.E.*, Farnsworth on Contracts – Vol II, New York, 2004, para 7.17.

Indeed, two varying approaches have been taken by the American courts. Some have taken a restrictive approach and imposed a judicially fashioned limitation under which the doctrine does not create independent rights separate from those created by the provisions of the contract. Thus the Third Circuit has said that 'courts generally utilize the good faith duty as an interpretive tool to determine "the parties' justifiable expectations", and do not enforce an independent duty divorced from the specific clauses of the contract.'[84] However, other American courts have not felt so constrained. The Ninth Circuit, in a franchising case, held that a franchisor's construction of a competing restaurant within a mile and a half of a franchisee's restaurant was breach of the good faith duty even though the franchise was not exclusive.[85]

The above discussion on the notion of good faith has sought to identify the meaning of this notion and its various nuances with regard to discrete contracts and collaborative contracts. We now turn to the third type of contractual relationship described in section B, namely the fiduciary relationship.

## D Is there a fiduciary relationship?

It may appear odd to discuss whether close collaborative networks like enterprise pools and virtual enterprises could give rise to fiduciary-like obligations, taking common law jurisdictions as a starting point, in view of the fact that few of the common law jurisdictions embrace the notion of good faith in contract performance. However, there is considerable literature by common law scholars discussing whether, and to what extent, joint venture participants are in a fiduciary relationship.[86] Reference is made to this

---

84 *Duquesne Light Co v Westinghouse Elec Co*, 66 F3d 604, 617 (3d Cir 1995). See further on this *Farnsworth, A.E.*, Farnsworth on Contracts – Vol II, New York, 2004, para 7.17.

85 *Vylene Enters v Naugles, Inc*, 90 F3d 1472 (9th Cir 1996). See further on this *Farnsworth, A.E.*, Farnsworth on Contracts – Vol II, New York, 2004, para 7.17.

86 See, for example, articles like *Corcoran, S./Tucker, J.C.*, Joint Venturers as Fiduciaries, Corporate & Business Law Journal (2) 1989, 34; *Chetwin, M.C.*, Joint Ventures – A Branch of Partnership Law?, University of Queensland Law Journal (16) 1990, 256; *Weissburg, A.B.*, Reviewing the Law on Joint Ventures with an Eye Towards the Future, Southern California Law Review, (63) 1990, 487; *Sharp, M.W.*, Fiduciary Duties owed by Co-Venturers in a Joint Venture, International

literature in an effort to see to what extent the issues discussed there are applicable to dynamic networks by analogy. The aim is to try to determine how the fiduciary principle differs from good faith, when a relationship is a fiduciary one, and what fiduciary duties are.

Mason holds that, of all the principles of equity, the fiduciary principle is the one which comes closest to approximating a duty of good faith, though he acknowledges that it is actually stronger than the good faith doctrine in that 'it gives primacy to the interests of the party to whom the fiduciary obligation is owed'.[87] Finn provides the following distinction between the notions of unconsionability, good faith and the fiduciary standard, taking as illustration the legitimate pursuit of self-interest: [88]

> 'Unconsionability' accepts that one party is entitled as of course to act self-interestedly in his actions towards the other. Yet in deference to that other's interests, it then proscribes excessively self-interested or exploitative conduct. 'Good faith', while permitting a party to act self-interestedly, nonetheless qualifies this by positively requiring that party, in his decision and action, to have regard to the legitimate interests therein of the other party. The 'fiduciary' standard for its part enjoins one party to act in the interests of the other – to act selflessly and with undivided loyalty. There is, in other words, a progression from the first to the third: from selfish behaviour to selfless behaviour.

When scholars, in particular common law scholars, discuss fiduciary duties, they generally speak of duties of loyalty and of 'strict duties of good

---

Company and Commercial Law Review (1992) 3(9), 321; *Bean, G.M.D.*, Fiduciary Obligations and Joint Ventures, Gloucestershire ,1995; *Mason, A.F.*, Contract, Good Faith and Equitable Standards in Fair Dealing, Law Quarterly Review (116) 2000; *Birchall, J.*, Duties of Good Faith in Commercial Joint Ventures? Contractual Duties, Fiduciary Duties and Shareholder Remedies, Journal of Business Law (269) 2005; books like *Finn, P.D.*, Fiduciary Obligations, Sydney, 1977 and *DeMott, D.A.*, Fiduciary Obligation, Agency and Partnership: Duties in Ongoing Business Relationships, Eagan (and others), 1991.

87 *Mason, A.F.*, Contract, Good Faith and Equitable Standards in Fair Dealing, Law Quarterly Review (116) 2000, 84.

88 *Finn, P.D.*, The Fiduciary Principle, in: Youdan, T.G. (ed), Equity, Fiduciaries and Trusts, Toronto,1989, p. 4. Mr Justice Finn's publications on fiduciary obligations, such as his classic Fiduciary Obligations (1977) have been cited extensively and with approval, also by the Privy Council in *Arklow Investments Ltd and Another v ID Maclean and Others*, 1 December 1999, an appeal from the Court of Appeal of New Zealand, (1999) UKPC 51.

faith, fairness and honesty',[89] sometimes termed 'utmost good faith'[90] in special fields of law like insurance law.[91] As Mason explains,

> [t]he good faith doctrine presupposes parties who contract on a footing of equality and are pursuing their own interests. By way of contrast, the fiduciary's fundamental duty:
> (1) not to use his own position to his own advantage or that of another party; and
> (2) not to place himself in a position in which his or her interest would conflict with his fiduciary duty
> arises when the relationship between the parties is such that, whether by reason of undertaking, vulnerability, dependence, the reposition of trust and confidence or otherwise, one person (the beneficiary) has a legitimate expectation that the other (the fiduciary) will act in the beneficiary's interest.[92]

The notion of fiduciary obligation is rather elusive as a concept since the particular duties it imposes vary, depending on the type of relationship. Some fiduciary relationships are more intense than others:

> The greater the independent authority to be exercised by the fiduciary, the greater the scope of his fiduciary duty. Thus, a trustee is under a stricter duty of loyalty than is an agent upon whom limited authority is conferred or a corporate director who can act only as a member of the board of directors or a promoter acting for investors in a new corporation. All of these, however, are fiduciaries and are subject to the fiduciary principle of loyalty, although not to the same extent.[93]

The term 'fiduciary' entered English law reports in the mid-nineteenth century, and was descriptive of relationships similar to that between a trustee and beneficiary. This term replaced 'trust' which in the same era came to have a precise technical meaning.[94] Thereafter, courts developed

---

89 See *Hewitt, I.*, Hewitt on Joint Ventures, London (and others), 1 para 11-19, referring to the US position.

90 See *Wilhelmsen, T. L.*, Duty of Disclosure, Duty of Good Faith, Alteration of Risk and Warranties, CMI Yearbook, 2000, pp. 84-85.

91 See section 17 of the English Marine Insurance Act of 1907, entitled 'Insurance is *uberrimae fidei*'.

92 This, as Mason acknowledges, is also the definition favour by Finn. See *Mason, A.F.*, Contract, Good Faith and Equitable Standards in Fair Dealing, Law Quarterly Review (116) 2000, p. 84.

93 *Scott, A.W.*, The Fiduciary Principle, California Law Review, (1949) 37, 539-542.

94 Namely that B had settled legal ownership of property on A to be used on behalf of B or others. See further *DeMott, D.A.*, Fiduciary Obligation, Agency and Partnership: Duties in Ongoing Business Relationships, Eagan (and others), 1991, p. 12.

rules for fiduciary types of relationships such as the relation of guardian and ward, agent and principal, attorney and client, executor or administrator and legatees and next of kin of the deceased. In most common law countries, the directors and officers of a company are in a fiduciary relation to the company, and in some of these countries also to some extent to the shareholders. Similarly, in many jurisdictions, in a simple or general partnership, each partner is in a fiduciary relation to the others, 'since, although he has his own interests to look after, he also has the power and the duty to look after the interests of the others'.[95] These are the established categories of fiduciaries. Difficulty arises when one tries to determine who is a fiduciary outside these established categories, not least of which because of the notion that being a fiduciary entails a certain amount of selflessness.[96]

In the United States, unlike in other common law countries such as England, joint venturers are deemed to be in a fiduciary relationship. The *locus classicus* is the 1928 case of *Meinhard v Salmon*, discussed above,[97] in which the New York Court of Appeals held:[98]

> Joint adverturers, like copartners, owe to one another, while the enterprise continues, the duty of the finest loyalty. ... Not honesty alone, but the punctilio of an honor the most sensitive, is then the standard of behaviour. As to this there has developed a tradition that is unbending and inveterate.

Some commentators have argued that the reason why the joint venture has been so popular in the United States is because in that country a corporation was not able, generally speaking, to join a partnership.[99] However, the

---

95 See further *Scott, A.W.*, The Fiduciary Principle, California Law Review, (1949) 37, 539-542.

96 As DeMott states, 'Fiduciaries are, in many different ways, obliged to act unselfishly and to give other persons the advantage of their knowledge and skill. Fiduciary obligation thus presupposes that persons subject to it are capable, at least in some respects, of selfless behaviour, that they are able, at least in defined circumstances, to abjure the immediate pursuit of self-interest.' See *DeMott, D.A.*, Fiduciary Obligation, Agency and Partnership: Duties in Ongoing Business Relationships, Eagan (and others), 1991, p. 2.

97 See section B-V.

98 See New York Court of Appeals, 1928, 249 NY 458, 164 NE 545.

99 See, for example, *Chetwin, M.C.*, Joint Ventures – A Branch of Partnership Law ?, University of Queensland Law Journal (16) 1990, 258; *Birchall, J.*, Duties of Good Faith in Commercial Joint Ventures? Contractual Duties, Fiduciary Duties and Shareholder Remedies, Journal of Business Law (269) 2005, 274.

significance of this distinction is today questionable because corporate participation in partnerships is now permitted by statute in almost all states.[100]

In the United States, as abovementioned, the courts have traditionally found that, like a partnership, members of a joint venture owe to each other strict duties of good faith, fairness and honesty and one member may not secretly advantage himself over his partner or partners. According to Hewitt, in the US 'this duty is even clearer when a party has a position of managerial control or stands in a position of trust and confidence in relation to, or control over, another's property.'[101]

In Australia, joint venturers are not deemed to be in a fiduciary relationship. However, there have been a string of cases where counsel with varying success relied on US case law to argue for *fiduciary duties* in joint ventures. The High Court of Australia reversed a finding of fiduciary duties by the Court of Appeal of New South Wales in *Hospital Products Ltd v United States Surgical Corp*, dealing with a distributorship relationship.[102] The appellant was the distributor in Australia of surgical equipment manufactured by the respondent. However, it turned out that the owner of Hospital Products Ltd had dishonestly intended to use the distributorship to manufacture copies of the respondent's equipment and sell those products in Australia. Although the court held that Hospital Products Ltd committed serious breaches of contract, the distributorship did not give rise to a fiduciary relationship for two reasons: (i) the arrangement was a commercial one entered into by parties at arm's length and on equal footing and (ii) the whole purpose of the transaction for Hospital Products Ltd was for it to make a profit. The court therefore held that an ordinary commercial contract made in such circumstances, even as a result of fraud, is unlikely to give rise to fiduciary obligations.

Mason J. dissented, holding that the categories of fiduciary relationships are not closed, and that such a relationship existed in this case, *albeit to a limited extent*, namely with regard to the appellant's obligation to pro-

---

100 The 1914 version of the Uniform Partnerships Act, drafted by the National Conference of Commissioners on Uniform State Laws, was enacted into law in every state except Louisiana. See further, *Weissburg, A.B.*, Reviewing the Law on Joint Ventures with an Eye Towards the Future, Southern California Law Review, (63) 1990, 520.

101 *Hewitt, I.*, Hewitt on Joint Ventures, London (and others), 2011, para 11-19.

102 High Court of Australia, 1984, 55 ALR 417.

tect and promote the respondent's goodwill in Australia. This is discussed in more detail in the next section.

Twenty months later the same court, with four of the same members, accepted that there was a fiduciary relationship between joint venture parties in *United Dominions Corp Pty Ltd v Brian Pty Ltd.*[103] The utility of this case to our discussion on contractual joint ventures is limited since the court found that the joint venture agreement was in fact a partnership agreement. Nevertheless, the court clearly stated that fiduciary relationships may be established in joint ventures that were not partnerships.[104]

A later unreported case by the Supreme Court of Queensland unambiguously stated that joint venturers, even though not partners, may owe *fiduciary duties* to each other. Ryan J. in *Pacific Coal Pty Ltd v Idemitsu Queensland Pty Ltd*[105] rejected the defendant's arguments (based on the majority view in Hospital Products Ltd) that a commercial agreement entered into by parties at arms' length precluded the existence of fiduciary duties.[106]

On the other hand, English judges tend to be sceptical about fiduciary duties in commercial contexts such as joint ventures,[107] though one author has held that 'there is no conclusive reason why they could not find parties to a contractual joint venture owe one another fiduciary duties.'[108]

## E. Fiduciary duties

It is opportune to examine closely, though succinctly, the fiduciary duties that partners and respectively, directors, owe when a formal partnership or

---

103 High Court of Australia, 1 August 1985, [1985] HCA 49, (1985) CLR 1.

104 As per Mr Justices Mason, Brennan and Deane, para 5.

105 Unreported, Supreme Court of Queensland, 21 February 1992. This case was extensively commented on by *Sharp, M.W.*, Fiduciary Duties owed by Co-Venturers in a Joint Venture, International Company and Commercial Law Review (1992) 3(9) 321.

106 See further *ibid* p. 323.

107 *Hewitt, I.*, Hewitt on Joint Ventures, London (and others), 2011, para 11-20 states that 'It is doubtful whether the English courts will go so far as to adopt any general implied duty of good faith in a contractual alliances (sic).'

108 *Birchall, J.*, Duties of Good Faith in Commercial Joint Ventures? Contractual Duties, Fiduciary Duties and Shareholder Remedies, Journal of Business Law (269) 2005, 276-277.

a company is set up. Common law countries, in particular England, have been pioneers in the field of fiduciary duties and the notion found fertile ground in the United States.[109] In Europe, there is a growing academic interest in the concept of directors' fiduciary duties, not least because of the increased importance of the notion of corporate governance as well as the view that company law has a role in furthering sustainable development.[110] Indeed, Fleischer observes that 'the concept of fiduciary duties has also proved highly influential' in continental Europe.[111] Reference will first be made to the notion as it was originally developed in Anglo-American law, following which the position in some civil law countries such as Germany, France and Norway will be examined.

We start first by looking at partnership law. As mentioned in the previous sections, partners in a partnership owe fiduciary duties towards each other. As Morse, writing on English law, puts it,

> The foundation of partnership is mutual faith and trust in each other and ever since the development of equity in the nineteenth century partners have always been regarded as being subject to the equitable duties, sometimes expressed in terms as the 'good faith' principle.[112]

He later on explains that, 'since the boundaries of equity in this respect are never closed it is impossible to provide a definitive list' of fiduciary duties.[113] The English Partnership Act, which dates back to 1890, lists three specific fiduciary duties in sections 28 to 30. The three fiduciary duties listed in the Act are:

1. *the duty to act honestly and make full disclosure*: Partnership is deemed to be an agreement *uberrimae fidei* and thus a partner's failure to disclose any relevant fact when dealing with the other partners is a breach of the duty to act honestly and make full disclosure – there is no need for proof of common law fraud or negligence. Section 28 of the

---

109 See further *Fleischer, H.*, Legal Transplants in European Company Law – The Case of Fiduciary Duties, (2005) 3 European Company and Financial Law Review, 381 *et seq.*

110 See *Sjåfjell, B.*, Towards a Sustainable European Company Law: A Normative Analysis of the Objectives of EU Law, with the Takeover Directive as a Test Case, Alphen aan den Rijn, 2009, p. 15.

111 *Fleischer, H.*, Legal Transplants in European Company Law – The Case of Fiduciary Duties, European Company and Financial Law Review (2005) 3, 382.

112 *Morse G.*, Partnership Law, Oxford , 2010, p. 153.

113 *Ibid*, p. 159.

English Partnership Act provides that: 'Partners are bound to render true accounts and full information of all things affecting the partnership to any partner or his legal representatives.'

2. *the duty not to make unauthorised profits*: Any unauthorised private gain, however innocent, which a partner makes as a result of being a partner must be accounted for to the other partners. The wording of section 29(1) of the English Partnership Act is very wide and includes clear-cut cases where one partner makes a personal profit out of acting on behalf of the partnership (e.g. negotiating a contract), or where a partner uses a partnership asset for his own benefit. However, as Morse notes, the question of liability is less certain when considering cases where a partner uses business connections of the firm.[114] The question that arises is whether a partner is prohibited from using information or contacts which he acquired from the firm's business, in another enterprise not directly connected with the firm's business. In *Aas v Benham*,[115] the Court of Appeal held that information gained in the course of a partnership business could not be used for a partner's own benefit in that type of business, but it could be used for purposes outside the scope of that business. In the court's view, it was the use of the information which counted and not the source.
3. *the duty not to compete*: This rule basically provides that a partner may not, without the consent of the other partners, operate a business in competition with the firm.[116] The question whether there is a competitive business is one of fact. In *Aas v Benham* mentioned earlier,[117] for example, the Court of Appeal held that there was no liability under this head.

Another question that arises is the interplay of fiduciary duties and the partnership agreement. Morse stresses that 'partnership is more than a fiduciary relationship, it is above all a contractual agreement and therefore subject to the terms of that agreement, which as in contracts generally may be express or implied.'[118] Many of the rules in the English Partnership Act are default terms which can be excluded or amended by either the express

114 *Ibid*, p. 168.

115 [1891] 2 Ch 244, CA. See further *Morse G.*, Partnership Law, Oxford , 2010, p. 169.

116 See section 30, English Partnership Act.

117 *Ibid.*

118 *Morse G.*, Partnership Law, Oxford, 2010, p. 154.

terms of the agreement or by the conduct of the partners. Section 19 of the Partnership Act states:

> The mutual rights and duties of partners, whether ascertained by agreement or defined by this Act, may be varied by the consent of all the partners, and such consent may be either express or inferred from a course of dealing.

However, Morse holds that section 19 cannot apply to all the fiduciary duties implied by equity since they do not necessarily arise either from the agreement or the Act, although there are three specific areas which are included as discussed above.[119] However, he holds, it is always a defence to a breach of fiduciary duty that the other party consented to the breach and such consent may be derived from the terms of the partnership agreement.[120]

Similar fiduciary duties apply in Norway, though the term used is 'duties of loyalty' or *lojalitetsplikt*.[121] Andenæs and Woxholth respectively explain that, according to an unwritten rule of law, partners in a general partnership owe each other and the partnership a duty of loyalty.[122] Though the same term as that used in general contract law is used – *lojalitetsplikt* (duties of loyalty) – as Andenæs explains, the partners' duty of loyalty goes further than the general *lojalitetsplikt* (good faith duties) between contracting parties.[123] This, I submit, is undisputed: the purpose of partnership is co-operation with one common business objective; that is not the purpose in an exchange contract where one, for example, buys a car. The partners in a partnership should co-operate loyally to promote the objects of the partnership in such a way that each individual partner must refrain from misusing his membership in the partnership to obtain for himself unreasonable advantages at the cost of the partnership or of the other partners.[124] The duty to promote the objects of the partnership also means that the partners' right to take part in the management of the partnership is

---

119 *Ibid.*

120 *Ibid.*

121 *Normann Aarum, K.*, Styremedlemmers Erstatningsansvar i Aksjeselskaper , Oslo, 1994, p. 353 also refers to the duty of loyalty as *lojalitetsplikten* when discussing this duty with regards to companies.

122 See further *Andenæs, M.H.*, Selskapsrett, Oslo, 2007, p. 111; *Woxholth, G., Selskapsrett,* Oslo, 2012, p. 79.

123 *Andenæs, M.H.*, Selskapsrett, Oslo, 2007, p. 111.

124 See *Woxholth, G.*, Selskapsrett, Oslo, 2012, p. 79 and *Andenæs, M.H.*, Selskapsrett, Oslo, 2007, pp. 111-112.

also, in effect, a duty.[125] Another aspect of the duty of loyalty is that a partner in a general partnership may not conduct or be a personally liable partner in any competing business – a rule enshrined in section 2-23(1) of the Norwegian Partnerships Act (*selskapsloven*).[126]

Turning to company law, in England, in terms of the recent Companies Act 2006, a director owes the company the following fiduciary duties:[127]

1. *The duty to remain within the scope of the powers which have been conferred upon him*: Section 171 deals with two manifestations of this principle, namely, that the director must 'act in accordance with the company's constitution' and must 'only exercise powers for the purposes for which they are conferred'.
2. *the duty to act in good faith to promote the success of the company*: This is the modern reformulation of the common law duty of directors to act in good faith in what they believed to be 'the best interests of the company'. Section 172(1) makes it clear that, as was the dominant view at common law, the shareholders or members are to be the primary object of the directors' efforts.
3. *the duty to exercise independent judgment* (section 173): At common law this issue was discussed under the heading of the director's duty not to fetter the exercise of his or her discretion.
4. *the duty not to put himself in a position in which his personal interests or duties to others conflict with his duty to the company*: The conflict could arise either (a) out of a transaction with the company (self-dealing transactions); (b) out of the director's personal exploitation of the company's property, information or opportunities; or (c) out of the receipt from a third party of a benefit for exercising their directorial functions in a particular way. Gower and Davies consider these three sub-headings as separate headings in their own right and thus suggest a category of six fiduciary duties, though they acknowledges that the no conflict' principle underlies each of these sub-headings. They consider them separately out of convenience because they have developed suffi-

125 See further on this *Andenæs, M.H.*, Selskapsrett, Oslo, 2007, p. 111.

126 Act of 21 June 1985 concerning unlimited liability partnerships and limited partnerships (The Partnerships Act) known in Norwegian as *Lov om ansvarlige selskaper og kommandittselskaper (Selskapsloven)*. See further *Bråthen, T.*, Selskapsrett, Oslo, 2008, p. 206.

127 See further on each of these categories, *Davies, P.L.*, Gower and Davies' Principles of Modern Company Law, London, 2008, pp. 497-576.

ciently separately.[128] They are treated in sections 175 to 177 of the Companies Act 2006.

In the United States, the classic definition of the directors' duty of loyalty was set out in *Guth v Loft, Inc* where the Delaware Supreme Court held that:[129]

> Corporate officers and directors are not permitted to use their position of trust and confidence to further their private interests. While technically not trustees, they stand in a fiduciary relation to the corporation and its stockholders. A public policy, existing through the years, and derived from a profound knowledge of human characteristics and motives, has established a rule that demands of a corporate officer or director, peremptorily and inexorably, the most scrupulous observance of his duty, not only affirmatively to protect the interests of the corporation committed to his charge, but also to refrain from doing anything that would work injury to the corporation, or to deprive it of profit or advantage which his skill and ability might properly bring to it, or enable it to make in the reasonable and lawful exercise of its powers. The rule requires an undivided and unselfish loyalty to the corporation and demands that there shall be no conflict between duty and self-interest.

Subsequently, the Section of Corporation, Banking and Business Law (now the Section on Business Law) of the American Bar Association explained this duty as follows:

> By assuming his office, the corporate director commits allegiance to the enterprise and acknowledges that the best interests of the corporation and its shareholders must prevail over any individual interest of his own. The basic principle to be observed is that the director should not use his corporate position to make a personal profit or gain other personal advantage.[130]

Then, in 1994, the American Law Institute extensively analysed the fiduciary duties of directors, controlling shareholders and the particular responsibilities in transfer-of-control situations in its *Principles of Corporate Governance.*[131] However, this publication avoids the use of the term 'duty of loyalty' when dealing with the obligation of a person who acts

128 *Ibid* p. 529.

129 As per Chief Justice Layton; see judgment published in 5 A2d 503 (Del 1939).

130 *American Bar Association*, The Corporate Director's Guidebook, Business Law (1978) 33, p. 1595. See further *Block, D.J./Barton, N.E./ Radin, S.A.*, The Business Judgment Rule: Fiduciary Duties of Corporate Directors, New Jersey, 1993, p. 124 *et seq.*

131 *American Law Institute*, Principles of Corporate Governance (ALI 1994), Part V, pp. 199-382.

with a pecuniary interest in a matter and instead uses the term 'duty of fair dealing'.

Many civil law jurisdictions impose a general duty of loyalty upon directors.[132] In France, the notion of fiduciary duties was introduced in French company law through classical legal concepts such as good faith, confidence and loyalty.[133] The French Court of Cassation, in fact, in a judgment of 27th February 1996, confirmed that a company director owes a duty of loyalty towards the shareholders. In that case, the president of a public, but unlisted company bought shares from shareholders for 3,000 F each and sold them a few days later for 8,800 F. The *Chambre Commerciale* held that, by not disclosing the shares' true value, he had violated his duty of loyalty which a director owes to each individual shareholder.[134]

Fleischer explains that in Germany, the German Stock Corporation Act (AktG) has codified the duty of loyalty of directors only in a rudimentary fashion in that section 88(1) prohibits management board members from competing with the company in its line of business and section 93(1) stipulates a statutory duty of confidentiality. He explains that:

> The general concept, however, is not mentioned in the Act. This caused considerable difficulties in shaping the duty of loyalty. However, over the years, contributions from comparative law scholarship have helped to fill in the gaps and flesh out the law of fiduciary obligations.

The duty of loyalty is, however, firmly entrenched in German court judgments.[135] Moreover, the *German Code of Corporate Governance* high-

---

132 See further *Fleischer, H.*, Legal Transplants in European Company Law – The Case of Fiduciary Duties, (2005) 3 European Company and Financial Law Review, 383.

133 See *Freedman, D.*, L'Américanisation du Droit Français par la Vie Économique, (2001) 45 Archives de Philosophie du Droit, 207, 209.

134 In the words of the Court, the director '*a manqué au devoir de loyauté qui s'impose au dirigeant d'une société à l'egard de tout associé*'. See Cass Com, 27.2.1996, JCP éd, E 1996 II, 838. See also *Fleischer, H.*, Legal Transplants in European Company Law – The Case of Fiduciary Duties, (2005) 3 European Company and Financial Law Review, 383.

135 See further *Fleischer, H.*, Legal Transplants in European Company Law – The Case of Fiduciary Duties, (2005) 3 European Company and Financial Law Review, 384.

lights some of its most important features.[136] Even in Germany, as Fleischer puts it,

> [s]ubstantially, it is generally agreed on that the duty of loyalty calls for a more demanding standard of conduct than the general obligation to act in good faith in contractual settings. Commentators explain that the stricter standards mirror the far-reaching influence and power of directors.[137]

Kershaw and Witz identify the following general fiduciary duties (*Treuepflicht*) which the management owes to the company, regardless of the type of company:[138]

1. duty of confidentiality: Though to some extent provided by statute,[139] this duty is also recognised by the courts;
2. prohibition of competition: This is the duty 'to abstain from entering into or promoting on behalf or in favour of [themselves] or of any third party any transaction or to pursue any other business which is within the scope of the company's business.'[140]
3. duty to take corporate opportunities: Managing directors have a general duty to take business opportunities in favour of the business of the company (*Geschäftschancenlehre*). This means that directors may not use such opportunities for their own purposes.

It is important to distinguish, in English law, between a partner's duty not to compete in the same line of business with the partnership of which he is a partner, from a director's duty not to put himself in a position of conflict

136 See, in particular, clause 4.3 on conflicts of interests of the management board. The Code, drafted by the Government Commission on the German Corporate Governance Code, is aimed at German listed companies, though it recommends that non-listed companies also respect it. It contains both 'recommendations' from which companies may deviate provided they disclose such deviation, and 'suggestions' which may be deviated from without disclosure.

137 *Fleischer, H.*, Legal Transplants in European Company Law – The Case of Fiduciary Duties, (2005) 3 European Company and Financial Law Review, 384-385.

138 See *Kershaw, D./Kitz, W.*, Protecting the Various Interests in the Joint Venture, in: Micheler, E./Prentice, D.D., (eds), Joint Ventures in English and German Law, Oxford, 2000, p. 74.

139 Section 85 (1) of Germany's Limited Liability Company Act (*Gesetz betreffend die Gesellschaften mit beschränkter Haftung* (GmbHG)); section 93(1) of Germany's Stock Corporation Act (*Aktiengesetz* (AktG)).

140 *Kershaw, D./Kitz, W.*, Protecting the Various Interests in the Joint Venture, in: Micheler, E./Prentice, D.D., (eds), Joint Ventures in English and German Law, Oxford, 2000, p. 74.

with the company. English courts do not recognise a general duty not to compete for directors, although the 'non-compete' rule goes a long way to serve as a substitute for a strict no-competition rule.[141] The German Stock Corporation Act, however, contains a strict no-competition rule in section 88 which prohibits members of the management board from engaging in any trade or dealing in the same branch as the company without having first obtained the consent of the supervisory board. In France, the Court of Cassation has recently established a judge-made duty not to compete even in the absence of contractual no-competition clauses.[142]

In Norway, the directors' duty of loyalty is a general principle of company law[143] and emanates *inter alia* from the principle in section 6-12(1) of the Norwegian Limited Liability Companies Act which provides that the board of directors is responsible for the proper (*forsvarlig*) administration of the company's business.

The Norwegian Limited Liability Companies Act prohibits conflicts of interest between a director's personal interests and those of the company.[144] Where a director or someone close to him or her has a personal or economic interest in a matter, such director is not competent to take part in discussions or decisions regarding that matter that is in front of the board of directors.[145] Nor can a director take part in a matter before the board regarding the provision of a loan or other credit to him or her or the provision of security for his or her debts.[146]

The board must also refrain from misusing its position. It must not obey any decision of the general meeting or of any other organ of the company if such decision is illegal or against the company's memorandum and articles of association. This requirement, emanating from section 6-28(2) can

141 See *Fleischer, H.*, Legal Transplants in European Company Law – The Case of Fiduciary Duties, (2005) 3 European Company and Financial Law Review, 395.

142 *Ibid*, 395-396.

143 See *Bugge Reiersen, H.*,Ansvarsbegrensning og Ansvarsfrihet i Aksjeselskaper: Forhåndsregulaering av Styremedlemmers Erstatningsansvar, Bergen, 2007, p. 91.

144 *Normann Aarum, K.*, Styremedlemmers Erstatningsansvar i Aksjeselskaper, Oslo, 1994, p. 351 explains that a director is deemed to have acted against the law (*rettsstridig*) if he has promoted his personal interests at the cost of the company.

145 See section 6-27(1) of the Norwegian Limited Liability Companies Act (*lov om aksjeselskaper*).

146 *Ibid*, section 6-27(2).

be understood as a requirement or duty on the directors to exercise independent judgment. Another facet of the rule that the board must not misuse its position is the provision that the board must refrain from doing anything which will give certain shareholders or others an unfair advantage at the cost of the other shareholders or of the company (section 6-28(1)). In other words, the board must act in the interest of the company, for the benefit of the shareholders as a whole, and not unfairly favour just some of them. Thus, a director is a trusted officer of the company and, in carrying out his duties, shall promote the interests of the company.[147] A director, in principle, has 'a duty to ensure that any business opportunities and advantages accrue to the interest of the company, and cannot appropriate them for himself.'[148]

## F. Fiduciary duties in dynamic networks

The classical fiduciary relationships are those which are also referred to as relationships of trust and confidence or confidential relations such as trustee and beneficiary, principal and agent, director and company, and partners. As Mason J. explains,

> The critical feature of these relationships is that the fiduciary undertakes or agrees to act for or on behalf of or in the interests of another person in the exercise of a power or discretion which will affect the interests of that other person in a legal or practical sense. The relationship between the parties is therefore one which gives the fiduciary a special opportunity to exercise the power or discretion to the detriment of that other person who is accordingly vulnerable to abuse by the fiduciary of his position.[149]

In *Hospital Products*, the appellant's capacity to make decisions and take action in some matters by reference to its own interests was held to be inconsistent with the existence of *a general fiduciary relationship*. However, as Mason J. rightly opined, 'this does not exclude the existence *of a more limited fiduciary relationship* [my emphasis] for it is well settled that a

---

147 See decision by the court of first instance of Glåmdal, Norway TGLOM 2007-135885.

148 See *Normann Aarum, K.,* Styremedlemmers Erstatningsansvar i Aksjeselskaper , Oslo, 1994, p. 351 also cited in TGLOM 2007-135885 abovementioned in footnote 166.

149 See *Hospital Products*, High Court of Australia, 1984, 55 ALR 417, para 68-69.

person may be a fiduciary in some activities but not in others.' As Mason J. stated in his dissenting opinion:

> ... it is altogether too simplistic, if not superficial, to suggest that commercial transactions stand outside the fiduciary regime as though in some way commercial transactions do not lend themselves to the creation of a relationship in which one person comes under an obligation to act in the interests of another. The fact that in the great majority of commercial transactions the parties stand at arms' length does not enable us to make a generalization that is universally true in relation to every commercial transaction. In truth, every such transaction must be examined on its merits with a view to ascertaining whether it manifests the characteristics of a fiduciary relationship.[150]

I submit that some of the dynamic networks that are the subject of examination of this paper could give rise to limited fiduciary obligations. One should here distinguish between a spontaneous temporary virtual enterprise and one which has been formed out of an enterprise pool. The former does not give rise to fiduciary-like obligations between the parties, but parties would be expected to carry out the contract in good faith (basic good faith), at least in those countries which recognise such a duty. The situation is different with regards to enterprise pools and virtual enterprises formed out of such pools. A typical feature of enterprise pools is the roles that some parties assume with regards to the enterprise pool.[151] Though the party assigned a particular role also has its own commercial reasons for being part of the enterprise pool, I would propound that, the obligations that come with performing *that specific role* are fiduciary obligations and should be performed in the interests of the enterprise pool. Similarly, the project manager who is entrusted with the day-to-day running of the project should perform those duties like a fiduciary. The analogy here is with the duties of a manager.

I also hold that members of a virtual enterprise that is formed out of an enterprise pool owe each other *certain fiduciary duties*, namely those identified above as additional good faith duties, that is, the (rather) limited duty not to compete, to the extent discussed above in section B-V, and the duty not to misuse confidential information discussed above in section B-IV.

---

150 See *Hospital Products*, para. 77.

151 These roles are explained in *Weitzenboeck, E.M.*, A New Legal Framework for Emerging Business Models: Dynamic Networks as Collaborative Contracts, Cheltenham, Northampton, 2012, pp. 42-46.

The question arises whether virtual enterprise participants could specifically opt for their relationship to be a fiduciary one. The classical notion of freedom of contract would certainly allow the parties to describe their contract, or a part thereof, as a fiduciary one. Indeed, the essence of most virtual enterprise contracts, especially those virtual enterprises formed out of an enterprise pool, is that they are collaborative contracts and not classical, adversarial exchange contracts. However, the virtual enterprise parties here would be well advised to exercise great caution since it is more likely that a contract with such a fiduciary clause will be deemed to be partnership, if a dispute arose before a court.[152]

To conclude, a virtual enterprise does not *per se* create a *general fiduciary relationship* between its participants. This statement is qualified with regards to virtual enterprises governed by US law since a court might deem it to be a joint venture and hence, giving rise to fiduciary duties between the parties. This depends on the particular facts, circumstances, and legal set-up of each virtual enterprise. However, with regards to other common law jurisdictions outside the US, it is likely that *limited fiduciary obligations* are created with regards to the performance of certain *trust-laden tasks* on behalf of the virtual enterprise such as where a specific party has been entrusted to promote the virtual enterprise thereby creating goodwill for the enterprise pool. In the performance of that task – and that task alone (except, of course, where he has been given other tasks of a fiduciary nature) – that party must act as a fiduciary.

Moreover, in civil law jurisdictions and those common law jurisdictions which recognise it, the principle of good faith in contract performance would apply, with its core good faith duties of co-operation and disclosure, as well as its additional, fiduciary-like duties of non-misuse of confidential information and non-competition, as discussed above.

152 For the consequences that would ensue if a dynamic network were to be deemed to be a partnership, see *Weitzenboeck, E.M.,* A New Legal Framework for Emerging Business Models: Dynamic Networks as Collaborative Contracts, Cheltenham, Northampton, 2012, pp. 268-284.

# A frame for business networks governance

*Dr. Carlos Gómez Asensio*

## A. Business networks as an economic structure

From an economical and organizational point of view business networks represent the result of both, vertical disintegration processes inside firm's boundaries and external convergence processes between economic agents.

Vertical disintegration processes are characterized by the shift from *taylorism* or *fordism* production models to autonomous work teams managing independent but linked tasks aimed to achieve a common goal[1]. Thus, the

1 This idea is stated by *Powell, W.*, The Capitalist Firm in the Twenty- First Century: Emerging Patterns in Western Enterprise, in: Di Maggio, P., (ed.), The Twenty-First-Century Firm, Changing economic organization in international perspective, Princeton, 2001, p. 33 (54-55).
About work team culture, *Sabel, Ch.*, El aprendizaje a través del monitoreo: los dilemas de la política económica regional en Europa, in: OCDE (ed.), Redes de Empresas y Desarrollo Local. Competencia y cooperación en los sistemas productivos locales, Paris, 1999, p. 25 (25): "New work coordination forms derived from Japanese's experience fosters an experimental and thoughtful revision of tasks allocation. Group members are concerned on specific goals including goods and services improvement, as well as technique's efficiency. Then group decides task organization, rotary member's assignation to each task and, grounded on reported experience, revises everything, including also relationships with other suppliers and consumers groups" (Translation given by the author).

blurring of hierarchical organization models[2] lead to *heterarchy*[3], where supervision tasks are reduced to merely coordinating autonomous[4], inter-

2 *Di Maggio, P.*, Conclusion: the futures of Business Organization and Paradoxes of change, in: Di Maggio, P., (ed.), The Twenty-First-Century Firm, Changing economic organization in international perspective, Princeton, 2001, p. 210 (215-217), systematises around two reasons the fall of hierarchical organization model: increasing amount of workers efficiency supervised by means of ICT, and Management own change as far as more tasks are assigned to self-organized horizontal groups. "Formalization fall", namely the reduction on number and binding character of production system ruling norms, is also pointed out. There is too a mention for "weakness of links between workers and companies" because of work less permanent character and higher mobility and dynamism on its conception. Altogether, these factors contribute to hierarchical organization model weakness.

3 In this sense *Teubner, G.,* Network as connected contracts, Oxford, 2011, p. 13-14: "Networks are instead 'highly unlikely reproductive correlations of heterogeneous elements". They fulfil the function of fostering interrelations between autonomous functional systems or between formal organisations. They promote the cross-boundary integration of autonomous operational logics, which also determine the potentialities and risks associated with the organisational forms that we are addressing...The evolution of *heterarchical* co-ordination determines that the organising principle is no longer one that is directed to a higher 'goal'. Rather, organisation is instead a strategic and contextual matter that no longer distinguishes between general public and particularistic private interests".

4 In this sense *Powell, W.,* The Capitalist Firm in the Twenty- First Century: Emerging Patterns in Western Enterprise, in: Di Maggio, P., (ed.), The Twenty-First-Century Firm, Changing economic organization in international perspective, Princeton, 2001 p. 58: "Teams can determine their own internal organization, communicate horizontally within the organization instead of up hierarchy, and build close relationships with suppliers , sharing information rather than hoarding it. Teams choose, within broad parameters, the necessary tools, services, and inputs needed to execute a task. Teams intensively monitor their own activities, thus in a key respect, they are self-managed. Critics, however, are right when they punt out that supervision, responsibility, and even discipline, is often shifted from managers to peers, without any parallel increase in compensation or security. Thus in many situations, workers are asked to do much more without any increase in pay".

dependent and linked work teams[5] as a way to enhance rationalism and efficiency in business management.[6]

Reproduction of inner coordination and supervision of relationships outside the firm's boundaries, represent one step further towards vertical disintegration processes.[7] In this sense, the autonomous execution of projects lead to broader market access and a rising of overall enterprise operation volumes,[8] furthermore, promoting outsourcing of former in-

---

5 *Westney, D.*, Japanese enterprise Faces the Twenty-First Century, in: Di Maggio, P., (ed.), The Twenty-First-Century Firm, Changing economic organization in international perspective, Princeton, 2001, p. 105 (p. 112), describing Japanese industry's characters referring to production organization, remarks the existence of "dense networks with suppliers embroiled in "just.in .time" logistics and the elimination (or drastic reduction) of inventory for final assembly, so that parts and subsystems are "pulled" onto the production line as needed, and suppliers are fully integrated into production planning and product design".

6 *Rosaria Maugeri, M.*, Reti contrattuali e abuso di dipendenza economica: alla ricerca di nuove discipline?, in: Iamiceli, P., (dir.), Le reti di imprese e i contratti di rete, G. Giappichelli, (ed.), Torino, 2009, p. 295 (p. 295-296), the author talks about "rationalism" of big integrated structures because of: "firstly, the need of cost and liquidity risk reduction, secondly the achievement of scale economies to become competitive and thirdly, globalization, which needs of more complex and articulate platforms unattainable to individual small and medium enterprises" (Translation given by the author)

7 In the same sense *Todeva, E.*, Business Networks: strategy and structure, Oxford, 2006, p. 1 (p. 5 and 9).
*Contractor, F.J./Lorange, P.*, Why should firms cooperate? The Strategy and Economic Basis for Cooperative Ventures, in: Contractor, F.J./Lorange, P., (eds.), Joint Ventures and Technology Partnerships between Firms, New York, 1988, p. 3 (p. 4-5): "Cooperation agreements are as numerous to suggest that our multinational company stereotype needs to be changed. Traditionally it has been perceived as a monolithic entity controlling or possessing its inputs and outputs and spreading then in foreign markets given its technological, management and market dominium… Nowadays as refers to industries, we are in a higher negotiation and competition world. In many situations, international enterprises are better seen as a coalition of interconnected relationships. Their strategic freedom is also increased by markets globalization and reduced by the need of bargaining cooperation agreements between enterprises and governments".

8 About these parameters influence on enterprises outsourcing, *Fernández Nogales, A./Martínez Castro, E./Rebollo Arévalo, A.*, La reorganización de los canales de distribución, Mediterráneo Económico, num.11, 182, (199) : "As well as markets size and companies operations volume increases, the possibility for several companies specialization on isolated tasks appears, frame in which execution would reach a nearer size to the optimal for the activity production, given the possibility to offer low prices to their clients in comparison with the conversely situation. Com-

house processes to external service providers, thus resulting in indistinct firm boundaries[9] and providing opportunities to SMEs specialized in outsourcing tasks execution[10].

As a consequence, changes in inner organizational structures have their own effect in ways enterprises interact with one another:[11] in a world with

---

panies would find more convenient to outsource no strategic tasks not only attending its low cost, but also because the possibility to place sources on core competitive functions. By this way, the more markets size increases, the more possibilities for outsourcing and joint efficiency. In the commercial distribution field this phenomena explains, for example, logistics companies and commercialization specialised companies work up named before". (Translation given by the author).

9 In this sense *Powell, W.,* The Capitalist Firm in the Twenty- First Century: Emerging Patterns in Western Enterprise, in: Di Maggio, P., (ed.), The Twenty-First-Century Firm, Changing economic organization in international perspective, Princeton, 2001, p. 58 : "Just as the changed conception of work, as organized around project teams, transforms firms internally, the growing involvement of firms in an intricate latticework of collaborations with "outsiders" blurs the boundaries of the firm, making it difficult to know where the firm ends and where the market or another firm begins. The former step redraws internal lines of authority, while the latter spreads the core activities of the firm across a much wider array of participants, which an attendant loss of centralized control".

10 In one article devoted to analyse the change on Enterprise organizing model from big companies to SMEs network structures, *Arzeni, S.,* Introducción, in: OCDE (ed.), Redes de Empresas y Desarrollo Local. Competencia y cooperación en los sistemas productivos locales, Paris, 1999, p. 16: "Growing interest on SMEs arises from industrial companies' changing structure facing more open economies. Traditional vertically integrated production units whose success depends on tasks disintegration, skills and work specialization, big production levels and scale economies, have stated its inflexibility in adapting to change of circumstances. Conversely, technology based small enterprises have demonstrated its capability to be viable, stable, flexible and adaptable to changing market demands even I the degree of assuming market's transnational character". (Translation given by the author)

11 This idea appears in the work *Westney, D.*, Japanese enterprise Faces the Twenty-First Century, in: Di Maggio, P., (ed.), The Twenty-First-Century Firm, Changing economic organization in international perspective, Princeton, 2001, p.115 and 142 where could be noticed the extension of inner network model of Japanese enterprises to market relationships by means of vertical or horizontal *keiretsu*, model identifiable with reciprocal interests corporate group and not with the business network concept assumed in this work.

In the western area, reciprocal interests and interlocking directorate in relation to business networks is analysed by *Zorzi, A.*, Reti di imprese e modelli societari di coordinamento, in: Cafaggi, F. (ed.), Reti di imprese tra regolazione e norme sociali. Nuove sfide per diritto ed economía, Bologna, 2004, p.174 (p. 179-185).

global competition, stable and long-term relationships between economic entities are needed to ensure economic efficiency through maximization of strategic advantages arising from synergies between firms.[12]

Therefore, this external convergence process reflects, in some way, inner coordination and interrelation links between the autonomous and independent work teams,[13] which consequently implies an overcoming of the traditional enterprise conception as an independent organizing unit playing in the market, shifting to a more relational conception defining it as a "market integrated centre of economic imputation and organization".[14]

In the production of complex goods, for instance, intermediaries, suppliers, distributors and retailers provide the main entrepreneur with strategic information about market conditions, thus, on the one hand influencing the development of commercial strategies for each country and market, and are, on the other hand, themselves indispensables for maintaining of

---

12 *Jacquemin, A.*, Cooperation ente les enterprises et droit economique, in: Jacquemin, A./Remiche, B. (eds.), Coopération entre entreprises, Entreprises conjointes stratégies industrielles et pouvoirs publics, Bruxelles, 1988, p.16 (p.19-20), sets principally benefits arising from stable cooperation between firms.

13 In a very pictorial way *Powell, W.*, Neither Market nor hierarchy: network forms of organization, Research in Organizational Behavior, Vol.12, 1990, 295 (301): "Many firms are no longer structured like medieval kingdoms, walled off and protected from hostile outside forces. Instead, we find companies involve in an intricate latticework of collaborative ventures with other firms, most of whom are ostensibly competitors. The dense ties that bind the auto biotechnology industries, discussed below, cannot be easily explained by saying that these firms are engaged in market transactions for some factors of production, or by suggesting that the biotechnology business in embedded in the international community science"

14 *Iamiceli, P.*, Dalle reti di imprese al contratto di rete: un percorso (in)compiuto, in: Iamiceli, P. (ed.) Le reti di imprese e i contratti di rete, Giappichelli, G., (ed.), Torino, 2009 p.1 (4), refers to the phenomena: "... practise, in its different forms seems to be the higher source for organizing innovation, tacking also into account enterprise international opening. Subcontract, distribution, franchising networks, joint ventures, strategic alliances and trademarks agreements constitute the roots for a rightful "network system" based on long-term collaborative relationships, specific investments intensity – specially human capital and knowledge –, trust and flexibility of governance tools as acts devoted to manage uncertainty characterized relationships survival". (Translation given by the author).
An example of the importance of relational component in business activity organization and strategy could be seen in the brilliant work of *Powell, W./White, R./ Koput, W./Owen-Smith, J.*, Networks dynamics and field evolution: The growth of interorganizational collaboration in the life Sciencies, American Journal of Sociology, vol. 110, núm. 4, 2005, 1132-1205. Available www.personal.umich.edu

quality and productivity – suppliers – and effective product commercialization – distributors–.[15]

Thence, business networks appear as a new economic structure placed between market and hierarchy as ideal models of business organization[16] whose main characters, from an economic point of view, are: interdependence between business benefits; stable, long-term and trust based rela-

15 Refering to the importance of intermediares, *Grundmann, S.,* Redes contractuales, ¿Contratos o sociedades personificadas?, in: Ruiz Peris, J.I., (ed.), Nuevas Perspectivas del Derecho de Redes Empresariales, Valencia, 2012, p. 127; *Id.* Contractual Networks in German private law, in: Cafaggi. F., (dir.), Contractual networks, inter-firm cooperation and economic growth, Cheltenham et. al., 2011, p. 111 (112): "Without network of contracts there is no market economy! It is the backbone of any value creation chain. This is evident for *production*, namely with supply contracts, among them the much discussed just in time contracts. All big branches such as the production of motor-vehicles, computers and more sophisticated electronic devices, but also tourism are designed in such a way that the ‚manufacturer' is surrounded by a certain number of suppliers... Traditionally, production is seen at the heart of the creation of values in market economies – although its contribution to the gross net income is no longer bigger than the one by its 'little sister', *trade and distribution*. The more products are complicated, the more this second sector becomes important also from a conceptual point of view, because information about the product and after sales service are more important here and typically provided by this second sector".

16 Following with the previous distinction between vertical disintegration and external convergence processes and clearly reaching a medium point as a distinctive for business networks organization, *Teubner, G.,* Network as connected contracts, Oxford, 2011, p. 20: "The crisis within the traditional hierarchically centralised organisation has not led to the true externalisation of activities within the market. Instead, it has given rise to the 'quasi-externalisation' of activities within networks of manufacturers, co-producers and distributors that also include customers and consumers within their wealth creating chains. By the same token, the process also sees formerly independent market firms integrated evermore closely within the wealth creating network without, however, ending in the establishment of integrated firms. Instead, increasing numbers of independent businesses have joined together within networks. In other words, there is no true internalisation within formal organisational terms, but rather a process of 'quasi-internalisation'. The trend is one of fragmentation into small business units and the emergence of common network usage. Just-in-time distribution systems, virtual businesses and franchising chains are the most commonly known network types. The new network enterprise thus stems from disintegration tendencies within the traditional firm on the one hand, and from quasi-integration tendencies within markets on the other".

tionships between its members; and, creation and/or sharing of industrial knowledge and know-how.[17]

## I. Interdependence between business benefits

Specialization and inter-firm collaboration constitute key factors for the development of new and more complex products and services, giving added value and differentiation capability from competitors.[18] However, to achieve these goals, especially intense inter-firm relationships, more accurately relationships with a stable and long-term character,[19] which also

---

17 This systemisation of business networks defining characters is essayed by *Powell, W.*, Neither Market nor hierarchy: network forms of organization, Research in Organizational Behavior, Vol.12, 1990, 295, 324; and also *Todeva, E.*, Business Networks: strategy and structure, Oxford, 2006, p. 14-15.

18 In this sense *Castaldo, S.*, Trust in Market Relationships, Cheltenham et. al., 2007, p.3 argues that: "Enterprises are incapable to manage independently environment complexity increasing and, therefore, require a specialization in the production of knowledge as well as in the development of trust relationships with their markets. Hence, the need to connect in networks and integrate complementarity competencies and expertise emerges, in order to face the new competitive contexts...Unilateral and instantaneous exchanges will have to become long-term bilateral relationships, in which the demand will actively interact with the firm's network, thus contributing to the knowledge development...In turn, clients become co-producers of the reticular knowledge base".
In the same sense, *Id.* Fiducia e relazioni di mercato, 2002, p. 15.

19 *Windahl, C./Lakemond, N.*, Developing integrated solutions: The importance of relationships within the networks, Industrial Marketing Management, num. 35, 2006, 806, (808 and 809) in relation with integrated products creation states that: "Integrated solutions creation is, overall, a question of combining multiple actor's value activities with the aim to develop final products "value creators"...Therefore, instead of focusing on the firm itself or even the industry, it becomes important to focus on the value-creating system where different actors (suppliers, business partners, allies, customers) work together to co-produce value; roles and relationships need to be reconfigured in order to create value in new forms, and a dynamic fit between competencies and customers becomes crucial... Taking into account a firm's embeddedness in the network and its indirect and direct connections and dependencies on other organizations is therefore likely to provide a more complete picture of the challenges connected to developing integrated solutions".

entail a higher stability degree in comparison with simple, instantaneous and sporadic market exchanges, are required.[20]

Thence, integration of performance processes – not of firms as a whole – between economic entities are the result. In this sense, the result of an enterprise hinges not only on its own inner management and organizational capabilities, but also on its external relationships – blurring of firm's boundaries –, namely, on the relations with other participating enterprises in the goods and/or services development and distribution. As a result, different entrepreneurs' business benefits are interrelated within the framework of an interdependent relationship aiming at one joint final product.

Therefore, interdependence implies the idea of connectivity between the various benefits, which means that, within the network, the outcome of one member activity is capable of affecting or influencing other network members, even in such cases where no direct relationship between the respective entities exists. Likewise, decisions and performances of subjects included in the network have their own influences on the whole project outcome, but also upon other member's freedom, since their benefits are reciprocally linked by means of interdependency.[21]

---

20 Refering to entrepreuner's reationships stabilization inside this framework, *Cafaggi, F.,* Reti di impresi, spazi e silenzi regolativi, in: Cafaggi, F., (ed.), Reti di imprese tra regolazione e norme sociali. Nuove sfide per diritto ed economía, 2004, p 1 (18-19): "The (business) network stabilises relationships narrowing negative effects from instability of single contractual relationships, opportunistic behaviour related to asymmetric specific investments and also the exigency of sources mobility securing enterprise flexibility and reaction. Stabilization also increases opportunistic exit costs as well as ensure reputational and non-reputational sanctions imposing. At the same time, specialization reduces efficient exit cost of singular contractual relationships holding from the network, thus, let a mobility of relational sources through cooperation systems warrant a trend optimum use". (Translation given by the author).

21 In this sense *Batt, P./Parchase, S.,* Managing collaboration within networks and relationships, Industrial Marketing Manager, num. 33, 2004, 169, (170): "As a network is a set of connected relationships between firms (Hakansson & Johanson, 1993), effects will flow through the various relationships that the focal firm has established with other connected actors. Connectedness is the extent to which exchange in one relation is contingent upon exchange in another (Cook & Emerson, 1978). Moreover, two connected relationships can be directly or indirectly connected to many other relationships that may have some bearing on each firm as part of a larger business network (Anderson, Hakansson, & Johanson, 1994). Thus, collaboration within one relationship will affect relationships with other closely connected actors, making the collaboration process and its outcomes con-

II. Stable, long-term and trust based relationships between network members

Continuous interaction between economic entities results in a learning curve by monitoring and assessing processes deriving from accumulated experience.[22] As a result, although no previous trusting relationship between the respective entities existed, particular significance corresponds to the relational component between said entities. Thus, informal links, based on past experience arise between the parties,[23] generating positive expectations – behaviour expectations – of a future satisfactory performance by the other counterparty.[24] These expectations constitute the basis for a trusting relationship between entrepreneurs in which each party relies on

tingent upon the goals of the network rather than the dyad. Hakansson and Ford (2002) describe how firms embedded in business networks are interdependent on other firms in the network. This interdependence implies that firms have limited discretion to act or to build independent strategy (Gadde et al., 2003). As a result, the outcomes of the firm's actions are strongly influenced by the attitudes and actions of those firms with whom the focal firm has relationships".

22 About economic incentives for entreprises to colaborate together in learning by monitoring, *Bosi, G.,* Modelli di autorreglamentazione nelle reti di imprese, in: Cafaggi, F., (ed.), Reti di imprese tra regolazione e norme sociali. Nuove sfide per diritto ed economia, Bologna, 2004, p. 233 (249-250).

23 *Perdersen, R.,* The gateway to successful business relationships in the 21st century, Pecnia, Monográfico, 2010, p. 165 (168), describes the pass of business relationship throughout five stadiums to reach informal trust links generation: "pre-relationship", including future counterpart research; "negotiations beginning", which is the period of higher inversions for both parties: meetings, discussions and information and energy sharing; "contractual relationship development", in which parts close each other as they get use to their work style and leadership; "deepening" in the relationship as a consequence of long time mutual knowing, when further details in information and coordination is not needed, which means also a danger for the contractual relationship in case of too much relax; "break down" of the relationship, when excess in relaxing, bankrupts trust".

24 The formation of this expectative is at roots of business networks where "the matted ties of reputation, friendship, interdependence and altruism become integral parts of the relationship". *Powell, W.,* Neither Market nor hierarchy: network forms of organization, Research in Organizational Behavior, Vol.12, 1990, p. 304 quoting *Macneil, I.,* Relational contract: What we do and do not know? Wisconsin Law Review, num. 3, 483-526.

the respective other to realise the benefits in accordance to the specificities previously known.[25]

At the same time, this trust framework boosts a higher degree of business collaboration, which means higher integration between productive activities of enterprises maintaining a stable relationship.[26] This desire of major integration further entails higher possibilities of trust generating, as well as opportunism risk reduction.[27] Therefore trust and integration appear to be linked throughout in a circular relationship, each one amplifying the other.

## III. Creation and/or sharing of industrial knowledge and know-how

Inside a business context where a higher degree of integration between independent entrepreneurs in complex and competitive goods and services' development exists, and also where the parties are interdependent and the possible benefits connected, the sharing of information and knowledge be-

---

25 Although it is true the higher degree of reciprocal trust reduce opportunism risk, capability of mutual reinforcement should also be taken into account as stress *Grandori, A.*, Interfirm Networks: Organizational mechanisms and economic outcomes, in: Grandori, A., (ed.), Interfirm Networks: Organization and Industrial Competitiveness, Oxford, 1999, p. 11, " Trust and opportunism could both been present not only inside a relationship but also strengthen each other as has shown Friedberg and Neuville in supply relationships. If one party has reached a reliable reputation this boost its opportunism as far as control of these behaviours is less common".

26 In a very pictorial way, *Todeva, E.*, Business Networks: strategy and structure, Oxford, 2006, p. 96-97, organizes around 6 stadiums the phases throughout a business relationships cross until get to the implication degree that a business network implies: 1 the potential relationship, where a co-presence of actor in the same field with feeds susceptible to be put on common exists; 2 pre-relationship, where one actor goes to another to get information and open a communication channel; 4 dyadic market relation, interaction has evolved to a share repetitive experience of goods exchange; 5 long-term relationship, which means a narrowing between production models; 6, networks relationship, when interdependence appears.

27 Analysing trust as network's feature *Powell, W.*, Neither Market nor hierarchy: network forms of organization, Research in Organizational Behavior, Vol.12, 1990, p. 326: "When there is a high probability of future associations, persons are not only more likely to cooperate with others, they are also increasingly willing to punish those who do not cooperate…As a result there is limited need for hierarchical oversight because the desire for continued participation successfully discourages opportunism".

tween the participants is vital for both, each member's activity management and the success of the whole operation.[28]

The sharing of information not only enhances each enterprises' ability to compete by means of strengthening reciprocal synergies (dynamic complementarity),[29] but also enables the execution of complex projects, which otherwise would not be feasible for said enterprises individually.[30] In addition, the sharing of information also enables the respective entities to fi-

---

28 The work of *Chen-Weng, C./M. Chiang/D. Fan-Yun,* Cooperative strategy in supply chain networks, Industrial Marketing Manager, 2012, 3 (6), reflects information sharing importance in diverse networks types, being specially telling the Toyota example: Toyota requires that its suppliers and dealers provide related production and sales ordering information such as demand forecasts, production planning, or inventory status to facilitate more network wide capacity and production planning. These knowledge-sharing routines result in increased efficiency for all partners, cost reductions, enhancement of information transparency, and the building of cooperative advantages. Consequently, Toyota develops information systems (i.e., Toyota Production System), which include advanced planning systems, supply chain management information systems, and global logistics management information systems. These integrate the information activities of all of the network members. In addition, Toyota improves the capability of the entire chain by, for example, training dealers or problem-solving for suppliers.

29 The term is used by *Nooteboom, B.,* A cognitive theory of the Firm. Learning, Governance and Dynamic Capabilites, Northampton, 2009, p.1 (135-136), referring in innovation frame to the convenience of jointing strengths and weakness of big and small enterprises: "Small firms have "behavioural" advantages: motivation to accept risks and low income in early stages of innovation, close contact with customers and employees, flexibility of small emergent firms that haven't yet hardened into organizational shapes to fit established, "dominant" practises. Large firms have advantages in resources: revenues from established activities to fund innovation, a wider range of activities to pool risks and cross-subsidize new ventures, specialized human and other resources, market access (distribution channels and brand names), and stablished political and social capital.
In view of dynamic complementarity, one would expect that large firms typically produce the scientific inventions that require lar R&D teams with specialists, while small, outside firms will be quicker in bringing inventions into practice, in new products (exploration), and large firms carry new products into efficient, large-scale exploitation".

30 In this sense, again, *Powell, W.*, Neither Market nor hierarchy: network forms of organization, Research in Organizational Behavior, Vol.12, 1990, 304: "Networks are particularly apt for circumstances in which there is a need for efficient, reliable information. The most useful information is rarely that which can be inferred from shifting price signals. Rather, it is that which is obtained from someone whom you have dealt with in the past and found to be reliable. You trust best information that comes from someone you know well…The open-ended relational features of net-

nance such research and technological developments, which, for each individual company, would not be viable.[31]

According to above requirements, characteristic trusting relationships between the network members constitute a suitable framework for sharing economic information between interrelated enterprises.[32]

## B. Business networks from a legal point of view: Main characters

The previous remarks regarding the economical and organizational aspects characterizing business networks as a new business model, substantially different from market and organization models, renders a specific analysis of this structure from a legal point of view necessary; namely, to identify

---

works, with their relative absence of explicit quid pro quo behaviour, greatly enhance the ability to transmit and learn new knowledge and skills".

31 *Nooteboom, B.*, The dynamic efficiency of networks, in:, Grandori, A., (ed.), Inter-firm Networks: Organization and Industrial Competitiveness, Oxford, 1999, p. 91, in a very interesting study devoted to analyse business network's efficiencies, analysing research and development factor highlights that, (p.105-106): "For lack of specialized researchers and due to a more practical, short-term orientation, small firms tend to be weaker in systematic, fundamental research, while they are better at applying and commercializing the results of fundamental innovations produced elsewhere....small independent firms in disintegrated structures tend to engage less in R&D, but when they do, they tend to do so more intensively and more efficiently. There is a dynamic complementarity: large integrated firms tend to do better in systemic and fundamental research, while small firms tend to be better at novel combinations in application and commercialization".

32 In this sense, *Teubner, G.*, Network as connected contracts, Oxford, 2011, p. 19 – 20: "The communication of non-marketable knowledge is more deeply anchored within long-term inter-personal cooperative relations and is less dependent on individual acts of impersonal exchange (the latter being characteristic for the production and distribution of material or tangible goods). As a direct consequence, businesses have been forced to restructure themselves as network type arrangements, within which trust-based co-operation forms the basis for enduring informational relations, recursive reinterpretation of events and for the collective construction of knowledge. At first glance, a formal organisation might appear more appropriate to meet these aims. However, an entrenched organisation is simply not in a long-term position to develop and cultivate the necessary knowledge that is dispersed far throughout the market. Accordingly, the current demand is for flexible, decentralised structures – beyond both market and organisation – that can comb the market for information sources and bind such sources together within co-operative relationships".

the suitable legal instruments in order to allocate duties and accountabilities of each part involved in said business network.

Taking into account the economic features named above, many legal scholars have offered different definitions what a business network, at least from a legal point of view, is.[33] In the following, we will use the definition given by Prof. Ruiz Peris: Business networks are defined as "a set of legal and economical independent entrepreneurs but legally linked – by means of collaborative long-term contracts, multilateral contracts, consortia, group or institutional structures – and economically linked – as consequence of its interdependence arising from its collaborative relationships –, that underpin a multiple, stable, relational structure which main characteristics are interdependency, stability or long-term character of network, company autonomy and unlimited accountability of its members in the sense that, each one, company or person, is unlimited liable of his own economic activity.

---

33 Among successive definitions given by the author we stressed here, *Cafaggi, F.*, Introduzione, in: Cafaggi, F./Vella, F., (eds.), Finanziamento delle PMI: cescere innovando, CEDAM, Padova, 2008, p. 8 (13-14): "Business networks constitute and organizational growing model, complementary to the group. In the neo-institutional ambit are qualified as hybrid between market and hierarchy. Are framed in the more general phenomena of enterprises' union and aggregation studied since century beginning. In the legal plane, as a difference to the group, they maintain full autonomy and independence of their members and admit only hierarchical forms in respect to contractual power but not property control...network's function mainly consists in giving raise to collaboration forms between complementary activities develop in one stage or involving several stages of production chain. Networks are constituted when both, market relationships are inadequate to organize complementarity and vertical integrated enterprise demands excessive cost and reduces flexibility" (Translation given by the author).
*Teubner, G.*, Network as connected contracts, Oxford, 2011, p. 17: "Business networks are defined as: "modes of organising economic activities that bind formally independent firms who are more or less economically dependent upon one another through stable relationships and a complex reciprocity that is more co-operative than competitive in form.'
*Iamiceli, P.*, Le reti di imprese: modelli contrattuali di cordinamento, in: Cafaggi, F., (ed.), Reti di imprese tra regolazione e norme sociali. Nuoves fide per diritto ed economia, Bologna, 2004, p. 125 (128) defines network as: "A set of cooperative and tending stable relationships between two or more enterprises formally and legally different although concurrent, in which activity exists or is generated any interdependence and so that, a coordination demand arises, to which network answers with diverse, formal and informal, contractual and non-contractual, governance mechanisms" (Translation given by the author).

Other typical characteristics of networks include sharing exploitation of goods, although not necessarily the direct or indirect ownership of each enterprise's intangible goods – trademark, technician or commercial know-how, goodwill, clients –; the allocation of I+D+I, productive, distributive or after sales functions; the existence of relationships between the network members' independently of its written foreseeability or not; and are based on trust relationships between their members".[34]

Defined this way, the development of a business network governance structure requires further detailed analysis on each one of the above characteristics beforehand in order to identify the main legal singularities resulting from this unique economic structure.

## I. Network stability and long-term character

Stable and prolonged relationships constitute the ground for the integration of business performances. As a result, a new form of entrepreneurial organization emerges, the network, an economic structure consolidated on time despite of members' exits and enters.[35]

Thus, for example, a distribution network could be originating from various similar contracts drawn up over time, whose long-term characteristics[36] result in the forming of a network as business organization form/model that, due to its status acquired on the market, maintains its consider-

---

34 *Ruiz Peris, J.I.*, Un Derecho específico para las redes empresariales, in: Ruiz Peris, J.I., (ed.), Nuevas Perspectivas del Derecho de Redes Empresariales, Valencia, 2012, p 73 (87).

35 In the same sense *Cafaggi, F.*, Redes contractuales y Small Business Act, in: Ruiz Peris, J.I., (ed.), Hacia un Derecho para las redes empresariales, Valencia, 2009, p. 21 (23): "Network stability, referring to the network as a whole, not to singular relationships (from head to rest of members), which can be more or less numerous. Network could be stable although the high number of enters and exits."

36 In Spain scholars, are unanimous in considering distribution contracts as long-term contracts and moreover, consider this long-term character as integrating in the cause of contracts: *Enciso Alonso-Muñuner, M.*, Duración de los contratos de distribución comercial, in: Alonso Ureba, A./Velasco San Pedro, L./Alonso Ledesma, C./Echevarría Sáenz, J.A./Jorge Viera González, A., (eds.), Los contratos de Distribución, La Ley, Madrid, monografía num. 3, 2010, 539 (546): "Parties concluding these contracts (distribution contracts), are looking to establish a stable and durable entrepreneurial collaboration link to promotion and commercialization of manufacturer products by the distributor… Are configured as durable contracts

ation as an organization in spite of changes in the identity of each subject participating in said network.

At the same time, business networks constitute a stabilizing factor for the entrepreneurs' relationships on both, external level – capability to react more efficiently to demand fluctuations –, and also on an internal level: higher integration triggers a more efficient and flexible mobility of resources, generating also higher exit costs for each member, which means a reduction of opportunism risk.[37]

In addition, due to the long-term character, there is the need for establishing auditing structures and modifying, managing and coordinating of member's relationship with the aim to ensure an efficient reaction to changes of market conditions.[38] In the case of contractual networks, this

---

and only towards time the effects looked by parties appears in opposition to instant execution contracts" (Translation given by the author).

To *Moralejo Menéndez, I.*, El contrato Mercantil de Concesión, Cizur-Menor, 2010, p. 56, which enables tacking about a wide category of distribution contracts is "Identity of contract cause inside this category, identity which is maintain a stable and durable coordination between entrepreneurs, producer and distributor tending to ensue products delivery from the first to the consumers". (Translation given by the author).

Specify about duration as integrating exclusivity distribution contracts cause, *García Herrera, A.*, La duración del Contrato de Distribución Exclusiva, Valencia, 2006, p. 358-363.

37 Network characterization as stabilization factor of relationships between entrepreneurs is taken from *Cafaggi, F.*, Reti di impresi, spazi e silenzi regolativi, in: Cafaggi, F., (ed.), Reti di imprese tra regolazione e norme sociali. Nuove sfide per diritto ed economía, 2004, pp. 18-20.

38 *Ruiz Peris, J.I.*, Del contrato bilateral a la relación de red, in: Ruiz Peris, J.I., (ed.), Hacia un Derecho para las redes empresariales., Valencia, 2007, p. 9 (13-14): " Network contracts are long term contracts that implies a durable relationship between its members, which place a set of question derived from differed execution on time towards contract life, contract modification due to the need of integration – for example as concerns to each season models or stock – identification of who determines modification terms and counterpart securities, need of adaptation to new market conditions arising during contract life". (Translation given by the author).

means challenges for writing,[39] integrating,[40] modifying[41] and terminating of contracts.[42]

39 About the question of long-term contracts drawn and terms concretion and capability to foresee conflict situations, *Choi, A./Triantis, G.*, Strategic Vagueness in Contract Design: The Case of Corporate Acquisitions, The Yale Law Journal, vol. 119, 2010, 848; *E. Scott, R., G./Triantis, G.*, Anticipating Litigation in Contract Design, The Yale Law Journal, vol.115, issue 4, January 2006, 816; *Gómez Pomar, F.*, Cooperation, long-term relationships and open-endedness in contractual networks, in: Cafaggi. F., (ed.), Contractual networks, inter-firm cooperation and economic growth, Nothampton, 2011, p. 21; *Bellantuono, G.*, I contratti incompleti nel diritto e nell'economia, CEDAM, Padova, 2000; *Montavini, M.*, Vizi incompleti del contratto e rimedio risarcitorio , Torino, 1995.

40 Integration according with good faith rules, network activity and relationships between its members. To a wide vision of the topic see *Kornet, N.*, Contract Interpretation and Gap Filling: Comparative and Theoretical Perspectives, Oxford, 2006.

41 "Change in activity conditions generally implies all network's members consent… the decision about submit any decisions about majority conditions – in the direction board or general assembly – concerns every members. In contractual networks conditions' change could be given to one party by a contract – network's head, for example in networks of parallel contracts as franchise –. In this case, the *ius variandi* concerns only one of the network members, being limited by abuse of right doctrine – not globally accepted – and objective novation doctrine" *Ruiz Peris, J.I.*, Business networks as a legal explanatory framework, in: Festschrift für Klaus J. Hopt zum 70.Geburtstag am 24. August 2010. Vol.2., Berlin, p. 2901 (2909).
In this context it is also interesting the idea stated by *Grandori, A.*, Contracts as organizational documents: designing flexible formalization, CROMA Working Paper, num. 11, 2002 where defends a "constitutional formalization" degree in business networks contracts drawing, which enable fix a frame of stable agreement between parts and gives high stability to the rest of content, making possible its renegotiation inside the frame established.

42 As concerns to nullity effects extension in the case of linked contracts, *Cauffman, C.*, The impact of voidness for infirgement of article 101 TFEU on linked contracts, in: Samoy, I./Loos, B.M., M., (eds.), Linked contracts, Cambridge, 2012, p. 29 – 54.
In a contractual level we refer to contract clauses coordinating contractual termination of network members, extinction as cause for linking contracts, form and effects of contractual extinction, especially which concerns to notice and damages, as well as post-contractual obligations of network members.

## II. Interdependence

Stable long-term relationships and integration of production cycles between companies – among others special notes[43] – result in the most defining and unique feature of business networks: interdependence between the members' benefits.[44]

---

43 An enumeration of interdependence sources appears *Cafaggi, F.*, Redes contractuales y Small Business Act, in: Ruiz Peris, J.I., (ed.), Hacia un Derecho para las redes empresariales, Valencia, 2009, p. 35.
States also the autor in *Cafaggi, F.*, Redes contractuales y teoría contractual: una agenda de investigación para un derecho contractual europeo, in: Ruiz Peris, J.I., (ed.), Nuevas Perspectivas del Derecho de Redes Empresariales, 2012, p.25 (32 and 35): "Bilateral linked contracts constitute the most common form of contractual networks. It is a network of contracts concluded by individual enterprises. They represent a flexible form of collaboration among multiple enterprises without the creation of a separate organizational entity. Certainly not all linked contracts constitute a network of contracts. The level of interdependence among individual contracts must be high and the overall scope must be unitary…It is not sufficient to have a multiplicity of linked contracts for a contractual network to emerge. As previously stated, there has to be (1) a strong collective interest to pursue, (2) a common objective, (3) a high level of interdependence among the contracts and the activities performed through contracts".

44 Generally speaking, about interdependence as own feature of business networks, *Ruiz Peris, J.I.*, Del contrato bilateral a la relación de red, in: Ruiz Peris, J.I., (ed.), Hacia un Derecho para las redes empresariales., Valencia, 2007, p. 14; *Ruiz Peris, J.I.*, "Business networks as a legal explanatory framework", in: Festschrift für Klaus J. Hopt zum 70.Geburtstag am 24. August 2010. Vol.2., Berlin, p. 2905; *Ruiz Peris, J.I.*, Un Derecho específico para las redes empresariales, in: Ruiz Peris, J.I., (ed.), Nuevas Perspectivas del Derecho de Redes Empresariales, Valencia, 2012, p. 88-89, especially on p. 88: " In our opinion, a clear conceptual delimitation between the general meaning of network as contact-network, and business networks founded in the idea of interdependence, should be made. Interdependence is the main feature which distinguish business networks from other types of networks, besides been constituted by entrepreneurs – enterprises following German law – or other economic agents developing economic or entrepreneurial activities for the market.
The frame and extension of interdependence may and shall be take into account as defining of network's frame, namely, identifying which part of network's members is under network coordination and takes profit of network synergies". (Translation given by the author).

Interdependence means, that the result of each members' actions depends again on the result of other network members' actions,[45] taking further into account that the amount of each party's share of overall activity between interdependent parties are not necessarily equal, but that it's rather the case, that the members vary in that point from one another.[46]

With respect to legal context, interdependence means that one contract execution is unilaterally or reciprocally dependent from others, a typical feature of linked or connected contracts,[47] in France "*l' interdependence*",[48] where execution of contractual benefits are affected in greater or

45 In this point it is important to distinguish between unilateral and multilateral interdependence. In the first case, one member benefit relies on other member's activity without any influence of its own activity upon other networks members. In contrast, multilateral interdependence entails a reciprocal influence between members conditioning each other his results. For more detailed explanation see *Cafaggi, F., Redes contractuales y Small Business Act, in: Ruiz Peris, J.I.*, (ed.), Hacia un Derecho para las redes empresariales, Valencia, 2009, p. 61 – 62.

46 In this sense *Ruiz Peris, J.I.*, Un Derecho específico para las redes empresariales, in: Ruiz Peris, J.I., (ed.), Nuevas Perspectivas del Derecho de Redes Empresariales, Valencia, 2012, p. 89-90: "Determination of interdependence frame enables to a network classification making possible to distinguish legal treatment in accordance with network's economic distinguishing features.
Thereby, we can identify network's members who's full or near full main activity is interdependent, members with their major activity part is interdependent, members in interdependence situation only in respect to a significant part of their main activity and members whose activities in interdependence situation are only secondary". (Translation given by the author).

47 Following *López Frías, A.*, Los contratos conexos, Barcelona, 1994, p. 282: "Contractual connection exists when, drawn different contracts, from a legal point of view it is not possible consider them as absolutely independent because either, their legal nature doesn't allow to this classification or this conception is at odds with the economic-legal business placed at the roots of them". (Translation given by the author).
To *Teubner, G.*, Network as connected contracts, Oxford, 2011,p. 58: We apply the term "connected contracts" to all mutually impacting contractual relations, whether of a bilateral or multilateral nature, whose interconnection gives direct rise to legal consequences (of a genetic, functional or conditional type), be it that one contractual relationship impacts upon another (or others), or be it that mutual impacts may be observed".

48 Article 13 *Avant-project Catala* and *Avant-project de l Chancellerie,* define *Contrats interdépendants* as: « contrats concomitants ou successifs dont l'execution est néxessaire à la réalisation de l'opération d'ensemble à laquelle ils appartiennent » y art. 100 project de réforme du droit des obligations, takes care of one *contrat interdépendant* nullity in art. 13 pointing that: « Lorsque l'un des contrats

lesser extent by other contract benefits, constituting altogether tools for legal formalization of a complex and multilateral economic structure.[49] This constellation enables to identify both, on the one hand the effects on individual contract performance resulting from the involvement in the network as a whole, i.e., as a factor of influence on duties and rights, and, on the other hand, the efficacy of the members' relationships with third parties, inside and outside the network.[50]

---

interdépendants est attient de nullité, les parties aux autres contrats du même ensemble peuvent se prévaloir de leur caducité si la nullité rend leur exécution impossible ou prive le contrat de tout intérêt pour les parties».
About this concept which appears in the draft of French contractual regulation, *Aubert de Vincelles, C.*, Linked contracts under French law, in: Cafaggi. F., (ed.), Contractual networks, inter-firm cooperation and economic growth, Edward Elgar, Nothampton, 2011, p. 163 (169-170): "Interdependence exits when each contract performance is needed inside a global transaction context. The originality of this question, which makes it interesting, is considering links between contracts in both, reciprocally and in relation with the whole transaction. The transaction is presented as a unity being each contract liked to it, namely, each contract is need for the whole achieving but isolates is not enough to reach the whole transaction aim". (Translation given by the author).

49 To *Van Dongen, S.*, Groups of contracts. An exploration of types and the archetype from a dutch legal perspective, in: Samoy, I./ Loos, B.M., (eds.), Linked contracts, Cambridge, 2012, p.8 (10): "In a wide sense the notion of "contracts' group" includes every situation in which several contract are not dependent but are part from a "bigger whole". This connection could be expressly previewed in contracts. To this end, it could be used so-called non-compliance cross clauses which entails that, one debtor's breach of contracts automatically leads to a breach under one or more contracts, turning automatically debts overdue and claimable and being possible to finish all contracts by the non-breach party".

50 In relation with this *Cafaggi, F.*, Redes contractuales y teoría contractual: una agenda de investigación para un derecho contractual europeo, in: Ruiz Peris, J.I., (ed.), Nuevas Perspectivas del Derecho de Redes Empresariales, 2012, p. 28, points out: "Contractual interdependence contrasts with a privacy regime, which imposes clear limits on the positive and negative effects that contracts can produce as regards other contracts and third parties. The boundaries of the firms are not rigid: flexibility increases efficiency but it requires a consistent legal framework. The production of complex goods and services often requires a contribution of several parties and their performances are interdependent, all being directed to achieving a common objective. This implies that conventional risk allocation, based on either/or mechanisms, does not fit the purpose of risk sharing within the contractual network: in this context, each party's breach may influence the feasibility of the common project, and that risk sharing has to been agreed upon by several parties who are not always directly bound by the same contractual relation-

Hence, a reviewing of independence of contracts principle in network relationships is needed due to the "reflect efficacy on third parties[51]" of business performances in this frame where dependence or connection rela-

---

ship. The domain of the common risk reaches beyond the boundaries of contractual relationships".

See also the theorist and speculative nature work by *Momnberg Uribe, R.*, Linked Contracts: elements for a General Regulation, in: Samoy, I./Loos M.B.M. (eds.), Linked contracts, Cambridge, 2012, p. 153, where perfectly reflects all the contractual link problematic as a consequence of contracts inclusion in a wider business structure than bilateral exchange relationship.

51 Following *Díez Picazo, L.*, Fundamentos del Derecho civil patrimonial, vol.I, Civitas, Madrid, 6ª ed, 2007, p. 530: "A reflected contract efficacy upon thirds parties exists when one contract rebounds in an alien sphere by means of a connexion phenomenon between many legal relationships. The reflected efficacy is not one "incidence" but a "rebound"… Rebound arises from connection between many pre-existing relationships. One connection between legal relationships can exist in three cases:…firstly, when these legal relationships are respectively *supra* and subordinated inside a worth hierarchical order (for instance, guarantor in respect to the relation between creditor and debtor); **secondly when different relationships coexist and reciprocal condition themselves (for instance, creditors concurrency in bankruptcy)**; thirdly, when one of the relationships derives and relies upon other which serves as basis (for example, sublease in relation to lease)". (Letters in bold and translation given by the author).

tionships arise from independent contracts[52], as a consequence of its benefit's interdependence situation[53].

---

52 As refers to contract classification arising from mutual repercussion as a consequence of their benefit's connection, *Díez Picazo, L.*, Fundamentos del Derecho civil patrimonial, vol.I, Civitas, Madrid, 6ª ed, 2007, p. 441: "A connection or dependence relationship between many contracts can exists in two concrete hypothesis: 1) By constituting one of these contracts a ground or a *conditio iuris* for the other full practical function development. For instance, the efficiency of a encumber contract constitution upon one thing depends on the contract efficiency by which encumber imposer had acquired the ownership or disposition power over the encumbered thing. 2) Both contracts simultaneously cooperate to an economic or economic-social result pursued by parties. We are in front of a complex business or colligated contracts phenomenon. For instance, when parties agree the transmission of a building site ownership, buyer's obligation of constructing, the obligation to transmit to the assigner certain flats as well as a set of securities (mortgages) to warrant the whole obligation".
Referring to complex or colligated contracts, the author points out in Dictámenes jurídicos, Civitas, Madrid, 1987, p. 73: "Colligated contracts are those in which parties juxtapose different contracts in one unique business with the aim to reach by means of everyone union, the pursued empiric aim. In contrast, in complex contracts, although each party's benefits, assumed obligations and pacts established isolated considered belong to a pre-existing contractual type, themselves shift from this type to take part of a unique business, thence without juxtaposition but merger of benefits in one sole contract...In "colligated contracts", a causal and functional link between different contracts exists but, maintaining each one its own autonomy and being summited to its own problems and having its own legal regime. Casual and functional identity exert certain repercussion. For instance: in applying the base idea or the *rebus sic stantibus* clause. Nevertheless, this repercussion should be considered exceptional and autonomy and independence normal. Besides, it should be taken into account that, by drawing different documents parties have produced, at least, formal contractual independence so, it seems not possible for them try to go against this interdependence".
To *López Frías, A.*, Los contratos conexos, Barcelona, 1994, p. 273: "There is a contractual connection phenomenon when many subjects draw two or more different contracts with a thin functional link between then by means of its own nature, or by means of the global aim informing them. This linking is or could be legally relevant".

53 About the overcoming of privacy principle, *Brownsword, R.*, Network contracts Revisited, in: Amstutz, M./Teubner, G., (eds.), Networks, Legal Issues of Multilateral Co-operation, Oxford, Portland, Oregon, 2009, p. 31; *González Castilla, F.*, En torno a las consecuencias de la conexión contractual en el crédito al consumo: la superación jurisprudencial de las exigencias de la Ley 7/1995, Revista de Derecho Mercantil, num. 279, 286. Id. La aplicación del principio de relatividad de los contratos a las redes de distribución, in: Ruiz Peris, J.I., (ed.), Hacia un Derecho para las redes empresariales, Valencia, 2007, p. 97-133; *Id.* Leasing fi-

## III. Members autonomy

This is the most distinguishing feature of business networks of companies and moreover of company groups. In this sense, entrepreneurs' integration in networks don't lead to the creation of a new legal entity, but members rather maintain their independence as entities, who simply decided to integrate part or whole of their business activity in a stable and continuous network of economic structure.[54]

---

nanciero inmobiliario, Madrid 2003; *Grundmann, S.*, Contractual Networks in German private law, in: Cafaggi. F., (dir.), Contractual networks, inter-firm cooperation and economic growth, Cheltenham et. al., 2011, p. 116-161; *Heerman, Peter W.*, The Status of Multilateral Synallagmas in the Law of Connected Contract , in: Amstutz, M./Teubner, G., (eds.), Networks, Legal Issues of Multilateral Co-operation, Oxford, Portland, Oregon, 2009, p. 103; *Hidalgo García, S.*, EL contrato y los terceros. Seguro, edificación, crédito al consumo, pactos de exclusiva y subcontratación, Valladolid, 2012; *Samoy, I./Loos, M.*, Linked contracts, Cambridge, 2012; *Martí Miravalls, J.*, El contrato de master franquicia, Aranzadi, Pamplona, 2009, p. 469-581.; *Teubner, G.*, Network as connected contracts, Oxford, 2011, p. 57-85; *Wellwnhofer, M.*, Third Party Effects of Bilateral Contracts within the Network, in: Amstutz, M./Teubner, G., (eds.), Networks, Legal Issues of Multilateral Co-operation, Oxford, Portland, Oregon, 2009, p. 119, *Whittaker, S.*, Contract networks, freedom of contract and the restructuring of privacy of contract, in: Cafaggi. F., (ed.), Contractual networks, inter-firm cooperation and economic growth, Northampton, 2011, p. 179-197.

54 In this sense, *Ruiz Peris, J.I.*, Del contrato bilateral a la relación de red, in: Ruiz Peris, J.I., (ed.), Hacia un Derecho para las redes empresariales., Valencia, 2007, p. 11, highlighting as differencing factors with partnership the existence in the network of a share interest as opposed to the common partnership interest; the different admitting and exclusion member's regime, focused in case of hegemonic networks in the network's head; regime of revenues' distribution in the absence of a common patrimony. In the same sense, regarding this distinction with partnership, *Teubner, G.*, Network as connected contracts, Oxford, 2011, p.44: "Networks do not create a corporate entity in its own right, rather, are simply formed out of connections made between decentralised decision-making centres. External contacts with the network do not take place as an agreement with a corporate entity, but rather follow out of bilateral connection to decentralised units. Usual management provisions and rules of agency are not appropriate since, in their guise as autonomous firms, network members are responsible for the consequences of their own decisions. Common property is not provided for, since network resources are not pooled, but remain within the purview of individual network nodes. Such structural distinctions between networks and corporate entities preclude the characterisation of business networks as partnerships, regardless of the degree of their centralisation. As a consequence, law must dispense with traditional corporate law

Thence, the entrepreneurs' legal independence means also legal autonomy from the other members and from the network itself, so that each member maintains its own business strategy – individual divergent interests – independent from the other ones, however their decisions might be influenced – interdependence and behaviour duties – as a consequence of his participation in the network.[55]

Independence and legal autonomy of network members are the reasons which preclude business networks classification as vertical or hierarchical company groups – holdings –, because of the lack of a "controlling influence" of each network participant upon the others.[56]

However, taking into account that the defining note for groups as a whole category – this is, including hierarchical and coordination groups – is the *unitary direction*,[57] it is possible to find out in the market economic

---

characterisations and find a new way appropriately to characterise the uncontrovertibly collective nature of networks".

55 In this sense, *Ruiz Peris, J.I.*, Un Derecho específico para las redes empresariales, in: Ruiz Peris, J.I., (ed.), Nuevas Perspectivas del Derecho de Redes Empresariales, Valencia, 2012, p. 90: "Network's members business decisions – whose execution determine their activity – are autonomous and not joint. Those decide its own business strategy in the market in an autonomous way, but shaped by network's inherent coordination and by the contractual or corporate boundaries agreed in respect of its own organization.
Network's members obtain their benefits from activity developed in network frame as a consequence of the exercise of its own individual activity to the market, whose results are conditioned by the synergies arising from network's belonging and, overall, maintain their unlimited liability in respect to their activity result".

56 As it is known, the main category of company group is defined as "a business set integrated by diverse legal subjects (usually companies) which, apart from their own legal personality, in the market performance are submitted to an *economic unified direction* by the group's head", *Embid Irujo, J.M./Fumás Salas, V.*, El gobierno de los grupos de sociedades, Fundación Alternativas, Documento de trabajo 64/2005, p. 1 (23).

57 *Girgado Perandones, P.*, La empresa de grupo y el derecho de sociedades, Comares, Granada, 2001, p. 200-201: "It is commonly pointed out between commercial law scholars at national and international level the role played by the unitary direction in corporate group formation, because it should be reminded dependence itself is not needed – coordination groups – or enough for the existence of a group, demanding one "additional element": unitary direction. This element has a predominant role in group formation, because as has been named before in relation with coordination groups, its existence itself is enough to the existence of a group, without any further requirement of dependence, control or domain that, if exists, it would be submitted under unitary direction; besides, it is necessary because with-

structures built only around the unitary direction note: distribution networks, construction and subcontractor networks, etc. All these structures could be classified as business networks, fact which suggest proximity between both institutions: coordination company groups and business networks. This proximity shall have been carefully observed and studied in the future.[58]

Apart from these conceptual questions it should also be noted, that members' autonomy results in a more burdensome situation for network members than in respect of the situation of shareholders in a company.

In this context, entrepreneurs are also considered parties in business relationships existing inside the network and are, as a consequence, bound to the duties and accountabilities arising from these relationships. Hence and paradoxically, legal autonomy implies for network members a major engagement in network management, playing an active role as stakeholders concerned about the success of the project they are supporting, more than mere shareholders taking profit of stock dividends.[59]

---

out unitary direction, we would place ourselves in scenarios previous to the group, but not in a proper group because it would miss the essential unity of any organization or enterprise" (Translation given by the author).

58 A very interesting delimitation between corporate group by subordination and coordination as way to organise a business network is made by *Echebarría Sáenz, J.A.*, Los grupos por coordinación como instrumento de red, in: Ruiz Peris, J.I., (ed.), *Nuevas Perspectivas del Derecho de Redes Empresariales*, Valencia, 2012, p. 249 (252-269); highlighting the author on p.263 that, in the case of coordination corporate groups: "It is needed to insisting again on the different situation (we are in coordination corporate groups) in respect to the control, characteristic feature of hierarchical or subordination corporate groups. Control techniques allow to exercise a decisive influence upon the enterprise, its IP rights, the asset's use, deliberations and organizing agreements...If we talk about peer structure groups, we talk about interdependence relationships. Here, unitary direction exercise is founded on the previous willing agreements between group members. Control capabilities are the result of one competences attribution and not of an economic dependence or subordination.
Another thing is – and here I doubt –, if the exercise of these competences not necessarily derives towards economic dependence and subordination. At least theoretically, in a unitary direction of a coordination group, decisions about group policy are taken with enterprises collaboration (usually in a proportional way to their participation, but occasionally, also by means of vote by head, unanimity or by consensus systems". (Translation given by the author).

59 The more intense role played by stakeholders in respect to shareholders inside enterprise's organization is stand out by *Cafaggi, F.*, Reti di impresi, spazi e silenzi regolativi, in: Cafaggi, F., (ed.), Reti di imprese tra regolazione e norme sociali.

Even though above mentioned characteristic of autonomy results in numerous forms of network organization,[60] it is possible to distinguish between two main categories: hegemonic networks (formerly known as hierarchical networks) and horizontal or peer networks:[61]

The hegemonic model is characterized by the existence of a network head or principal node, usually embodied by that entrepreneur who provides the network with considerable assets: enterprise model, know how,

---

Nuove sfide per diritto ed economía, Bologna, 2004, p. 29-30: "Thought from one part of economist and sociologist reflect that network's comparative advantage in respect of other enterprise organizing models arise from the higher engagement of these subjects (stakeholders) in the decision process, which is addressed to boost cooperation, cut down transactions costs and opportunism behaviours. View from the alternative between stakeholder-shareholder, this profile would point the need to considerer with higher attention the different stakeholder's role from owner or managers in the decisional process defining as well as the effects on accountability allocation". (Translation given by the author).

60 *Ruiz Peris, J.I.*, Del contrato bilateral a la relación de red, in: Ruiz Peris, J.I., (ed.), Hacia un Derecho para las redes empresariales., Valencia, 2007, p. 14; *Cafaggi, F.*, Redes contractuales y teoría contractual: una agenda de investigación para un derecho contractual europeo, in: Ruiz Peris, J.I., (ed.), Nuevas Perspectivas del Derecho de Redes Empresariales, 2012, p. 24;
An enumeration of diverse network's types attending to business sectors is pointed by *Gaudin, J.H.*, Structures internes des entreprises conjointes et intérêts privés, in: Jacquemin, A./Remiche, B. (eds.), Coopération entre entreprises, Entreprises conjointes stratégies industrielles et pouvoirs publics, Bruxelles, 1988, p. 31, (p. 32), distinguishing 3 types of joint enterprises: "The joint research and development enterprise, which at least in theory, can preserve industrial and commercial independence of each one of its participants; the joint enterprise on industrial manufacturing, in further than is usual outputs can allow to its members certain commercial independence, or, at contra, constitute a quasi-merge; the commercialization joint enterprise where the exact position between "merger" and "simple cooperation" depends on the activity of founder enterprises". (Translation given by the author).

61 This distinction is sooner proposed by *Cafaggi, F.*, Il goberno della rete: modelli organizzativi del coordinamento inter-imprenditoriale, Cafaggi, F., (ed.), Reti di imprese tra regolazione e norme sociali. Nuove sfide per diritto ed economía, 2004, p. 57, (p. 63 and 64), who later on insis in this idea on Id. Product safety, private standard –setting information and Networks, in: Cafaggi, F./Muir Watt, H., (eds.),The Regulatory function of European Private Law, Cheltenham, 2009, p. 207 (236-241), in respect to different ways to transmit information inside a network.
In the same sense, *Ruiz Peris, J.I.*, Business networks as a legal explanatory framework, in: Festschrift für Klaus J. Hopt zum 70.Geburtstag am 24. August 2010. Vol.2., Berlin, p. 2902.

intellectual property, etc., and who exercises his influence over the business organization.[62]

Preference for the term "hegemonic" instead "hierarchical" is because the latter implies an implicit graduation of subjects attending to proprietary control relationships between them, a factual situation unknown in business networks, due to the legal autonomy of its participants. However, big corporations or those corporations providing the network with substantial contributions do exist and, consequently, are in a better strategic position compared to the other members.

Therefore, it could be said, that these participants are in a "hegemonic" position, exercising their own influence over the network organization and activity, even though they don't have any controlling influence over any of the independent participants.[63] In practice, these networks are rather organised by bilaterally linked contracts[64] providing the network's head with

62 *Baudry B./Chassagnon, V.,* The vertical network organization as a specific governance structure: what are the challenges for incomplete contracts theories and what are the theoretical implications for the boundaries of the hub-firm?, Journal of Management Journal, num. 16, 2012, 285 (289-290), in one section devoted to describe vertical network's characters, define it as: "The VNO (vertical network organization) is a productive entity that unifies a set of legally independent firms that are vertically integrated and coordinated by a main firm called the ''hub-firm'', ''which is the firm that, in fact, sets up the network and takes a proactive attitude in the care of it'' (Jarillo 1988, p. 32). The hub-firm, as a ''core network'' (Robertson and Langlois 1995), is situated either upstream or downstream of the production process".

63 In this sense, *Ruiz Peris, J.I.,* Business networks as a legal explanatory framework, in: Festschrift für Klaus J. Hopt zum 70.Geburtstag am 24. August 2010. Vol.2., Berlin, p. 2906: "In every network there is a direction centre – network's direction – which can be the enterprise head of the network, one producer – outsourcing – o services supplier – franchisee or credit cards.
Network direction could also be placed in the entity who structures the network – joint ventures, cooperatives or consortia –, or in a stable committee, personified or not, representative of all or several network's members".

64 About the definition of this type of networks *Cafaggi, F.,* Redes contractuales y Small Business Act, in: Ruiz Peris, J.I., (ed.), Hacia un Derecho para las redes empresariales, Valencia, 2009, p. 47: "A contractual network exists where there are two or more linked contracts between three or more contracting parties (heterogeneity). Various linked contracts between the same two parties (homogeneity), don't constitute a contractual network but, from my perspective, a chain". Stressing in p. 49 three types of linked contract's networks, namely: chain model, halo model and distribution or franchisee model.

power and factual influence over the direction and coordination of said network.[65]

As opposed to peer models, it further describes networks where a hegemonic position doesn't exist and network participants, in most cases entrepreneurs from the same sector and production chain level, in spite of maintaining interdependent relationships, are in a more equal hierarchical level, making it possible to be collaborators working together towards the network goal and competitors outside the network structures at the same time.

---

Furthermore the author in Introduzione, in: Cafaggi, F., (dir.), Il contratto di rete, Bologna, 2009, p.16, states that: "Not any type of business link between a plurality of contracts constitute a network. For the network arising it is need an instrumental complementarity relationship between enterprises' feature, being the contractual link drawn in the network contract an expression of this relationship. Thence, the mere reference to an unitary economic operation is not enough, it is also need the existence of linking elements between colligated contracts under the object causal profile making evident interdependence between activity as a consequence of business risk" (Translation given by the author).
About situation that trigger a contractual network constitution, *Cafaggi, F.,* Redes contractuales y teoría contractual: una agenda de investigación para un derecho contractual europeo, in: Ruiz Peris, J.I., (ed.), Nuevas Perspectivas del Derecho de Redes Empresariales, 2012, p. 55-56: "Networks of bilateral contracts are generally deployed where there is an initially lower degree of interdependence, less uncertainty and parties wish to enjoy a higher level of freedom and autonomy to exit the network. They emerge when lower level coordination is necessary but they require higher coordination costs than multilateral contracts. Structurally it is a relatively decentralized model, often deployed on the supply chain, where coordination power is the facto exercised by the main contractor, who subcontracts the main tasks to other parties not contractually linked to each other. Networks of bilateral contracts often include a common clause, imposing a duty to coordinate performances, encompassing monitoring and reporting. Monitoring is decentralized and often, reciprocal duties to report to the main contractor are devised in order to facilitate coordination" (Translation given by the author).

65 About configuration of this contractual origin power in networks, *Ruiz Peris, J.I.,* Business networks as a legal explanatory framework, in: Festschrift für Klaus J. Hopt zum 70.Geburtstag am 24. August 2010. Vol.2., Berlin, p. 2906 – 2907: "The ground for direction power in contractual networks lies in bilateral contracts. These generally parallel adhesion contracts with great homogeneity reduce member's commercial autonomy...These contracts also provide of supervision powers to define the major or minor organization degree of each network member's enterprise, allowing the network's head to exercise a *ius variandi* by giving instructions to the other network's members and to underpin moderation power between network's members in reference to the network inner organizing documents".

These networks are common in structures with a high collaboration degree between the parties developing a joint project, where each party's benefits are integrated to a large extent and in which complementarity is so substantial that it becomes difficult to distinguish individual benefits from the overall result. They are common in research and technological developments, but also in structures, where complementarity between produced goods exists, resulting in a more frequent occurrence of strategic alliances or consortia.[66]

## IV. Coexistence of contradictory interests

The existence of both, members' autonomy and the possibility of relationships defined by cooperation and competition, results in other unique features of business networks:[67] namely the coexistence of parallel and diver-

66 *Cafaggi, F.,* Redes contractuales y teoría contractual: una agenda de investigación para un derecho contractual europeo, in: Ruiz Peris, J.I., (ed.), Nuevas Perspectivas del Derecho de Redes Empresariales, 2012, p. 30-31.

67 This point has been highlighted by *Ruiz Peris, J.I.,* Un Derecho específico para las redes empresariales, in: Ruiz Peris, J.I., (ed.), Nuevas Perspectivas del Derecho de Redes Empresariales, Valencia, 2012, p. 115 -116; *Ruiz Peris, J.I.,* Business networks as a legal explanatory framework, in: Festschrift für Klaus J. Hopt zum 70.Geburtstag am 24. August 2010. Vol.2., Berlin, p. 2904. *Ruiz Peris, J.I.,* Del contrato bilateral a la relación de red, in: Ruiz Peris, J.I., (ed.), Hacia un Derecho para las redes empresariales., Valencia, 2007, p. 11; *Cafaggi, F.,* Redes contractuales y Small Business Act, in: Ruiz Peris, J.I., (ed.), Hacia un Derecho para las redes empresariales, Valencia, 2009, p. 24; *Cafaggi, F.,* Redes contractuales y teoría contractual: una agenda de investigación para un derecho contractual europeo, in: Ruiz Peris, J.I., (ed.), Nuevas Perspectivas del Derecho de Redes Empresariales, 2012, p. 18.
Distinguishing business networks from partnerships, *Teubner, G.,* Network as connected contracts, Oxford, 2011, p. 38 – 39: "In fact, all business networks pursue a 'common purpose'. It is nevertheless true that they should still not be characterised as partnerships. Why should this be? The reason is not a fictional distinction between 'unitary' and 'common' purpose, but the simultaneous presence of individual and common interest pursuit. This simultaneous presence is contrary to corporate law by definition, but, strikingly, is also the creative characteristic exhibited by networks. Law must respond to the contradiction as such; not by making the contradiction disappear through artificial distinctions, but by deploying more complex legal qualifications which furnish internal creative tensions within networks with firm institutional backbone… p. 43-44: This leads us back to the issue of 'common purpose' discussed above. It is no accident, but inherent in net-

gent interests between network members, both in a dialectical relationship and both absolutely lawful,[68] and which can also be divided into two big categories: Firstly, the parallel interest of all members in value creation for the network (*Netzzweck*), namely interest on success and efficiency of the same; and, secondly, each member's divergent interest to retain the created value by excluding the others, is the latter being the real interest when joining a business network.[69]

Both interests should be in a balanced state, however, in some cases one of the mentioned interests might outweigh the other, as long as proportion-

---

work structure, that the issue of 'common purpose' can only be responded to with a contradiction. Network participants must adapt to a contradictory double challenge: following their own individual interest and realising the overarching network purpose in one and the same operation. In contrast to this, traditional corporate law entails a strong presumption that operations within the collective action sphere (e.g. management, voting rights) must be pursued with sole reference to the 'common purpose'. Network members may only pursue their individual interests in non-collective action spheres (e.g., profit rights, individual rights of review) *Tertium non datur*. Within corporate law, management functions must not be exercised in an individual interest, but only to the benefit of the common purpose. 'Collective interests do not, to be sure, take absolute precedence; there is room for the pursuit of individual interest, but only to the degree that this does not violate the corporate interest".

68 This idea of interest dialogue is pointed by *Ruiz Peris, J.I.*, Un Derecho específico para las redes empresariales, in: Ruiz Peris, J.I., (ed.), Nuevas Perspectivas del Derecho de Redes Empresariales, Valencia, 2012, p. 115 -116; *Id.*, Business networks as a legal explanatory framework, in: Festschrift für Klaus J. Hopt zum 70.Geburtstag am 24. August 2010. Vol.2., Berlin, p. 2904. *Id.*, Del contrato bilateral a la relación de red, in: Ruiz Peris, J.I., (ed.), Hacia un Derecho para las redes empresariales, Valencia, 2007, p. 11; *Cafaggi, F.*, Redes contractuales y Small Business Act, in: Ruiz Peris, J.I., (ed.), Hacia un Derecho para las redes empresariales, Valencia, 2009, p. 24; *Id.* Redes contractuales y teoría contractual: una agenda de investigación para un derecho contractual europeo, in: Ruiz Peris, J.I., (ed.), Nuevas Perspectivas del Derecho de Redes Empresariales, 2012, p. 65 a 68.

69 This interest typology is in relation with the diverse interest concurrent in corporate groups, thus, following, *Moro Visconti, R.*, La governance nei gruppi e nelle reti di imprese, Conflitti fra stakeholsers e diffusione di valore, Milano, 2011, pág. 83: "The unitary direction in corporate group comes from the existence of one economic agent who formally is opposite to diverse legal subjects which, in turn, correspond with each one of the corporates which conform the group. Three diverse interest exist inside the group: Holding's controller interest, controlled corporate's interest and group interest. The last is the equilibrium point, the convergence centre or coordination axis between the controller and interest of group's corporate". (Translation given by the author).

ality is ensured and adequate compensation for said outweighed interest is provided.[70]

## V. Intellectual property sharing

Very often, the reason for the constitution of business networks is the share interest of its members in using an intellectual property right, for instance, a trademark or a patent. The sharing of intellectual property rights is merely an additional consequence resulting from integration into a business network.[71]

---

70 Thus for instance, *Ruiz Peris, J.I.,* Un Derecho específico para las redes empresariales, in: Ruiz Peris, J.I., (ed.), Nuevas Perspectivas del Derecho de Redes Empresariales, Valencia, 2012, p. 115-116: "Share interest's performance by network's direction, as a general rule, shall not unnecessarily injure divergent interests – to value appropriation – of its members as are contractual defined or arises from contractual interpretation or integration according with good faith rules.
An eventual injury to divergent interest is only justified when is strictly necessary – there are not less injuring alternatives – to protect share interest and to obtain an economic legitimate network aim. In addition, injury shall be proportional in respect of the benefit obtained to the network by share interest playing. It is not possible to give a non-justified and unequal treatment injuring one's network member divergent interest in different way from the others.
Network's member whose interest is injured shall be properly compensated with the network's profits obtained with the performance in share interest which has caused the injury to divergent interest". (Translation given by the author)
*Cafaggi, F.,* Il governo della rete: Modelli Organizzativi del Coordinamento Inter-Imprenditoriale, in: Cafaggi, F. (ed.), Reti di imprese tra regolazione e norme sociali, 2009, p. 75: "One first aspect of conflict of interests refers to the scenario in which the enterprise or single corporate's interest could be sacrificed in network's favour as well as compensation tools are pre-stablished. From this view, some corporate groups' tools could be applied by analogy to networks. An unfair sacrifice is compensated, a sacrifice upon which is a consent is indemnified. However it is obvious that the different weight of the hierarchical variable may influence upon compensation *an* ad *quantum*, especially in the prospective of a more symmetric cost and revenues distribution referring to network's belonging in respect to the corporate group". (Translation given by the author).

71 In this sense, *Ruiz Peris, J.I.,* Un Derecho específico para las redes empresariales, in: Ruiz Peris, J.I., (ed.), Nuevas Perspectivas del Derecho de Redes Empresariales, Valencia, 2012, p. 88; *Id.,* Del contrato bilateral a la relación de red, in: Ruiz Peris, J.I., (ed.), Hacia un Derecho para las redes empresariales., Valencia, 2007, p.14.

The share use of an intellectual property right generates interdependence among networks members who use it, as well as reproduces network interest's dialectic: each one of the members pursues the objective to increase and/or preserve IP rights, goodwill or efficiency, aiming to ensure a competitive advantage of the network but, at same time, aim to maximize their individual profits deriving from the use of joint asset.[72]

Principal challenges arising from a shared use of IP rights in networks are the unequal lengths of the IP license periods and the duration of the network relationships on the one hand, as well as the adequacy of its legal regime to business network featureson the other hand: In the first case, the main challenge is to avoid opportunistic behaviour of those solely participating in the network in order to gain access to and benefit from the IP rights before the exclusive rights of the patent holder expire.[73]

In the second case, especially in second degree networks (master franchise), the main issue is to coordinate the consequences arising for network members – being IP licensees at the same time –, in case of changing on the franchisor of the master franchisor who granted the licenses in question. Other challenges refer to the possibility for licensees to take actions against other licensees in case of trademark law infringement.[74]

---

72 The description about immaterial goods role in business networks is made in relation to distinctive signs by *Martín Aresti, P.*, Signos distintivos y redes de distribución, Ruiz Peris, J.I. (ed.), Nuevas Perspectivas del Derecho de Redes Empresariales, Valencia, 2012, p. 547-572.

73 *Iamiceli, P.*, Le reti di imprese: modelli contrattuali di cordinamento, in: Cafaggi, F., (ed.), Reti di imprese tra regolazione e norme sociali. Nuoves fide per diritto ed economia, Bologna, 2004, p.171-172, points out that: "The more relationship's duration near to right's duration the more relief cooperative dimension of the relationship acquires. Equally, during relation performance, the temporary distance to right's extinction term increases licensee exit option value, as concerns the relationship, influencing on incentives to invest in the relationship and its truthfulness because the threat a confrontation with licensees implies". (Translation given by the author).

74 For a deeper analysis from a Spanish and European perspective, see *Martín Aresti, P.*, Signos distintivos y redes de distribución, Ruiz Peris, J.I. (ed.), Nuevas Perspectivas del Derecho de Redes Empresariales, Valencia, 2012, p. 547-542; *González Castilla, F.*, Caracterización de la relación negocial entre los integrantes de la red secundaria y la marca, in: Viera González, J. A./Echebarría Sáenz, J. A., (eds.), Distribución comercial y Derecho de la competencia, La ley, 2011, p. 321-334; and more specifically *Martí Miravalls, J.*, El contrato de master franquicia, Aranzadi, Pamplona, 2009, p. 295-357.

## VI. Intuitu character of network member's relationships

The long-term character of the contractual relationships in the network and interdependent benefits result in, as pointed out in the previous economic approach a relationship built on trust between the participants.[75] Thereby, the relationships between network participants are characterized by an *intuitu* note, where not only technical qualities (*intuitu instrumenti*), but also personal qualities (*intuitu personae*) are valued. Additional factors of importance are coordination, supervision and sharing of information which are considered also essential within the network.[76]

The *Intuitu* character doesn't constitute personal obligations between the parties – though, due to the fact that critical information are being shared in networks, contracts include termination clauses in case of party changes,[77]– however, due to the influence of trust in the organization and integration of members in the network, parties maintain specially qualified

75 *Ruiz Peris, J.I.,* Intromisión en la clientela ajena y redes de distribución (Encroachment), Cizur-Menor, 2007, p. 101: "Contracts used to constitute networks are long-term contracts giving place to continued relationships between parts along time which aim is reaching a common aim pursued by all network's members – selling certain products or services – collaborating the parties to achieve it – collaboration contract –.
Consequently, in this type of contracts the other contractual part identity is extremely relevant – *intuitu personae* contracts –, generating special trust relationships – contracts rule by trust principle –, which as we have seen, triggers a reasonable expectation to each part in the other's performance without hidden defects and considering the other's interests– *ubérrima bona fidae* –". (Translation given by the author).

76 One distinction between both types of characters, referring to the classification of legal relationships maintained by parties in the master franchise frame, is found in *Martí Miravalls, J.,* El contrato de master franquicia, Aranzadi, Pamplona, 2009, p. 164-169, where referring to the trust character of relationships inside this contracts, the author states that: "...the master franchise contract shall be framed inside trust contracts named *intuitu personae*, this not mean that the franchisor in contracting takes into account besides the trust triggered by the physical person or the administrators of the legal person, the enterprise objective qualities, for instance, infrastructure or logistics". (Translation given by the author).

77 In this sense, *Ruiz Peris, J.I.,* Del contrato bilateral a la relación de red, in: Ruiz Peris, J.I., (ed.), Hacia un Derecho para las redes empresariales., Valencia, 2007,p. 14, defines network contracts as: "*intuitu personae* contracts although been drawn in the big amount of cases by corporates who stablish as resolution clause the change in share's property or corporate control or the exit of the directive in attention to which the contract have been drawn". (Translation given by the author).

relationships governed under *uberrima fides* principle.[78] This fact results in a unique organizational and governance structure characterised by the qualified role that fiduciary duties play in ruling network member's behaviour[79]The most important of the overall duties resulting from above structure is to observe the principles of good faith, which impose two main duties: diligence and loyalty. The obligation to exercise diligence refers to

78 *Ruiz Peris, J.I.*, Intromisión en la clientela ajena, in: Ruiz Peris, J.I., (ed.), Hacia un Derecho para las redes empresariales., Valencia, 2007, p. 94-95: "Contracts used to build networks and, between then distribution networks, are collaboration contracts where *intuitu personae* plays a main role, deriving our case law an acknowledgment of specific loyalty duties between parties and the submission of these contracts to trust principle. Hence, the claim for a good faith behaviour by parties un this type of contracts is specially high, being possible to qualify then as *uberrima bona fide*, because existing trust relationship between parties as well as a common shared main aim derived from the exercise of share business activity to which consecution parties cooperate independently of interest confrontation before others persistence, reinforces each party trust in each other performance according to good faith, namely, according with the claimable standards of who runs - organises and coordinates – an entrepreneurs network to which is joint by a set of bilateral contracts and without hidden aims apart from collaboration in the share common aim achieving expressed in the negotiation process". (Translation given by the author).

79 *Cafaggi, F.*, Reti di impresi, spazi e silenzi regolativi, in: Cafaggi, F., (ed.), Reti di imprese traregolazione e norme sociali. Nuove sfide per diritto ed economía, 2004, p. 24-25: "Network's specificity from market relies on the capability to govern interdependence throughout fiduciary relationships. This interdependence, in absence of an ideal organizing model generating trust, could trigger opportunism behaviours risk leading even to dishearten initially investments". (Translation given by the author).

"Collaboration character of network's contracts, long-term as far as a continued entrepreneurial collaboration is previewed, sometimes during decades, in occasion as is the case of franchisee, concession or outsourcing determining the major part of the entrepreneurial organization, their intuit personae character, the existence of immaterial shared elements, between them, good will and clients, brings as an inescapable consequence that this elements play with great intensity in vertical and horizontal relationships regulation and, as a consequence, these principles play equally with major intensity in network's contracts interpretation and integration than other bilateral contracts". *Ruiz Peris, J.I.*, Del contrato bilateral a la relación de red, in: Ruiz Peris, J.I., (ed.), Hacia un Derecho para las redes empresariales., Valencia, 2007, p. 15.

information duties – pre-contractual information duties, disclosure duties during the contract period and the duty to keep confidential.[80]

The duty of loyalty implies the harmonization between share and divergent interests, given raise to other secondary duties for network members: duty to act in "network (share) interest"; duty to refrain themselves from behaviours that, pursuing divergent own interest, may affect to network interests achieving; encroachment and *tortius interference* banning, among others[81]

## C. Conclusions

Long-term and continuous relationships, the interdependence of benefits, each participant's autonomy, the coexistence of contradictory interests, shared assets and the *intuitu* character of the participant's relationships, place networks in an eclectic position between contract and organization governance mechanisms.

---

80 Duties enumeration is made by *Ruiz Peris, J.I.*, Del contrato bilateral a la relación de red, in: Ruiz Peris, J.I., (ed.), Hacia un Derecho para las redes empresariales., Valencia, 2007, p. 16-19; *Id.* Un Derecho específico para las redes empresariales, in: Ruiz Peris, J.I., (ed.), Nuevas Perspectivas del Derecho de Redes Empresariales, Valencia, 2012, p. 116 -118; *Id.*, Business networks as a legal explanatory framework, in: Festschrift für Klaus J. Hopt zum 70.Geburtstag am 24. August 2010. Vol.2., Berlin, p. 2908; *Cafaggi, F.*, Organizational Loyalties and Models of Firms: Governance Design and Standard of Duties, Theoretical Inquires in Law, vol.6, 2005, 463; *Id.* Organizational Loyalties and Models of Firms: Governance Design and Standard of Duties, EUI Working Paper, Law, núm. 5, 2005.
Especially, about duties arising from good faith principle, *Ruiz Peris, J.I.*, Intromisión en la clientela ajena,
About economic dependence abuse on business networks, *Estevan de Quesada, C.*, El abuso de dependencia económica en las redes de distribución, in: Ruiz Peris, J.I., (dir.), Hacia un Derecho para las redes empresariales, Valencia, 2007, p. 187-221.

81 This enumeration and classification is made by *Ruiz Peris, J.I.*, Un Derecho específico para las redes empresariales, in: Ruiz Peris, J.I., (ed.), Nuevas Perspectivas del Derecho de Redes Empresariales, Valencia, 2012, p. 116-118.
At general level, as concerns to loyalty duty on business networks, *Cafaggi, F.*, Introduzione, in: Ruiz Peris, J.I., (ed.), Hacia un Derecho para las redes empresariales, Valencia, 2009, p. 19 "At general level it could be argued the existence of a reciprocal loyalty level between network participants and an individual level, of each participant towards the networks as a whole".

Thus, classic contractual governance mechanisms are not applicable, due to the special governance requirements resulting from the network's economical and organizational features, leading further to challenges in all the network specific characteristics mentioned above.

Therefore, instead of trying to fit networks into the various pre-existing contractual models, it appears be more convenient to carefully analyse the network's legal demands before proposing a contractual instrument for its governance.

This article represents the first step in this task, pointing out vital aspects and focusing on, in my opinion, the decisive factor in understanding business networks governance requirements: the identification of rights and duties which bind the parties in their actions as network members.

Hence, the goal is the development of a business networks governance theory, identifying the rules of conduct originating in the good faith principles, and being in accordance with network features and aims, which bind the parties in their contract's execution as members of the network.

The development of a governance theory around general duties – as has been done before with corporate managers and fiduciary duties – allows designing a wide frame presenting the network participants with the opportunity to interact in many different ways over a period of time, as well as establishing precise boundaries, declaring certain behaviour patterns occurring outside set boundaries and being opposed to the overall network features and goals unlawful.

The construction of a proposal for business network governance including all features and challenges mentioned in this article will be addressed in an upcoming second article completing this general view on business network governance.

# Contractual business networks: Interpretation criteria and axiological perspective

*Prof. Dr. Camilla Crea*

## A. Introduction

To talk of business networks in terms of concepts that are well known in the legal tradition such as 'contract' or 'firm' seems to express a form of Kantian and inexorable *sapere aude* aimed at overcoming perceived forms of hostility or scepticism[1].

Law follows practice seeking to accompany the development of economic and social systems with more or less regulatory constructions. An approach intent on stabilising and ordering the necessarily dynamic complexity[2] of reality into legally relevant notions. The network phenomenon stigmatises complexity and hence shuns any 'absoluteness', any rigid classification of categories and concepts and any subsystems inside the legal order. Within a law that is ever more fluid and flexible, there are no auto-referential and independent branches (law of contract vs. law of business

---

1 *Collins, H.*, Introduction to Networks as Connected Contracts, in: Teubner, G., Networks as connected contracts, trans. Everson, M., Oxford, Hart Publishing 2011, p. 1; *Buxbaum, R. M.*, Is the Network a Legal Concept?, 149 Journal of Institutional and Theoretical Economics, No. 4, 698, 704 (1993). The issue has now assumed key importance in legal scholarship debate: *Brownsword, B.*, Networks as Connected Contracts, 75 Modern Law Review, No. 3, 559-460 (2012).

2 On the theory of complexity: *Taylor, M.C.,* The Moment of Complexity. Emerging Network Culture, University of Chicago Press 2001, 17. From a legal perspective, *Falzea, A.*, Complessità giuridica, in Enc. dir., Annali, I, Milan, Giuffré 2007, 201 – 202, as an epistemological challenge at the base of society and every category of knowledge, which calls for a constructive renewal of legal science in order to reconcile the modern and postmodern tension with the tradition of concepts and categories (*Pagallo, U.*, Teoria giuridica della complessità, Turin, Giappichelli, 2006). In social science, *Lhumann, N.*, Sistema giuridico e Dogmatica giuridica, Bologna, Il Mulino 1978; *Id.*, Sistemi sociali. Fondamenti di una teoria generale, Bologna, Il Mulino 1990).

associations or corporations[3], or torts or competition law[4]) incapable of communicating with one another.

Network has a variety of underlying meanings, at times divergent but in some cases also convergent. The variability depends on two factors: the science selected to evaluate networks and the effectiveness of facts and their peculiarities. The first point entails a choice: the selection of law and a prescriptive language as a context and method of analysis in preference to others (in particular, economics and sociology) [5]. This preference does not imply exclusion. Indeed, it is through a non-opposition comparison among the sciences of evaluation that a correct cognitive process arises and develops regardless of the perfectible result that one arrives at[6]. In that way legal analysis re-imagines and rationalises facts and behaviour within itself without being a prisoner to dogma and by adapting to the complexity.

The reaction of the outside world to the chaos and uncertainty - that characterise markets and legal systems themselves - produces relationships of economic cooperation. Networks, especially among businesses,

---

3 *Teubner, G.*, Coincidentia oppositorum: Hybrid Networks Beyond Contract and Organization, in Amstutz, M./Teubner, G. (eds), Networks: Legal Issues of Multilateral Cooperation, Oxford, Hart Publishing 2009, pp. 3-32.

4 *Martinek, M.*, Networks of Contracts and Competition Law, in: Grundmann, S. *et al.* (eds) The Organizational Contract: From Exchange to Long-Term Network Cooperation in European Contract Law, Ashgate, Farnham 2013, pp. 163-178; *Crea, C.*, Reti contrattuali e organizzazione della attività di impresa, Naples, Esi 2008, pp. 144-160.

5 *Perlingieri, P./Femia, P.*, Nozioni introduttive e principi fondamentali del diritto civile, Naples, Esi 2000, p. 12. In relation to business networks, see *Gentili, A.*, Una prospettiva analitica su reti di imprese e contratti di rete, Obbl. contr., 87-90 (2010). On the meanings of network between economics and sociology, see *Crea, C.*, Reti contrattuali e organizzazione della attività di impresa, Naples, Esi 2008, p. 105 *et seq.*, 112-119; see also, *Collins, H.*, Introduction: The Research Agenda of Implicit Dimension of Contracts, in *Campbell, D. et al.* (eds), Implicit Dimension of Contract. Discrete, Relational and Network Contracts, Oxford, Hart Publishing 2003, p. 1, 19 *et seq.*; in a similar sense *Iamiceli, P.*, Le reti di imprese: modelli contrattuali di coordinamento, in: Cafaggi, F. (ed), Reti di imprese tra regolazione norme sociali, Il Mulino, Bologna 2004, p. 128.

6 *Collins, H.*, Introduction to Networks as Connected Contracts, in: *Teubner, G.*, Networks as connected contracts, trans. Everson, M., Oxford, Hart Publishing 2011, p. 21 (referring to the Teubnerian sociological jurisprudence approach).

express forms of hierarchy[7] linked to a process of self-organisation, a "spontaneous order sui generis"[8] that interfaces – without dialectic conflicts and without an accomplished synthesis – with the anarchy of the pure market of transactions and the hierarchy of the firm[9]. Hierarchy, in the Platonic sense of the word as viewed through the lens of the Taylorist concept of firm[10], is based on the division, on the pyramidal centralisation of decision-making power, dependence, inertia and uniformity. There is always a cause, in a material (and legal) sense, with an effect. There is always a top and bottom, a superior and an inferior, that in a linear way explains the structure of the firm and how it acts in the midst of the legal traffic, without any possibility at all to change and adapt to the external chaos and dictates that it adopt a rigid closed approach. On the other hand, a network aggregates, expresses and at the same time is based on collectivity and co-existence: each node can represent the whole in accordance with a path of continuous interaction, trust and a generally decentralised and multiple sharing of power (independence inside interdependence) and hence flexible, open and modifiable on the basis of external shocks. Pluralism of members, relationships that are more or less contractualised and legal models for evaluation and justification.

And this brings us to the last factor (articulated in itself and non exhaustible): effectiveness[11]. A network is an expression of this principle,

---

7 *Amstutz, M.*, Contract collision: an evolutionary perspective on contractual networks, 76 Law and Contemporary Problems, No. 2, 169, 179 (2013) and note 7.

8 *Teubner, G.*, "And if I by Beelzebub Cast out Devils, ...": An Essay on the Diabolics of Network Failure, 10 German, L. J., 395, 401 (2009).

9 The contractual network expresses and conserves its functional contradictions (cooperation/common interest vs. competition/conflict of interests) and structural ones (market/bilateral exchange/contract vs. hierarchy/organisation/multilateralism; stability vs. flexibility): *Teubner, G.*, Networks as connected contracts, trans. Everson, M., Oxford, Hart Publishing 2011, pp. 182, 210, 238.

10 *D'Amico, E.*, Motivazioni, dinamismo ambientale e reti tra imprese, in *Lopes A. et al.* (eds), Reti di imprese, scenari economici e giuridici, Turin, Giappichelli 2007, p. 287; *Thorelli, H.*, 7 Networks between Markets and Hierarchies, Strategic Management Journal, No. 1, 1986, 37-51; *Powel H. H.*, Neither Market nor Hierarchy: The Network Forms of Organization, in Straw, B.M/Cummings, L.L (eds), Research in Organizational Behaviour, JAI-Press Inc., Greenwich, 1990, pp. 295-336; *Geiss, G.*, The Space Between Markets and Hierarchies, 95 Virginia L. R., 99-153 (2009).

11 Effectiveness as a "dynamic criterion for legitimacy" (*Piovani P.*, Effettività, in Enc. dir., XIV, Milan, 1965, 420) exalts the interior force of concrete facts [*Grossi, P.*, La formazione del giurista e l'esigenza di un odierno ripensamento

just like the business activities on which it is generally based and which it contributes to creating and regulating.

Commencing from such a premise it is necessary to select the analysis by first distinguishing between the different legal forms a network can take. The analysis should focus on the specific features of the concrete case, valuing the 'normativity' of complex facts and behaviour. Indeed, business networks require jurists to give answers that are not unequivocal but rather ones that differ depending on the functional and structural pluralism and heterogeneity of the network concerned: linked contracts (generally bilateral, with a long term and involving an exchange) that create a multilateral organisation of relationships, including *de facto* ones[12]; a single multiparty contract, generally endowed with a certain level of relevant organisation vis-à-vis third parties; an actual network entity (similar to a network company). The real combinations of these typical forms are potentially unlimited considering further possible variables (e.g. the nature/legal form of the network participants, the purpose and object of the activities of each firm and the network as a whole, the relevant goods and geographic market, etc.). This work will focus in particular on contractual networks among firms as compared to the traditional concept of linked contract and in light of recent Italian legislation on network contracts. The goal is to argue the centrality of both the effectiveness of business activity and of party autonomy (and organisational freedom) that expresses itself in selecting legal models, possibly enriching them with further elements of complexity, or also in choosing not to subject the network (totally) to law (in the sense of a body of specific rules). Thereafter we evaluate the consequences on the techniques of interpretation and on the value parameters capable of justifying the legally relevant fact-network on a functional and teleological level and from an axiologically well-founded perspective.

---

metodologico, Quad. fiorentini, 38 (2004)]. It is at the heart of the concept of business activity (*infra* footnotes 26-27).

12 *Gilson, R./Sabel, C./Scott, R.*, Braiding: The Interaction of Formal and Informal Contracting in Theory, Practice and Doctrine, 110 Columbia L. R., 1377-1447 (2010); on the metaphor of connected contracts *Gulati, G.M/ Klein, W.A/ Zolt, E.M,* Connected Contracts, 47 UCLA L. Rev., 887 -948 (1999-2000).

### B. Open-endedness of cooperative competition: from traditional linked contracts to contractual business networks

The key feature of a network among firms and its goal of organising cooperative competition is pluralism, of participants (formal or material parties) and, often, of contracts.

In truth a contract is in itself a pluralistic concept, which expands and adapts to contexts old and new. A sort of elastic and all-inclusive category, a filter through which to conceive every human relationship in a deeply contractualised society. And so the typical contract becomes irregular[13], mixed, complex or atypical but always one; this through extensive interpretation and/or interpretation by analogy seeking to simplify complexity by reduction to a unit (just one contract). However, the modern market economy[14] has a surplus that a single and unique contract cannot cover even if stretched to the limit: metacontractual realities that escape categorisation since they represent insurmountable cognitive limits[15]. The latter are a reflection of party autonomy itself in as much as a power of self-regulation to be viewed ever more in its social dimension.

A single bilateral contract no longer suffices. The creation and implementation of the overall economic transaction requires a plurality of contracts, not independent and isolated but linked – contemporaneously or sequentially – by a nexus of unilateral dependence or mutual interdepen-

---

13 The dialectic between the form and substance/nature of the contract [(*Grossi, P.*, Sulla natura del contratto, Quad. fiorentini, 593, 603-613 (1986)], between regularity – from a legal standpoint – and irregularity and between the implied and the express reflect the ongoing development of law to take account of the reality of human behaviour. This consciousness of the historical evolution of the contract category and above all its social dimension connected to the economic system and action by the regulatory authorities (*Collins, H.*, Regulating Contracts, Oxford, Oxford University Press, 1999).

14 *Grundmann, S.*, Contractual Networks in German Private Law, in: Cafaggi, F. (ed), Contractual Networks, Inter-Firm Cooperation and Economic Growth, Cheltenham, UK - Northampton, MA-USA, Edward Elgar 2011, pp. 111, 112.

15 *Femia, P.*, Nomenclatura del contratto o istituzione del contrarre? Per una teoria giuridica della contrattazione, in: Gitti, G./Villa, R. (eds), Il terzo contratto, Bologna, Il Mulino 2006, pp. 265, 274. The cognitive limits of contract lead to a consideration of its social multidimensionality, *Teubner, G.*, In the Blind Spot: The Hybridization of Contract, 8 Theoretical Inquiries in Law, 51–55 (2006).

dence[16]. This occurs on the basis of an express or implied will to link (in the absence of precise norms regulating the matter); increasingly so, irrespective of any manifestation of will. The series of agreements (the whole) is not and could not be contained in the single contract (a part) but it is necessary to explain its true meaning and vice versa.

The contractual nexus is simplified when it is objectively possible to identify a single exchange/synallgma among the performances of the various contracts[17] and when the parties in a technical sense are the same[18].

When, however, the persons are different – a triangle in which it is necessary to protect the third party given the cognitive limit of the *inter partes* effects of the contract (privity of contract[19]) and the measures adopted by the adjudicatory body (judge or arbitrator) – a further element of complexity raises its head. This does not hinder the link and especially any characteristic remedy (for example, an exchange contract possibly to the benefit of a third party). That said, whoever wishes to avail of the link (if established in their exclusive interests) must prove its existence and the proof required is very stringent. An express will is necessary, a so-called 'saving clause'[20] to protect the third party who is not interested in the nexus but

---

16 On (simplified) contractual links, from the monistic perspective of the unitary contract, see *Lener, G.*, Profili del collegamento negoziale, Milan, 1999, p. 163 *et seq.*; *Sacco, R.*, Contratto collegato, Dig. disc. priv., Sez. civ., Agg. VI, Turin, Utet 2011, pp. 238, 241. On the protection of third parties: *Colombo C.*, Operazioni economiche e collegamento negoziale, Padua, Cedam 1999, p. 166 *et seq.*, 224 *et seq.*, 252. On diversifying the hypotheses in the light of the contractual function as a synthesis of the essential legal effects, see *Maisto, F.*, Il collegamento volontario tra contratti nel sistema dell'ordinamento giuridico. Sostanza economica e natura giuridica degli autoregolamenti complessi, Naples, Esi 2002, 252-257.

17 Some authors speak of "circular exchange" (*Villa, R.*, Inadempimento e contratto plurilaterale, Milan, Giuffré 1999, 26-32) or of an extension of the reciprocity of a single bilateral contract to linked contracts (*Amadio, G.*, Inattuazione risoluzione: la fattispecie, in Roppo, V. (ed), Rimedi-2, V, Tratt. contr. Roppo, Milan, Giuffré 2006, 62) or in terms of multilateral sinallagma (*Heermann, P.*, Drittfinanzierte Erwerbsgeschäfte, Tübingen 1998, p. 92 *et seq.*, 200 *et seq.*).

18 *Cafaggi, F.*, Contractual Networks and the Small Business Act: Towards European Principles?, 4 European Review of Contract Law, 493, 519 (2008).

19 *Adams, J.N./Brownsword, R.*, Privity and the Concept of a Network Contract, 10 Legal Studies, 12-37 (1990); *Wellenhofer, M.*, Third Party Effects of Bilateral Contracts Within the Network, in Amstutz, M./Teubner, G. (eds), Networks: Legal Issues of Multilateral Cooperation, Oxford, Hart Publishing 2009, p. 119 *et seq.*

20 Italian Supreme Court judgment no. 3645 of 16.2.2007, Contratti, 156 (2007); Court of Appeal of Florence judgment of 14.9.2011, Obbl. contr., 147 (2012).

may be damaged by the contract that he is not party to. Does this mean returning to the rule of party autonomy as an expression of a will declared in an *ad hoc* contractual clause? In reality, if a trilateral economic transaction is objectively characterised by a single interest pursued in the context of an overall closed and circular exchange, that interest is relevant for the law. Accordingly, the exercise of the right of termination, the remedies for breach (actions or defences even though founded on a distinct contract), the unfairness of a clause or a possible *fraudem legis* or *creditorum* are assessed in light of the entire contractual arrangement[21] and hence the evaluation is extended to the linked contracts.

A network of contracts among firms is an evolution in terms of complexity. A simple link is traditionally associated with the function of exchange. The cognitive limit of the exchange is not bilaterality since the exchange can be made also in a situation of multilaterality[22]. Neither does it lie in the duality of relationships involving obligations. It consists in the exponential growth of centres of interest (more than three), contracts (three, four, and so on) or informal relations, and especially in the need to adapt the plural economic transaction to an associative-type goal (common purpose/project underlying the organisation itself that is *de facto* attained, for example, in the supply chain or in franchising systems[23]).

A contractual business network, compared to a simple link, is characterised by a greater spatial-temporal open-endedness as regards the actions of the members, how many there are and how they interact with one another. There is also the fact that the network is not only an exchange but a multilateral organisation for cooperative competition. The network participants cooperate in some markets and compete in others, thereby possibly giving rise to conflicts of interest between the interests of single partici-

---

21 *Buonocore, V.*, Contratti di impresa e collegamento, in: AA.VV., I collegamenti negoziali e le forme di tutela, Milan, Giuffrè 2007, 40; *Crea, C.*, Connessioni tra contratti e obblighi di rinegoziare, Naples Esi, 2013, 25 *et seq.*, 39-50. For caselaw, see Italian Supreme Court judgment no. 14244 of 28.7.2004, Giur. it., 1827 (2005); Italian Supreme Court judgment no. 11240 of 18.7.2003, Contratti, 120 (2004); Italian Supreme Court judgment no. 12733 of 12.12.1995, Foro it., 1996, I, 2162 (1996).

22 *Barba, V.*, Appunti per uno studio sui contratti plurilaterali di scambio, Riv. dir. civ., 531 (2010); *Villa, R.*, Inadempimento e contratto plurilaterale, Milan, Giuffrè 1999, pp. 25, 133.

23 *Teubner, G.*, Networks as connected contracts, trans. *Everson, M.*, Oxford, Hart Publishing 2011, p. 184.

pants and the interests of the network (collective interests[24] or interest of the network itself if it takes the form of a legal entity). There is also an internal open-endedness: quantitative and structural (number of contracts, long-term and incomplete[25], and of persons/firms/activities) and, especially, qualitative (function of contractual fragments vs. function of the whole with an ensuing increase in conflicts of interest despite the cooperation). This is explained by the very concept of business activities and their natural indefinite duration in time.

A firm is in itself an activity[26]: an ensemble of acts and behaviour, including heterogeneous but unified, on a teleological level, by a common purpose (production and/or distribution). It exists on the level of effectiveness[27], actual carrying on of business, as a portion of socio-economic reality. It is a legally relevant and complex fact that serves to assess the single acts even if the latter are independent, considered individually. Therefore, the contractual network, as a whole, organises firms in the sense of complementary activities (even if attributable to separate enterprises). This

---

24 *Cafaggi, F.*, Contractual Networks and the Small Business Act: Towards European Principles?, 4 European Review of Contract Law, 493-539, 502 (2008).

25 Long term contracts have become synonymous with relational contracts: *Gomez, F.*, Cooperation, Long-term Relationships and Open-endedness in Contractual Networks, in: Cafaggi, F. (ed), Contractual Networks, Inter-Firm Cooperation and Economic Growth, Cheltenham, UK-Northampton, MA-USA, Edward Elgar 2011, 21, 25 and 31. In general, in the rich literature, see *Macneil, I.R*, Contracts: Adjustment of Long-Term Economic Relations under Classical, Neoclassical, and Relational Contract Law, 72 Northwestern U. L. R., 854-902 (1977-1978); *Goetz, G. /Scott, R.E*, Principles of Relational Contracts, 67 Virginia L. R., No. 6, 1089-1150 (1981); *Eisenberg, M.A*, Why There Is No Law of Relational Contracts, 94 Northwestern U. L. R., No. 3, 805-21 (1999-2000). For the issues of incompleteness, *Schwartz, A.*, Incomplete Contracts, in: Newman, P., The New Palgrave Dictionary of Economics and the Law, II, London, Macmillan Publishers, New York, Stockton Press 1998, 277-283; *Valentino, D.*, Incomplete Agreements: a Comparative Law Analysis, 20 European Business L. R., 6, 819-34 (2009). On the correlation with networks, see *Geiss, G.*, The Space Between Markets and Hierarchies, 95 Virginia L. R., 107-123 (2009).

26 And hence 'fattispecie' as a complex legal fact that can produce effects: *Auletta, G.*, Attività, in Enc. dir., III, Milan, Giuffré 1958, pp. 981-982; *Oppo, G.*, L'impresa come fattispecie, Riv. dir. civ, I, 109 (1982).

27 *Buonocore, V.*, L'impresa, Tratt. dir. comm. Buonocore, I, 2.1, Turin, Giappichelli 2002, 89, 92; *Ascarelli, T.*, Corso di diritto commerciale: introduzione e teoria dell'impresa, Milan, Giuffré 1962, pp. 147, 155 *et seq.*; *Alcaro, F.*, La categoria dell'attività: profili ricostruttivi, in *Id.*, L''attività' profili ricostruttivi e prospettive applicative (Saggi), Naples, 1999, pp. 22, 33.

network creates interdependencies[28] - or, at times, also dependencies – not only between the bilateral contracts and between the related performances but in particular between the various business activities and between the capacities and resources instrumental to the business activities of each node, in view of attaining a common interest/goal. A produces eco-sustainable substances and has a contract with B for the supply of those substances that B uses inside machines that it manufactures. B has a contract with C for the supply of further components of the finished product. A has a contract with D, which assembles the machines and tests their capacity. D has a contract with E, which handles sales on the final market. And so on and so forth. Complementary activities (more or less non-fungible or essential) or compatible ones for the attainment of a shared objective (for example, cooperation in manufacturing and selling a high-quality product). The latter constitutes a specification or evolution of the purpose of each firm-node.

Business activity is potentially endless, the number and the complexity of the networks that organise firms as activities are potentially inexhaustible. They can increase and diversify the products, the services, assembly techniques, the combination of activities (distribution, production of goods or services, or even just R&D for process and/or product innovations), the relevant market, the number of co-producers, the suppliers, etc.

The internal open-endedness then develops and is justified in view of the indeterminateness and uncertainty of the outside environment, dynami-

28 *Teubner, G.*, Coincidentia Oppositorum: Hybrid Networks Beyond Contract and Organization, in: Amstutz, M./Teubner, G. (eds), Networks: Legal Issues of Multilateral Cooperation, Oxford, Hart Publishing 2009, pp. 3-32; *Heermann, P.*, The Status of Multilateral Synallgmas in the Law of Connected Contracts, in: Amstutz, M./Teubner, G. (eds), Networks: Legal Issues of Multilateral Cooperation, Oxford, Hart Publishing 2009, p. 103. The physiognomic nature of contractual networks is the interdependence (justified by mutual specific investments). But it is not a necessary requirement considering that a network is not a typical phenomenon (*Collins, H.*, Introduction to Networks as Connected Contracts, in: Teubner, G., Networks as connected contracts, trans. Everson, M., Oxford, Hart Publishing 2011, p. 11). A nexus of dependence (or if, one prefers, asymmetric interdependence) can also exist between one firm and another (for example, quasi-hierarchical network based on an *ex contractu* power of control in the absence of ties associated with the ownership of equity *Crea, C.*, Reti contrattuali e organizzazione della attività di impresa, Naples, Esi, 2008, pp. 244-253).

cally considered, in the context of globalised markets, especially if this environment is a high-tech and innovative one [29].

However, the network of long term contracts among firms is not and could not be a legal effect in a technical sense of the single contracts but it is a material economic effect stemming from the interaction of the legal effects (functions) produced by each contract of the series. No contract, if viewed in isolation, is necessary or sufficient compared to the others but the legal effects of each contract, in combination, actually produce the network. The latter is thus in turn a complex legal fact that can be reconstructed in accordance with the paradigm of strict legal relevance[30]. The legal order commences from the network in the construction of the norms governing the single contracts that comprise the whole. Therefore, the function of each part (the effects/subjective legal situations and their regulation) cannot be identified if not in light of the function of the whole.

A link between contracts can envelop a consumer and exist between contracts, typical or atypical, not necessarily long term ones . The network of connected contracts (and/or de facto relationships) tends to consider consumers as third parties[31]. The former is characterised by a need to link one contract to another as regards cessation such that defects in one have

29 *Gilson, R./Sabel, C./Scott, R.*, Contracting for Innovation: Vertical Disintegration and Interfirm Collaboration, 109 Columbia L. R., 431-502 (2009).

30 *Irti, N.*, Rilevanza giuridica, in Noviss. dig. it., XV, Turin, Utet, 1968, p. 1094 *et seq.*; *Falzea, A.*, Il soggetto nel sistema dei negozi giuridici, Milan 1939, 7 *et seq.*, 24. The concept of 'legal relevance' enables juridicity to be attributed to socio-economic phenomena (contractual networks) without crystallising them in precise legal rules: *Crea, C.*, Reti contrattuali e organizzazione della attività di impresa, Naples, Esi, 2008, p. 143.

31 On the possible reception of networks, from the English law perspective, in the context of both consumer and commercial contracts, see *Brownsword, R.*, Contract with Networks Effects: Is the Time now Right?, in Grundmann, S. *et al.* (eds.) The Organizational Contract: From Exchange to Long-Term Network Cooperation in European Contract Law, Ashgate, Farnham 2013, pp. 146, 151. In favour of a European contract law that includes those aspects are *Cafaggi, F./Grundman, S.*, Towards a Legal Framework for Transnational European Networks, *ivi*, p. 363. However, this present analysis focuses solely on networks among firms.

repercussions on the other leading to its fall (*simul stabunt simul cadent*) [32]. On the contrary, in the latter, the need to preserve the network prevails, or even its single parts (long term contracts) if not essential to the attainment of the aim of the network[33].

The functional and structural surplus likens the two cases although with different intensity, forcing the interpreter to identify the whole (multiple unit) – with a consequent surplus of interpretation – and its single parts (each bilateral contract), verifying how the former impacts on the selection of the regulation of the latter and vice versa.

However, while for a simple nexus the conflicts that emerge in concrete cases could be resolved by treating the series of contracts as a single one (mixed, atypical, for the benefit of a third party or with protective effects for the third party[34]), very often such a classification is insufficient when there is an indeterminate (persons, contracts, business activities) multiplicity (multilaterality) like a network.

In this case it is possible to stipulate *ex ante* a multiparty contract. Otherwise, *ex post*, at the time of interpretation, one could proceed either to fragment the plurality seeking to select complex sub-portions (e.g.: within the sequence-combination of contracts, one identifies two, as in a simplified nexus) or to reclassify as a multilateral contract or a unitary organisa-

---

32 Amongst many see Italian Supreme Court judgment no. 7255 of 22.3.2013, Mass. Giust. civ., 229 (2013); Italian Supreme Court judgment no. 13164 of 5.6.2007, Resp. civ., 204 (2008); Italian Supreme Court judgment no. 14611 of 25.7.2005, Giur. it., 2064 (2006).

33 *Crea, C.*, Connessioni tra contratti e obblighi di rinegoziare, Naples Esi, 2013, 67-75. In the antitrust sphere, for example, the cumulative effect of parallel distribution networks (with the ensuing application of the rules outlawing restrictive agreements) is premised also on the essentiality or not of the single agreement for the purposes of generating the alleged effect. If it is not so essential, the agreement remains valid: ECJ judgment of 7.12.2000, in case C-214/99, Neste Markkinointi Oy v. Yötuuli Ky, in [2000] ECR I-1121. See also the leading ECJ judgment of 28.2.1991, in Case-234/89, Stercios Delimitis v. Henninger Bräu AG, Foro it., 1993, IV, p. 29 *et seq*.

34 *Teubner, G.*, Networks as Connected Contracts, trans. *Everson, M.*, Oxford, Hart Publishing 2011, pp. 222, 250. On third party beneficiaries in construction contracts, see inter alia *Cafaggi, F.*, Contractual Networks and Contract Theory: A Research Agenda for European Contract Law, in: Cafaggi, F. (ed), Contractual Networks, Inter-Firm Cooperation and Economic Growth, Cheltenham, UK-Northampton, MA-USA, Edward Elgar 2011, pp. 78-79.

tion relevant towards third parties. In the final analysis, liability in tort may come to the rescue.

The function produced by the legally relevant fact-network (organisation of cooperative competition) enables one to achieve an added economic and social value: this requires conformation of the subjective legal situations stemming from each contract, their exercise and implied provision of additional rights-duties connected to persons who are not contractually bound. In this way, performance could turn out to be essential not only for the purpose of the single contract but for the protection of the economic and social value of the network (for examples, duties of confidentiality, of disclosure, of care or of warning, etc.). Conduct could prove to be opportunistic (or otherwise) in light of the value of the network (for example, withdrawal from one of the contracts). Duties of loyalty and collaboration are created among the various members and intensify in view of the attainment of the function of the network even when a single contract is terminated (but the network continues): this enables the actionability of remedies in contract and tort or under the law of partnership or corporations depending on the case, in a social and relational context informed by the solidarity among the members of the aggregation as a whole.

The network of bilateral contracts, just like a simple link, is not as a whole a typical situation (capable of being evaluated merely in terms of legality/illegality or validity/invalidity). But it is a legally relevant fact, which must be worthy and socially useful – compared to the two adjoining legal paradigms (single contract vs. organisation) – in a perspective that contemplates effectiveness and normativity of complex facts. The network must be suited to attaining the socio-economic value underlying its creation and development. This is an assessment of efficiency, axiologically based on solidarity and on the sociality of solidarity.

### C. Multiparty organisation-oriented network contract and network legal entity: surplus of party autonomy, organisational freedom and flexibility of Italian legislation

In each legal system[35] the phenomenon of business networks is governed by principles and rules and multiple methods of evaluation through which one resolves, though not always entirely satisfactorily, the concrete problems raised by such networks (internal and external liability, distribution of profits or losses, mechanisms for partial or total dissolution, governance and control).

At European level and in attempts at harmonisation and uniform law (DCFR and UNIDROIT Principles) there is no regulation of multilateral agreements, long term contracts and linked contracts, if not at the level of research agenda for the future[36].

---

35 For a comparative framework *Grundmann, S.*, Contractual Networks in German Private Law, *Vincelles, C.*, Linked Contracts Under French Law, *Whittaker, S.*, Contract Networks, Freedom of Contract and the Restructuring of Privity of Contract, in: Cafaggi, F. (ed), Contractual Networks, Inter-Firm Cooperation and Economic Growth, Cheltenham, UK - Northampton, MA-USA, Edward Elgar 2011, respectively 111, 163, 179; and also *Weitzenboeck, E.M.*, A Legal Framework for Emerging Business Models. Dynamic Networks as Collaborative Contracts, Cheltenham, Edward Elgar, 2012.

36 *Cafaggi, F.*, Contractual Networks and the Small Business Act: Towards European Principles?, 4 European Review of Contract Law, 498. Some sporadic reference can be found in DCFR: article II.–1.101 on multilateral juridical acts: *Von Bar C./Clive E.* (eds), Principles, Definitions and Model Rules of European Private Law. Draft Common. Frame of Reference (DCFR), I, Oxford, Oxford University Press, 2009, pp. 125-129. Also in some provisions on consumer credit (article II–5:106; as well as Directive 2008/48/EC) and on franchising systems (part IV E: e.g. IV E-4:101 and 4:102). On these aspects and on the methodological difficulties of European contract law in selecting an adequate regulation for essential contractual nexus, see *Amstutz, M.*, Nemesis of European Private Law: Contractual Nexus as a Legislative Conundrum, in: Grundmann, S. *et al.* (eds.) The Organizational Contract: From Exchange to Long-Term Network Cooperation in European Contract Law, Ashgate, Farnham 2013, pp. 319-356, and 323 note 17. See also the proposal for an optional Common European Sales Law, the text including the amendments that the European Parliament approved on 26 February 2014 available at www.europarl.europa.eu/sides/getDoc.do?type=TA&reference=P7-TA-20 140159&format=XML&language=IT (latest visit on 27th June 2014): in particular, the amendments to article 6(1), on the possible extension of the applicability of the CESL to certain linked contracts. Within the context of uniform law, the 2014–2016 Work Programme adopted by the UNIDROIT General Assembly,

Italy recently introduced *ad hoc* legislation on network contracts[37], unique in the international field. The legislation in question expresses a progressive attempt at a flexible but incomplete stabilisation. Flexible because it is still anchored to soft law techniques[38] aimed at valuing party autonomy (and organisational freedom) according to a logic of legal standards[39] and at implementing European initiatives to protect above all SMEs[40]. Incomplete because it does not select a type of self-sufficient contract[41]: it is necessary to refer, adopting a systemic approach, to the domestic law of contracts (general principles or single contracts: e.g. franchising, subcontracting, temporary association of enterprises, sale, agency, etc.) and above all to the law of business organisations (partnerships, com-

---

72nd session, 5 December 2013 proposes a study on multilateral and associative contracts and on the related issue of relational contracts (respectively available at www.unidroit.org/about-unidroit/work-programme?id=1575; and www.unidroit.org/english/governments/councildocuments/2014session/cd-93-03-e.pdf, latest visit on 10th July 2014). The system of private international law would also appear to be inadequate in addressing the phenomenon: *Cafaggi, F./Clavel, S.*, Toward a European system of decentralized rules?, in: Cafaggi, F. (ed.), Contractual Networks, Inter-Firm Cooperation and Economic Growth, Cheltenham, UK - Northampton, MA-USA, Edward Elgar 2011, pp. 201, 205-245.

37 Article 3, paragraphs 4-*ter* and 4-*quater*, of Law Decree No. 5 of 10.2.2009 converted by parliament with amendments into Law No. 33 of 9.4.2009 and amended on a number of occasions these past few years.

38 *Di Robilant, A.*, Genealogies of Soft Law, 54 The American Journal of Comparative Law, No. 3, 499-554 (2006); *Gersen ,L.E /Posner, E.A*, Soft Law, 61 Stanford L. R., No. 3, 580, 587 *et seq.* (2008).

39 *Zanelli, P.* , La rete è, dunque, della stessa natura del gruppo di società?, Contr. impr., 543 (2011).

40 EU Commission, 23.2.2011, CO(2011) 78 final, Review of the "Small Business Act" for Europe. Businesses and Entrepreneurs Charter (Law No. 180 of 11 November 2011), article 2, subparagraph n, and article 1.

41 There is talk of a "transtypical" regulation (*Cafaggi, F./Iamiceli, P.*, Le reti produttive: spunti ricostruttivi da una indagine empirica, in Reti di impresa tra crescita ed innovazione organizzativa. Riflessioni da una indagine sul campo, Bologna, Il Mulino 2007, p. 432); or of the lack of a typical (and nominated) contract in view of the intrinsic atipicality of cooperation and the multiform nature of the phenomenon: *Macario,* F., Il "contratto" e la "rete": brevi note sul riduzionismo legislativo, *Contratti*, 951-953 (2009); *Perlingieri, P.*, Reti e contratti tra imprese tra cooperazione e concorrenza, in Iamiceli P. (ed.), Le reti di imprese e i contratti di rete, Turin, Giappichelli 2009, pp. 389-391. On including network contracts within the flexible paradigm of consortia or consortium companies, see *Santagata R.*, Il contratto di rete fra (comunione di) impresa e società (consortile), Riv. dir. civ., I, 332 (2011).

panies and consortia *in primis*)[42] depending on the concrete case. This hinders a legal transplant[43] to other legal systems.

The rules introduced do not seem to cover contractual networks. This latter situation continues to be governed by legal models that predate the new law and still currently operate and by the concept of (simple) linked contracts. The regulation on network contracts does not exclude the specificness contained in other specific rules of the legal order, with the need in concrete cases to resolve possible conflicts between them; but it could well offer criteria for evaluating the general phenomenon of business networks.

After an initial approach tending towards contract, Italian lawmakers changed tack and opted for a more organisationally structured model to the point of contemplating a network with 'legal personality' (*soggettività giuridica*). The network contract is in any case associative (with a common purpose) and normally, but not necessarily, multiparty right from the very signing of the contract or subsequently (if there are clauses for later adhesion). The multilateral form thus enables the interdependencies (or dependencies) among the various activities of the firms and associated performances to be captured.

The common purpose, borrowed from economic language, is 'the individual and collective increase of the potential for innovation and competitiveness' of the members and the network as a whole. The firms – whatever their legal form (individual or collective) and irrespective of the sector that they operate in (agriculture or industry, production or distribution) – remain legally independent but devise a common programme (*i.e.* the network's activity, the rights and duties of the participants) consistent with common predetermined strategic objectives. The object of the network is cooperation and/or the exchange of information or performances of various types (industrial, commercial, technical or technological) and/or the carrying on of business together (like associative contracts in a broad sense).

---

42 Involving both joint groups [*Onza, M./Salamone, L.*, Le nuove forme di integrazione tra imprese: dai contratti di rete ai gruppi paritetici (e ritorno), Ric. giur., 221, 248-261 (2012)] and hierarchical ones: *Maugeri, M.*, Reti di imprese, contratto di rete e reti contrattuali. *Non minor virtus est tueri et perficere rem inventam... quam reperire*, Obbl. contr., 951, 955-962, (2009).

43 *Graziadei, M.*, Legal Transplants and the Frontiers of Legal Knowledge, 10 Theoretical Inquires in Law, No. 2, 693 – 713 (2009).

The contract specifies an order, a set of rules whose implementation is a matter for the parties' subsequent executory behaviour or, if there is a corporate-type organisational structure, it selects the division of competencies and functions among whatever organs (or pseudo-organs) there may be[44] .

Capital and organisational requirements are optional: common fund and common governance organ[45]. The first is an independent pool of assets separate from those of the member firms, is created through initial or subsequent contributions from the members and is governed by the rules on consortia with third party dealings in so far as they are compatible (articles 2614 and 2615, paragraph 2, of the Italian Civil Code). It cannot be divided up for the entire term of the contract and a member's own creditors cannot levy execution on the member's share of the fund. The benefit of limited liability is bolstered by the express provision that as regards the obligations assumed by the common organ in connection with the carrying out of the network's programme, third parties (*i.e.* the network's creditors)

---

44 The content of the contract must indicate: the particulars of the parties; the strategic objectives for innovation or increasing the competitive potential of the parties and the criteria for measuring progress towards those objectives; the common programme (rights and obligations of the single firms) and the method of attaining the common purpose; the term of the contract, the parameters and procedures governing adhesion by other firms; the rules on how members are to make decisions on all matters or aspects of common interest (that do not fall within the management powers vested in the common organ, if one has been established); and – if the contract provides that the network programme can be modified by majority vote – the rules on adopting decisions regarding making changes to the network programme. Exit and termination procedures are a matter for party autonomy, although there is pleonastic reference to the general rules on the dissolution of multilateral contracts. For a detailed analysis of the technical aspects of the rules and the criticalities thereof, see *Cafaggi, F. et al.* (eds), Il contratto di rete per la crescita delle imprese, Milan, Giuffré 2012; *Id. (*ed*)*, Il contratto di rete. Commentario, Bologna, Il Mulino 2009; *Zanelli, P.*, Reti e contratto di rete, Padua, Cedam 2012; *Genovese, A. et al* (eds), Riflessione sul contratto di rete. Profili privatistici e fiscali, Bari, Cacucci 2013; *Briolini, F. et al.* (eds), Il contratto di rete. Un nuovo strumento di sviluppo per le imprese, Napoli, Esi 2013; *D'Amico, G./Macario, F. (*eds*)*, Contratti di rete: prime applicazioni pratiche, Contratti, 799-836 (2013).

45 The existence of those optional organisational requirements has an impact on the content of the contract, which in that case must indicate in particular: the amount of the initial contributions and valuation criteria for them and for possible subsequent ones and the rules for managing the fund; the particulars of the person appointed to hold the office of the common organ for the performance of the contract and the latter's powers of management and representation (and the principle governing that person's replacement).

may levy execution solely on the common fund. The common governance organ, if there is one, is vested with power to manage, regulate and pursue the network's strategic objectives and acts as an agent of the firms that are party to the contract unless otherwise agreed by the parties. However, if the network acquires 'legal personality', the common organ acts as an agent/manager of the network itself as a whole[46].

The creation of a network as a legal entity is optional: it is a matter for the parties to decide (without prejudice to compliance with requirements as to form, content, organisation and registration). Such a personality does not seem to differ significantly from the corporate one of companies but diverges as regards the mandatory and peremptory nature of the procedures for enrolment in the register of enterprises[47]. A network that takes the form of a legal entity entails a completely independent body to which rights and duties can be attributed[48]. Internally, the skimpy legislative provisions afford ample freedom in selecting organisational rules on the division of power and the distribution of profits or losses that are much more flexible than those applicable to companies. While companies are rooted to a typical scheme, networks – even if in the form of a legal entity – can escape from that rigidity. Depending on the specificness of the network contract, the interpreter will have to establish which regulatory framework is most appropriate, applying directly or by analogy rules from the law governing companies (when the network has a corporate-type structure), partnerships, associations or consortia with third party dealings (when the organisational structure is more personal in nature).

The legislative framework enables one to achieve a multiplicity of different network aggregations (profit or non-profit, concerning cooperation, exchange or the carrying on of business together): in addition to entity-type networks purely contractual networks are also included(generally no

46 The written form is a burden (not an obligation) for public notice requirements (enrolment in the register of enterprises by all of the members if the network does not take the form of an actual entity or by just the network entity: *Maltoni, M.*, Le pubblicità del contratto di rete: questioni applicative, Cons. Naz. Notariato, Studio di Impresa No 5-2013/I, 8-10).

47 *Guerrera, F.*, Il contratto di rete tra imprese: profili organizzativi, Contratti, 397-401 (2014).

48 Article 3, paragraphs 4-*ter* and 4-*quater*, of Law Decree No. 5 of 10.2.2009 converted by parliament with amendments into Law No. 33 of 9.4.2009, as recently amended by article 36, paragraph 4, of Law Decree No. 179 of 18.10.2012, converted by parliament into Law No. 221 of 17.12.2012.

interaction with third parties and devoid of a common fund or common organ of governance), in which case liability towards third parties, if any, is joint and unlimited.

Networks that are a mix of contract and organisation have a common fund and a governance organ that acts on the basis of a collective mandate as agent for the single members. They also enjoy limited liability[49]. Such networks are the expression of a 'lesser' degree of personality [50], consistent with already tried and tested schemes like consortia with third party dealings: a hybrid scheme, potentially multiparty, which allows for a separate pool of assets without however reaching the level of full legal personality.

Each network contract is and cannot but be different from the other considering the *vis* creative of party autonomy and organisational freedom and also because the law requires, as a minimum common denominator, that the contract be justified by a broad common purpose-goal of an individual and collective increase in the potential for innovation and competitiveness and by a "common programme" consistent with shared "strategic objectives": all elements capable of translating an economic idea of business into legal language, a value that potentially creates an advantage for the network as a whole and its members.

---

49 In the sense of the possibility of graduating liability between limited liability and joint and common liability: *Villa, G.*, Il contratto di rete, in *Gitti, G. et al.*, I contratti per l'impresa, II, Bologna, Il Mulino 2013, p. 500. On the creation of a legal entity without separate assets if there is no common governance organ, see *Granelli, M.*, In margine alla ricerca della "Fondazione Bruno Visentini" sulle prassi applicative del contratto di rete, in: D'Amico, G./Macario, F. (eds), *D'Amico, G./ Macario, F.* (eds), Contratti di rete: prime applicazioni pratiche, Contratti, pp. 835-36 (2013).

50 Commencing from an analysis of the language [*D'Alessandro, F.*, Persone giuridiche e analisi del linguaggio, Padua, Cedam 1989; *Gentili, A.*, Una prospettiva analitica su reti di imprese e contratti di rete, Obbl. contr., 90 (2010)], a (network) contract can become an entity when it acts through a permanent establishment creating an order that governs the interdependent activities and ascribes inside it powers and duties of behaviour.

### D. Lack of stable hierarchy of canons of interpretation and adaptation to the complexity of business networks

The regulatory framework, whose essential features have been outlined above, does not and could not preclude the possibility of constructing networks devoid of the statutory requirements: the law has selected just one (in itself covering numerous options) of the possible schemes for organising cooperative competition (business network).

The network contract may also be bilateral, purely contractual, contractual but organisation-oriented (up to an entity-type network), entailing exchange, cooperation or the carrying on of business together. Initial practice bears witness to that. Moreover, where multiple functions (and programmes) are pursued, it is theoretically possible to create networks of networks. In other words, a network contract that envisages a link between bilateral network contracts: the purpose of each firm must thus be consistent with the purpose of each network contract and all must be suited to achieving the ultimate aim of the basis network contract. If a multiparty contract of this type is lacking and if each bilateral network contract is not expressly connected to the others, the problem of the multilateral organisation of contractual networks arises.

In this case it is necessary *ex post* to identify criteria for ascertaining a network of contracts and selecting the regulatory framework to govern the whole and the single parts. In the past some spoke of a split between function and structure[51], mentioning the commercial distribution sector as an example of where an anomalous common purpose could be achieved

51 *Auletta, G.*, Un saggio di economia del diritto, Riv. trim. dir. e proc. civ., 1091-1099 (1980). From the standpoint of bilateral-governance, *Williamson, O.E.*, Transaction-cost Economics: The Governance of Contractual Relationship, 22 Journal of Law and Economics, 233, 250 (1979); consequently, *Grundmann, S./ Cafaggi, F./ Vettori, G.*, The Contractual Basis of Long-Term Organization-The Overall Architecture, in: Grundmann, S. *et al.* (eds.) The Organizational Contract: From Exchange to Long-Term Network Cooperation in European Contract Law, Ashgate, Farnham 2013, pp. 3, 6-38 propose a reconstruction of network contracts in light of a new atypical paradigm of organisational contracts, considering their governance features and the role of cooperation. On those issues: *Scott R.E. / Triantis G.G.*, Incomplete Contracts and the Theory of Contract Design, 56 Case Western Reserve L. R., 2005, 187-201; *Jennejohn, M.C*, Collaboration, Innovation, and Contract Design, 14 Stanford Journal of Law Business & Finance, 83 (2008); *Gilson, R./Sabel, C./Scott, R.*, Contracting for Innovation: Vertical Disintegration and Interfirm Collaboration, 109 Columbia L. R., 431.

through a plurality of contracts of exchange. In such cases a linear itinerary of complexity would require multilateral contracts (or organisations): all of the holders of a legally relevant interest should participate in the structure of the juridical act. When this does not occur – also due to the transaction costs that condition the choices of economic actors – it is necessary to seek other answers in the legal system however 'irritating' that may be.

The network of linked bilateral contracts may be constructed through multiple express mechanisms, creating interdependence between or dependence on activities (e.g.: linking clauses or conditions [52] that highlight the nexus because they make the effectiveness of a contract dependent on a subsequent one[53]) such as to warrant an organisational system, at least in part multilateral. In those cases, both *ex ante* and *ex post*, *i.e.* at the time of interpretation, the connection can – with varying degrees of intensity – be traced back to a manifestation of an express or even implied will. The subjective interpretation criteria assist in the dual process of verifying the existence of a network of contracts and identifying the consequences for the resolution of conflicts, according to the specificness of both the legal systems involved and the concrete case.

Much more often, however, the network is simply real (*de facto*) but no objective will can be found in the content of the various contracts. Such lack of will could be 'pathological', when the parties seek to artificially

---

52 In France *Vincelles, C.*, Linked Contracts under French Law, in: Cafaggi, F. (ed), Contractual Networks, Inter-Firm Cooperation and Economic Growth, Cheltenham, UK - Northampton, MA-USA, Edward Elgar 2011, 168; in Italy, Italian Supreme Court judgment no. 1333 of 3.2.1993, Foro it., 1993, I, 3086 (1993); *Amadio, G.*, Inattuazione risoluzione: la fattispecie, in Roppo, V. (ed), Rimedi-2, V, Tratt. contr. Roppo, Milan, Giuffrè 2006, 62. For the distinction between linking clauses (that connect two or more contracts) and conditions, see *Colombo C.*, Operazioni economiche e collegamento negoziale, Padua, Cedam 1999, p. 264. See also the very early contribution by *Giorgianni, M.*, Negozi giuridici collegati, Riv. it. scienze giur., 275, 333 (1937).

53 Also relevant are cooperation clauses, exclusivity clauses (which are specific cases of non-compete clauses: *Decker, D./Filipp, M.*, Covenants Not To Compete, 3rd ed, New York, Aspen Publisher 2009, p. 239 *et seq.*), multiparty management clauses, termination clauses in the sense of protecting the network purpose, and indemnity clauses: *Cafaggi, F.*, Contractual Networks and Contract Theory: A Research Agenda for European Contract Law, in: *Cafaggi, F.* (ed), Contractual Networks, Inter-Firm Cooperation and Economic Growth, Cheltenham, UK - Northampton, MA-USA, Edward Elgar 2011, pp. 75-76.

fragment a unitary entity, to separate internal and external (to the network) risks and liability through splitting up the contracts (clauses of separateness of the contracts, clauses limiting or excluding liability[54] and clauses limiting legal action or defences). This means eluding some branches of law: tax law[55], labour law, in general mandatory rules. The will to separate may *ex adverso* constitute an indicator of the relevance of the nexus. Other times the lack of will is 'physiological', a result of the impossibility of foreseeing *ex ante* the evolution of the network (internal and external dynamic open-endedness) and the cooperative competition among an exponential multiplicity of firms. What can the interpreter do and what should he do? The subjective interpretation criteria, especially if correlated in a literal sense to the words used in the single contractual text, are not sufficient or indeed may prove to be misleading (if for example a clause of *divisibilité* of objectively linked contracts is unilaterally imposed by the party with the greater bargaining power[56]). But yet an economic unity has to be identified, a value of the 'whole' has to be considered.

Concrete and repetitive cooperative behaviour that exhibits, in objective terms, a function of the network as instrumental to satisfying shared collective objectives (e.g. common purchasing or selling, joint brand, manufacturing of a complex product, etc.) of the whole even if fragmented[57]. Formal contracts that braid material behaviour: the effectiveness of the legally relevant fact-network. The making of specific investments is achieved through contractual or material acts that justify (especially on an economic level) interdependencies or dependencies within the network.

---

54 *Brownsword, R.*, Network Contracts Revisited, in Amstutz, M./Teubner, G. (eds), Networks: Legal Issues of Multilateral Cooperation, Oxford, Hart Publishing 2009, p. 31.

55 In Italian caselaw, Italian Supreme Court judgment no. 1465 of 21.1.2009, n. 1465, Banca dati-Foro It. (April 2009). In the international context, see *Cafaggi, F.* (ed), Contractual Networks, Inter-Firm Cooperation and Economic Growth, Cheltenham, UK - Northampton, MA-USA, Edward Elgar 2011, p. 75.

56 *Crea, C.*, Connessioni tra contratti e obblighi di rinegoziare, Naples Esi, 2013, pp. 61-67.

57 Fragmentation often means pluralism of contracts, which as a whole are referable to the body of rules governing a single contract: *Azzaro, A.M.*, Contratto e negozio nel "frazionamento" del rapporto giuridico, Turin, Giappichelli 2009, p. 11 *et seq.*, 225, 255 *et seq.* In contractual networks the multiplicity of contracts entails a collision of contract rules, resolved in the light of the functionality of the network as a whole: *Amstutz, M.*, Contract Collision: An Evolutionary Perspective on Contractual Networks, 76 Law and Contemporary Problems, No. 2, 182 (2013).

The feature of the linked contracts, whether simplified or network, is hence in the *quid pluris* of the interpretation and classification, from a functional perspective. All of this has consequences. Primarily, the object of interpretation is not the single contractual text but all of the contractual texts (as well as the possible deeds establishing the firms that participate in the network): a sort of overall macro-text[58], as regards both the totality that it expresses and its single parts, intrinsically uncertain not only on a semantic but also legal level. The literal rule of interpretation loses its priority and its exclusionary role in the very task of interpretation.

Subjective interpretation criteria - based on the will of the parties and that are often considered as hierarchically superior to objectives ones - can prove to be unsuitable or insufficient[59]. At the very least, these parameters should shed light on the value of the whole compared to the individual interests (of the formal parties) and the collective interest (of the network), between the function/effects of each contractual fragment and the function of the network in its entirety: hence a functional and teleological approach, taking interests into account and axiologically justified.

In this direction it is possible to value the objectification of the subjective interpretation criteria considering the sequence and interaction of the contracts and relationships as ascribable to the "behaviour" of the parties and/or also to the relevant "circumstances" [60] that are necessary for reconstructing the deep sense and purpose of the overall economic operation.

The context of each contract is the network, which favours a contextual[61] rather than a textual approach (if by text that of the single contract is

---

58 *Velluzzi, V.*, Interpretazione sistematica e prassi giurisprudenziale, Turin, Giappichelli 2002, p. 185, and note 27.

59 *Pennasilico, M.*, Metodo e valori nell'interpretazione dei contratti, Naples, Esi 2011, 229-260; *Colombo C.*, Operazioni economiche e collegamento negoziale, Padua, Cedam 1999, pp. 252, 254, referring to (simplified) linked contracts.

60 *Crea, C.*, Connessioni tra contratti e obblighi di rinegoziare, Naples Esi, 2013, 39-44. For international trade contracts see *Vogenauer, S.*, Article 4.3, in S. Vogenauer/J. Kleinheisterkamp (eds), Commentary on the Unidroit Principles of International Commercial Contracts (PICC), Oxford, Oxford University Press 2009, p. 510.

61 On new contextualism see *Brownsword, R.*, Contract with Networks Effects: Is the Time now Right?, in: Grundmann, S. *et al.* (eds.) The Organizational Contract: From Exchange to Long-Term Network Cooperation in European Contract Law, Ashgate, Farnham 2013, pp. 138, 151; *McLauchlan, D.W*, The New Law of Contract Interpretation, 19 New Zealand University L. R., 147 (2000). From a different perspective, *Gilson R.J./ Sabel C.F./ Charles R.E.*, Contract and Innovation:

meant). And it is a dynamic context, internally and with respect to the relevant market. Therefore, the legal assessment cannot be tied to the moment of the conclusion of one or more contracts: it is necessary to undertake an evolutive interpretation centred on the implementation phase of the overall regulation of interests (as they are long term contracts, often following one another in time).

The canon of the totality of the interpretation of clauses having regard to the others is suited to the complexity. The single clause is weighed up in light of the whole, in other words, the series of contracts and the clauses in each of them. The holistic approach extends expanding the part-whole correlation and vice versa[62].

The objective interpretation criteria that are a traditional feature of contracts with a common purpose[63] flank or override the subjective interpretation criteria (in the absence of a will and in order to protect third parties) if such proves to be useful or necessary for a correct understanding of the peculiarities of the case. What is at stake here are firms-activities, contracts that organise interdependencies between (or at times dependencies on) business activities. Reference to customs and the market helps in se-

---

The Limited Role of Generalist Courts in the Evolution of Novel Contractual Term, 88 New York University L. R., 170 – 215 (2013).

62 *Pennasilico, M.*, Metodo e valori nell'interpretazione dei contratti, Naples, Esi 2011, p. 53; *Colombo C.*, Operazioni economiche e collegamento negoziale, Padua, Cedam 1999, p. 53. The French experience of *ensemble contractuel* or *groupe des contrats* oscillates between a concept of *indivisibilité* and *interdépendance*, at times prioritising the will of the parties and at other times preferring an objective interpretation based on the *economie generale du contrat* and on a principle of consistency and rationality of the clauses of each contract (in particular clauses on *divisibilité*) in light of the aims of the overall deal (article 1137.2 Project Català and article 13 Project de la Chancellerie): *Bros, S.*, Les contrats interdependants: actualité et perspectives, Rec. Dalloz, 2009, 14, 965 (2009); *Vincelles, C.*, Linked Contracts under French Law, in: Cafaggi, F. (ed), Contractual Networks, Inter-Firm Cooperation and Economic Growth, Cheltenham, UK - Northampton, MA-USA, Edward Elgar 2011, p. 163; *Fauvarque-Cosson, B.*, L'interdépendance contractuelle dans une opération incluant une location financière. A propos de deux arrêts de chambre mixte de la Cour de cassation, 22 European Review of Private Law, 253-260 (2014).

63 *Oppo, G.*, Profili di interpretazione oggettiva del negozio giuridico, Bologna, Zanichelli 1943, 150; *Angelici, C.*, Appunti sull'interpretazione degli statuti di società per azioni, Riv. dir. comm., I, 797 *et seq.*, 811 (1993); *Ibba, C.*, L'interpretazione degli statuti societari fra criteri oggettivi e criteri soggettivi, *Riv. dir. civ.*, 525 (1995).

lecting the 'reasonable' expectations[64] of the network participants even if technically third parties as regards a single contract. Cooperation is supported by an interpretation informed by good faith[65] (itself founded on the principle of solidarity), which can supplement and correct the content of the contract, shedding light on implied duties.

Clauses that separate what is objectively inseparable, where unilaterally imposed by the party with greater bargaining power, should be interpreted *contra proferentem*. The balancing of the multiple interests involved operates from a multiple perspective: inside the single contract and outside of it, but internal or external to the network as regards third parties since legitimate expectations must be safeguarded.

Therefore the objective and subjective interpretation criteria work together. The network of connected contracts is an effective multilateral organisation: the hybridisation of the reference legal models goes hand in hand with a hybridisation (or at least an evolution) of hermeneutical techniques and parameters for assessment. Accordingly, the hierarchy between criteria is not static but variable and dynamic. It must adapt to the peculiarities of the concrete case[66] (network), fostering a coherent interaction among the canons of interpretation and not a rigid and predetermined

---

64 *Brownsword, R.*, Contract with Networks Effects: Is the Time now Right?, in: Grundmann, S. *et al.* (eds.) The Organizational Contract: From Exchange to Long-Term Network Cooperation in European Contract Law, Ashgate, Farnham 2013, pp. 421, 427-429. *Herbots, J.H*, Interpretation of Contracts, in: Smits, J.M (ed), Elgar Encyclopaedia of Comparative Law, 2nd ed., Cheltenham, UK/Northampton, MA, USA, Edward Elgar 2012, 421, 427-429.

65 *Di Nella, L.*, Mercato e autonomia contrattuale nell'ordinamento comunitario, Naples, Esi, 2003, p. 370 *et seq.*; *Olivieri, G.*, L'interpretazione del contratto, in: Olivieri, G./Zoppini, A. (eds), Contratto e antitrust, Rome, Laterza 2008, p. 84; *Barcellona, M.*, Clausole generali e giustizia contrattuale. Equità e buona fede tra codice civile e diritto europeo, Turin, Giappichelli 2006, p. 257 *et seq.*; *Herbots, J.H*, Interpretation of Contracts, in: Smits, J.M (ed), Elgar Encyclopaedia of Comparative Law, 2nd ed., Cheltenham, UK/Northampton, MA, USA, Edward Elgar 2012, pp. 442-445.

66 *Rizzo, V.*, Interpretazione del contratto e la relatività delle sue regole, Naples-Camerino, 1985, 498-499; *Pennasilico, M.*, Metodo e valori nell'interpretazione dei contratti, Naples, Esi 2011, 219; *Cafaggi, F.*, Contractual Networks and the Small Business Act: Towards European Principles?, 4 European Review of Contract Law, 528 (2008).

gradualism as well as the definitive superseding of the limit of literalness/clearness[67].

## E. Functional, teleological and axiological approach

Party autonomy is central to the phenomenon of networks: it creates rules of organisation for the activities among the firms or can express itself through the decision not to be subject (in part) to law. But such autonomy, in order to lawfully bear fruit, must be exercised in line with the framework of values and principles underlying the legal system that it belongs to [68] (constitutionally oriented and open to European and international influences), not only with the mandatory rules. The interpretation of contractual networks and their classification - *i.e.* identification of the regulatory framework to be applied - should be done from an axiological, teleological and functional standpoint.

Networks of bilateral contracts do not have a common purpose with inputs pooling and profit sharing according to a pre-established *ratio* (as under company law and multiparty contracts endowed with a corporate-type organisation). But in any case there are shared objectives, a common interest that the network is successful and realises its value as a unitary socio-economic entity. This leads to implied duties of behaviour and the conformation of some subjective legal situations – technically stemming from the single contracts – for network function.

Italian legislation envisages organisation-oriented cooperative network models but the activities among the members may simply be one of exchange. At the same time it highlights that a network, whatever its form, is instrumental to a strategic objective that the parties must share: a common programme/project[69], which can vary depending on the case but which in

---

67 *Herbots, J.H*, Interpretation of Contracts, in: Smits, J.M (ed), Elgar Encyclopaedia of Comparative Law, 2nd ed., Cheltenham, UK/Northampton, MA, USA, Edward Elgar 2012, p. 438.

68 On the centrality of private autonomy as a core of private law and the fundamental basis of both the law of contract and company law/law of corporations, see *Grundman, S.*, On the Unity of Private Law from a Formal to a Substance-Based Concept of Private Law, 18 European Review of Private Law, 1055, 1063-1077 (2010).

69 *Teubner, G.*, Networks as Connected Contracts, trans. *Everson, M.*, Oxford, Hart Publishing 2011, p. 92.

any event is aimed at achieving an individual and collective increase in the potential for innovation and/or market competitiveness by the members and the network considered as a whole.

The words "competitiveness and innovation" [70] are incorporated into the law from the socio-economic system if and to the extent that they have positive effects (or at least not negative ones) on the network and the single nodes. Thus the norm selects from within the value to be realised and its dual axiological orientation (individual/collective interest) in order to balance economic efficiency and social solidarity: but it does not exhaust and nor could it the modalities and intensity (organisational and contractual structures) through which this value can be realised because it leaves ample freedom to party autonomy. However, this value becomes a parameter of evaluation not of the strict legality of a network made up of bilateral connected contracts (if devoid of the requisites, especially the organisational ones, laid down by the overarching rules) but of the worthiness[71] and socio-economic utility of the function in concrete pursued (in the single contracts in light of the network as a whole).

The decision of the parties to shun the law – opting for a hybrid and atypical network of contracts compared to the traditional scheme: firm/ organisation vs. single isolated contract – cannot contrast with the value protected by law even if the level of implementation is different. If this does not occur, the network is unworthy because useless (and inefficient),

---

70 Competitiveness and innovation underlie European policy on supporting business: Regulation (EU) No 1287/2013 of 11 December 2013, Programme for the Competitiveness of Enterprises and Small and Medium-Sized Enterprises (COSME) (2014 - 2020), in particular, on business networks, article 11.3.a.; and Regulation (EU) No 1291/2013 of 11 December 2013, Horizon 2020 - The Framework Programme for Research and Innovation (2014-2020).

71 Party autonomy is neither a dogma nor a value in itself but is subject to the necessary assessment of worthiness (*meritevolezza*: article 1322 of the Italian Civil Code): in other words, conformity with the general principles of the Italian-EU system of sources of law from an axiological and teleological standpoint (*Perlingieri, P.*, Il diritto civile nella legalità costituzionale, secondo il sistema italo-comunitario delle fonti, Naples, Esi, 2006, pp. 322, 337, 347). Hence, this type of control is beyond the mere legality of the function/cause of the single contracts (conformity with specific rules: law as a statute). See: Italian Supreme Court judgment no. 14343 of 19.6.2009, Rass. dir. civ., 99 *et seq.* (2011); Italian Supreme Court judgment no. 8038 of 2.4.2009, Not., 40 *et seq.* (2010); *Villa, R.*, Il contratto di rete, in: Gitti, G. *et al.*, I contratti per l'impresa, II, Bologna, Il Mulino 2013, pp. 503-504.

from the very perspective of the market itself since that value protects the network, its members and third parties (business competitors[72] and consumers). The rights and duties technically stemming from the single bilateral contract and the correctness of their exercise find their justification in realising the value of the network as an economically unitary and legally relevant fact in the sense mentioned above.

Single rules or bodies of rules, no matter how flexible, are difficult to transfer to different legal systems. On the other hand, the value identified could constitute the ratio (in terms of principle) for justifying rules that vary and could be the instrument for a potential path towards harmonisation. Above all, this value can offer the interpreter a form of guidance in resolving conflicts arising out of the very existence of the network itself, a criterion for selecting the most appropriate regulatory framework[73] in keeping with respect for the centrality of self-regulation[74]. All without compressing the complexity of facts and interests but guaranteeing *juridicité* that is axiologically well founded.

---

72 Italian Competition Authority decision no. 22362 of 16.5.2011, Boll. No.17-201.

73 And hence the choice of remedies: *Femia, P.*, Desire for Text: Bridling the Divisional Strategy of Contract, 76 Law and Contemporary Problems 151, 168 (2013).

74 *Collins, H.*, The Weakest Link: Legal Implication of the Network Architecture of Supply Chains, in: Amstutz, M./Teubner, G. (eds), Networks: Legal Issues of Multilateral Cooperation, Oxford, Hart Publishing 2009, pp. 187, 205-206; *Perlingieri P.*, Reti e contratti tra imprese tra cooperazione e concorrenza, in: Iamiceli, P. (ed), Le reti di imprese e i contratti di rete, Turin, Giappichelli 2009, p. 396; on the complexity of self-regulation in relation to the problem of 'multi-level governance' (in developed business networks): *Krebs, P. / Jung, S.*, Governance structures in business networks, p. 118 (129 et seqq.) (in this volume).

# Virtual enterprises: liability problems in one- and multi-level networks[1]

*Katja Aedtner, Prof. Dr. Dr. h.c. mult Gunther Teubner*

## A. One- and multi-level cooperations

Virtual enterprises are a successful new type of business entity.[2] In many sectors individual companies which intend to concentrate on their core competences affiliate in a cross-company virtual cooperation. The cooperation is virtual since its participants operate spatially separated from each other, but compensate for this separation with an intensive working relation by means of communication technology.[3] In the German-speaking countries, VirtuellBau, virtuellefabrik.ch, AMZ (automobile supplier Saxony) and Silicon Saxony have become known.[4] On the European level, several projects are closely examining the organisational form of virtual cooperation.[5] Especially medium-sized companies use the advantages offered by such forms of cooperation. The cooperation organised in complex networks may occur in different legal regimes such as contract, company

1 This paper is a translated version of a German article („Virtuelle Unternehmen: Haftungsprobleme in ein- und mehrstufigen Netzwerken") that was published in the German journal „Kölner Schrift zum Wirtschaftsrecht" (KSzW 2015, p. 109-113).

2 Fundamental for the microeconomic analysis of virtual cooperation see: *Davidow, W. H./Malone, M. S.*, The Virtual Enterprise: Structuring and Revitalizing the Corporation for the 21st Century, New York 1992; recently: International Journal of Computer Integrated Manufacturing, Special Issue: Collaborative Networks as Modern Industrial Organisations: Real Case Studies, Issue 1-2, 2013, p. 1 et seqq.; *Durugbo, C./Riedel, J.*, International Journal of Production Research 2013, Vol. 51 Issue 2, p. 598 et seqq.

3 On the individual definitions see *Lange, K. W.*, Virtuelle Unternehmen, Heidelberg 2001, p. 44 et seq.

4 www.amz-sachsen.de; www.silicon-saxony.de; www.virtuellefabrik.ch; www.virtuellbau.ch (last visited 23.03.2015); for details on the examples see *Weitzenboeck, E. M.*, A Legal Framework For Emerging Business Models, Oslo 2012, p. 42 et seq., 56 et seq.

5 Cf. GloNet: www.glonet-fines.eu as well as Bivee: www.bivee.eu (last visited 23.03.2015).

or special relation (German "Sonderverbindung"). These do not exclude each other, but they coexist. The model "The modular system of network activities" illustrates the multi-dimensionality of different legal regimes in various business modules and within the framework of the network.[6]

The multi-dimensionality of company networks becomes apparent in the two main forms of virtual cooperation.[7] Firstly, there are the one-level virtual cooperations (in the following: Virtual Enterprises), which are formed due to a spontaneous connection without previously existing formal relations between the participants. In these Virtual Enterprises, individual companies get together only temporarily to cooperate in a project. Frequently, no company form is chosen for the coordination within the Virtual Enterprise. Rather, the individual companies conclude a series of bilateral contracts.[8]

Secondly, the circumstances become more complex if a superordinate organisation is added to the one-level Virtual Enterprise. Now the cooperation occurs on two levels. Regularly, this superordinate cooperation forms a pool of companies as is also the case in the examples mentioned above. The pool of companies combines the individual companies participating in the network as a kind of platform. The pool generates cooperation advantages for the participants, such as the reduction of transaction or search costs. Once various legally independent companies from the pool wish to pursue a common project, they affiliate in a Virtual Enterprise.

The one-level as well as the multi-level virtual cooperation presents the law with difficult liability problems, which cannot readily be solved by the traditional instruments of contract law or company law.

---

6 *Krebs, P./Jung, S./Aedtner, K./Schultes, M.*, The modular system of network activities, in this volume, p. 75-117.

7 For detailed manifestations of virtual cooperations see *Lange, K. W.*,Virtuelle Unternehmen, Heidelberg 2001, p. 53 et seqq.

8 *Weitzenboeck, E.M.*, A Legal Framework for Emerging Business Models, Oslo 2012, p. 189.

## B. Liability problems

### I. Two questions

In the following we examine in detail which liability problems arise in such one- and multi-level networks. We focus on constellations in which both the pool of companies as well as the Virtual Enterprise consists of bilateral contracts,[9] since these are the cases in which legally difficult network effects occur.[10] Entering such a network cannot be compared to joining a corporation, which means concluding a contract with the whole corporate entity. Rather, entering a network is the result of a bilateral contact with one of its network members. This distinctive feature poses the legal problem if those network members who are not connected by bilateral contracts nonetheless stand in a legal relation to each other with specific obligations, i.e. in a special relation ("Sonderverbindung").[11] Empirical observations indicate that particularly this loose form of multi-level networks, which consist of a series of bilateral contracts, is also the most common in practice.[12] The reason may lie in low transaction costs, a high degree of informality, and the resulting flexibility of companies.

In this constellation, the problem arises in all three action units – in the pool of companies as well as in the individual Virtual Enterprises and lastly also in the relation between both – that factual cooperation relationships exist whose legal qualification is highly problematic, since they cannot merely be defined neither as contract nor as a corporate entity. Instead, special legal relations ("Sonderverbindungen") are emerging whose factual conditions and legal consequences are controversial. Sometimes, arrangements under company law or multi-lateral contracts do occur. However, in the following, they are only addressed marginally, since their liability concerns follow secured rules under contract law and company law.

Two questions are paramount. The first question arises *within* the network of individual companies in a Virtual Enterprise. How is the special

---

9 Accordingly, multi-lateral contracts and arrangements under company law are not examined here.

10 Cf. *Uribe, R. M.*, in: Samoy, L/Loos, M. (eds.), Linked Contracts, Cambridge, Mortsel 2012, p. 153 (160 et seqq.).

11 Fundamental for third party special relations: *Krebs, P.*, Sonderverbindung und außerdeliktische Schutzpflichten, München 2000, p. 339 et seqq.

12 *Weitzenboeck, E.M.*, A Legal Framework For Emerging Business Models, Oslo 2012, p. 189.

relation ("Sonderverbindung") to be qualified in legal terms due to which the participants are probably liable?

The second question, in contrast, arises from the relation *between* the pool of companies and the Virtual Enterprise. Both are networks which again for their part align to a network of a higher order. In this case, the interesting problem of higher-level networks arises. Which liability concerns are posed by such an affiliation of networks?

Both questions regard the internal liability of the network as well as the external liability toward third parties.

## II. Liability within Virtual Enterprises

It is highly controversial how special relations ("Sonderverbindungen") within networks are to be constructed legally. Three basic tenets are discernible. Firstly, the existing legal framework is widely dismissed and a new legal framework is designed for networks. One example is the audacious construct of an independent "network contract" ("Netzvertrag"), which has to assume an implied representation of all participants for all participants as well as numerous implied agency powers so as to finally be able to construct a complete multi-lateral contract.[13] Secondly, the problems are, in relying upon the completeness of the legal system, considered solvable by means of the existing legal framework. In this case one of the available legal institutions is selectively chosen and ad hoc modified until satisfactory results are achieved. One example is the "implicit basis of a contract" ("Geschäftsgrundlage"), according to which the existence of the one contract in the network provides the implicit basis for the other contract due to which – in clear contrast to the legal consequences intended in § 313 BGB – duties can be "extrapolated" for parties which are not contractually connected.[14] The third position also takes up the existing legal institutions, but chooses amongst them according to the aspect which best

13 *Rohe, M.*, Netzverträge – Rechtsprobleme komplexer Vertragsverbindungen, Tübingen 1998, p. 85 et seqq.; opposed to this see only *Canaris, C. W.*, Bankvertragsrecht, first part, 4th ed. Berlin 2005, recital 393; *Stoffels, M.*, Gesetzlich nicht geregelte Schuldverträge, Tübingen 2001, p. 268 seq.; *Einsele, D.*, Archiv für die civilistische Praxis 199 (1999), 145 (172 et seqq.); *Martinek, M.* , Moderne Vertragstypen III, München 1993, § 30 II.3.c.4.

14 *Grundmann, S.*, Archiv für die civilistische Praxis 207 (2007), p. 718 (740 et seqq., 759 et seqq.).

meets the particularities of networks and then develops a comprehensive approach. One example is the "connected contract" ("Vertragsverbindung"). It would be applied to other networks beyond the financed contracts and would define legal consequences based on the connection of the contracts.[15]

The debate will not be illustrated in detail here.[16] Rather, we will suggest a liability model which rejects the first position as unsustainable fiction,[17] but takes up the positive aspects of the second and third position and integrates them in a consistent legal institution. The normative foundation for network liability is the principle of reliance, which was developed in a long discussion and which has now become positive law in § 311 para. 3 sentence 1 and 2 BGB.[18] Accordingly, quasi-contractual obligations can be established between persons not bound by a contract if a legally relevant relationship of trust exists between them. This general clause of liability based on reliance requires meticulous specification for the various circumstances.

In order to be applicable to networks § 311 BGB has to be adapted to this new situation in several ways. Firstly, § 311 BGB is obviously tailored to bilateral relationships and yet has to be rethought for *multilateral relationships*. Secondly, within the network a specific kind of trust emerges, i.e. not trust in particular persons, but trust in the *system* generated by the network, which is connected to the network-specific cooperation and the general reciprocity in networks.[19] Thirdly, the commitment out-

15 *Weitzenboeck, E. M.,* A Legal Framework For Emerging Business Models, Oslo 2012, p. 313 et seqq.; *Schacherreiter, J.*, Das Franchise-Paradox, Tübingen 2006, p. 125 et seq., 243 et seq.; *Teubner, G.*, Netzwerk als Vertragsverbund, Baden-Baden 2004, p. 101 et seqq. (English translation: Networks as Connected Contracts. Oxford 2011 with an introduction by Hugh Collins).

16 On this *Teubner, G.,* Netzwerk als Vertragsverbund, Baden-Baden 2004, p. 182 et seqq., 217 et seqq.

17 Detailed arguments against the construct of a network contract in *Krebs, P.*, Sonderverbindung und außerdeliktische Schutzpflichten, München 2000, p. 314; *Picker, E.*, in: Beuthien, V./Fuchs, M./Roth, H. (eds.) Festschrift für Dieter Medicus: Zum 70.Geburtstag, Köln 1999, p. 397 (429); *Schmidt, K.* , Handelsrecht, 5th ed. , Köln 1999, § 35 III.

18 In detail *Emmerich, V.*, in: Münchener Kommentar zum Bürgerlichen Gesetzbuch, 6th ed., München 2012, § 311 recital 185 et seqq. with further references.

19 On systemic trust see *Luhmann, N.*, Vertrauen: Ein Mechanismus der Reduktion sozialer Komplexität, 4th exp. ed., Stuttgart 2000, p. 47 et seqq., 60 et seqq. For a thorough examination of fiduciary duties resulting from the relationship of trust in

side the bilateral contracts is not yet generated by the relationship of trust per se. The network participants commit themselves to a legally relevant *network aim*, ("Netzzweck") which is neither identical to the mutual aim of company law ("Gesellschaftszweck") nor to the exchange aim of contract law ("Vertragszweck").[20]

The emerging special relations ("Sonderverbindungen") are to be specified in a way that consults the underlying legal principles of relevant doctrinal constructs so as to determine the specific rules for various liability constellations. Therefore, the legal principles of culpa in contrahendo (§ 311 para. 2 BGB), the basis of contract ("Geschäftsgrundlage") (§ 313 BGB), the contract with protective effects for third parties ("Drittschutzvertrag") (§ 311 para. 3 sentence 1 BGB analogue), the trustee liability ("Sachwalterhaftung") (§ 311 para. 3 sentence 1 and 2 BGB) and of connected contracts ("Vertragsverbindung") (§ 358 para. 2 and 3 BGB) need to be considered. However, contrary to those voices in literature that underestimate the problem[21] none of these norms can be directly applied to networks. These constructs have to be reformulated for the particularities of networks – i.e. for network-specific trust, network purpose and multi-laterality – before they can meet the specific problems posed by networks.

## III. Liability in the relation between Virtual Enterprises and the pool of companies

Virtual cooperations additionally raise a special problem which has not been systematically examined in literature or case law. The networks of the different Virtual Enterprises and their underlying pool of companies

---

the network see *Crea, C.*, Reti contrattuali e organizzazione dell'attività d'impresa, San Dorligo della Valle 2008, esp. p. 189 et seqq.

20 On the differences in detail: *Teubner, G.*, Netzwerk als Vertragsverbund, Baden-Baden 2004, p. 148 et seqq.; *Rohe, M.*, Netzverträge – Rechtsprobleme komplexer Vertragsverbindungen, Tübingen 1998, p. 358 et seq., 407 et seqq, 437 et seqq. On the autonomy of the network purpose as company purpose *Baumgarten, A.*, Das Franchising als Gesellschaftsverhältnis: eine Studie zur spezifischen zivilrechtlichen Qualität des Rechtsverhältnisses zwischen Franchise-Geber und Franchise-Nehmer, Göttingen 1993, p. 114 et seqq.; esp. 146 seq..

21 *Grundmann, S.*, Archiv für die civilistische Praxis 207 (2007), p. 718 (718 et seqq.).

do not stand as such unconnectedly on their own, but are themselves closely linked to each other. In this case, networks arise out of networks, i.e. multi-level networks. If such an affiliation of networks is created by the participants does this then have consequences for liability issues?

A side glance at other legal fields makes clear that the law of corporate groups distinguishes not only between two, but three entities (parent company, subsidiary company, the entire group as poly-corporate enterprise)[22] and also public law assumes three entities for the German federal state (federation, states (Länder), federal state)[23]. Accordingly, with regard to Virtual Enterprises not only two, but three action units may have to be distinguished (the individual Virtual Enterprise, the pool of companies and the entire network of Virtual Enterprises that develops between the individual companies and the pool). This complication has legal consequences in practice.

A first consequence can be seen for the network purpose. When taking a closer look then all three networks pursue different legally relevant purposes. The individual Virtual Enterprise pursues the purpose of implementing the specific project as close cooperation of partners who remain autonomous. The pool of companies, in turn, follows the purpose of exploring business opportunities, recruiting potential project members and carrying out matters of mutual interest such as marketing and image branding. The entire network, i.e. the network consisting of both networks, finally, pursues the purpose of coordinating the individual projects and the pool's project. Just as the exchange purpose in contract law or the mutual purpose in company law influences the duties of the participants, these different purposes of the three networks also have clear effects on the rights and duties of the network members to one another.

But also in terms of third party relations of the Virtual Enterprise this affiliation of networks plays an important part. Neither do merely the individual Virtual Enterprises nor merely the pool of companies act as an independent competition and image unit, but also the virtual cooperation it-

---

22 *Bälz, U.*, in: Festschrift für Thomas Raiser, Berlin 1974, p. 287 (330).

23 *Herzog, R./Grzeszick, B.*, in: Maunz, T./Dürig, G., Grundgesetz: Loseblatt - Kommentare, as of 67. Supplement 2013, Art. 20 IV. recital 141 with further references.

self may be perceived as an independent action and liability unit in legal relations.[24]

In the following, the relevant liability problems – (I) liability for culpa in contrahendo, (II) liability for breach of contract, and (III) liability to third parties - are examined respectively with regard to one-level and multi-level Virtual Enterprises.

## C. Liability within the network

### I. Liability for culpa in contrahendo in the Virtual Enterprise

#### 1. Liability of the members of the Virtual Enterprise

The difference between one-level and multi-level virtual cooperations is already legally important when an individual Virtual Enterprise is founded, but also when a new member accesses the network. It makes a difference for culpa in contrahendo whether the Virtual Enterprise is simply based on a spontaneous cooperation or whether a connection, in form of a pool, has already existed in advance from which the members of the Virtual Enterprise are recruited.

A one-level Virtual Enterprise is, as already mentioned, most of the time not founded via a general multi-lateral agreement, but via several bilateral individual contacts. These contacts can be "horizontally" established by the members or the connection of the individual network members exists "vertically" to another member who takes on the role of a coordinator.[25] These contacts are to be qualified legally as a series of bilateral contracts. This creates the paradigmatic network situation, namely that only some members are connected by bilateral contracts whereas no contractual relation exists between many network members.[26] If conflicts arise

24 Naturally, not as legal person, but as economic entity. In more detail *Martinek, M.*, in: Martinek, M./Semler, F.-J./Habermeier, S./Flohr, E. (eds.), Vertriebsrecht, 3rd ed., München 2010, § 1 recital 18 et seqq. as well as § 2 recital 89.

25 On the centrally coordinated forms of Virtual Enterprises further see *Lange, K. W.*, Virtuelle Unternehmen, Heidelberg 2001, recital 56 et seq.

26 On the general opinion see only *Grundmann, S.*, Archiv für die civilistische Praxis 207 (2007) p. 718 (720); *Wellenhofer, M.*, Die Kritische Vierteljahreszeitschrift für Gesetzgebung und Rechtswissenschaft 2006 p. 187 (188); *Nicklisch, F.*, Betriebs-Berater 2000 p. 2166 (2166 seq.).

during the negotiating phase then the rules of culpa in contrahendo apply to the partners of the bilateral contracts without special problems caused by the network character.

The legal situation is more difficult if the conflicts arise between those participants of the intended Virtual Enterprise who are not connected by a bilateral contract. They cannot make use of the culpa in contrahendo unless the rules of trustee liability ("Sachwalterhaftung") are applicable. If a participant not connected by a contract breaches the duties as a trustee then the network character takes legal liability effects. For both prerequisites of trustee liability – self-interest and power over the contract – are much more likely to be fulfilled in a situation in which a close association, intensive cooperation and the mutual purpose of implementing the project is intended between the participants. As generally illustrated above, the network character legally transforms the general rules of trustee liability.

However, if the members of the specific Virtual Enterprise are recruited from an already existing pool then the question arises whether also the affiliation of the networks, i.e. the relation between pool and Virtual Enterprise, effects the liability based on culpa in contrahendo. Indeed, the existence of the pool impacts the negotiating situation in the planned Virtual Enterprise.[27] Its future members already are pool members. Therefore, they are subject to more vigorous negotiation duties.[28] The legal situation is similar to the familiar situation in ongoing business relations ("Geschäftsverbindung").[29] In clear contrast to the merely one-level Virtual Enterprise, the participants are subject to the following quasi-contractual duties already during negotiations: exclusivity, no parallel negotiations, increased informational duties and confidentiality obligations. In any case,

---

27 *Lange, K. W.*, Virtuelle Unternehmen, Heidelberg 2001, p. 202 et seqq. does not take the pool's influence on the negotiating duties of the project participants into consideration.

28 The intensification of the culpa in contrahendo duties in principal exists with all forms of the pool as corporation, as multi-lateral contract or as a series of bilateral contracts. Besides the breach of duty resulting from culpa in contrahendo, it will constructively be referred back to the breach of duty resulting from the duties of the pool members (be it from contract or company relations).

29 Cf. Fundamental Entscheidungen des Reichsgericht in Zivilsachen R 27, 118 (121); further see Entscheidungen des Bundesgerichtshof in Zivilsachen 13, 198 (200); *Ernst*, W., in: Münchener Kommentar zum Bürgerlichen Gesetzbuch, 6th ed. München 2012, § 280 recital 129; *Martinek, M.*, in: Staudinger-BGB, Berlin 2006, § 675 recital C 22 et seqq.

these duties apply as soon as sensitive information has been disclosed or first investments have been made in the Virtual Enterprise.[30]

## 2. Joint liability of the pool?

As the most difficult liability problem in this constellation the additional question arises whether the pool members are also to be included in the liability based on culpa in contrahendo, which originates within the Virtual Enterprise. Also in this case the affiliation of networks has legally relevant effects in modifying the general rules of trustee liability. Regularly, the rules according to which Virtual Enterprises are to be formed are mandatorily determined in the pool.[31] Often the pool also exerts specific influence on the planning of the project. If in this case duties are breached the rules of trustee liability based on culpa in contrahendo are to be applied in a way modified to the pool. The close connection between pool and Virtual Enterprise entails that the pool's power over the contract and its personal interests in the negotiations can be proved relatively quickly in the intended Virtual Enterprise. As a consequence, the breach of duty in formulating the rules of the game or otherwise exerting influence causes joint liability.[32]

## II. Liability for breach of contract

### 1. Liability of the members of the Virtual Enterprise

If the contract is breached during the stage of implementation in one-level Virtual Enterprises then again the question arises whether liability exists between the participants who are not bound by bilateral contract. Again, § 311 para. 3 BGB is relevant, which imposes contractual fiduciary duties

30 In detail on these duties *Weitzenboeck, E. M.,* A Legal Framework For Emerging Business Models, Oslo 2012, p. 103 seq.

31 *Weitzenboeck, E. M,* A Legal Framework For Emerging Business Models, Oslo 2012, p. 90, 294 et seqq.

32 Cf. *Benz, H.,* in: Forschungsinitiative Virtuelle Organisationen im Dienstleistungsbereich (ed.): Erfolgreich arbeiten mit virtuellen Kooperationen/Praxisbeispiele, Baden-Baden 2002, p. 29 (31).

as well as commitment to the network purpose.[33] In this case, some authors draw on the legal concept of the contract with protective effects for third parties ("Drittschutzvertrag"). [34] The construction is somewhat forced: a protective effect in favour of the other members not bound by contract would have to be attributed to every individual bilateral contract. There is a broad consensus that the contract with protective effects with respect to a third party cannot comprise the manifold reciprocations.[35] At best, merely the basic idea of the contract with protective effects for third parties may be drawn upon to support the joint liability resulting from the modified § 311 para. 3 BGB.

In multi-level virtual cooperation, however, fiduciary duties from non-connected ties are not only established due to their special relation ("Sonderverbindung"), but are additionally increased since the legal relationships resulting from the underlying pool effect the Virtual Enterprise.[36] As a result, the cooperation duties are intensified. In contrast to one-level Virtual Enterprises, where the network purpose merely requires to balance individual and collective purposes, the ties of the participants to the pool require the collective purposes to be the priority. This, however, only applies to the pool duties which also have their effects in the Virtual Enterprise, but not to the genuine duties resulting from the individual Virtual Enterprise. As specific, intensified fiduciary duties the following can be named: duty of co-operation, of information, of nondisclosure as well as the prohibition to compete. Moreover, the fiduciary duties may also substantiate the prohibition of free-riding, cheap-riding and crowding.[37]

---

33 *Weitzenboeck, E. M.*, A Legal Framework For Emerging Business Models, Oslo 2012, p. 327.

34 *Lange, K.W.*, Virtuelle Unternehmen, Heidelberg 2001, p. 188 et seq.; *idem*, Das Recht der Netzwerke, Frankfurt am Main 1998, p. 195 et seqq.; *Larenz, K./Wolf, M.*, Allgemeiner Teil des Bürgerlichen Rechts, München 1997, p. 470.

35 *Schmidt, K.* ,Handelsrecht, 5th ed. , Köln 1999, § 35 III., p. 1019; *Lange, K.W.*, Virtuelle Unternehmen, Heidelberg 2001, p. 200; *Rohe, M.,*, Netzverträge – Rechtsprobleme komplexer Vertragsverbindungen, Tübingen 1998, p. 104 et seqq.

36 *Krebs, P./Jung, S./Aedtner, K./Schultes, M.*, The modular system of network activities, in this volume, p. 75-117.

37 On these specific network problems see *Glückler, J./Hammer, I.*, in: Glückler, J./ Dehning, W./Janneck, M./Armbrüster, T. (eds.), Unternehmensnetzwerke, Heidelberg 2012, p. 139 (148 et seqq.).

## 2. Joint liability of the pool?

Concerning the breach of contract in Virtual Enterprises, the question regarding the joint liability of the pool arises. Do situations exist in which the pool has to be included in the liability of the Virtual Enterprise? In this case, the contract with protective effects for third parties is of little use, because then one would have to follow the daring construction that the fiduciary duties, which exist in the special relation between the pool and the Virtual Enterprise, are for their part equipped with protective effects for third parties. The liability resulting from § 311 para. 3 BGB discussed above also has to be consulted here. For further specifications the legal concept of trustee liability ("Sachwalterhaftung") is to be considered, namely in the modified way in which it was sketched out by the German Federal Court of Justice (BGH). Case law has expanded trustee liability beyond the stage of negotiating a contract to the stage of implementation. If independent companies appear not only as "negotiating parties", but also as "implementing parties" then trustee liability exists for them especially if they use trust for the implementation of the contract, exert a sort of power over the contract and economically pursue their own interest.[38] In this context, the pool is jointly liable in the case of fault based on the construct of trustee liability.

# III. Third party liability to clients of the Virtual Enterprise

Ultimately, it has to be examined how Virtual Enterprises are liable to external clients based on their contracts.

## 1. Liability of the members of the Virtual Enterprise

If the Virtual Enterprise breaches duties to the client during the stage of negotiation, then the member who is intended to conclude the contract with the client is primarily liable. The general rules of culpa in contrahendo apply. However, if a different member of the Virtual Enterprise is involved in the negotiations and breaches the negotiation duties then it is

38 Verification in *Teubner, G.*, Netzwerk als Vertragsverbund, Baden-Baden 2004, p. 235 recital 73-75.

again worth considering the personal liability according to the principles of trustee liability if the requirements are met.

During the stage of implementation the contractual partner from the Virtual Enterprise who concluded the contract with the client is again primarily liable. Other members are liable due to the contract with protective effects for third parties if one is willing to assign protective effects for third parties to the bilateral contracts between the members. This, however, entails certain problems for members not bound by contract since protective effects for third parties would have to be assigned to their special relation.

Or they are, similarly to trustees, liable, if they, as mentioned above, are "implementing parties" and have breached their contractual duties.

## 2. Joint liability of the pool?

This case poses the question whether the pool has to be included even in the third party liability to clients if a close connection exists between the pool and the Virtual Enterprise and the pool has had significant impact on the implementation of the contract. Here again, the principles of the trustee liability are to be applied if the pool has either functioned as "negotiating party" or as "implementing party" and has breached a duty.

As a result, the members of both the one-level and the multi-level Virtual Enterprise, but sometimes also the pool members are included in the liability to third parties. It has to be emphasised that they are not subject to the joint and several liability under company law, which makes all associates responsible for the damage regardless of their involvement, but that a liability restricted to individual persons will occur. Only those members who have a contractual duty to the clients based on the special relation ("Sonderverbindung") existing in the network and who have breached their duty should be jointly and severally liable. This means that in certain constellations even members of the pool who on their part have not become a member of the specific Virtual Enterprise are liable if they have breached an incumbent contractual duty.

As a result, this amounts to a special form of liability which stands between the joint and several liability of the partnerships (joint and several liability of all members) and the personal liability of the contract (liability of only one member). It only applies to those members who culpably have breached an incumbent contractual duty. Such a liability to third parties restricted to individual persons seems most appropriate for the degree of networking of Virtual Enterprises. Since no jointly owned assets emerge and no legal entity with own assets is formed such a joint liability restricted to the contract infringers is appropriate also in this comparison. The results can be regarded as a system running parallel to the tortuous producers' liability, which includes the participating members as "producers".[39] Furthermore, the sensitive gap of the missing tortuous liability of service providers would be closed and at the same time an adequate restriction of the liable group of persons ensured.

## D. Summary

Virtual Enterprises as a successful cooperative form of the future cannot be completely comprised under the scope of classic contract law and company law. For the network specific liability questions that arise in virtual cooperations a network adequate liability model was developed here, which is based on contract law, but includes in addition the special network effects which stem from the special relations ("Sonderverbindungen") in networks. The liability model moreover takes into account the so far neglected problem of the affiliation of networks. As a result, the participants in a Virtual Enterprise have increased internal as well as external duties. If the members of the Virtual Enterprise are recruited from a pool of companies then the duties are again intensified. The participant is liable if, and only if, he individually breaches the therefrom resulting duties.

---

39 Cf. *Wagner, G.*, in: Münchener Kommentar zum Bürgerlichen Gesetzbuch, 5th ed. München 2009, § 823 recital 592 et seqq.; *Hager, J.*, in: Staudinger-BGB, Berlin 2009, § 823 recital F 1 et seqq.

# Interface-liability. Tortious joint liability towards third parties of network-like cooperating companies, and at the same time a contribution to liability in cases of multi-causation

*Jun.-Prof. Dr. Maximilian Becker*

## A. Introduction

The cooperation of companies in the scope of a business network or a network-like connection is a form of organisation that allows carrying out larger projects together with several independent companies. Some examples of this are large construction contracts such as building an airport, subway or power plant. Likewise, the implementation of a business project or the long-term cooperation of several companies in their daily business also comes into consideration.

The legal order holds different company forms with a defined liability regime for the organised interaction of several. Within a network which is not organised in a legally regulated company form or whose individual members evade being assigned to company law despite their existent company form within the network,[1] the degree of organisation varies among the participating companies; it is often very low. This has several advantages for the participants. Besides saving transaction costs they also include, among others, a reduced risk of the individual's liability towards third parties. This risk reduction results from difficulties concerning the proof of evidence arising for the aggrieved party, which is according to the *general* civil law liability regime compelled to prove to potential indemnity debtors their specific share in the event that caused the damage. These difficulties typical for the liability of several parties are only partially met by law. In the following, matters are addressed that can be most likely assigned to the context of alternative causation[2], i.e. close to the situation

1 The question regarding company law is of subordinate significance since company law knows only few exceptional tortious regulations (e.g. the characteristic § 31 BGB is typically enough applied by analogy).

2 On this *Brüggemeier, G.*, Prinzipien des Haftungsrechts, Baden-Baden 1999, p. 158 et seq.

described in § 830 para. 1 s. 2 BGB in which the party responsible for the damage cannot be determined among several participants. However, the cases dealt with here cannot simply be assigned to the constellations considered in § 830 BGB. Therefore, a law developing solution is to be suggested.

## B. Problem

The following constellation serves as introductory example: a group of companies is employed. The companies belong to a larger compound of numerous participants, who merge in modules depending on to the needs.[3]. The affiliation in said project may occur under a purchaser who himself is a general contractor for the client for whom the building is built.

Especially at the interfaces of different tasks the interaction of the individual participants poses the risk of coordination weaknesses. Specifically, this may include e.g. the faulty coordination of jobs on a construction site. The liability thereby is at best only contractually limited to the contractor. Regarding tortuous liability towards third parties, the individual participants are also liable in addition to the general contractor. As far as the necessary requirement to observe instructions is provided in the individual case then § 831 BGB is effective. This, however, does not impede the parallel liability of the participants, principal included.[4] § 831 BGB shows, amongst others, a liability deficit for the aggrieved party if the general contractor is insolvent. Since the damages caused by business networks occasionally amount to some hundreds of millions of Euros a special need for a broad basis of liability exists here.[5]

Cases of multi-causation and liability of several in the broadest sense are under consideration. It is indeed questionable as well as the object of the following whether the law of torts in this respect provides adequate liability towards third parties for network constellations and if this is not the case whether an adequate liability towards third parties is justified as well as how it should be shaped *de lege lata.*

3 Cf. *Krebs, P./Jung, S./Aedtner, K./Schultes, M.*, The modular system of network activities, p. 75 et seqq., in this volume.

4 *Sprau, H.*, in: Palandt, 73. ed., München 2014, § 831 recital 2.

5 The damage may also be smaller and the general contractor may become insolvent rather coincidentally, i.e. irrespective of the occurrence of the damage.

## C. On the nature of the network's tortious liability towards third parties

The liability towards third parties of the business network and network-like connections is best characterized as *interface-liability*. The uncoordinated interaction of several without the necessary degree of organisation is causal for the damage of third parties: damages occur at the interfaces of different tasks, whose responsibilities are not sufficiently clarified or inadequately communicated, whose work and risk precautions are not sufficiently coordinated and/or not uniformly checked for breaches so that considerable monitoring gaps may occur. The *causal* problem lies in the excess complexity of the network-like cooperation and in that it is hardly transparent from the outside. This causes a lack of evidence on the part of the aggrieved party, which is faced with the privilege of the individual tortfeasor as long as the legal principle of tort liability is adhered to, namely that the aggrieved party bears the burden of proof for the tortious damage caused by every individual.

Before this problem can be dealt with, the constellations of multi-causation have to be examined for which the German legal order holds statutory and partially also case law rules governing liability.

## D. Relevant liability substantiation in cases of multi-causation

### I. On the separation of causation and the form of liability

Cases of multi-causation are characterised by complex matters. Accordingly, different forms of causation have to be isolated first which give reason for increased liability towards the aggrieved party in different ways (cf. below D. II. Forms of causation). Even though liability is closely linked to the forms of causation, the differentiation between causation and liability nevertheless has to be considered since the former is merely one determinant of the eventually applicable form of liability. This, for instance, is shown in § 830 para. 1 s. 1 BGB, which defines joint and several liability not due to the specific problem of causation, but above all due to the mutual will to act. The forms of causation at first only describe the causal relation of the different contributions. Accordingly, it is neither about causation nor about the attribution of liability or even liability substantiation. Nonetheless, typical pairings of causation and liability exist. For instance, pure doubts about the originator ("Urheberzweifel") in cases of alternative perpetration regulated in § 830 para. 1 s. 2 BGB presuppose competing,[6] or at least alternative causations. Valuations that are tied to life problems and interests which are connected to diverse causalities link causation to liability and especially to liability facilitation.

The presentation of the various bases of liability and liability facilitation with multi-causation in the scope of interface-liability is not only required to determine liability gaps, but also because the forms of liability described may be relevant in their original area of application.

## II. Forms of causation

Regarding the forms of causation it has to be taken into consideration that only those variants requiring explanation are mentioned here. Further constellations of multi-causation exist. They may not only occur separately, but also in combination (e.g. competing partial causation).

### 1. Complete causation / partial causation

The distinction between complete causation and partial causation is central. The *suitability* of an action to be completely or merely partially causal for the damage caused is decisive for liability and for possible facilitations regarding the proof of causation. Suitability always matters if it cannot be proven whose contribution eventually (partially) caused the damage.

### 2. Alternative and, if applicable, competing causation

*Alternative causation* is particularly known under the name of alternative perpetration.[7] Causation and the basis for liability are mixed here. Alternative perpetration presupposes alternative causation: the members of the

---

6 When taking a closer look, this ideal constellation applies rather infrequently. At least the first damage does often not exclude a second damage to the legal good. The cases of truly competing causality are narrower than the scope of application of the doubts about the originator ("Urheberzweifel") in line with § 830 para. 1 s. 2 BGB.

7 Cf. e.g. *Deutsch, E.*, Neue Juristische Wochenschrift 1981, 2731, 2732 et seq.; *Fuchs, M./Pauker, W.*, Deliktsrecht, 8. Ed., Heidelberg 2012, p. 237 et seq.; *Brüg-*

circle of perpetrators each have to take responsibility for an action which may be causal for the overall damage. In its purest form alternative causation means that only one of several actions suitable for complete causation was causal for the overall damage. [8] Liability for alternative perpetration in § 830 para. 1 s. 2 BGB, however, also includes cases of doubts about the share ("Anteilszweifel") (c.f. below D. III. 3.) where several activities suitable for complete causation have proportionately led to the overall damage.

*Competing causation* is more narrowly conceptualised: the realization of the causation lying in the first action excludes the realization of the similarly widely defined causation of the second action.[9]

**Example:** Two companies discharge the waste water accrued from petroleum drills into a river, which leads to the destruction of grassland situated downstream. Since the waste water discharged by both companies was sufficient to cause the overall damage, they cannot rely on the fact "daß auch noch von anderen dortigen Petroleumbohrgesellschaften derartige Abfallwässer gleichzeitig [sic!] in den Fluss eingeleitet werden"[10] ("that also other companies drilling for petroleum discharge such waste water into the river at the same time"). The grassland can only be destroyed once. Even more plausible are cases at different times: if a drunk driver runs over and kills a dog then a second drunk driver who also runs over the dog, may indeed act unlawfully, but he does not cause any damage, which is why only the first driver is liable to the dog's owner.

### 3. Cumulative (=complementary) causation

Cumulative causation is "dadurch gekennzeichnet, daß es erst durch das Zusammenwirken zweier oder mehrerer, gleichartiger oder ungleichartiger Gefährdungsbeiträge, die jeder für sich allein haftungsrechtlich irrelevant geblieben wären, zu dem haftungsbegründenden Erfolg der Interessenverletzung kommt" ("charcterised by the fact that only the interaction of two

---

*gemeier, G.*, Haftungsrecht – Struktur, Prinzipien, Schutzbereich, Heidelberg 2006, p. 188 et seq.

8 *Brüggemeier, G.*, Haftungsrecht – Struktur, Prinzipien, Schutzbereich, Heidelberg 2006, p. 186.

9 *Brüggemeier, G.*, Prinzipien des Haftungsrechts, Baden-Baden 1999, p. 157.

10 RGZ 16, 144 – Wasserinterdikte.

or several similar or disparate risk contributions, which each for themselves would have remained irrelevant for liability, leads to the infringement of the interests, which is the basis of liability"). Only the contributions together meet the prerequisites for a basis of liability, it is neither "Einzel- noch Mehrtäterschaft, sondern gewissermaßen *Gesamttäterschaft*"[11] ("individual nor several perpetration, but in a way *overall perpetration*").

**Example:** Firm A fails to set up the lift for roofing work in an orderly way; firm B wrongly adjusts the brake linkage; both mistakes together lead to an accident. [12] The so called "children's tea cases" are also prominent in which children's tea containing sugar caused caries in children only in connection with the plastic drinking bottles also sold by the defendant. Separately, no damage would have been caused.[13] In a different case, the German railroad company provided wagons with lead residues for transportation, in which animal food was transported without further examination by the sender (a sugar factory). This caused the death of several cows due to lead poisoning.[14]

### 4. Additive causation

Additive causation is characterised by the fact that several contributions are added to a single, unified, indivisible overall damage. In contrast to cumulative causation each individual contribution itself already causes damage. By adding the contributions, however, an indivisible overall damage is formed.

**Example:** A is injured by B through a blow to the head. Shortly after, C knocks A over in a grossly negligent way. Due to the previous injury the

---

11 *Brüggemeier, G.*, Prinzipien des Haftungsrechts, Baden-Baden 1999, p. 156.

12 Cf. Oberlandesgericht München VersR 1984, 342; *Lange, H./Schiemann, G.*, Handbuch des Schuldrechts - Schadensersatz, 3rd ed., Tübingen 2003, p. 158; *Brüggemeier, G.*, Prinzipien des Haftungsrechts, Baden-Baden 1999, p. 156.

13 Cf. Entscheidungen des Bundesgerichtshof in Zivilsachen 116, 60 = Neue Juristische Wochenschrift 1992, 560 – Kindertee I; BGH, Neue Juristische Wochenschrift 1994, 932 – Kindertee II; BGH, Neue Juristische Wochenschrift 1995, 1286 – Kindertee III; *Brüggemeier, G.*, Haftungsrecht – Struktur, Prinzipien, Schutzbereich, Heidelberg 2006, p. 186.

14 Entscheidungen des Bundesgerichtshof in Zivilsachen 17, 214 = Neue Juristische Wochenschrift 1955, 1314.

fall causes the death of A. The unlawful action of B and C each causes individual damage; by adding the injuries, however, an even greater indivisible overall damage is caused.

## III. Delinquent attribution of liability

### 1. Complicity, § 830 para. 1 s. 1, para. 2 BGB

§ 830 para. 1 s. 1 BGB bridges *causation gaps* in cases of complicity. Prerequisite is (according to § 25 para. 2 StGB) a jointly committed action. Following criminal law, jointly *committing* an action presupposes a corresponding joint influence.[15] Therefore, § 830 para. 1 s. 1 BGB is limited to intentional offences. It sanctions the intentional joint committing of an action by expanding the circle of those liable also to those who have not necessarily contributed to the damage in a direct way, but who have participated in the action under direct intent or conditional intent. The causation of the individual contribution to the damage is not required;[16] the common will takes its place and justifies attributing the effect of the infringement to all accomplices.[17] The will of the participant directed towards the action compensates "(unwiderlegbar) etwaige Unsicherheiten oder Lücken der Kausalität"[18] ("(irrefutable) for possible insecurities or gaps of the causation"). The "tatsächliche Zusammenwirken fahrlässigen Handelns" ("actual interaction of negligent actions") does not meet the requirements of § 830 para. 1 s. 1 BGB.[19]

**Example:** Eight demonstrators separate from the demonstration in order to demolish a police car. Three of those involved kick the car while the others are standing aside and encouraging them.

---

15 Cf. *Steffen, E.*, in: Reichsgerichtsräte-Kommentar, 12. ed., Berlin 1989, § 830, recital 4.

16 BGH, Neue Juristische Wochenschrift 1982, 40, 41 et seq.

17 BGH, Neue Juritische Wochenschrift 1982, 40, 41 et seq.; *Eberl-Borges, C.*, in: Staudinger, Berlin 2012, § 830, recital 13 et seq., cf. also the criticism in recital 21 et seq.

18 *Steffen, E.*, in: Reichsgerichtsräte-Kommentar, 12. ed. Berlin 1989, § 830, recital 1.

19 *Steffen, E.*, in: Reichsgerichtsräte-Kommentar, 12. ed. Berlin 1989, § 830, recital 4.

For business networks § 830 para. 1 s. 1 BGB is not suitable; the participants are indeed more or less connected by a joint project, but the participants are not linked by a "auf Rechtsverletzung gerichtete[s] Wollen"[20] ("will directed at the violation of the law").

## 2. Negligent independent perpetration

In the next step, cases of *negligent independent perpetration*[21] have to be taken into consideration. Independent perpetration occurs if several persons commit illegal actions regardless of each other, whose success however is realised in a *uniform damage*. Accordingly, *Brüggemeier* speaks of "Einheitsschadenverursachung durch mehrere"[22] ("uniform damage caused by several"). In contrast to complicity and participation the perpetrators come from different sides or are active one after the other and none of the actions of the independent perpetrators has to be causal for the overall damage; it suffices if all participants have partially contributed to the success. It is, however, necessary that all of the contributions are indispensable so that otherwise the damage would not have occurred. Accordingly, the causation of the actions that caused the damage has to be certain.[23] The decisive difference to single perpetration and the partial cause of damage lies in the fact that the independent perpetrators are linked by the uniformity of the damage caused by them. [24] It is thereby not about suitability for partial or complete damage causation, but about whether the contribution of the individual can be omitted without changing the overall damage. Theoretically, however, cases of uniform damages suitable for complete damage causation should be contained in § 830 para. 1 s. 2 BGB, which under these circumstances includes not only doubts about the originator, but also about the share (c.f. below III. 3. c.).

If several partial contributions complement each other and thus result in a uniform, i.e. indivisible overall damage, then particularly additive as

---

20 Cf. *Steffen, E.*, in: Reichsgerichtsräte-Kommentar, 12. ed. Berlin 1989, § 830, recital 5.

21 Cf. e.g. *Wagner, G.*, in: Münchener Kommentar zum Bürgerliches Gesetzbuch, 6. ed., München 2013, § 840 recital 2 et seq.; *Krause, R.*, in: Soergel, BGB, 12. ed. Stuttgart 2005, § 840, recital 8 et seq.

22 *Brüggemeier, G.*, Prinzipien des Haftungsrechts, Baden-Baden 1999, 164.

23 *Eberl-Borges, C.*, in: Staudinger, Berlin 2012, § 830, recital 67.

24 Cf. *Larenz, K./Canaris, C.*, Schuldrecht II/2, 13. ed. München 1994, p. 580 et seq.

well as cumulative causalities come into question.[25] In cases of suitability for complete causation the separately discussed alternative perpetration applies, as already mentioned, which includes cases of alternative and competing causation.

Independent perpetration applies secondarily to complicity and participation,[26] which both presuppose a certain kind of connection among the perpetrators. Independent perpetrators, in contrast, are according to § 840 BGB directly jointly and severally liable whereby § 840 BGB must not be understood as the underlying basis for the claims (this results from §§ 823 et seq. BGB for each individual action); the provision merely regulates the "how" of the liability, not the "if".[27]

**Example:** The cases mentioned above regarding children's tea and railroad wagons are at the same time cases of negligent independent perpetration.

This constellation only rarely applies to business networks. – Damages caused by coordination difficulties at interfaces in business networks can be traced back to missing or faulty arrangements of the participants. Accordingly, the damage is not caused by separate individual actions, but by specific, yet faultily organised interaction.

### 3. Alternative perpetration, § 830 para. 1 s. 2 BGB

§ 830 para. 1 s. 2 BGB covers a special case of negligent independent perpetration, for which it reduces the required standard of proof to the mere suitability for causation of the action in question. [28] § 840 para. 1 BGB, in contrast, presupposes that the various contributions of the individual perpetrators to the damage are already proven and the perpetrators are therefore already "responsible side by side". It regulates the "how" of the otherwise fixed liability in favour of a joint and several obligation. If a specific

25 *Deutsch, E.*, Allgemeines Haftungsrecht, 2nd ed., Köln 1996, recital 502.

26 *Deutsch, E.*, Allgemeines Haftungsrecht, 2nd ed., Köln 1996, recital 502 fn. 20.

27 Cf. *Wagner, G.*, in: Münchener Kommentar zum Bürgerliches Gesetzbuch, 6. ed., München 2013, § 840 recital 2 et seq.

28 *Wagner, G.*, in: Münchener Kommentar zum Bürgerliches Gesetzbuch, 6. ed., München 2013, § 830 recital 55.

share in the damage can be assigned to individual perpetrators then the extent of the joint and several liability decreases accordingly.[29]

§ 830 para. 1 s. 2 BGB therefore goes one step further in that it releases the aggrieved party of the proof of causation – the responsibility required for § 840 para. 1 BGB is refutably presumed ("ist (...) für den Schaden verantwortlich") ("is responsible for the damage"). The requirements are accordingly demanding: § 830 para. 1 s. 2 BGB applies if several persons *each* have committed a tortious offence and the action *of every individual* was suitable to cause the entire damage that occurred[30] – only cases of "multipler Gefährdung und unaufklärbarer Einzeltäterschaft"[31] ("multiple hazards and unsolvable individual perpetration") are regulated, i.e. cases of alternative and competing causation. It deals with categorising the "Risikos der Nichtfeststellbarkeit des Schadensverursachers"[32] ("risk of the perpetrator of the damage being undiscernible").

The aggrieved party is merely released from proving *whose* actions eventually caused the damage.[33] The circle of participants defines the persons who come into consideration as perpetrators.[34] So as to differentiate this circle the jurisdiction requires that "der sich aus mehreren selbständigen unerlaubten Handlungen zusammensetzt und in dessen Bereich der rechtswidrige schädigende Erfolg fällt"[35] ("it consists of several independent, illegal actions and that the illegal and damaging success falls within its scope"). The aggrieved party indeed has to prove that each individual acted illegally. Likewise, it has to prove that the actual perpetrator is among the accused participants. Lastly, none of the participants must succeed in proving that their action was not causal for the damage. Accordingly, it is necessary for the alternative perpetration that the action comes into consideration in a complete causal way.

---

29 Cf. *Wagner, G.*, in: Münchener Kommentar zum Bürgerliches Gesetzbuch, 6. ed., München 2013, § 840 recital 13.

30 *Steffen, E.*, in: Reichsgerichtsräte-Kommentar, 12. ed., Berlin 1989, § 830, recital 16, 23.

31 *Brüggemeier, G.*, Prinzipien des Haftungsrechts, Baden-Baden 1999, p. 158.

32 *Weckerle, T.*, Die deliktische Verantwortung mehrerer, Karlsruhe 1974, p. 121.

33 *Steffen, E.*, in: Reichsgerichtsräte-Kommentar, 12. ed., Berlin 1989, § 830, recital 17.

34 *Brüggemeier, G.*, Prinzipien des Haftungsrechts, Baden-Baden 1999, p. 159.

35 BGH Neue Juristische Wochenschrift 1957, 1834 (1835) = Entscheidungen des Bundesgerichtshofs in Zivilsachen 25, 271; see also Entscheidungen des Reichsgerichts in Zivilsachen 58, 357, 361.

**Example:** Three construction workers each negligently drop a tile from the roof. One of the three tiles injures a passer-by. [36]

The relevant problem regarding the interface-liability lies, if at all, in the scope of the application of § 830 para. 1 s. 2 BGB. However, it may often be difficult, if not impossible to prove that the contribution of each individual can be *causal for the overall damage* especially since the uncertainty regarding network-like actions often concerns the question of who has provided which contribution.[37] Besides the doubts about the originator, if it is certain that one of the perpetrators has caused the overall damage alone, § 830 para. 1 s. 2 BGB according to the leading opinion also includes doubts about their share.[38] These exist, if the circle of perpetrators who have caused the damage is known, but it cannot be clarified whether only one perpetrator or several have jointly caused the damage.[39] Also in this case, the prerequisite is that the action of each individual can be causal for the overall damage.[40] The constellation of the individual contribution that can be causal for the damage only in interaction with the others, i.e. especially not alone, is not included.

So as to fathom why § 830 para. 1 s. 2 BGB does not include these cases and whether this may result in a barrier effect for law developing liability or if such an effect could – reversely – be based on an analogy to § 830 para. 1 BGB, the purpose of § 830 para. 1 s. 2 BGB has to be taken into consideration. § 830 para. 1 s. 2 BGB ultimately ascribes the "Lasten einer Beweisnotgemeinschaft jedem der an ihr Beteiligten" ("burden of a community of lack of evidence to each of the participants"), because it "gerechter erscheint, daß die für sie Verantwortlichen die

36 According to *Wagner, G.*, in: Münchener Kommentar zum Bürgerliches Gesetzbuch, 6. ed., München 2013, § 830 recital 13.

37 In a similar way on environmental damages caused by emissions of several facilities, *Hager, G.*, Neue Juristische Wochenschrift 1991, 134, 139 et seq.

38 BGH Neue Juristische Wochenschrift 1976, 1934, 1935 = Entscheidungen des Bundesgerichtshof in Zivilsachen 67, 14; BGH Neue Juristische Wochenschrift 1994, 932, 934; *Fuchs, M./Pauker, W.*, Deliktsrecht, 8. ed., Heidelberg 2012, p. 237; *Steffen, E.*, in: Reichsgerichtsräte-Kommentar, 12. ed. Berlin 1989, § 830, recital 23.

39 *Eberl-Borges, C.*, in: Staudinger, Berlin 2012, § 830 recital 70.

40 BGH Neue Juritische Wochenschrift 1976, 1934, 1935 = Entscheidungen des Bundesgerichtshof in Zivilsachen 67, 14; BGH Neue Juristische Wochenschrift 1994, 932, 934; *Fuchs, M./Pauker, W.*, Deliktsrecht, 8. ed. Heidelberg 2012, p. 237; *Steffen E.*, in: RGRK, 12. ed., Berlin 1989, § 830, recital 23.

Kausalitätszweifel nicht mit dem Geschädigten, sondern untereinander ausmachen"[41] ("seems fairer that those responsible clarify the doubts about causation not with the aggrieved party, but amongst themselves"). In this way, the purpose still matches the interface-liability. However, why does it not suffice when the contribution *by itself cannot be causal* for the overall damage?

*Deutsch* holds that the attribution cannot only depend on the lack of evidence of the aggrieved party, but that there has to be a connection to the person of the several liable; it may be aimed at whether "der Haftpflichtige weiß oder damit rechnen muß, daß sich ein Dritter im Schädigungsbereich befindet"[42] ("the party liable knows or has to expect that there is a third party in the damaged area"). "Der Alternativtäter muß das parallele Verhalten des anderen erkennen können; andernfalls kann ihm dessen interferierende Kausalität nicht zugerechnet werden." [43] ("The alternative perpetrator has to be able to recognise the parallel behaviour of the other party; otherwise his interfering causation cannot be attributed to him.") Accordingly, it would be decisive that the members of the community of lack of evidence ("Beweisnotgemeinschaft") were able to know that they run the risk of establishing a community of lack of evidence with parallel acting parties. Thereby, the lack of evidence on the side of the aggrieved party is initially an advantage for the liable party, which is turned into a disadvantage by the legal order in § 830 para. 1 s. 2 BGB. Merely the *burden of information*[44] (burden of proof) is redirected, namely by the *assumption* (not the distribution!) of *causation* of the actions *of the specific defendant party*.[45] It is not about attributing someone's action to another, but about "Umkehrung der Beweislast hinsichtlich der Kausalität"[46] ("inversing the burden of proof regarding the causation"). The regulation only wants to alleviate the lack of evidence on the side of the aggrieved party, which was caused by the complexity of the situation.[47] This is the dogmatic reason

41 *Steffen, E.*, in: Reichsgerichtsräte-Kommentar, 12. ed., Berlin 1989, § 830, recital 14.

42 *Deutsch, E.*, Juristen Zeitung 1972, 105, 106.

43 *Deutsch, E.*, Allgemeines Haftungsrecht, 2nd ed., Köln 1995, recital 519.

44 Cf. *Steffen, E.*, in: Reichsgerichtsräte-Kommentar, 12. ed., Berlin 1989, § 830, recital 14.

45 *Larenz, K./Canaris, C.*, Schuldrecht II/2, 13. ed., München 1994, p. 572.

46 *Larenz, K./Canaris, C.*, Schuldrecht II/2, 13. ed., München 1994, p. 571.

47 Cf. also *Wagner, G.*, in Münchener Kommentar zum Bürgerlichen Gesetzbuch, 6. ed., München 2013, § 830, recital 37.

for limiting the circle of persons capable of being sued to actions which are suitable to cause the *overall* damage. In this way, it remains open to the defendant party to prove exoneration. If a participant can prove that his actions could have only become causal for a part of the damage and not for the overall damage, then he is only severally liable for this part[48] – his action lacks the "specific suitability for damage" ("konkrete Schadenseignung"[49]) regarding the overall damage. Besides this somewhat dogmatic reason there is also a further reason for the limitation: § 830 para. 1 s. 2 BGB applies to *every* illegal action. The scope of application includes the entire range of the general civil law of torts and can already lead to hardships in individual cases here. A general joint and several liability for mere contributions would reach too far. Accordingly, § 830 para. 1 s. 2 BGB is limited to potential single perpetrators.

Methodically, this all leads to a barrier effect for general (refutable) several liability for partial causation. It is, however, not barred for narrower cases.

### 4. Causing partial damage

Causing partial damage is not a case of independent perpetration (c.f. D. III. 2.). There is no uniform damage here: several contribute their own share each, which lead to separate damages respectively, but are *not* added to an overall damage that is greater than the individual parts.[50] If the individual actions can thus no longer be considered as suitable for complete causation by definition, § 830 para. s. 2 BGB is eliminated. Likewise, a unique damage required for individual perpetration liability does not exist; therefore, the damage is to be distributed according to § 287 ZPO.[51]

**Example:** A, B and C use an unlocked back door and plunder a warehouse one after the other and independently of each other.[52]

---

48 Cf. on the principle *Wagner, G.*, in: Münchener Kommentar zum Bürgerlichen Gesetzbuch, 6. ed., München 2013, § 830, recital 58.

49 On this *Larenz,K./Canaris, C.*, Schachenrecht II/2, 13. ed., München 1994, p. 578.

50 *Brüggemeier, G.*, Prinzipien des Haftungsrechts, Baden-Baden 1999, p. 163 et seq.

51 *Eberl-Borges, C.*, in: Staudinger, Berlin 2012, § 830 recital 71; see also *Wagner, G.*, in: Münchener Kommentar zum Bürgerlichen Gesetzbuch, 6. ed., München 2013, § 830 recital 36.

52 According to *Eberl-Borges, C.*, in: Staudinger, Berlin 2012, § 830 recital 71.

In general, everyone is liable for the damage they have caused. The difficulties of proof resulting from this have to be accepted by the aggrieved party. Facilitation is only available in exceptional cases, in German law it is limited to the joint and several liability intended in § 89 WHG (c.f. III. 3. e. § 89 WHG, § 6 UmweltHG).[53]

### 5. § 89 WHG, § 6 UmweltHG

Other constellations are again included in § 89 WHG (§ 22 WHG old version.), which is developed as strict liability and which due to its low interference barriers takes into consideration several cases at the same time, partially also cases included in regulations already mentioned above:[54] § 89 para. 1 s. 2 WHG lays down joint and several liability for water pollution irrespective of negligence if the interaction of the individual contribution "allein oder im Zusammenwirken mit den übrigen Handlungen geeignet ist, den eingetretenen Schaden herbeizuführen"[55] ("is suited on its own or in interaction with the other actions to cause the damage that occurred"). The "suitability for co-responsibility" ("Eignung zur Mitursächlichkeit") suffices.[56] By way of a teleological reduction the BGH in this case, however, spares *small emitters*. [57] This nonetheless very strict regulation is justified due to its narrow scope of application and the purpose of water conservation which is predominantly important to the legal community (c.f. § 1 WHG).

---

53 *Brüggemeier, G.* (Prinzipien des Haftungsrechts, Baden-Baden 1999, p. 163 et seq.) moreover refers to the application of § 830 para. 1 s. 2 BGB to the doubts about the shares ("Anteilszweifel"). Prerequisite for this, however, is the share's suitability for complete causality, as mentioned above, which significantly limits the scope of application.

54 Accordingly, parallel applicability exists, *Petersen, N.*, in: Landmann, R./Rohmer, G., Umweltrecht, 71. supplement. München 2014, § 89, recital 10.

55 *Petersen N.*, in: Landmann, R./Rohmer, G., Umweltrecht, 71. supplement München 2014, § 89 WHG, recital 58; Beck'scher Online-Kommentar Umweltrecht / *Hilf, J.* (Ed. 26, 2013), § 89 WHG, recital 44.

56 *Petersen, N.*, in: Landmann, R./Rohmer, G., Umweltrecht, 71. supplement 2014, § 89 WHG, recital 79; BGH Neue Juristische Wochenschrift 1972, 205, 208 = Entscheidungen des Bundesgerichtshof in Zivilsachen 57, 257.

57 BGH Neue Juristische Wochenschrift 1972, 205, 208 = Entscheidungen des Bundesgerichtshof in Zivilsachen 57, 257; *Brüggemeier, G.* , Prinzipien des Haftungsrechts, Baden-Baden 1999, p. 165.

With regard to the liability for environmental damage the situation is similar. § 6 UmweltHG lays down the facilitation of the burden of proof for doubts about the originator as well as doubts about the share ("Urheber- und Anteilszweifel") by linking the presumption of a causal connection to the suitability to cause damage regarding the facilities listed in annex 1 of the law, provided that the facilities are run improperly (cf. § 6 para. 2 UmweltHG).[58] The aggrieved party merely has to prove a certain probability of causing the damage ("Verursachungswahrscheinlichkeit"). Therefore, the illustration of the facility's causal effect is firstly required, whereby it is questionable whether the proof of the release of pollutants has to be fully provided. Subsequently, the aggrieved party has to prove the suitability of the environmental impact for causing its damage by demonstrating that it was exposed to the emissions in question and that a relation of cause and effect exists between the pollutant and the violation of legally protected interests. [59] Besides cases of suitability for complete causation the presumption of causation of § 6 UmweltHG shall also apply if merely a partial responsibility can be suspected and the damage cannot be estimated according to § 287 ZPO.[60]

## IV. Provisional results

The constellations presented may indeed become relevant for the liability towards third parties of business networks. The interface-liability, which is the focus here, is, however, not included:

§ 830 para. 1 s. 1 BGB appears unsuitable for cases of networks; usually a complicity in intentional offences does not exist, but a negligent independent perpetration. Whereas § 840 para. 1 BGB in other cases links negligent independent perpetration (additive and cumulative causation) of certain perpetrators to joint liability, § 830 para. 1 s. 2 BGB bridges causation doubts – also persons are liable who have acted illegally and in a way suitable for complete causation, even though their actions have not materi-

---

58 *Hager, G.*, in: Landmann, R./Rohmer, G., Umweltrecht, 71. supplement München 2014, § 6 UmweltHG, recital 3.

59 *Hager, G.*, in: Landmann ,R./Rohmer, G., Umweltrecht, 71. supplement München 2014, § 6 UmweltHG, recital 16 et seq.

60 *Hager, G.*, in: Landmann, R./Rohmer, G., Umweltrecht, 71. supplement München 2014, § 6 UmweltHG, recital 35 et seq.

alised in the damage. § 830 para. 1 s. 2 BGB, which regulates an exceptional case of negligent independent perpetration, is so clear and strict, because it renders the proof of causation unnecessary. The transfer lies in the fact that not only doubts about the share in the damage, but also doubts about causation are bridged and conferred to the internal relations. Accordingly, the prerequisites for the liability of the *potential perpetrator* according to § 830 para. 1 s. 2 BGB are therefore very high: the aggrieved party has to prove that a) all accused have committed a tortious offence and b) that their actions were each suitable for complete causation.

Bridging doubts about causation is of particular interest to network liability. The aggrieved party only knows that the accused have cooperated in a network-like way and that this caused the damage. Neither can it prove the contributions to the damage and therewith the responsibility required for § 840 para. 1 BGB nor can it demonstrate that all or individual participants have committed a tortious offence which is suitable for complete causation (so that § 830 para. 1 s. 2 BGB would spare it the proof of causation).

## E. Coordination weaknesses as reason for joint and several tortious liability towards third parties in the network

The evaluative question now is whether it is justified to privilege the aggrieved parties with liability facilitation at the suspense of the network participants. The aspects that may suggest this and how far this privilege should go will be illustrated in the following.

### I. Desired legal consequences and hoped for actual consequences

The purpose of the considered liability facilitation does not lie in changing the legal consequences, but (as always in law) in the therewith created actual consequences.[61] The desired legal consequences and the hoped for actual consequences can be sketched out as follows:

---

61 Cf. *Lübbe-Wolff, G.*, Rechtsfolgen und Realfolgen: Welche Rolle können Folgenerwägungen in der juristischen Regel- und Begriffsbildung spielen?, Freiburg 1981.

Legally, the aggrieved party shall only be subject to the burden of proof regarding the *participation* of the accused in the damage; it has to prove that the network member in question participated in the planning or the implementation of the task in question. It does not have to prove that and which transaction duty the network member has breached, that the actions were causal for the damage and to what extent the member was involved in causing the damage. The accused is free to refute these presumptions. The members liable to pay compensation eventually have to prosecute each other internally. This situation occurs if (this may most of the time be the case) the members lack consensus or if one member has paid the aggrieved party and now raises claims against the others.

The hoped for actual consequences of liability facilitation include the significantly improved control and documentation of processes, organisation, supervision and task distribution, especially the determination of intermediate steps which help locate possible defects or menacing risks and, in particular, a heightened awareness of the individual network members to fulfil the organisational tasks under the responsibility of the network. The lack of coordination of the interfaces shall be remedied by the preventive effect of liability.

## II. Overview of the considered liability

A first prerequisite for tortious liability is the here unproblematic existing damage to a legal good protected in tort. Since the demanding requirements of § 826 BGB for the subjective circumstances are only rarely met and are untypical for the underlying problem at hand the focus shall lie on the use of § 823 para. 1 BGB (which does not exclude the infringement of proprietary rights according to § 823 para. 2 BGB). Especially the infringement of property, life, body and health come into question.

The required infringing activity is more problematic. In the "usual" cases of multi-causation the insolvability of the consequences of a *known action* is at issue such as e.g. the discharge of waste water into a river. Likewise, the *breach of transaction duties* is also relevant e.g. when the cleaning of the contaminated railway wagons is neglected before handing them over to be used. The accusation against the network companies here concerns the excess complexity created by the network-like cooperation, which leads to a third party damage due to the lack of adequate coordination. Accordingly, there would have to be a *legal obligation to coordinate* whose breach leads to the attribution of the infringement of legal goods. Dogmatically, it is about network-specific tortious transaction duties. In particular, *organisation duties* are to be discussed regarding the coordinated interaction in the network. Since the aggrieved party only rarely has insight into the internal affairs of the business network the reversal of the burden of proof in favour of the aggrieved party is appropriate.

The actual focus here, however, is the question whether and if so how the facilitation of the causation proof may be justified. Even if the organisational duty was breached causing damage, the aggrieved party – and sometimes also the network members – often cannot prove which actions were causal for the damage. If someone suffers damage caused by an accident on a neighbouring construction site he may indeed be able to determine the circle of participants, but he cannot reconstruct the exact occurrence of the damage. The above illustration has shown that waiving the proof of causation regarding the liability of several is, however, the absolute exception and its justification is furthermore controversial as well as presupposes suitability for complete causation. After all, also those will risk joint and several liability whose action has indeed remained without consequences. Therefore, a precise consideration is required whether such a strict liability is adequate considering the interests and the sums occasionally in question when it comes to damages caused by business networks.

## III. Arguments for a stricter liability of the network towards third parties

The measures considered here (network-specific transaction duties, reversal of the burden of proof, facilitated proof of causation) amount to a significantly stricter liability for business networks. Some evaluative aspects may be combined since they are crucial to several aspects of the stricter liability in question. In principal, two arguments speak for a stricter liability of networks towards third parties.

The first argument is of a general nature and is based on the fundamental principles of the law of damage: in the way that the tortfeasor has to compensate for the damage caused by him in a culpable and illegal way it may be just and equitable to impose the compensation for the problems of proof on the perpetrator. It may, however, be objected that it infringes the system if the party causing the problems of proof is supposed to compensate for the damage which he has definitely not caused. The legal order only mandates such a waiver of causation in especially serious constellations, particularly in § 830 para. 1 s. 1 BGB. This objection, however, does not hurt the core argument; the compensation for problems of proof can be also carried out in a milder way.

As alternative to this tortious principle the *polluter pays principle* (to be found e.g. in § 122 para. 1 BGB) may also be used: in as much as the mistaken party is entitled to avoid its declaration regardless of any fault (§§ 119 et seq. BGB), but then bears "die Gefahr seines eigenen Verhaltens"[62] ("the risk of its own behaviour") – also irrespective of its own fault or the fault of the opposite side[63] – the freedom to interact uncoordinatedly as a network may be linked to a corresponding liability irrespective of the fault for thereby occurring problems of proof of possible perpetrators. This can be met – similarly as in § 830 para. 1 BGB – with an expanded circle of persons liable.

Probably more significant for the network-specific context is the second argument, which is close to the idea of the *guarantor's liability*: if networks feature an immanent excess complexity from an external point of view and if this bears risks for third parties then stricter liability can be imposed on the network members to this extent. The roots of the guarantor's liability lie in criminal law: for sources of particular risk or law infringement a special responsibility is laid down in narrowly defined legal cases. However, this contribution only deals with the argument as such and not with the introduction of strict liability. Network-specific transaction duties would take its place. Tortious transaction duties are more flexible than the guarantor's liability and are linked to the beginning of a transaction. Such transactions may also be seen in a network, i.e. in the creation of social links, which indeed make the network-like activities possible.

Both arguments are based on the disadvantages which the network-like cooperation may entail for third parties. As is often the case in law of obligations, one party's disadvantage is another party's advantage: the difficulties of proof, which cause problems for the aggrieved party when making use of individual network members, offer protection for the network participants. This thought shall be included below in the detailed differentiation of the suggested solution.

---

62 *Enneccerus, L./Nipperdey, H.*, BGB AT I/2, § 171 (p. 1057 et seq.).

63 *Enneccerus, L. /Nipperdey, H.*, BGB AT I/2, § 171 (p. 1057 et seq.) (at fn. 4).

After all, an addition to tortious liability can only be indicated where a deficit in liability exists in that tortious law does not or only insufficiently fulfil its function. At first glance, this idea may be displaced by the question about the *worthiness of protection* of third parties: if the aggrieved party in a bilateral relation already receives adequate (e.g. contractual) compensation for the damage in question, then its worthiness of protection and the need for supplementing the legal liability regime could be doubted.[64] One function of damage compensation is, at least with regard to fault-based liability and – even though to a lesser extent – strict liability, the *prevention* in addition to the compensation.[65] The legal order is interested in preventing damages which may occur in the future by culpable, illegal or simply dangerous actions. Accordingly, not only does a deficit in liability exist in the cases in which the aggrieved party does not possess an adequate claim to compensation for the damage, but also in those in which the actually desired liability for an illegal or dangerous action is omitted due to practical reasons.

## IV. Methodical questions

Methodically, the considered stricter liability is a further development of law *extra legem*, which is closely oriented along the lines of the legal prerequisites for tortious liability of several: for the damage of third parties caused by business networks the legal liability facilitations in favour of the aggrieved party do not apply. The simple tortious liability has a functional deficit in light of the lack of proof on side of the aggrieved party. Accordingly, this is an unintended regulatory gap in the legislation – it cannot be imagined that the legislator wanted to unburden the aggrieved party regarding multi-causation with regulations such as § 830 para. 1 BGB; but on the other hand impose the entire burden of proof on the aggrieved party for constellations with similar interests, which, however, do not meet the required conditions of § 830 para. 1 BGB. It has been shown above that a gap exists in the thickets of tortious liability of several for damages caused by business networks, which requires a law developing closing. However,

64 Accordingly, the contract with protective effect for third parties requires that the third party holds no claim against the tortfeasor, who compensates for his damage.

65 *Larenz, K.*, Schuldrecht I, 14. ed., München 1987, p. 423 et seq.; *Lange, H./Schiemann, G.*, Schadensersatz, 3rd ed., Tübingen 2003, p. 11 et seq.

there is no norm which could be considered for an application by analogy. Accordingly, a further development of the law *extra legem* offers itself, which is further illustrated in the following.

## F. Structure

### I. Organisation duties in the network

In general, a legally relevant omission to act only exists if the breach of the legal duty to act lies in inactivity and if the person concerned is indeed capable of averting the legal infringement.[66] The argumentation for the general introduction of strict liability in form of network-specific organisation duties was outlined above. At this stage, this legal duty to act is to be specified. The possibility to avert the infringement of legal goods is addressed in the next stage, i.e. in connection to the circle of persons liable.

Besides the *problem of proof* the excess complexity in networks bears a central danger for third parties and shall be termed *interface problems* here: due to the lacking coordination of collaborative interaction risks emerge at the interfaces of different tasks of various network participants, which would be avoided with well-coordinated interaction.

Liability for breaches of organisation duties in networks is based on the theory of *operational organisation faults*: in the organisation of his company the entrepreneur is subject to the *organisation duty,*[67] which is to be characterised as "besondere Verkehrssicherungspflicht für den Betrieb" ("special duty of transactional safety for the company"), to observe "bei der Organisation des von ihm zu betreuenden Verkehrsbereichs die erforderliche Sorgfalt" ("the necessary diligence in the organisation of the transaction area that he supervises") and in this way prevent risks for third parties.[68]

In order to prevent the risks emerging at the interfaces, areas of accountability and responsibility have to be determined. In particular, it should be prevented here that "gaps" emerge in which the question of accountability and responsibility remains unclear. Such gaps especially emerge in the area of interfaces between the individual performances. Ac-

66 *Staudinger, A.*, in: Schulze, R., BGB, 8. ed., Baden-Baden 2014, § 823, recital 56.
67 *Hassold, G.*, Juristische Schulung 1982, 583, 584 et seq.
68 *Belling, D.*, in: Staudinger, Berlin 2012, § 831, recital 21.

cordingly, the individual single performances have to be coordinated with each other in a way that the areas of accountability and responsibility continue seamlessly. It is imaginable for business networks to establish a coordinating body, which in accordance with the implementing network participants defines and distributes tasks as well as checks the adherence to the responsibility regulations. It is particularly necessary in the scope of coordination that in the case of individual performances based on one another the successful implementation of the previous performance is documented and the subsequent performance is only commenced after the approval of the coordinating body. At the same time, the individual network members should not be exempt from influencing the coordination if they recognise deficits. Documenting the individual performances not only serves the orderly network activity, but at the same time facilitates identifying the causalities between individual performances and damages in hindsight.

The content of the organisation duties has to be adapted to the specific circumstances of the network (structure, size, extent of services). Of course, content and extent of the transaction duties can only be determined based on the circumstances of the individual case.[69] However, it is imaginable to identify risk-prone interfaces in advance based on experience.

A hoped for real consequence of this organisational duty is a better coordination of the network participants at the interfaces and the communication of organisational doubts among each other. Impending joint and several liability creates the necessary pressure.

## II. Liable network participants

### 1. Principle

In principle, all those network participants are jointly liable if the aggrieved party is able to prove that they have contributed to the project's part[70] in question. Temporal restrictions can only be made very carefully

69 *Staudinger A.*, in: Schulze, R., BGB, 8. ed., Baden-Baden 2014, § 823, recital 65.

70 The term is problematic, but serves to demarcate the *circle of participants* as does the no less precise temporal and local connection of actions (see BGH Neue Juristische Wochenschrift 1957, 1834 (1835) = Entscheidungen des Bundesgerichtshofs in Zivilsachen 25, 271; see also Entscheidungen des Reichsgerichts in Zivil-

here since at these interfaces usually only the combination of different performances, which are sometimes wide apart time-wise, lead to the damage. Usually, the causation is not disproved by the fact that the accused had no longer been working at the scene of the accident at the time the damage occurred. Exculpation is most likely possible if the accused proves that his task stood in no content-wise connection to the part of the project in which the damage occurred.

## 2. Worthiness of protection of the network participants with external coordination?

The principle of protection of legitimate expectations forces to address the question whether there are constellations in which a network is coordinated in a way so that the network participants in their expectation of this coordination are worthy of protection, i.e. they must not be burdened with individual organisation duties. The question is closely linked to the already presupposed actual possibility of preventing the infringement of legal goods. This defines that it would be inequitable to impose organisation duties on network participants which are unreasonable to fulfil; if fulfilling them is indeed impossible, then the obligation ceases anyhow (§ 275 Abs. 1 BGB).

A case in point is especially the case in which the organisational agreement within the network conflicts with the provisions of the contractual partner. If, for instance, a general contractor has ascribed clear tasks to five companies in the scope of a specific construction project then their internal organisation duty has to be modified. Contractual and tortious duties collide here. This collision can go hand in hand with an economic imbalance in power between the general contractor and the individual companies.

Regarding the question dealt with here about joint and several liability the general contractor should at first be included in the circle of liable persons. A reason for this is that he most likely can be expected to determine

---

sachen 58, 357, 361.), which is stipulated by jurisdiction in the scope of § 830 para. 1 s. 2 BGB. If lacking consultation between several craft businesses leads to damage it would be inequitable if those companies were liable that are also involved in the overall project, but definitely have nothing to do with the damage, e.g. a painters company that works on another building.

the accountability and responsibility areas, because he himself usually is or appoints and instructs the coordinating body addressed above. The specificities in business networks, however, speak against leaving it at liability according to § 831 BGB. The exculpation by a qualified choice of the top-level management is not suitable if the principal in this way discharges his central tortious duties in a particularly hazardous area. Also the coordinating body probably appointed by him should be liable with regard to the hoped for actual consequences since it is here where the decisive activities concerning the organisation of the interface are implemented or omitted. This would correspond to the valuation of § 831 para. 2 BGB – he who takes on the principle's duties of choice and monitoring by contract (e.g. a general contractor) is liable in addition to the principle, who remains responsible for the right choice of the transferee.[71] Here as well as there it is a special case of liability for the transfer of tortious transaction duties.[72]

If the acting companies used to be tied to the provisions of a general contractor or of a different coordinating body the question still remains to what extent they can refer to their faulty instruction. It would be inequitable to make the construction company readily liable for the faulty instructions of a client. Therefore, after initial inclusion in the circle of the persons liable exculpation should be possible by proving that a) only the instructions of the coordinating body were followed and b) they were not obviously faulty.

## III. Liability facilitation

### 1. Reversal of the burden of proof for liability substantiation

Even if the network activity and therewith the actions of network participants are indisputably causal for the damage of a third party then the causal connection between the action of an individual and the damage does not remain provable or provable with great difficulties. The deeper

71 *Wagner, G.*, in: Münchener Kommentar zum Bürgerlichen Gesetzbuch, 6. ed., München 2013, § 831 recital 51; *Staudinger, A.*, in: Schulze, R., BGB, 8. ed., Baden-Baden 2014, § 831 recital 15.

72 Cf. *Belling, D.*, in: Staudinger, Berlin 2012, § 831, recital 178.

reason for this problem of proof is the network typical *excess complexity*, which results from the range of actors and their separate performances.

Whereas the assumption of causation addressed in the following step unburdens the aggrieved party from the burden to prove the causal connection between the illegal action and the damage, the reversal of the burden of proof serves the relief of the proof of a culpable breach of duties. A connection exists to the assumption in § 831 BGB. § 831 BGB assumes actual fault as well as a connection in the incorrect choice, control, management etc. of a vicarious agent (assumption of causation and fault) that caused the damage.[73] Moreover, in the case of liability for operational organisation fault in favour of the aggrieved party the proof facilitation is common by approval of prima facie evidence.[74] Thereby, a specific set of experience is assumed – as part of the judicial evaluation of evidence – according to which a causal connection exists between the breach of duties and the damage occurred.[75] The reversal of the burden of proof also serves here to assume the culpable breach of the duty of the accused network members and to leave their refutation to them. The exculpation may occur by means of adequate documentation and organisation of the network-like interaction. In the ideal case the occurrence of the damage can be precisely reconstructed in this way that the circle of people liable is minimized to those people whose breach of duty was indeed causal to the damage.

## 2. Assumption of causation

In tortious liability the aggrieved party generally carries the burden of proof "für sämtliche Tatbestandsmerkmale der Norm, also nicht nur für die Haftungsbegründung und insbesondere für die häufig zentrale Voraussetzung der Sorgfaltspflichtverletzung, sondern auch für sämtliche Fragen der Haftungsausfüllung"[76] ("for all aspectual features of the norm, i.e. not

---

73 Cf. *Spindler, G.*, in: Beck'scher Online-Kommentar, BGB, 11/2013, § 831, recital 2.

74 BGH, Beck-Rechtsprechung 1973, 30378315, judgement of 6. 11. 1973, Az. VI ZR 76/72; *Hassold, G.*, Juristische Schulung 1982, 583, 585 (refers to decisions of the Reichsgericht).

75 *Prütting, H.*, in: Münchener Kommentare zur Zivilprozessordnung, 4. ed., München 2013, § 286, recital 48 et seq.

76 *Wagner, G.*, in: Münchener Kommentar zum Bürgerlichen Gesetzbuch, 6. ed., München 2013, § 823, recital 71.

only for liability substantiation and especially for the often centrally required breach of the duty of care, but also for all questions of the extent of liability"). Accordingly, the aggrieved party has to prove to the network which network member has caused which share of the damage. For the aggrieved party it is particularly difficult to reconstruct the course of the damage due to the network-like interaction. These problems of proof are also caused by the tortfeasor alone. Besides the reversal of the burden of proof regarding liability substantiation the causation facilitation should therefore apply in the liability of the business network. This could, as in § 830 para. 1 s. 1 BGB, be structured as a real assumption of causation; alternatively, it would be possible to require at least the proof of *suitability* of complete causation, as in § 830 para. 1 s. 2 BGB. A further option would be a refutable assumption of causation, such as contained in § 831 para. 1 BGB.

§ 830 para. 1 s. 1 BGB bridges causation gaps in that it lets the mutual will of the accomplices, to realize the action causing damage as own action, suffice as grounds for attribution (cf. D. III. 1.).[77] Adequate grounds for attribution would also be required here. The purpose behind § 830 para. 1 s. 2 BGB is as already mentioned less clear, but in the end it aims at achieving the relief of the burden of proof of the aggrieved party at the expense of those who have to take responsibility for the damages and the lack of proof in as much as all illegal actions which are suitable for complete causation are imposed on them.

Grounds for attribution, whose weight would comply with those in § 830 para. 1 s. 1 BGB, do apparently not exist regarding damages to third parties caused by business networks. Indeed, the participants already cause the excess complexity and therewith the lack of proof on the side of the aggrieved party through their network-like interaction. However, for a legal waiver of causation more serious reasons would have to exist such as a typically visible and probable risk to third parties. As milder option the refutable assumption of causation remains, which if necessary could be further diminished by the prerequisites for a suitability of causation. In my opinion, synchronisation with § 831 para. 1 BGB is at hand here: the aggrieved party should not have to prove that the actions of the participants were each partially or completely suitable for causation. The addressed excess complexity within business networks makes this proof for external

77 Cf. *Eberl-Borges, C.*, in: Staudinger, Berlin 2012, § 830, recital 12.

parties extremely difficult. Rather, the assumption of causation should apply here, which the aggrieved parties can refute. Since causation is assumed the aggrieved party does not have to prove that the actions of the accused were partially or completely suitable for causation. In reverse, this leads – due to the lack of waiving the causation – to the fact that exculpation can occur in that the accused proves that his action was neither partially nor completely suitable for causation.

### IV. Joint and several liability

The legal consequence in form of joint and several liability of the participants results from § 840 para. 1 BGB, i.e. if it is clear that the network members are "responsible side by side" for the damage. This mutual accountability follows from the whole of the suggested measures for strict liability: in that the proof of exoneration is imposed on the network members and the causation is refutably assumed the circle of people liable is expanded. If the accused do not manage to illustrate their innocence or the missing causation of their actions for the damage then they are tortuously responsible. The connection ("side by side") – which is missing in the partial cause of damage (cf. above D. III. 4.) – follows from the network-like interaction: whereas in the cases of § 830 para. 1 BGB a temporal and local connection is required, the thematic connection to the section causing the damage links the participants here to a liable community. § 840 para. 1 BGB holds joint and several liability for such cases so that the law can be followed.

## G. Result

Among the different figures of tortious liability also cases can be found which can be applied to damages to third parties caused by business networks. However, for the case of interface-liability discussed here they are typically not useful: damages to third parties caused by negligent uncoordinated interaction of several companies are neither cases of complicity (§ 830 para. 1 s. 1 BGB) nor of partial damage cause, but are to be classified as a special case of negligent individual perpetration. The exceptional case of negligent individual perpetration regulated in § 830 para. 1 s. 2 BGB does not fit since it presupposes the suitability of an action to be completely causal for the damage. Due to this reason a law development *extra legem* was suggested: the lack of proof on the side of the aggrieved party caused by the damage creating business network should be at the expense of the business network alone. Considering the typical excess complexity in network actions – from view of the aggrieved party – this lack of proof does not only apply to the illustration of the precise causation (such as in § 830 para. 1 BGB), but also already exists with regard to the damage causing action. Therefore, the aggrieved party should only have to prove that a) its damage refers back to the network-like action of several companies (so that the scope of application of the liability suggested here is opened) and b) which members have participated in the place in question. Liability grounds are the breach of network-typical organisation and coordination duties, which are to be classified as special effects of tortious transaction duties. The possible general contractor and the coordinators appointed by him are to be included in the circle of persons who are jointly and severally liable. All persons liable have the possibility to exculpate themselves for which the proof of the missing suitability for causation of their own actions suffices among others.

# Authors

**Katja Aedtner**
Risk and contract manager at a global leading company in power and automation technologies and Doctoral candidate at University of Siegen at the Chair of Civil Law and Business Law of Prof. Dr. Peter Krebs.

**Jun.-Prof. Dr. Maximilian Becker**
Junior Professor at University of Siegen, Civil Law and IP-Law

**Prof. Dr. Camilla Crea**
Associate Professor at University of Sannio, Private Law

**Hermann Dück**
Research fellow and Doctoral candidate at University of Siegen at the Chair of Civil Law and Business Law of Prof. Dr. Peter Krebs.

**Dr. Alexander Eufinger**

Legal counsel in a public foundation and visiting lecturer at University of Siegen at the chair of Civil Law and Business Law of Prof. Dr. Peter Krebs

**Prof. Dr. Johannes Glückler**
Professor of Economic and Social Geography at the Institute of Geography and Fellow of the Marsilius Centre for Advanced Study at Heidelberg University

**Dr. Carlos Gómez Asensio**
Associate at Cuevas & Carbonell abogados. Arbitrator at the Valencia Arbitration Court
Associate Professor at Catholic University of Valencia

**Ingmar Hammer**

Research fellow and Doctoral candidate at the Institute of Geography at Heidelberg University

**Dr. Stefanie Jung, M.A. (CoE)**
Postdoctoral researcher at University of Siegen at the Chair of Civil Law and Business Law of Prof. Dr. Peter Krebs.

**Prof. Dr. Peter Krebs**
Professor at University of Siegen, Chair of Civil Law and Business Law

**Jonatan Prosenjak**
Desk officer at the Federal Office of Economics and Export Control
Doctoral candidate at University of Siegen at the Chair of Civil Law and Business Law of Prof. Dr. Peter Krebs.

**Marion Schultes**
Transaction Support Lawyer at an international law firm and Doctoral candidate at University of Siegen at the Chair of Civil Law and Business Law of Prof. Dr. Peter Krebs.

**Prof. Dr. Dr. h.c. mult. Gunther Teubner**
Professor Emeritus, Private Law and Legal Sociology, at Goethe University Frankfurt

**Dr. Emily M. Weitzenboeck**
Senior Associate, Wikborg Rein & Co, Advokatfirma DA, Norway
Postdoctoral Research Scholar, Norwegian Research Centre for Computers & Law at University of Oslo.

For Product Safety Concerns and Information please contact our EU representative GPSR@taylorandfrancis.com
Taylor & Francis Verlag GmbH, Kaufingerstraße 24, 80331 München, Germany

www.ingramcontent.com/pod-product-compliance
Ingram Content Group UK Ltd.
Pitfield, Milton Keynes, MK11 3LW, UK
UKHW022004180926
475701UK00003B/196
*9780367598563*